Toward Defining and Improving Quality in Adult Basic Education

The RUTGERS INVITATIONAL SYMPOSIUM ON EDUCATION Series

Belzer, Ed.
Toward Defining and Improving Quality in Adult Basic Education:
Issues and Challenges

Rubin/Giarelli, Eds.
Civic Education for Diverse Citizens in Global Times: Rethinking
Theory and Practice

O'Donnell/King, Eds.
Cognitive Perspectives on Peer Learning

Vitello/Mithaug, Eds.
Inclusive Schooling: National and International Perspectives

Golbeck, Ed.
Psychological Perspectives on Early Childhood Education:
Reframing Dilemmas in Research and Practice

Shimahara/Holowinsky/Tomlinson-Clarke, Eds.
Ethnicity, Race, and Nationality in Education: A Global Perspective

O'Donnell/Hmelo-Silver, Eds.
Collaborative Learning, Reasoning, and Technology

Toward Defining and Improving Quality in Adult Basic Education

Edited by

Alisa Belzer
Rutgers, The State University of New Jersey

2007

Lawrence Erlbaum Associates, Publishers
Mahwah, New Jersey   London

For Jon, Joseph and Nathan

Camera-ready copy for this book was provided by the editors.

Lawrence Erlbaum Associates, Inc., Publishers
10 Industrial Avenue
Mahwah, NJ 07430

Cover design by Tomai Maridou

Library of Congress Cataloging-in-Publication Data

Toward defining and improving quality in adult basic education / edited by Alisa
Belzer.
    p. cm.
 Includes bibliographical references and index.
 ISBN 0-8058-5545-9 (case : alk. paper)
 1. Adult education--United States. 2. Fundamental education--United States.
I. Belzer, Alisa.
 LC5251.T69 2007
 374'.012--dc22

                            2006017907

Books published by Lawrence Erlbaum Associates are printed on acid-free paper, and
their bindings are chosen for strength and durability.

Contents

PREFACE

The Rutgers Invitational Symposium on Education (RISE), held in the fall of 2003, gave researchers, practitioners, and policy makers a rare opportunity to come together and focus on issues of quality in adult basic education (ABE). While this volume can not capture the synergy created by the presentation of the researchers' papers, interspersed with panel and participant discussion sessions at the two-day gathering, it does make the invited papers available to a wider audience. Hopefully, through the publication of this book, they can continue to serve as vehicles to further our understanding of what constitutes quality, how we can achieve it, and what barriers we must overcome to attain it.

Most discussions about providing quality services in ABE eventually come around to the challenges of doing so in a context of scarcity; the field is under funded, it is staffed by an inconsistently-trained workforce, and policy, administration, and instruction is implemented with little empirical knowledge to inform them. The lack of resources is a given that can not be brushed aside. Until the field has the financial, human, and knowledge resources it needs, quality will always be elusive. Yet the eighteen researchers who presented papers at the RISE conference refrained from belaboring this issue. They focused instead on what we do know, what we can do, and what we should try. They made an effort to cover new ground by reexamining previous work or reframing new work through the lens of defining and improving quality in ABE.

My colleague, Hal Beder, who co-organized the conference with me, and I invited the authors to consider what constitutes a quality system and quality instruction, and what is needed to operationalize this vision. In our invitation to present at the conference, we acknowledged that a challenge to the field is sometimes competing goals and agendas of various stakeholders. Although we can safely assume that all are united in their desire to provide effective and efficient learning opportunities for adults who seek them, specifically what and how we are trying to accomplish this is contested. For example, policymakers and funders often have special goals for ABE that may be quite different from the personal goals of learners. Meanwhile, practitioners may have a third set of goals that are aimed at broadening students' perspectives on the potential of learning. The issue of competing goals is only one of the many factors and complications in fully defining and putting into action what it means to offer quality services in ABE.

Thanks to the National Center on Adult Literacy (NCAL), the National Center for the Study of Adult Learning and Literacy (NCSALL), the research centers of Penn State, and other publicly and privately funded initiatives, the knowledge base in the field has expanded. However, much of this work has not been explicitly tied back to issues of quality. This volume attempts to do so. It neither offers a unitary definition of quality, nor does it fully articulate all the elements needed to attain a quality ABE system. It does point to some very specific actions that we can take in practice, policy, and research, that can potentially improve the quality of the work we do. Not strictly prescriptive, however, it also pushes us to think in new ways about what we do and how we do it. It is my hope that it can prompt us to act in new ways, to see things differently, and to ask new and better questions about how we can improve the quality of what we do.

OVERVIEW OF THE BOOK

In selecting the researchers to present at the conference and then author chapters for this book, we tried to be comprehensive in our scope of topics. We invited researchers that work in the realms of policy and practice. We wanted to encompass the major instructional areas — reading, writing, and math — but we also tried to keep our eye on the larger issues of literacy, learning, and adulthood. As in all situations when we must reconcile limits on time and space, with a multitude of possibilities, we had to make hard choices. Conference participants and readers of this volume may quibble with what (and whom) was included and excluded. We know we did not cover everything, but we believe that the range of topics and ideas that are included in this volume is amply sufficient to raise the level of discussion, knowledge, and ideas regarding issues of quality in ABE.

Once the papers were presented and the chapters revised, it became clear that the authors' work fell into three major areas which are the basis for the sections of this book. Part 1 addresses accountability, standards, and the challenges of executing scientific research and meaningful documentation in adult basic education. The focus here is on defining and increasing quality through systematic and rigorous performance and content standards, the collection of meaningful data, and a clear understanding of how it can be used to improve practice. The Workforce Investment Act of 1998 raised the bar on accountability for all stakeholders, but in this chapter Condelli argues that accountability measures only influence quality when specific implementation conditions are met. He looks at three eras of accountability in the field through the analytic lens of these conditions. His work is helpful in making clear the interrelated links between requirements for the systematic documentation of learner outcomes, contextual factors at the policy level, and the actual improvements to the system. Similarly, Stein argues that content standards like those established by Equipped for the Future can only succeed in attaining higher levels of learning when there is alignment among standards, assessments, and accountability. Even with congruence among these three elements, increased levels of learning can not be achieved without the intervening condition of substantive professional development that is supported at all levels of the system. Greenberg's chapter on conducting scientific research in ABE illustrates that conditions in the field make problematic even the best laid out, systematic, and planful research efforts. She makes some of the challenges of conducting scientific research transparent, and suggests that we can do a better and more realistic job of collecting data that more accurately reflects the realities of teaching and learning in adult basic education. By doing so, researchers have a better chance of doing work that can impact quality. In their chapter, Bingman and Smith focus on how professional development can be used as a tool to encourage and support teachers to be consumers of research that is meant to inform and improve practice.

Part 2 addresses itself to issues of practice. Beder sets the stage by reminding us that different approaches to instruction suggest different measures of quality. Without advocating for one approach over another, he does make clear that defining quality is at least as much about articulating the values we attribute to the acquisition of literary skills as it is about identifying measurable outcomes. Belzer and Comings and Cuban look at structural factors at the program level that can enhance quality in ABE. Belzer focuses in particular on the ways in which volunteer-based programs train and support tutors. Comings and Cuban argue that persistence in formal learning should be understood as a process that may be episodic, and sometimes alternates between periods of self-study and participation in a program. They also identify different participation patterns and suggest that programs should support learners in their long-term efforts in different ways depending on the participation "pathway".

The remaining three chapters in this section focus on the traditional instructional focus of ABE: reading, writing, and math. Gee explores explanations of reading failure by examining different assumptions about the learning process. He suggests that learning to read is a cultural process and instruction should be based on this assumption. This means that the learning process should be connected to literate cultural practices that are of importance to the learner. Gillespie argues that much greater attention needs to be paid to writing instruction, suggesting that it is currently "the forgotten R" in the reading, 'riting, 'rithmetic triumvirate of academic basics. She also makes concrete recommendations for how to improve writing instruction. Similar to Gillespie, Schmitt and Merson claim that math education is often neglected in ABE instruction. They suggest that not only is it ignored in policy and practice, math instruction that does take place in ABE is often out of step with the knowledge base on how math is learned and used.

The chapters in part 3 suggest that an important ingredient in defining and improving quality is going beyond our business as usual understandings and concepts of literacy, learners, and programs. Hayes helps us understand that if ABE is going to serve as a successful mechanism for bridging the "digital divide," technology can not merely be assimilated into traditional classroom practice. By drawing on examples from computer gaming, she suggests the importance of expanding notions of literacy in general and digital literacy in particular. Wrigley, Askov and her colleagues, and Reder all make a case in their chapters for rethinking the structures and goals of programs. Wrigley focuses on the ESL population and suggests that changing immigrant demographics, workplaces, and naturalization policies indicate that programs must do more than teach survival English. Askov and her colleagues have begun the process of tying research to practice in the realm of family literacy as an important step in conceptualizing best practices in the field. Reder documents that under-educated adults engage in a range of learning opportunities in and out of programs, and argues for "bringing literacy to people" to support these efforts. This means that we need to determine ways to support literacy development that work outside of program walls. In their chapters, Gadsen and Hull, Jury, and Zacher turn our attention to the importance of identity, development, and context for literacy learning. Gadsden, in particular, focuses on the ways in which gender contributes to learners' impetus for participating, interactions in the classroom, and ways of using literacy in their lives. Hull, et al., focus on the ways in which adult development and identity formation intersect with the social contexts in which individuals use and develop their literacy skills. These two chapters illustrate well the complex and layered lives of adult learners, and argue for the importance of expanding our understandings of, and building classrooms and programs that respond to, the diversity of learners that we serve. In our desire for quality and the imperative to be "research based" we must resist the impetus to seek recipes for cookie cutter instruction, program planning, and assessment and evaluation.

A NOTE ABOUT TERMINOLOGY

Adult Basic Education, in the title of this book, refers to beginning and intermediate reading, writing, and numeracy, preGED, GED/Adult Secondary Education And ESL instruction that takes place in a range of contexts including schools and community-based programs, community centers, and workplaces and workplace development programs. The chapter authors use other terms including adult literacy education and the adult literacy and education system. Although some would argue that these terms do not mean the same thing and should not be used interchangeably, for the purpose of this book, they should all be taken to refer to the broad range of services for adults who seek to improve their literacy and language skills.

ACKNOWLEDGMENTS

I want to thank my colleague, Hal Beder, who has been a constant help and support to me from the beginning of this process to the end. I greatly appreciate his willing assistance whenever it was asked for and his gracious deference when it was not. He has been my go-to man, agreeing without hesitation to co-direct the RISE conference with me, and providing advice on this book when I wanted it. I also thank the chapter authors for agreeing to participate in the conference and contribute to the book. The process was a departure from business as usual both as a conference and as a writing task. The authors all rose admirably and amiably to the task. Lastly, I want to thank former Rutgers University Graduate School of Education Dean Louise Wilkinson for instituting the RISE conference and for agreeing to focus the 20th annual meeting on the important topic of adult basic education. She enabled an unusual and appreciated opportunity for researchers and practitioners to come together to focus on the important issue of defining and improving quality.

— *Alisa Belzer*

Why Quality? Why Now?

Alisa Belzer
Rutgers University

Given the fact that most adult basic education (ABE) stakeholders have always cared about, thought about, and talked about quality with regard to ABE, it is important to say why, when we began to think about a theme for the RISE conference, defining and improving quality still seemed like a fresh, provocative, and important topic on which to focus. We wondered if there would really be anything new to say. What we realized is that although questions about quality in adult literacy education--what it is, how to do it, and how to document it-- might be the same now as they have always been, the context in which they are asked has shifted significantly in recent years. This has dramatically changed the discourse, the stakes, the challenges, and the opportunities. This chapter briefly traces the changes in the policy context that have had a significant impact on our evolving thinking about quality, and the way we respond to various stakeholders' expectations of it, and where we stand now with it. It concludes with a discussion of the ways in which the papers presented at the RISE conference help us think about the opportunities we now have to define and improve quality within the current climate.

A RETROSPECTIVE ON QUALITY

The purpose of this section is to establish a comprehensive performance accountability system, comprised of the activities described in this section, to assess the effectiveness of eligible agencies in achieving continuous improvement of adult education and literacy activities funded under this subtitle, in order to optimize the return on investment of Federal funds in adult education and literacy activities.

Workforce Investment Act, Title II, Section 212(a) (1998)

1

With the 1998 passage of the Workforce Investment Act (WIA), the section of the law quoted earlier demonstrates clearly Merrifield's (1998) assertion that, for the first time in its history as a federally funded program, ABE must now show demonstrable outcomes as a way to justify funding. She suggested that this requirement is a result of the confluence of social, economic, governmental, and education system changes which all point to a focus on standards, assessment, accountability, and concrete evidence of significant performance. The presumed goal is to improve quality by holding providers responsible for their perform-ance. Literacy education, like many other sectors of social service and educa-tion, must show a "return on investment" that goes well beyond the development of human potential. This climate suggests that providing quality services for adult learners has finally become a policy priority. This move can be viewed as a mixed blessing. On the one hand, the field has been forced to consider what it can do to most efficiently and effectively serve learners in ways that can be en-coded in official documentation procedures. On the other hand, top-down, sys-tem-wide efforts like that generated by WIA can improve documentation of cer-tain aspects of learner achievements without necessarily improving quality. More importantly, definitions of quality are contested. Quality in the official, bureaucratic sense may very well not mean the same thing for all stakeholders. Venezky (1992) illustrated this point well when he suggested that "Students who enroll in literacy courses to learn how to read to their children may not care at the end of instruction what their reading levels are relative to national standards. However, policy makers do" (p. 8). Additionally, insufficient political commit-ment, resources, and infrastructure may mean that the field simply gets better at reporting what it is already doing because it must, but may not be able to pro-vide significantly better educational services because it does not have the capac-ity to do so. In other words, mandated, surface level reforms do not necessarily lead to deep change and improved quality. This is not to say that the field cannot improve the quality of its services; it continually strives to do so. Rather, it is to say that it is handicapped by a weak infrastructure (Beder, 1996), and made all the more crippled by time and labor consuming accountability demands that sometimes focus on documenting outcomes that may seem less important or relevant to practitioners and learners than they do to policymakers and funders.

A focus on issues of quality probably could not occur until some infrastruc-ture--a program system—existed, which includes elements such as political commitment to dependable and significant funding; governmental agencies to oversee, monitor, and provide guidance and direction; a professional workforce; curriculum and instructional materials; and established programs. Although a history of what quality means in adult basic education has not been written, sev-eral scholars have tracked both the development of the system (Sticht, 2002), and the shifts in purpose of various stakeholders over time (Merrifield, 1998; Quigley, 1997; Sticht, 2002). These histories suggest that for much of the cen-tury, just getting basic education for adults on the radar screen of funders was the main focus of its advocates. Until the 1960s when adult basic education first received federal funding, with rare and nonpublicly funded exceptions, the importance of literacy and the prevalence of low literate adults only came in to focus during times of crisis, for example, during both world wars and the Depression. However, targeted responses during these times were developed as a way to address specific needs quickly, and just as quickly they faded away when the need was no longer pressing. These bursts of activity did little to build a system with an infrastructure to support it.

At the same time, the broader field of adult education was beginning to organize and practitioners worked to professionalize their endeavors. Here a struggle emerged, played out over many years, between those who saw adult education as serving a broad, liberal, general educational agenda, and those who saw it as serving a vocational or human resources development need; between those who felt it should be targeted broadly toward anyone who had time and interest, or focused primarily on the neediest and least advantaged (Sticht, 2002). Neither faction had significant success at gaining public funding. It was not until Johnson launched the "Great Society" funded by the 1964 Economic Opportunity Act that ABE received federal money. By virtue of its funding source, ABE was initially a poverty reduction program. Two years later, the administration of ABE federal funds was moved over to the U.S. Office of Education. However, its purpose has continued to be debated by way of various policy requirements and expectations, and even by the ways in which it has been defined in federal funding statutes.

Efforts over the next 20 years of ABE went toward growing the system by increasing participation and funding. As the social program it was originally conceived to be, simply serving as many of the neediest as possible was the quality marker at the federal level. Adult literacy educators were probably as concerned then as they are now with quality at the classroom and program level, but were not expected to demonstrate or document it. Little systematic effort at the federal level was applied to determining what quality is and how it could be measured. Requirements at both the state and local levels to demonstrate efficacy were relatively undefined. 1988 saw the first federal requirements related to quality, but these focused on program management issues rather than learner outcomes. Learner levels were articulated in the legislation at that time, but were poorly defined and very broad (beginning, intermediate, and advanced, which corresponded roughly to elementary, middle, and high school), so they could not be used effectively to measure quality or to report on the outcomes of funding to Congress (Condelli, 2000). States were required to report learner outcomes, but no real evidence was required to demonstrate their achievements and reporting was often based on a combination of learners' claims of accomplishments and teachers' judgments. Quality in ABE was still essentially undefined.

The 1991 National Literacy Act (NLA) began to bring the question of quality more sharply into focus in at least two ways. First, the Act gave rise to an initial attempt to build systematic approaches to accountability by requiring states either to develop *Indicators of Program Quality* or to adopt the model developed by the U.S. Department of Education. The requirement, although unevenly implemented, did encourage many states to articulate what processes and outcomes define quality, as well as how to achieve and measure it (Condelli, this volume). Although not representative of every state's efforts, the U.S. Department of Education's model Indicators included both student outcome measures and program processes, suggesting that learner accomplishments are unlikely without excellent programs supporting their efforts. However, what this actually meant in practice was relatively loosely defined and had little uniformity across states.

The second important initiative regarding quality that the NLA gave rise to was the development of content standards for the field. The National Institute for Literacy (NIFL) was funded by the NLA, and the Equipped for the Future (EFF) Initiative has been one of its most significant and sustained efforts. This standards-based reform initiative was begun as a response to NIFL's assignment to measure progress toward achievement of National Education Goal 6. The Adult Literacy and Lifelong Learning Goal aimed for every adult to be literate and have "the knowledge and skills necessary to compete in a global economy and exercise the rights and responsibilities of citizenship" (Retrieved July 12, 2006, from http://www.ed.gov/legislation/GOALS2000/TheAct/sec102.html) by the year 2000. The difficulty of meeting this challenge was underlined by a General Accounting Office Report (General Accounting Office, 1995) which indicated that, not only does the field lack accurate data for measuring progress toward this goal, it also lacks a coherent vision of what defines literacy and therefore would have difficulty identifying and measuring program results.

EFF developers took on the coherence task by concretizing literacy definitions through the development of content standards. Using a combination of field-based research, consensus building, and research in the learning sciences, EFF developers identified key (adult) purposes for learning and defined the knowledge and skills that adults need to know and be able to do to carry out a full range of adult roles and responsibilities. The development of 16 content standards was guided by the developers' understanding of the importance of being specific and clear enough to be understandable by all stakeholders, guide instruction, assessment, and be measurable (Equipped for the Future, n.d.-b). Most importantly, the standards had to focus on results that matter (Stein, 2000) to the diverse range of stakeholders in this field. By taking this approach, the developers worked toward a definition of quality that was resonant with the real-world responsibilities of adults, and would be viewed as significant and important to funders and policymakers. Veering away from traditional academic definitions of quality education, EFF standards focus on literacy uses in the execution of communication, decision-making, interpersonal, and lifelong learning skills as they pertain to adult roles as citizens, workers, and family members.

Concurrent with the development of this standards-based systems reform effort, in response to a WIA mandate, the American Institutes for Research was hard at work on the development of a national, standardized system for documenting learner outcomes along more traditional lines: academic achievement and job attainment and retention. Once WIA became law, the so-called National Reporting System (NRS) was launched to accomplish this. Participation in EFF was voluntary; 10 years after its inception 18 states are working to integrate aspects of EFF into their adult education and training systems (Equipped for the Future, n.d.-a). In contrast, adoption of the NRS at every level of the system served by federal Title II money was mandated by law. Training for EFF is extensive and in-depth. Adoption of various aspects of it has been understandably slow and incremental, given the complexity and richness of the process; states and local programs were required to quickly adapt to the demands of the NRS. NRS training and resources for capacity building needed to respond to its requirements were variable from state to state, depending in large part on how the state agency director perceived his or her role in acting as a mediating influence between federal requirements and local programs (Belzer, in press). Although Condelli (this volume) argues that the NRS was developed with the characteristics that give it the potential to improve quality, its focus is more procedural than substantive in that it establishes a system for reporting learner outcomes, but does so within the context of existing standardized tests and other traditional measures of adult education outcomes such as job attainment. It does not address how programs, practitioners, and learners might best achieve improved outcomes. In other words, it was not built with the same kind of systems reform goals with which EFF began. It was a pragmatic response to a federal mandate that the ABE system show a return on its investment. As a mandated system, it does have the "teeth" that EFF lacks. Unfortunately, although efforts are currently underway, there is no substantive interconnection between these two initiatives. In other words, achievement toward EFF standards can not currently be measured using NRS documentation procedures.

QUALITY NOW

So now that ABE has content standards as well as a standardized reporting system (albeit unrelated to each other), what have we got now that we did not have before with regard to defining and improving quality? As funding for adult literacy education increased in the 1990s and the field was mandated to demonstrate a "return on investment," it has become more integrated with and perhaps more like the broader educational system, because it has had to respond to many of the same kinds of demands for accountability. Belzer and St. Clair (2003) suggested that in moving toward more institutionalized and systematic approaches to defining and documenting quality (as well as many other aspects of the field), there are both new opportunities and new limits. On the one hand, "limits are helpful when they outline effective and efficient practice" (p. 6). On the other hand, systematization can shut down innovation and dampen responsiveness to what learners actually want to learn and what practitioners have to offer as teachers. One challenge that continues to dog the field, even as it has matured in many ways, is that it has insufficient evidence (regardless of how evidence is currently defined) to say that much of anything is best for any one learner. It is imperative then, that just as our understandings of literacy and adult learners should remain open and multiple, so too should our ideas about what quality is and how to improve it.

This is not to say that we should not continue to sharpen definitions of quality as well as our understandings of how to measure and improve it. However, when it comes to sharpening our images, we should choose our metaphors carefully. We should not think of it like the process of sharpening a knife in which the blade gets finer and finer as it is honed (as definitions get narrower and narrower). Instead, we ought to think of sharpening as more like cutting precious stones so that the defined edges of facets emerge. Here sharpening implies clarifying many angles. Faceting is used to bring out the brilliance of the gem. In gem cutting, faceting "has the greatest profit potential" (Clark, n.d.).

Thinking of quality in this way will help us maximize the brilliance of what is possible in ABE. The chapters in this volume do this by considering many different facets of what defines quality and how to improve it. They do not offer any one standard definition of quality. Instead they explore the challenges and opportunities, what we do know, and what we can do to provide the best for learners who seek ABE, what we can try to do better, and what we need to know more and think about further. In some chapters, the authors explore how to do this within the traditional, institutional, and political boundaries of our field by including discussions of research, professional development, and structural aspects of the system. Other authors help us take a new look at learners, and teaching and learning as a way to expand our thinking about quality in the classroom. Some chapters also help us see that we can expand our thinking about quality in ways that go beyond the places and ways we have traditionally thought of for providing quality ABE. All of these perspectives can help the field reach higher levels of quality, but none suggest that there is only one way to do so. Each help to cut a new facet in our understanding of quality in ABE.

REFERENCES

Beder, H. (1996). *The infrastructure of adult literacy education: Implications for policy* (Tech. Rep. No. TR96-01). Philadelphia, PA: National Center on Adult Literacy.

Belzer, A. (in press). Implementing the Workforce Investment Act from in-between: State agency responses to federal accountability policy in adult basic education. *Educational Policy.*

Belzer, A., & St. Clair, R. (2003). *Opportunities and limits: An update on adult literacy education* . (Information series No. 391). Columbus, OH: ERIC Clearinghouse on Adult, Career, and Vocational Education.

Clark, D. (n.d.). *Gem cutting terms.* Retrieved December 3, 2005, from http://www.gemsociety.org/info/igem3.htm

Equipped for the Future. (n.d.-a). *About the EFF Initiative.* Retrieved December 22, 2005, from http://eff.cls.utk.edu/fundamentals/about.htm

Equipped for the Future. (n.d.-b). *EFF Fundamentals: Content standards.* Retrieved December 22, 2005, from http://eff.cls.utk.edu/fundamentals/eff_standards.htm#skills

General Accounting Office. (1995). *Adult education: Measuring program results has been challenging* (Report No. GAO/HEHS-96-153). Washington, DC: Author.

Merrifield, J. (1998). *Contested ground: Performance accountability in adult basic education* (NCSALL Report No. 1; 423 450 ed.). Cambridge, MA: National Center for the Study of Adult Learning and Literacy.

Quigley, B. A. (1997). *Rethinking literacy education: The critical need for practice-based change.* San Francisco: Jossey-Bass.

Stein, S. (2000). *Equipped for the future content standards: What adults need to know and be able to do in the 21st century.* Washington, DC: National Institute for Literacy.

Sticht, T. G. (2002). The rise of the adult education and literacy system in the United States: 1600-2000. In J. Coming, B. Garner, & C. Smith (Eds.), *The annual review of adult literacy and literacy* (Vol. 3, pp. 12-43). San Francisco: Jossey-Bass.

Venezky, R. L. (1992). *Matching literacy testing with social policy: What are the alternatives?* (Policy brief, document No. PB92-1). Philadelphia, PA: National Center on Adult Literacy.

Workforce Investment Act (1998). Retrieved July 12, 2006, from http://www.doleta.gov/USWorkforce/wia/wialaw.txt

PART ONE

ACCOUNTABILITY, STANDARDS, AND THE USE OF DOCUMENTATION AND RESEARCH

Chapter 1

Accountability and Program Quality: The Third Wave

Larry Condelli
American Institutes for Research

Over the last 20 years, accountability has grown to be a central force in public policy. Driven by political concerns, uncertain funding, and pressure to resolve difficult social problems, the demand for publicly funded programs to demonstrate that their services lead to positive outcomes for their clients has increased steadily. At the federal level, demands for accountability led in 1993 to the passage of the Government Performance and Results Act, the first accountability legislation that required federal agencies to develop a set of performance measures to judge whether they were meeting their legislative mandates. Many states passed similar legislation for their education, welfare, and job training programs, often mandating that programs demonstrate successful client and programmatic outcomes, or risk financial sanctions or complete loss of funding.

In no area have pressures for accountability been greater than in education. A series of sharply critical studies of the state of education and failing schools led to the rise of a host of school reform efforts at the state and federal levels, which often included mandatory student testing and sanctioning of low-performing schools. Accountability demands for public schools culminated in 2002 with the enactment of the No Child Left Behind legislation, which included mandatory testing of all students.

Although lacking the politically charged atmosphere surrounding public schools, the adult basic education (ABE) system has faced similar demands for accountability. Mirroring the broader public policy arena, concerns over ABE program quality and demands for accountability arose in the late 1980s. In 1998, with the passage of the Workforce Investment Act (WIA), a state-level accountability system for ABE, with an incentive system tied to performance measures, was federally mandated for the first time. The National Reporting System (NRS), established by the U.S. Department of Education to implement the WIA accountability requirements, went into effect in July 2000.

Permeating debates around the value of accountability systems is the assumption–usually implicit--that they provide information about, and help improve, the quality of programs. For example, a school with high test scores is presumed better than a school with poor scores; an ABE program where most students pass the General Educational Development (GED) test is viewed as being of higher quality than one in which fewer students pass. Whether this assumption is true depends on the nature of the accountability system and how it is implemented.

This chapter explores the relationship between program quality and accountability in the context of federal efforts toward promoting accountability in the ABE program. These efforts have occurred in three distinct phases or waves over the last decade. In Wave 1, accountability focused on program inputs and process, whereas in Wave 2, student outcomes are the main focus. It appears that Wave 3, which is now emerging, will have elements of both processes and outcomes, balancing the two prior waves. The chapter discusses the approach toward accountability for each wave, evaluates its affect on program quality, and concludes with observations on how the accountability process can be improved to strengthen the accountability-quality link.

A FRAMEWORK FOR EVALUATING ACCOUNTABILITY AND PROGRAM QUALITY

To help us explore the relationship between accountability and program quality, I first describe general characteristics of accountability systems and review the literature on aspects of accountability systems that are most likely to affect program quality. I use this research as a framework to help us evaluate how federal approaches toward accountability in ABE have affected program quality.

Key Characteristics of Accountability Systems

As described by Stecher (1995) and Elmore (1997), a system of program accountability provides a systematic way to gauge whether a program is meeting its goals and mandates. Accountability systems can document how a program operates, or its *processes;* what a program produces or its clients achieve, or its *outcomes;* or both processes and outcomes. Most accountability systems currently in use are "top-down"–systems that have been legislatively mandated to serve the interests and policies of funding agencies. In these types of systems, policymakers and program directors set measures, methods, and procedures. Accountability systems also can be field driven, or "bottom-up." Practitioners or service providers take a major role in devising the accountability system, under this approach.

Information from the accountability system is often used as a factor in funding decisions, although the data can also be used for program improvement efforts. Legislatively mandated, top-down approaches to accountability are usually more focused on the use of quantitative accountability data to inform a general system of performance-based funding. Bottom-up approaches typically have a more explicit and direct focus on program improvement, often include qualitative measures, with less emphasis on performance-based funding. A distinctive feature of the current trend in accountability has been the almost exclusive focus on outcome-based, top-down approaches, using quantitative measures.

The Job Training Partnership Act (JTPA) established the first major accountability system of this type. The JTPA program, which funded state and local adult job-training efforts from 1983 to 1998, required states and local programs to report on a range of participants' employment outcomes. In their study of this accountability system, Baj, Sheets, and Trott (1995) used business management theory to identify four essential characteristics of all accountability systems:

- An underlying set of *goals* that the program is to achieve, such as promoting learning, literacy, self sufficiency or employment.
- A common set of m*easures* that reflect the goals and that are reported and aggregated. The measures must be clearly defined and can be qualitative or quantitative.
- *Performance standards* tied to measures, which set a level or target of performance that programs must achieve.
- *Sanctions or rewards* for programs, tied to performance.

Only accountability systems that have all of these characteristics in place can successfully meet their goals of providing accurate measures of program performance and can positively influence program quality. To be implemented successfully, accountability systems need "buy-in" and acceptance from local programs, and sufficient resources to provide local programs with technical assistance and tools (e.g., computer hardware and software for data collection, documentation, and analysis) to make it feasible to implement requirements. Gaining acceptance is particularly important with "top-down" accountability systems that are defined and established by funding or oversight agencies for their grantees.

Accountability systems not only serve as a way to measure program performance, but they can affect program processes and outcomes. This dynamic nature of accountability systems makes them important policy tools: they can be used to implement policy and measure whether policies are effective. For example, emphasizing specific measures can define what stakeholders believe is important and focus programmatic efforts on improving performance on these measures. The same measures then become the means by which program success is evaluated. The clearest example of this dynamic is the emphasis on standardized testing in elementary and secondary education. Producing high test scores is a major focus of most schools, and high scores are the main criteria by which schools are judged (Elmore, 1997).

Accountability Factors Affecting Program Quality

Implicit in this approach toward accountability is that good performance means high program quality: a good program is one that has good performance measures. Most policymakers and the general public tend to believe in this relationship. However, outcome-based accountability systems usually lack direct measures of program processes or operations that define program quality. Little attention is usually given to *how* programs achieve these outcomes. Quality is only indirectly affected in this type of accountability system. Whether good outcomes, as measured through an accountability system, reflect program quality depends on how the four characteristics of an accountability system are implemented.

Over the last 15 years, several studies have explored how this policy-accountability dynamic affects local service quality by examining federal employment training programs, notably programs funded through the JTPA, the first major federal program to have an outcome-based accountability system (Condelli & Kutner, 1992; National Commission on Employment Policy [NCEP], 1987; Trott & Baj, 1996). These studies concluded that each of the four defining characteristics of accountability systems affect how local program services are provided and the success of the system in achieving the policy goals for the program.

The extent to which the accountability system reflects the goals of programs is central to how well the system can affect program quality. Although authorizing legislation defines programmatic goals for most social and education programs, a successful accountability system requires agreement between policymakers and practitioners on these goals and their priority in service delivery. For example, the level of importance of employment as a goal for ABE is often debated among policymakers, teachers, and employers. Due to its central importance, creating consensus on program goals among stakeholders is usually the first step in developing an accountability system.

Once the program goals the system will reflect are defined, one of the most difficult and contentious issues in the development of an accountability system is defining measures that match the goals. Although it may be relatively easy to build consensus that "literacy development" is a central goal of ABE, for example, determining how to measure it poses a much greater problem. Not only do measures faithfully reflect goals in an effective accountability system, but good measures also are closely tied to the services a program provides. A close link between services and outcome measures means that programs can more directly affect the measure and that the accountability system more accurately reflects program performance and program quality.

Performance standards in accountability systems are numeric targets that define the performance levels a program must meet to be judged a success. The level at which standards are set is a critical factor in whether the standards reflect program quality. Standards that are set too low are usually unable to affect quality because programs do not have to change what they do to meet them, and therefore do not need to take low standards very seriously. Standards that are set too high also do not usually improve program quality because they are too difficult to meet. Although there is often a tendency to set performance standards to high numeric levels in the belief that higher program quality will result, experience indicates that programs achieve excessively high standards by making changes that actually hurt program quality. For example, programs may enroll students with higher literacy levels who will progress faster and turn away lower literacy students; or programs could provide less comprehensive instruction that focuses on achieving quick outcomes. These "unintended consequences" can completely subvert the accountability system by preventing programs and students from achieving their goals and can end up actually *reducing* program quality. Finding the appropriate level at which to set standards to avoid unintended consequences usually means adapting them to local circumstances, such as the type of student enrolled and community conditions (NCEP, 1987).

Monetary incentives or sanctions are tied to performance standards to reward programs that exceed standards or punish those that fail to meet them. The amount of the rewards and sanctions can have a significant affect on program quality. In its study of the JTPA system, NCEP (1987) concluded that rewards and sanctions that are set too low are unlikely to affect quality, because they do not motivate providers to make programmatic changes. However, when they are set too high, rewards--and particularly sanctions--can greatly exacerbate unintended consequences. Faced with a significant or total loss of funding, for example, a program may resort to any number of strategies to achieve its numeric performance standards--strategies that can hurt or have little to do with program quality. Dishonest reporting is also more likely, as the recent case in the Houston public school system illustrates. Several schools exaggerated, and in at least one case falsified, data on student dropout rates due to fear about the sanctions involved in being labeled "low performing" (Winerip, 2003).

EVALUATING QUALITY THROUGH ACCOUNTABILITY IN ADULT BASIC EDUCATION

Research has demonstrated that outcome-based accountability systems can affect program quality through the program goals they define, the measures and performance standards they require, and the rewards and sanctions they provide to local programs (e.g., Elmore, 1997). Systems where stakeholders agree on goals that accurately articulate program purposes, that have measures that reflect these goals, and that are closely tied to the services programs provide, have realistic performance standards, do not have excessive sanctions or rewards for performance, and are most likely to affect program quality positively.

Using this research as a guide, I evaluate how federal approaches toward accountability in ABE have affected program quality. I first examine the U.S. Department of Education's initial attempt at accountability, which was not a formal system. It relied on a set of suggested, but not mandated, indicators to define program quality (Wave 1). My main focus is on Wave 2, the NRS which is the ABE program's formal accountability system, and on an upcoming third wave of accountability, legislative proposals to change the NRS. In my evaluation of the first two waves, I look at the purpose and rationale behind the accountability requirements, judge the success of their implementation, and reflect on their impact on program quality in ABE. In my discussion of the third wave, I speculate about the likely impact proposed changes will have on quality and suggest ways to enhance accountability to create a more explicit link between accountability and quality.

Wave 1: Quality Indicators

The ABE program's first legislative step toward formal accountability requirements appeared in the 1988 reauthorization of the Adult Education Act, which required states to evaluate local programs in six areas and to use standardized tests as part of their evaluation system. However, it was not until the passage of the National Literacy Act of 1991 that the Department of Education (ED) began its first major effort toward instituting an accountability system. The Act required states to develop "indicators of program quality" and to use them "to judge the success of [local] programs" as a way to assess program quality. The indicators were meant to measure "efficient and effective performance" of ABE programs in seven areas related to student outcomes and program processes: educational gains, recruitment, retention, support services, staff development, curriculum and instruction, and program planning. ED developed eight model indicators (two for educational gains) and required all states to use them, or to develop and use their own indicators, to evaluate local program effectiveness (U.S. Department of Education, 1992).

ED required states to define each indicator with a descriptive statement reflecting quality, and to attach measures to them. The model indicators and measures for curriculum and instruction and for retention, for example, included the following:

- *Indicator:* Program has curriculum and instruction geared to individual student learning styles and levels of student needs.
  - *Measures:* Instructional content addresses individual student needs (measured by classroom observation or self-report); student goal setting processes are linked to instructional decisions.
- *Indicator:* Learners remain in the program long enough to meet their educational needs.
  - *Measures:* Hours in program by learning gain; percentage of students returning after specified time period.

ED also encouraged states to develop performance standards for each measure. States were to use the measures as a means to assess program effectiveness, identify program improvement and technical assistance needs, and make funding decisions.

A review of states' efforts in implementing quality indicators found that about two thirds of states developed and were using them in the intended ways. States reported that the development process itself had a positive effect on programs, as the process raised awareness of program quality issues and gave state and local staff the opportunity to define and reach consensus on the characteristics of effective, quality programs. Defining the measures and standards along with the indicators gave states direction on how to evaluate and improve local programs (Condelli, 1996).

Assessment of the Quality Indicators Approach

The quality indicator approach was not a fully realized system of accountability as it is defined by the four essential characteristics described earlier. Although the approach included goals or statements of what is important to ABE, measures and performance standards were not universally set, and the approach lacked a system of rewards and sanctions. In addition, measures were not consistently collected and implementation was voluntary. Because the National Literacy Act defined quality indicators and how they were to be measured and used in only very general terms, the ED lacked a mandate to impose an outcomes-based system. However, the approach of defining and using quality indicators embodied many of the positive aspects of accountability as it can affect program quality, including an emphasis on program processes, state and local flexibility, wide acceptance, and lack of excessive sanctions (NCEP, 1987).

The indicator development process helped states and local programs approach accountability in a serious way by focusing on the processes and outcomes that define quality. In addressing each of the indicator topic areas, state and local staff had to decide how quality could be realized and measured, and then incorporated into a system of accountability. The indicators became statements of what makes a good ABE program, defined ways to measure quality, and encouraged local and state adult educators to set levels of acceptable quality to evaluate program operation and outcomes. Because there were only general requirements on how to establish the indicators, states were free to define and measure them in ways that were most suited to their delivery systems and students. States could use the indicators in ways that worked best for them.

Although mandated "from above" by legislation, the indicator development process in most states included substantial involvement and leadership from the local level. Many states also included adult learners in the development process, as did ED in the development of the model indicators. This involvement promoted local ownership of the indicators, which led to wide acceptance and adoption of them in most states.

Unlike systems of accountability currently in use, which focus almost exclusively on participant outcome measures, the indicators explicitly recognized the importance of program content, structure, and operation in affecting quality. Although not lacking in student outcome measures–the model federal indicators included two student educational gain measures and two retention measures–the indicator framework gave equal attention to program processes such as planning, curriculum, instruction, and professional development, as central to a quality program. In contrast, outcome-based accountability systems that now prevail imply only an indirect connection to program quality.

Despite these positive aspects of the quality indicator approach toward accountability, it is difficult to determine whether it was successful in improving ABE program quality. The only study that examined its effects (Condelli, 1996) focused on the impact of indicator development process, not the success of their implementation or their affect on quality. States also did not systematically document programmatic changes resulting from indicator implementation. Nonetheless, some lasting effects of this approach are evident. Many states, including Arkansas, Connecticut, and Iowa, incorporated quality indictors into their local program monitoring and evaluation systems. Other states, such as Pennsylvania, continued to use indicators to assess local program quality, eventually incorporating them into a broader accountability system that included NRS measures.

The use of quality indicators as the basis for accountability in ABE ultimately failed. As a national accountability system, the approach was flawed because it was voluntary and did not have a uniform set of measures or standards. Consequently, several states did not participate and there was no way to aggregate information across states to develop a national picture. The lack of rewards or sanctions tied to the indicators also was problematic, because states had little incentive, other than their own interest, to implement and enforce the indicators. In the end, however, it was the political environment of the 1990s, with its demands for measuring quantitative outcome measures, that made the indicators approach untenable. The indicators emphasized the importance of quality in program processes, but did not focus sufficiently on measuring outcomes. Without such measures, the ABE program could not survive the accountability pressures facing all education and human service programs.

Wave 2: The National Reporting System

The WIA created the first true accountability system for the ABE program, requiring a set of measures and performance standards in the areas of educational gain, attainment of a secondary credential or equivalent certification, advancement to further education and training, and employment. WIA tied incentives to the standards through awards of up to $3 million to states that exceeded standards, and by requiring states to consider local program performance in awarding grants to local programs. ED established the NRS to implement the accountability requirements by defining the measures, methods, and reporting procedures and to establish a system of training and technical assistance aimed at helping states implement the system. The NRS went into effect in July 2000, although ED required states to set performance standards in the previous year.

WIA established the legislative basis for it, but the need for an outcome-based accountability system was already apparent in 1995. At that time, federal funding for the ABE program faced elimination through absorption into a proposed state block grant approach to funding it and employment training programs. U.S. Congressional demands for data on outcomes of participation on ABE students, along with similar accountability pressures within the states, caused state ABE directors and ED to begin planning a reporting system that would provide these data. ED initiated a 2-year planning and development process in 1996, which ultimately led to the NRS.

Design of the Accountability System

Before commenting on the NRS's ability to affect program quality, and evaluating its success in doing so, it is worth examining the extent to which the NRS was designed in a way that it had the potential to influence program quality. I use the research-based framework presented earlier to guide this assessment. This framework identified how the four main components of an outcome-based accountability system—goals, measures, performance standards, and rewards and sanctions—can affect quality in program design and performance.

Through a series of meetings in 1996 and 1997, state directors of adult education, federal staff, and other national leaders in the field reached consensus on four main purposes or goals of ABE that they believed should be reflected in a national accountability system (Condelli & Kutner, 1997). The goals identified were as follows:

- Educational improvement and lifelong learning.

- Enhancement of employability.

- Improvement of civic participation.

- Improvement of literacy and education within the family.

These four purposes correspond with the roles of ABE expressed in most other general frameworks and was thus a good basis for the design of an accountability system that could affect quality. Agreement on these goals was essential because the stakeholders recognized that the accountability measures would reflect the goals and that the measures would affect instruction and other program activities. However, such broad goals implied the need for a complex accountability system with multiple measures that made development of an accountability system very difficult.

Once the goals to be reflected in the accountability system had been clarified, draft measures were developed. In anticipation of the emerging requirements of accountability systems, ED and state directors required that the measures for the planned system should be outcome-based and quantitative. In addition, draft measures were designed to have a clear relationship to goals, be likely to reflect program performance, provide information to help inform decisions, and be easy to understand (Condelli, 1998). Measures with these characteristics are likely to minimize unintended consequences and have a high probability of positively affecting program quality (Trott & Baj, 1996).

The goal identification and measurement development process created far too many measures for the proposed accountability system. However, the passage of WIA required four sets of measures, educational gain, advancement to postsecondary education, attainment of a secondary credential, and employment entrance and retention, which became the required measures of the NRS. Because many stakeholders objected to this lowering of the importance of community and family measures, these measures were retained as secondary, optional measures in the system.

WIA also required that performance standards be tied to a reward system, the final component of an accountability system designed to improve the quality of services. First, ED required states to set performance standards based on estimates of mean past performance. Setting standards in this way is a moderate approach that is likely to minimize unintended effects, as by definition, half of programs already meet or exceed the average standards. WIA also set an incentive reward system for states exceeding standards, but did no sanctioning. States do not lose federal funding for failing to meet standards, although states are given the option of cutting funds to local programs that do not perform. Because high sanctions are a major cause of unintended effects in local programs (NCEP, 1987), the lack of formal sanctions removes a significant barrier from the NRS's potential to affect quality. Setting standards too low, on the other hand, minimizes the accountability system's affect on quality.

The ability of states and local providers to adjust accountability requirements in response to local conditions, however, can minimize unintended effects and positively affect quality. The NRS allowed some state flexibility in setting performance standards and in implementation of requirements. States could use the optional measures and add their own, determine the level of local sanctions, and set student assessment and goal setting policies, for example, as long as the policies conformed to NRS guidelines (U. S. Department of Education, 2001).

Assessing the National Reporting System and Program Quality

This review of NRS design illustrates that it was developed with an eye toward minimizing unintended effects and maximizing its ability to improve quality. However, as an outcome-based accountability system, the NRS can only affect program quality indirectly, through its measures, performance standards, and sanctions, and by how well states and programs accept and implement the system. There are no direct measures of program processes or procedures with which to directly examine the question of quality, although Belzer (2003) examined how states implement federal policy using WIA as an example.

Based on discussions with ED staff in the adult education and literacy division, staff from eight states, and the author's experience with developing the NRS and providing assistance on its implementation to state and local staff, there is no doubt, however, that accountability requirements have substantially affected the ABE delivery system. WIA requires states to fund programs that provide instruction with "sufficient intensity and duration … to achieve substantial learning gains" [Workforce Investment Act of 1998, Section 231 (e) (1)] and this requirement, coupled with the need to demonstrate learner outcomes, has resulted in many states funding fewer small providers and replacing them with larger providers that offer more intensive services. Small providers, at least initially, were unable or unwilling to meet state accountability demands. Accountability has also led to a substantial reallocation of resources to developing data collection and reporting systems. Although there was in increase in overall federal funding for ABE when WIA was enacted, in part to offset the costs of developing accountability systems, these funds often did not keep pace with state and local program needs. Their increased costs included the need for new or additional computer systems, software development, and data processing. Local programs in most areas lacked sufficient staff to collect and enter data (especially employment and other follow-up data), and provide additional time for student assessment, goal setting, and student tracking. In many states, significant amounts of professional development time and activities were also directed toward data management and accountability issues. Many programs were overwhelmed by the time and energy needed for the process, especially in the first years (Belzer, 2003). This sometimes led to resentment and resistance toward accountability requirements among local providers in many states.

In spite of these difficulties, there have been many positive results from the increased focus on accountability. There has been significant movement in the field away from counting numbers of students served and hours of attendance to putting in place systems that focus more on individual student needs and student achievements. NRS reporting has created a body of data that states can use to demonstrate the value and effects of ABE instruction. These data have helped maintain funding in many states and have also helped ABE programs build better relationships and leverage funding with other agencies to expand instruction. Accountability data also give local programs information they can use for program management and improvement. States and local programs have been able to gain insight on the effects of class size, instructional hours, staffing patterns, and student characteristics on performance and other aspects of program operation.

Although the NRS has had substantial impact on the field, I now turn to an assessment of how NRS requirements have affected specific aspects of local program quality over the last 3 years. The dimensions of quality on which I focus include recruitment of students in need of instruction, student retention, student goal setting, and instruction and student assessment. I assess the NRS's possible effect on quality in each of these areas.

Students and retention in adult basic education

When the NRS was first implemented many providers were concerned that the accountability requirements would lead programs to neglect students of lower literacy levels in favor of students at higher levels, so that states could show learning gains more readily. Indeed, this "creaming" effect of enrolling more prepared students is a serious concern of all outcome-based accountability systems. However, to help prevent this, ED required states to set separate performance standards for each educational functioning level. States could set lower standards for student advancement at the lower educational functioning levels, for example, so that programs serving such students could continue to do so without adversely affecting their overall performance standards. In addition, rewards and sanctions at the federal level were not tied to performance at individual levels. Although many states did not set significantly different standards for the lower educational levels than for higher levels, it appears unlikely that NRS requirements led programs to stop serving lower level students. A review of national data on the percentage of students entering at the lower educational levels also provides little evidence of a problem. The proportion of students enrolled in the two lowest literacy levels remained about one third of ABE students and slightly more than one half of English as a Second Language (ESL) students for both 2000 and 2001, the first 2 program years of the NRS (it is very difficult to compare NRS data with those from prior years). Total program enrollment has also changed little over the last 3 years under WIA. Enrollment in the federal ABE program dropped from 2.9 million in 1999 to 2.7 million in 2000, but rose to 2.8 million the next year.

Average attendance hours of students, however, have increased under WIA, as most states have reported sharp increases in mean hours attended from 1999 to 2001. Nationally, the rise has been from a mean of 86 hr in 1999 to 111 hr in 2001. ESL students have shown the sharpest increase in attendance, up 33% from 1999 to 124 mean hr in 2001 (excluding Florida, which did not accurately report total attendance hours). The reasons students are attending more hours are not fully known, but may reflect programmatic changes designed to meet WIA's mandate to fund programs of sufficient intensity and duration to achieve learning gains to meet accountability requirements.

Student goal-setting

Although most ABE programs have always assisted students in goal setting as part of good instructional practice, there has been an increased emphasis on its importance due to NRS requirements to report student postparticipation outcomes related to employment, entry into postsecondary education, and passing the GED test. Local programs must track students who set these outcomes as a goal for attending and report the proportion of those students who achieved the outcome. Consequently, programs have become much more judicious in how they set and report student goals. Most states reported a lower proportion of students with these goals in 2001 than in 2000. In addition, many states often set two types of goals for students, one for accountability purposes and a second goal to guide instruction. Although these changes may reflect better goal setting processes, it is also apparent that in some states, fewer students have set the goals of passing the GED, employment, and entry into postsecondary education than appears plausible.

Assessment and instruction

Undoubtedly one of the biggest changes resulting from WIA accountability requirements has been in the area of student assessment. Programs must pretest and posttest students to determine their gains across NRS-defined educational functioning levels, the main outcome measures in the NRS. The NRS requires states to set assessment policies, including specifying which standardized tests to use and policies on when to pretest and posttest students. States and local programs have spent considerable resources establishing assessment systems through training local staff on test administration, purchasing tests, actual administration of the tests, and developing systems to track student performance on the assessments.

Besides the strain on resources that assessment requirements have brought on local programs, the short average duration of participation of ABE students has created additional problems for programs. Many students do not attend long enough to be posttested, making it difficult for programs to measure the extent of their learning. An additional challenge is the fact that the number of assessment instruments available for adult students is very limited, especially for low-literate learners, and are often not well aligned with what is taught in the classroom. Consequently, states and programs have had to select assessments that meet accountability requirements, regardless of their instructional approaches or the needs of students, rather than developing instructional standards and assessments aligned to them to measure student learning. This approach is the reverse of good educational practice, and has diverted the focus on using assessment information primarily as a means to evaluate students and inform instruction, to using assessment as an accountability tool to measure ABE program and system performance.

On the positive side, assessment requirements have focused much more attention on the need for programs to consider more deeply curriculum and instructional practices and the role of assessment in instruction. Many states have worked on improving both assessment and instruction by developing instructional standards, new approaches to assessment, and ways to use assessment for instructional decisions. Recent federal initiatives are designed to help states move in this direction through technical assistance to develop instructional content standards (see especially http://www.adultedcontentstandards.org), use data for program improvement (Condelli, 2003), and develop performance-based assessments (Condelli & Baker, 2003; Mislevy & Knowles, 2002).

Summary

The accountability requirements of the NRS have clearly affected retention, goal setting, and assessment procedures in ABE. On average, students appear to be staying longer, there is a stronger focus on goal setting, and student assessment has become a more critical element for programs. However, it is very difficult to ascertain how these changes have affected program quality in terms of improving instruction, program services, student development of literacy skills, and other outcomes. The NRS was developed deliberately in a way that it could increase its ability to influence program quality, but its actual effect on quality is undoubtedly state specific. Belzer's (2003) research found that states' ability to implement WIA requirements depended on the degree to which they anticipated the changes, their approach toward supporting local programs, and the quality of their professional development systems. State capacity and political context also affected the success and level of implementation. Thus, in states that recognized the potential of using the accountability system as a tool to influence quality and that were able to direct resources to implement NRS requirements by building the necessary systems and training, it appears likely that better programs have resulted. In states that lacked resources and implemented requirements in a pro forma fashion, it is unlikely that quality was much affected. In both cases, the requirements shifted substantial resources and attention toward reporting outcomes of ABE and indirectly on program quality.

Wave 3: Reauthorization of the Workforce Investment Act

As ABE concluded its final year under WIA, both houses of the U.S. Congress passed new legislation reauthorizing the ABE program. The proposed legislation kept the accountability requirements defined through the NRS largely intact, but made some important changes although it is unclear whether this new legislation will be implemented, I will speculate how these changes could affect program operation, and ultimately program quality. After first reviewing the proposed changes, I use the accountability framework of what we know about effective accountability systems to make an assessment of their possible impact on quality. I also offer some suggestions on how to affect program quality more directly through accountability.

Proposed Changes in Accountability

In this upcoming third wave of accountability, the general approach defined under WIA through the NRS remains intact. However, there are two significant proposed changes at the federal level and additional requirements at the state and local levels that may affect program quality. First, the two employment measures–entered and retained employment–may no longer be required core measures, meaning that state performance on these measures is no longer part of the basis for incentive awards. States would also be free to set performance standards on these measures without getting federal approval for the level set, as they do for the remaining core measures of educational gain, secondary level attainment, and advancement to postsecondary education. These changes mean that the employment measures may have much less importance at the federal level, under the proposed new system.

The second change at the federal level is the possible addition of a new employment-related measure, quarterly wages. ABE programs soon may be required to collect data on the wages of students with employment goals to determine whether they have increased after participation in ABE. This measure would be defined identically to the measure used by WIA Title I (job training) programs and would be collected in the same way as the current employment measure, through a system of data matching with employment records or through a telephone survey of learners.

The most significant proposed changes affecting accountability are at the local level. For the first time, states could be required to set performance standards for all local programs and to establish rewards and sanctions based on performance. WIA now only requires states to "consider" past performance when selecting providers. In addition, proposed legislation could require states to conduct annual reviews of programs not only to assess performance, but to ensure that programs are providing quality instruction in reading, writing, speaking, and math, based on "scientific research." Furthermore, states may be required to ensure that teachers are well trained, and, as under WIA, instruction is of sufficient quality and duration that it will lead to measurable gains. These requirements are noteworthy for their explicit focus on instruction and program operations, which have a direct influence on quality.

Significance of Changes for Program Quality

Although the new changes may not take effect, I can once again rely on the accountability-quality framework to speculate about the impact this third wave of accountability might have on ABE program quality. The proposed changes affect setting of performance standards, measures, sanctions, and how local programs are evaluated, and have both positive and negative potential effects.

At the federal level, the removal of employment status from the core measures is likely to have a positive effect. Accountability systems work best when they include measures directly related to program performance and most ABE programs can only indirectly affect whether their students get or retain jobs. Further, in most programs, only a relatively small percentage of students have an employment-related goal. Therefore, the employment measures by themselves are not very good indicators of the overall performance of most ABE programs and de-emphasizing them is not likely to affect quality adversely. On the other hand, the addition of a new employment-related measure, wage increase, is likely to have a negative effect. Not only do programs have little direct influence on affecting this measure, making it a poor performance measure according to accountability principles, but it will be almost impossible to collect in a valid way, except through data matching with wage records, something many states are unable to do.

The use of sanctions both at the state and local levels to punish poor performance can be effective, but is also dangerous. The research reviewed earlier suggests that when sanctions are set too high, unintended consequences that negatively affect student recruitment and instruction, as well as reporting practices, are more likely, with highly negative consequences for quality. How high sanctions are set and applied is therefore critical. Similarly, it is also important for states to set local performance standards at appropriate levels. When set too high, they result in negative consequences, and when set too low, they are not taken seriously and may be ineffective as indicators of performance and program quality.

The one proposed change with the greatest potential to impact program quality positively is the requirement for states to conduct annual reviews of program performance to determine whether they are providing quality instruction and professional development. As I have argued, outcome-based accountability systems can only affect quality indirectly. However, these new accountability requirements explicitly focus on what programs do. They have the potential to affect quality directly, and thus are a significant enhancement of the accountability system. This new requirement brings us full circle back to the quality indicators of Wave 1, as states will need to develop similar criteria for quality with which to evaluate what local programs do. Local programs and states will need to define and articulate high quality instruction, recruitment, support services, and professional development. The success of this renewed direct focus on program quality will depend in part, however, on states having the resources and capacity to implement this requirement--not something always to be taken for granted. Indeed, Belzer (2003) found that states cannot implement policy changes of this type without sufficient resources.

IMPROVING QUALITY THROUGH ACCOUNTABILITY

ABE now has 4 years of experience under a formal accountability system and has succeeded in establishing a successful system that has helped it survive federal funding cuts in this era of accountability. Although there have been many benefits resulting from the implementation of accountability requirements, the NRS remains a work in progress, with many weaknesses and areas for further development. However, as we enter this third wave of accountability, adult educators have an opportunity to focus more directly on guiding the system to have a greater impact on program quality. I conclude with some suggestions for achieving this goal.

Set Performance Standards Appropriately

Initially, states had little experience and prior information that would have enabled them to set appropriate performance standards. To ensure their programs would meet them, many cautiously set them at a relatively low level. Consequently, almost all states exceeded all their standards, some by very high margins. As I have discussed, performance standards set too low affect the overall credibility of the performance data, as they imply that the performance system is not taken seriously. In addition, when standards are set too low, they have a low probability of affecting program operations and quality, as programs can easily meet them without making changes.

The proposed requirement for states to set performance standards for local programs provides an opportunity to use standards more effectively. By setting them at appropriate levels, states can use standards as a means to promote policy goals and program quality. For example, states could set lower educational gain standards to encourage programs to serve low-literacy students or adjust standards for GED attainment to encourage programs to serve greater numbers of adult secondary students. Employment standards for programs serving students with employment goals could be set according to the local economic conditions.

To set standards appropriately, however, states will need to learn to use their data more effectively to answer policy questions.

Use of Additional Outcome Measures

Although much attention is focused on federal accountability requirements of the NRS, most states also must meet their own accountability requirements, which often differ. States may use additional educational levels, other measures, and place different emphases on measures than at the federal level. Because measures reflect program and policy goals, states can define additional measures that reflect their unique policy goals and delivery systems. For example, a state can set performance standards for family literacy measures or citizenship attainment to require programs to provide these services. In this way, the use of additional measures allows for greater expansion of the purposes of ABE and the services it provides, helping to mitigate against the narrower focus of the NRS outcomes, which has been the source of concern and considerable angst among many practitioners.

Explicit Focus on Program Processes

States need to take advantage of the new proposed requirements to review local programs annually to establish their own program operational requirements that define a quality ABE program. As was done under Wave 1, states need to develop (or revive) something like the quality indicators to set criteria for what constitutes a quality program and then tie these standards into the accountability systems. Several states already do this as part of their program monitoring process. However, the ability of states to set and monitor compliance with these types of standards will be limited by the resources they have available to conduct reviews.

As there are limited resources for reviewing local programs and because much work has already been done on developing quality indicators and standards, one approach toward ensuring quality in an accountability system could be to adopt a system of program accreditation, as is used in higher education and other social service programs (Comings & Stein, 1991). Under an accreditation process, the field would adopt an accepted set of operational standards and an independent body, usually consisting of peers from other programs, would review programs to determine their adherence to the standards. The accreditation could be voluntary and funded by the states and programs that are interested in achieving the accreditation. The chief advantage of this approach is that it establishes a uniform, and therefore, more efficient system of quality that saves the expense of each state having to develop its own standards and review process. Early childhood programs have developed an accreditation process that could serve as a model for ABE, given the similarity of delivery systems and funding mechanisms of the two programs (for details on the process, see http://www.na eyc.org/accreditation/naeyc_accred/info_general-components.asp).

Assessment

One of the major difficulties in accountability for ABE remains the lack of availability of assessment instruments and the difficulty of tying the results from current assessment to instruction. There is no quick or easy solution to this problem. The field needs a wider variety of literacy and language assessments for adults which are aligned with instructional standards. Although ED has provided some resources toward this effort, including convening a national symposium on developing performance-based assessments (Mislevy & Knowles, 2002), and a project to assist states in developing instructional content standards (U.S. Department of Education, 2005), continued support is needed. Several states are developing innovative approaches to assessment, which also should be supported and continued.

Although much attention has been focused on developing standardized assessments, another approach that might be considered is to adopt a system of learner accreditation, similar to approaches used in Great Britain (Hamilton & Merrifield, 1999). Under this approach, learners can obtain credit and a credential for work completed, based on a set of performance indicators and accepted standards of learning. Alternatively, independent authorities (similar to Britain's Open College Network) could accredit specific courses of instruction that teach essential basic skills within an established set of skill standards. Learners that satisfactorily complete the accredited courses are presumed to have the skills. Within the NRS framework, this approach could work by better defining the skills inherent within the educational functioning levels and then determining indicators of performance within the levels. The difficulty with this approach, both here and in Britain, has been to develop consensus and acceptance on the skills that would define the educational levels. However, if accountability is to result in improved program quality in ABE, continued resources and support must be given to creative and innovative approaches like these.

REFERENCES

Baj, J., Sheets, R., & Trott, C. (1995). *Building state workforce development systems based on policy coordination and policy assurance.* Washington, DC: National Governors' Association.

Belzer, A. (2003). *Living with it: Federal policy implementation in adult basic education. The cases of the workforce investment act and welfare reform* (NCSALL Report No. 24). Cambridge, MA: National Center for the Study of Adult Learning and Literacy.

Comings, J. P., & Stein, S. (1991). Would accreditation work for ABE programs? *Adult Learning, 3,* 23-24.

Condelli, L. (1996). *Evaluation systems in the adult education program: The role of quality indicators.* Washington, DC: U.S. Department of Education, Office of Vocational and Adult Education.

Condelli, L. (1998). *Measure definitions for the national reporting system for adult education.* Washington, DC: U.S. Department of Education, Office of Vocational and Adult Education.

Condelli, L. (2003). *Using NRS data for program management and improvement.* Washington, DC: U.S. Department of Education, Office of Vocational and Adult Education.

Condelli, L., & Baker, H. (2003). *Developing performance assessments for adult literacy learners: A summary.* Washington, DC: U.S. Department of Education, Office of Vocational and Adult Education.

Condelli, L., & Kutner, M. (1992). *Quality indicators for adult education: Lessons learned from other programs.* Washington, DC: Pelavin Research Institute.

Condelli, L., & Kutner, M. (1997). *Developing a national outcome reporting system for the adult education program.* Washington, DC: Office of Vocational and Adult Education.

Elmore, R. (1997). Accountability in local school districts: Learning to do the right things. *Advances in Educational Administration, 5,* 59-82.

Hamilton, M., & Merrifield., J., (1999). Adult learning and literacy in the United Kingdom. In J. Comings, B. Garner, & C. Smith (Eds.). *The annual review of adult learning and literacy* (Vol. 1, pp. 243-303). San Francisco: Jossey-Bass.

Mislevy, R., & Knowles, K. (2002). *Performance assessments for adult education: Exploring the measurements issues.* Washington, DC: National Academy of Sciences, National Research Council, Board of Testing and Assessment.

National Commission on Employment Policy. (1987). *The Job Training Partnership Act.* Washington, DC: National Commission on Employment Policy.

Stecher, B. (1995). *Improving performance measures and standards for workforce education.* Berkeley, CA: National Center for Research in Vocational Education.

Trott, C., & Baj, J. (1996). *Building state systems based on performance: The workforce development experience. A guide for states.* Washington, DC: National Governor's Association.

U.S. Department of Education. (1992). *Model indicators of program quality for adult education programs.* Washington, DC: Office of Vocational and Adult Education.

U. S. Department of Education. (2001). *Measures and methods for the national reporting system for adult education: NRS implementation guidelines.* Washington, DC: Office of Vocational and Adult Education.

U. S. Department of Education. (2005). *The adult educators guide for establishing state content standards.* Washington, DC: Office of Vocational and Adult Education.

Winerip, M. (2003, August 13). The 'zero dropout' miracle: Alas! Alack! A Texas tall tale. *The New York Times*, Late Edition, Section B, p. 7, Column 1.

Chapter 2

Equipped for the Future and Standards-Based Educational Improvement: Achieving Results that Matter for Adult Learners

Sondra G. Stein, Ph.D.
Equipped for the Future
National Institute for Literacy

The history of standards-based reform of education in the United States began, in 1983, with the publication of *A Nation at Risk,* the report of the National Commission on Excellence in Education (NCEE, 1983). One of dozens of responses by governments around the world to the first impact of globalization and the information age, the report, subtitled "The Imperative for Educational Reform," begins with an excoriation of "a rising tide of mediocrity" that is "eroding the educational foundations of our society" and "threatening our very future as a Nation and a people" (NCEE, 1983, p. 5). Finding that "our society and its educational institutions seem to have lost sight of the basic purpose of schooling and of the high expectations and disciplined effort needed to attain them," the report called for "schools, colleges, and universities to adopt more rigorous and measurable standards, and higher expectations for academic performance and student conduct [in order to] help students do their best educationally with challenging materials in an environment that supports learning and authentic achievement" (NCEE, 1983, p. 27).

Six years later, President George Herbert Walker Bush called together all 50 governors for the first National Summit on Education since George Washington was President. At the summit, the governors put in place the political mechanism for a standards-based approach to raising educational achievement across the country. They established a set of common, national performance goals in education, and each state committed to launch serious efforts to improve educational performance in relation to those goals. One of those goals focused on adult literacy and lifelong learning. In 1991, when Congress established the National Institute for Literacy (NIFL) as part of the National Literacy Act, they called on this new agency to report on progress within the states and across the nation toward achievement of what is now Goal 6 of the National Education Goals: "Every adult American will be literate, and possess the knowledge and skills necessary to compete in a global economy and exercise the rights and responsibilities of citizenship" (National Education Goals, 2000).

Equipped for the Future (EFF), the NIFL's standards-based educational reform initiative, grew out of this mandate to measure progress toward our national goal (Stein, 2000). This chapter draws on the experience of the EFF development team over the past decade to examine the premises behind standards-based reform as an approach to educational improvement, and the conditions under which it can make a contribution to the quality of educational systems and educational interventions and lead to higher levels of learning for students.

WHY STANDARDS-BASED REFORM?

> Knowledge, learning, information and skilled intelligence are the new raw materials of international commerce and are today spreading throughout the world as vigorously as miracle drugs, synthetic fertilizers, and blue jeans did earlier. If only to keep and improve on the slim competitive edge we still retain in world markets, we must dedicate ourselves to the reform of our educational system for the benefit of all … " (NCEE, 1983, p. 6)

Because a key impetus for educational reform in the 1980s was the impact of the global economy and the fear that the United States would somehow be left behind if we did not improve our schools, it is fitting that the method proposed for educational reform–the emphasis on using standards to drive reform throughout the system—mirrored the approach adopted by U.S. corporations at the same time as a way to improve productivity and competitiveness. Throughout the business world, there was a new interest in the Japanese approach to quality, based, in fact, on the methods of W. E. Deming, an American statistician and management consultant (Deming, 1982). At the heart of this new approach to building better products more efficiently was the recognition that as long as quality control was left to the end of the production line, it could not improve the percentage of quality products produced. Instead, it could only sort high quality from inferior products. To minimize waste of time and materials, Deming proposed that quality control be integrated into every stage of the production process. In this way, variance from the quality standard could be detected as soon as it occurred, and a higher percentage of quality products would result.

Translated to the world of education, the quality approach has been characterized by an emphasis on what Deming talked about as "fact-based" management: getting clear on what the results are that you want to achieve (developing standards), aligning all your systems and processes to achieve those results (making sure that everyone in the system knows what those standards are and their role in achieving them), and then carefully measuring your progress toward achieving those results (using tests, instead of statistical process control, to measure variance from the standard). Figure 2-1 shows how educational policymakers expected standards-based reform to work.

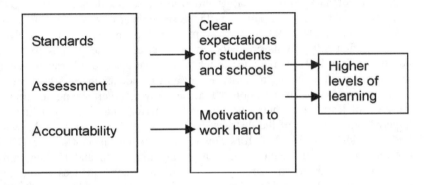

Figure 2.1. Basic model, theory of action of standards-based reform

No Child Left Behind (NCLB), the Bush Administration's signature education reform initiative, represents a straightforward application of this mechanism. NCLB focuses on assessment of "high standards" in reading and math, introducing more testing, for more students, at earlier points in the educational process, to provide earlier opportunities for identifying how well students are performing in relation to the standard. NCLB also includes strong accountability provisions, holding schools accountable for achieving higher levels of learning by introducing the threat of lost or reduced funding for any school that does not meet the established performance criteria. The use of serious sanctions against schools that are labeled as "low performing" is intended to provide the motivation for students, teachers, and schools to work harder and perform better so that "no child is left behind."

Over the past 2 years, there has been a widening critical response to NCLB, from teachers and school superintendents, and, increasingly, from parents and elected officials. They argue that rather than encouraging higher levels of learning, the primary accountability mechanisms introduced by NCLB have in fact worked against them. Many educators argue that the frequent high stakes testing has shifted instruction in the classroom from a broader focus on building conceptual foundations to a narrower focus on preparation for the test, and from a focus on a broad range of academic subjects–reading, math, social studies, history, geography, arts, music–to an almost exclusive focus on reading and math-- the only subjects tested. Although students may score higher on NCLB-related

tests, these educators argue, their overall preparation for life–their level of learning–may be lower than before.

Most recently, the critique of NCLB has focused on its accountability provisions. Under NCLB, a school can be labeled *low-performing* regardless of
how well the majority of students perform on the required tests in reading and
math, if less than 95% of any target group in the school does not take the assessment in a given year. This was the case for many of the 26,000 public
schools (out of a total of 93,000) that were labeled low performing by the law in
2003, the first full year its provisions were in effect. Although this particular
provision of the law was intended to make sure that a school district served all
its students well, including minority and disabled students, the *unintended* consequence has been to label schools that are actually high performing–in terms of
the level of learning of their students--as low performing. Dr. Elliott Landon,
Superintendent of one of the districts that "failed" the NCLB test in this way,
told the following to *The New York Times:* "It really bugs me that we got a black
eye for a mechanical reason rather than for anything legitimate" (Dillon, 2004,
p. A31). Although acknowledging these unintended consequences of the law,
Eugene Hickok, Deputy U.S. Secretary of Education, defended NCLB: "the
point of the law is not to label schools … [but] to find out which students are not
performing well, and to do something about it" (Dillon, 2004, p. A31).

Secretary Hickok's statement echoes the goals of standards-based reform.
But in fact, the way in which the law defines standards-based reform might very
well prohibit it from ever achieving its intended goal of helping more students
do better. According to *Testing, Teaching, and Learning: A Guide For States
and School Districts,* a 1999 report by the National Research Council's (NRC's)
Board on Testing and Assessment, the basic model (discussed earlier) of how
standards-based reform works does not address all the elements necessary for
successful achievement of higher levels of learning. Careful examination of state
efforts to implement standards-based reform in the kindergarten through 12th-
grade system in the 1990s revealed that it was not sufficient to build a system
which aligned high standards, assessment, and accountability, in the hope that
clearer expectations matched with powerful sanctions would lead to achievement of better results. Another element is critical to produce those higher levels
of learning–professional development specifically targeted at providing teachers
with the opportunity to learn how to use the best research on how to improve
learning for all students. The NRC report offered an amended model of the theory of action of standards-based reform that reflected this finding.

This amended model of how standards-based reform works comes closer to
reflecting the systemic nature of the approach to quality originally advocated by
Deming in his 14 principles for quality management. Often described as continuous improvement through total employee involvement, this more holistic
approach to quality is what the U.S. Department of Commerce has adopted as
the foundation for the Malcolm Baldrige Criteria for Performance Excellence
(Baldrige National Quality Program, 2004). In this approach to system quality–

whether in the realm of business, health care, or education–the focus is not on achievement of specific performance goals but on engaging all the workers in an organization in a systematic, fact-based process of quality improvement. Viewed through this lens, standards, assessments, and accountability–the triumvirate that has become the hallmark of a standards-based approach to education improvement–are not the focus of the effort. Rather, they are primarily tools for helping teachers and administrators do a better job.

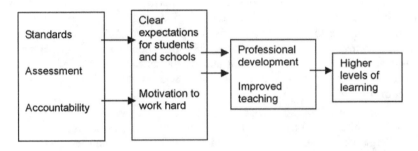

Figure 2.2. Evidence-based model, theory of action of standards-based reform

This is the model of standards-based reform adopted by EFF. In advocating standards-based reform, EFF approaches it as a continuous improvement process in which standards and assessments are tools that provide all the workers in the system, teachers as well as administrators, with information they need to periodically review how well the system is doing to achieve desired results. Where there are gaps, system workers identify and put in place possible improvements to help the system achieve higher, or more equitable results.

This chapter draws on the experience of implementing EFF standards in adult education since 2000 to argue that standards-based reform can be a successful strategy for building a higher quality adult literacy and basic skills system that systematically produces better results for adult learners if three conditions are met:

1. If the standards focus on results that matter to adult learners.
2. If professional development policies and practices engage teachers in an active process of standards-based improvement.
3. If there is an institutional environment that supports standards-based reform.

THE EQUIPPED FOR THE FUTURE STANDARDS: RESULTS THAT MATTER

Content standards are the heart of any standards-based reform system. The NRC diagram of the theory of action of standards-based reform (discussed earlier) illustrates how standards drive the system. They define what students need to know (content standards), and how well or when they need to know it (performance standards). These expectations for student performance shape all the rest of the system—the assessments, the accountability, the teaching and learning—and, of course, the results. For this reason, standards-based reform works, in the sense of achieving goals we care about, *only* if the content standards define results that matter, only if the content and performance standards reflect broad consensus on what is important for students to know and be able to do (Wurtz & Malcom, 1993).

This is one of the key criteria for defining educational and occupational standards in the United States. It is why every standards development initiative in kindergarten through 12th-grade content areas and in industry sectors has been broadly inclusive, making every effort to represent key strands of thinking, key perspectives, key stakeholders. Those initiatives that succeed, like the mathematics standards developed by the National Council of Teachers of Mathematics, do so because they have been successful in building that broad consensus. Those efforts that have more troubled histories, like the English Language standards and the American History standards, fail because they are unable to build consensus on what is most important.

Building consensus on standards for the adult literacy and basic skills system has been more difficult than for the primary and secondary education system. In the case of kindergarten through 12th-grade standards, there was broad agreement that the starting point for the development of standards was academic disciplines—mathematics, science, geography—and the goal was to build a foundation of knowledge and skills, grade by grade, that would enable students to fully participate in American life when they became adults.

The starting point was not so clear for the adult literacy and basic skills system, largely because of differences between the adult and kindergarten through 12th-grade populations. Most adults who enter this system have already been through a primary and in some cases a secondary education system. They already have a foundation of knowledge and skill, based on both formal and informal educational opportunities throughout their lives. They return to formal education as adults to achieve a particular learning goal, often because of a change in life circumstances that has given rise to that goal. How do you frame standards for a system that aims to serve such a diverse student body, with such diverse learning needs? How do you approach building competence in content domains when each student has different baseline knowledge and few students remain in learning programs for even 50 hours of instruction, the equivalent of two weeks in school at the kindergarten through 12th-grade level? At the time that NIFL first launched EFF, the only consensus in the field was that there could be no consensus: the only responsible approach to adult learning was for instructors to address each learner individually.

The National Adult Learning Goal gave NIFL a new place to start in thinking about standards for adult learning. Instead of focusing on academic knowledge domains, as the other national goals did, this goal focused on critical adult roles, on what adults need literacy *for*. When NIFL asked adult learners to help us launch a process that could turn that goal from an idealized statement of a desired end to a practical measure of learning, they responded by endorsing the focus on roles and identifying four fundamental purposes for learning, related to helping them achieve goals and purposes in their adult roles (Stein, 1995).

NIFL was able to build broad consensus around this framework of roles and purposes, as a first step in the standards-development process, because it offered a way to think about adult literacy education that was consonant with educators' view of themselves and the needs and interests of their students. The goal of defining a "body of knowledge and skills adults need … to address the four purposes throughout their lives as they move from one context to another" (Stein, 1995, p. 10), suggested a shift in both the what and the how of adult education: from a focus on remediation, characterized by a school-based model of decontextualized instruction in academic content areas, to a focus on adult development, characterized by a contextualized approach to instruction, aimed at building competence in learners' ability to use a core set of generative skills and knowledge to accomplish a wide range of purposes in their lives. This was an *adult* approach to education that would be judged by how well it helped adults achieve purposes that mattered in their own lives, rather than on whether it enabled adults to "show learning gains" according to a school-based model of preestablished, standardized levels of competence.

Armed with broad agreement from literacy stakeholders that this focus on what adults need literacy *for* was the right one for adult learning, the EFF development team turned to the emerging body of research on the learning sciences to define standards that were congruent with cognitive science research on how people learn and develop expertise. This research, like EFF, began from the assumption that learning is a goal directed, purposeful human activity (Scribner, 1987). As a result, the best way to facilitate learning with understanding and transfer of learning from one context to another was to organize knowledge in purposeful chunks: teaching "facts" in the context of "concepts and principles" and "procedures" that are conditioned according to when they are useful (Glaser, 1991).

In keeping with this approach, each EFF standard was defined as an integrated skill process that was always launched by attending to the purpose which required using the skill (whether the skill was reading, using math, or resolving conflict). That purpose also provided the context for learning new facts and procedures, learning and practicing cognitive strategies that enabled goal-oriented organization of knowledge (Glaser, 1991), and learning and practicing metacognitive strategies that enabled monitoring and evaluation of performance (Greeno, Resnick, & Collins, 1997). By building these key elements of cognitive science theory into EFF standards, the EFF development team provided a research-based rationale for expanding the focus of adult education to explicitly address cognitive and metacognitive strategies. This gives adult learners the tools they need to revise and build on prior knowledge (Bransford, Brown, & Cocking, 1999), so they could use the target skills with greater fluency, independence, and range.

By developing applied learning standards and focusing the standards specifically on what adults need to know to use the standard to achieve meaningful goals and purposes in everyday life, the EFF team made sure that the driver of our system for standards-based reform was a good one: it would matter if we achieved the goals EFF defined--to adult learners, our key customers, and to many of the stakeholders of our system, including employers and other partners in the workforce investment system, and partners in the public education system who are concerned about adults' role in helping their children succeed in school.

THE POWER OF PROFESSIONAL DEVELOPMENT: ENGAGING TEACHERS IN STANDARDS-BASED REFORM

Although standards define what a system aims to achieve, professional development specifically aimed at improving the quality of teaching and learning is the primary vehicle for assuring that educational programs actually achieve these results. In their review of states' efforts to implement standards-based reform, the National Research Council Committee on Title I Testing and Assessment found that teachers were limited in their ability to implement standards-based reform in the classroom because they did not know what changes to make in their instruction. The committee also found that the amount and kind of professional development opportunities available were not sufficient to support such changes. Their conclusion, reflected in the report cited earlier, was that "standards-based policies can affect student learning only if they are tied directly to efforts to build the capacity of teachers and administrators to improve instruction" (NRC, 1999).

The importance of addressing professional development needs of practitioners emerged early in the life of the EFF initiative. Because EFF was committed to standards-based reform as a tool to improve the quality of the adult literacy and basic skills system, the development team adopted a field-based approach to developing and refining our standards and related products. As soon as the first draft of the standards was complete, we invited state directors of adult education to join us in helping to ensure that EFF standards could work within the day-to-day realities of programs and classrooms. Over the next 5 years we engaged these "field development partners" in a highly structured program of practitioner research, involving up to 100 practitioners at a time, working in more than 25 programs in 12 states. The goal of this practitioner research effort was to collect data from practitioners to help us determine whether EFF standards were specific enough to inform instruction and assessment and whether our approach to assessment and accountability met the needs of program and state administrators. To make sure that the data we collected was as useful as possible, we had to design and provide an organized program of professional development in standards-based instruction.

The model of practitioner research as professional development that we developed and refined reflects many of the elements of professional development that Richard Elmore identified as necessary for the purpose of engaging teachers in the process of standards-based improvement (Elmore, 2002). In *Bridging the Gap Between Standards and Achievement: The Imperative for Professional Development in Education* (2002), Elmore synthesized the following consensus list of key elements:

- Focuses on a well-articulated mission or purpose anchored in student learning of core disciplines and skills.

- Derives from analysis of student learning of specific content in a specific setting.

- Focuses on specific issues of curriculum and pedagogy, derived from research and exemplary practice and connected with specific issues of instruction and student learning … in the context of actual classrooms.

- Embodies a clearly articulated theory or model of adult learning.

- Develops, reinforces and sustains group work through collaborative practice within schools and networks across schools.

- Involves active participation of school leaders and staff.

- Sustains focus over time – continuous improvement.

- Provides models of effective practice delivered in schools and classrooms.

- Uses assessment and evaluation for active monitoring of student learning and to provide feedback on teacher learning and practice. (p. 7)

As Elmore pointed out, very few of these elements of effective practice come into play in the approach to professional development that is dominant in education today. The more typical approach to professional development is grounded in policies that treat the teacher as a *solo practitioner* who is expected to accumulate academic credit for courses to advance in rank or salary. This approach operates on the assumption that *any improvement in teacher knowledge and skill will benefit student learning.* Because the content of professional development is wholly at the discretion of the individual, who gets the same benefit in rank or salary regardless of whether the courses are connected to his or her daily work, there is no systematic way to tell whether the professional development has an impact on student learning. Changing professional development so that it is a fully integrated element in a system of standards-based improvement is critical, according to Elmore, to the kind of improvements in teaching and learning that are necessary to achieve higher levels of learning for students.

Because the EFF field development effort was highly structured and collected data on teacher knowledge and behavior over a multiyear period, it functioned as a laboratory in which we were able to try out and observe the impact of many of the elements of professional development identified by Elmore. By the third year, through analysis of the data we collected, we were able to refine a model for practitioner research as professional development that we articulated in a series of formal agreements with practitioners, program administrators, and state administrators (See Bell & McGuire, 2002 for full text of these agreements). This model included five critical elements from Elmore's (2002) list. First, and most important, the model brought teachers, program administrators, and state administrators together in a common, collaboratively defined effort to improve adult learning. Second, by requiring that each participant be part of a four-person program team and that the team meet together regularly, the model shifted the focus from individual professional development to program improvement. Third, by defining the research task to focus on classroom-based activities, the model required teachers to step outside of their usual practice, try out new instructional strategies, and collect data and reflect on the process and outcomes. Fourth, to assure that teacher-researchers developed the knowledge and skills needed to try out the new practices in their classrooms, the model replaced one-shot workshops with a range of professional development activities over a sustained period of time. Finally, the model did not overlook the need to build in institutional supports (such as paid individual and group planning and preparation time) that are critical to creating an environment that supports teacher innovation and change. Each of these elements is discussed in more detail later.

The agreement with teachers laid out the specific requirements of the research project at the heart of the professional development. From 1999 to 2000, the focus of the research task was collecting data on student performance to help build the EFF assessment framework. This focus meant that participating teachers were engaged in purposeful activity anchored in analysis of student learning of specific content–two elements that Elmore (2002) identified as central to professional development for standards-based improvement. To enable us to aggregate data across the 80-plus participating teachers, we structured the process carefully. Teachers were asked to use a step-by-step approach to working with students to plan what we called "well-structured" learning activities, to document for us the process of planning and implementing instruction, and to describe and provide evidence of the results of that instruction for three cycles of planning-instruction-assessment of student learning.

The research was centered in the classroom, requiring teachers to focus on instructional strategies that supported student learning of knowledge and skills. To ensure that the research enhanced student learning, teachers were asked to choose the standards on which they wanted to concentrate. We encouraged them to focus on areas of knowledge and skill that were most critical to their students. We also encouraged participating teacher-researchers and administrators to make sure that at least two teachers from the same program were working with the same EFF standard. Because part of the professional development was aimed at building teacher expertise in working with the knowledge base of a particular standard, having more than one teacher focused on the same content, as well as the same process, meant teachers could support each other in their learning.

In *Bridging the Gap between Standards and Achievement,* Elmore (2002) reminded us why these aspects of professional development are so important:

> Direct linkages between professional development and accountability ... will succeed to the degree that they engage teachers and administrators in acquiring knowledge and skills they need to solve problems and meet expectations for high performance. To the degree that people are being asked to do things they don't know how to do and, at the same time, are not being asked to engage their own ideas, values and energies in the learning process, professional development shifts from building capacity to demanding compliance. (p. 12)

Professional development activities for participants in the EFF project were designed to address both aspects of capacity building. Over the course of a year, teachers were provided with instruction in the EFF approach to purposeful, contextual instruction aimed at building students' expertise in using particular standards to carry out meaningful tasks in their everyday lives. The process included three intensive training institutes. One, at the start of the process, was conducted at the state level to ground the work in state-specific requirements. Midyear and end-of-year meetings included participants from all partner states to enrich the exchange of ideas and to begin to build a national network of teachers, program administrators, and state leaders committed to standards-based improvements.

Because we knew the training provided through these institutes was not sufficient to build the level of competence participants needed to carry out new approaches to teaching, our agreements required participating programs to establish regular meetings of all practitioner researchers in a program, and states to provide stipends to teachers and programs to cover the costs for such extra staff time (discussed later). The regular biweekly research team meetings supplemented what was learned through the institutes, providing an opportunity for participating teachers to review each other's work and to help each other figure out effective ways to approach problems that emerged during implementation. EFF project staff conducted two site visits early in the year when participants were likely to need on-site help the most. Project staff members also were available by conference call and e-mail to support the learning process.

Two elements of the teachers' task were at the center of their learning: the requirement to follow a new approach to planning and instruction, and the requirement to document the process and provide feedback on the usefulness of the tools the EFF team developed for teachers, and on the ways in which using them changed what happened in the classroom. By and large teachers were willing to try out this new approach to instruction, although it involved substantial changes in their daily practice, because it was part of something larger that made sense to them. They understood the goal of what we were trying to achieve, and the theory behind the approach we were using (Elmore, 2002). The fact that they were being compensated for the extra planning and documentation time (although the level of compensation was more an honorarium than actual hourly payment) also contributed to teachers' willingness to try something new (Smith, Hofer, & Gillespie, 2001). When the work became difficult, it helped that they were part of a team, that their program administrator and the state director supported the work, and that carrying out the work enrolled them in a larger "community of practice" (Wenger, 1998) made up of teachers across the country who, like them, were committed to trying out this approach to standards-based instruction to see whether it might help them do a better job of reaching and teaching their students.

At state, and especially, at national project meetings, the excitement was contagious, the buzz of learning continuous. EFF staff always constructed these sessions as working meetings. Teachers and administrators were given lots of opportunities to work in small groups with others from across the country teaching the same standard or working with the same population of adult learners. During the first day of the meeting, the assignment for these groups was usually to share learnings, compare processes and results, and identify key questions and challenges. The small group sessions were followed by a whole group synthesis exercise in which everyone had the opportunity to see how their individual work contributed to the whole, and through which we arrived at a negotiated group consensus on the way forward. The whole group sessions were followed by more work in small groups, this time focused on building and practicing the skills needed for the next phase of the research task. As a result, participants left these meetings exhausted and exhilarated, with new tools for working with their own students, enhanced understanding of the theory and action of standards-based instruction, and with a sense of themselves as part of a community of teacher-researchers who were discovering how to improve their practice and make a difference for their students. In this way, the research project created an environment that supported and encouraged what Elmore (2002) called the "practice of improvement."

The documentation provided by teachers and administrators enabled us to have a window on the kinds of changes teachers were making in their practice and the impact of these changes on their classrooms and students. As a result, teacher documentation provided data on what the teachers had learned well enough to implement and where they needed more support. Changes that were reported by almost all teacher participants can be summed up in the words of one teacher as "focusing on … facilitating student learning rather than teaching the 'right answers.'" Teachers talked about "thinking more about students' prior knowledge–what they bring to the learning environment from their previous experience–and planning in ways that will build on this prior knowledge." This was related to "thinking ahead" in lesson planning. Before they began a lesson, teachers were asking themselves what evidence of student performance they expected to see from an activity. They were thinking about how the student performance would be documented and how to involve students in the process of developing criteria for the evidence of learning. Even more important, teachers were beginning to think about what they needed to know to build students' cognitive and metacognitive strategies and engage them in thinking about their own learning processes–thinking about thinking. Finally, teachers reported more critical reflection on their own teaching. As one teacher wrote, "I am continually asking if the learning activity has real-life meaning and will result in transferable skills for the learner" (Bell & McGuire, 2002, p 27).

Administrators' quarterly reports identified similar changes in teacher behavior (EFF/NRS Joint Data Collection Project, 2000-2002). The largest proportion of administrator comments focused on increased intentionality in planning and teaching. One administrator wrote the following:

> Teachers continue to have good discussions with students about ways to apply knowledge and ways to integrate prior knowledge and experience. They are very aware of the need to determine the students' prior knowledge before they begin the task. It takes a lot of preparation and planning.

Another described how the teachers in her program were "gathering more feedback from the students and giving them more opportunity to reflect upon what and how they are learning. This data has been helpful in identifying what changes need to be made to the lessons." A third administrator noted the following:

> One of the most heartening signs emerging from our research is having witnessed the transformation of the [teacher] researchers' approach to their teaching. For example, the [teacher] researchers have all stated that they have been more analytical and better organized not only in their teaching but in their lives as well.

Such changes in participating teachers led another administrator to reflect the following: "A lot of things have changed this year. The teachers involved in the EFF project do many things differently.... I'm not sure the normal teacher interacts with students with the level of awareness that seems to be required."

In their quarterly reports, administrators also were asked to describe any changes they observed in learner behavior in classes where teachers were trying out these new approaches to instruction. Although our efforts were focused on teacher change, we wanted to encourage administrators from the start to pay attention to the goal of this change process—improvements in student learning. What administrators consistently noted were increases in student involvement and persistence. According to an administrator from an Oregon program, "Learners attend class much more consistently, and are more attentive in class due to increased interest in activities that related to the goals they have articulated." Similar comments came from administrators in the other participating states: Maine, Ohio, Tennessee, and Washington. For example, one administrator wrote the following: "While learners still get frustrated and discouraged and talk about quitting, they seem wed to seeing activity-based learning opportunities through to their end, and get re-charged for the next challenge when one activity is successfully completed." Another commented on similar changes: "Students are taking an active role in their own learning …. Students are also asking each other for help and working together to accomplish tasks. The classroom climate is much more collaborative." And yet another found that "students seem to persist when they consistently are given the opportunity to think about what they are learning and why, and to relate it to something meaningful in their own lives. It seems closely related to the instructors' struggle to understand how to teach and help others learn."

THE INSTITUTIONAL ENVIRONMENT: MEETING THE CONDITIONS FOR HIGH PERFORMANCE

One of the persistent problems we face in instituting large-scale improvement of the adult literacy and basic skills system is a lack of the necessary resources to support the kind of substantive change that EFF advocates. Adult literacy and basic skills programs often operate in substandard, makeshift facilities and borrowed classrooms, with predominantly part-time staff who work varied hours in a range of instructional sites. All these institutional factors make it difficult for programs to support the kind of sustained professional development required for teachers to develop expertise using standards to guide teaching and assessment. In their study of professional development and teacher change in adult education, Smith, Hofer, and Gillespie (2003) found a strong correlation between such factors as access to benefits and paid planning and preparation time, and teacher motivation and ability to integrate new practices into their teaching. Yet, roughly half of the teachers in their sample had no access either to benefits, or paid planning time. Although 77% of the teachers received some paid professional development time, for nearly half, this was only 1 to 12 hours per year. Given these conditions, the EFF development team knew that our requirements for participation in EFF field research needed to do more than acknowledge these institutional barriers. We had to put in place structural supports designed to ameliorate their impact. Agreements signed by state and program administrators were designed to create an environment within the state and the program that supported teacher innovation and change.

At the state level, the agreements put an emphasis on financial and programmatic support. In addition to providing financial support for three to five programs, state adult basic education directors also were asked to " ... keep well informed about what is happening in the field development process by attending all trainings and meetings or sending representatives," and, even more important, to " ... think about how to integrate what is happening with EFF field development into the ongoing work of the statewide adult basic education system" (Bell & McGuire, 2002, p. 39). Because so many teachers were hourly employees who did not receive paid planning time, the financial support provided by the state to each participating program was, of course, a critical element. Just as important, however, was the state administrator's willingness to participate in the process. In some cases, state directors of adult education went one step further, signaling their support for the work participants were engaged in by exempting participating programs from other reporting requirements.

Requirements for program administrators were just as essential to the success of the effort. In addition to attending all training and technical assistance sessions, they were asked to actively support the participation of a team consisting of several instructors in several ways: observing teachers' instruction and documentation activities, convening regular team meetings to assure that the members of the team worked collaboratively as much as possible, encouraging other professional development opportunities such as teacher cross-visitation and observation, observing and documenting the effects of EFF implementation in the program, and keeping state agency contacts informed about progress and outcomes (Bell & McGuire, 2002).

Probably the most critical aspect of the program administrator's role was arranging the schedules of participating teachers so that they could attend biweekly meetings to discuss the progress of their work. The value of these meetings quickly became clear. Teachers and program administrators consistently reported that the team meetings were one of the greatest benefits of participating in the process, because they provided the first regular opportunity to interact with other teachers around curriculum and instruction (Schimmenti et al., 2003). One administrator wrote the following:

I think the EFF project has been very beneficial in strengthening the relationships among the teachers. They work very well together. They plan together and they share ideas to strengthen their classes and help their students learn. They really support each other, which has been very important to get all the work done.

A second administrator was even more positive about the value of team meetings. She wrote the following:

Team meetings are a joy as instructors share and explore instructional practice. It is like going back to school together. There is a shared ownership in outcomes and a shared pride in the struggle and accomplishment of moving forward in their profession. There is legitimacy to their practice and shared purpose. They seem to feel a greater ownership in the outcomes for their students and a greater confidence that what we are measuring, as progress for students is recognizable to all. It is very empowering.

Program administrators came to appreciate the importance, and the value, of other requirements over the course of the year. For example, although every administrator agreed that observing teachers was important both for quality control and for signaling their interest in supporting what goes on in the classroom, until they were required to do so few administrators had actually made time for classroom observation.

The requirements of the project made clear both the benefits and the difficulties of putting in place the structural supports for program improvement. Although administrators saw how regular teacher meetings were helping to transform their programs into learning organizations, and making a real difference in the ability of the programs to deliver high quality services, most felt it would be difficult to maintain these practices once the research project ended. Although the resources required were not great (a stipend of about $2,500 per teacher per year for the extra hours), programs could not foresee being able to implement these practices across the whole program without a policy mandate at the state level and resources particularly focused on implementing those mandates. One program administrator wrote the following:

I am very concerned about the number of programs that offer classes four hours a week, usually two hours, two days a week. I think it is very hard to implement EFF in this type of setting. I am also concerned about the number of part time staff members who only work four hours a week. Would I be willing or able to implement EFF in a class that met four hours a week if I only worked four hours a week at what is probably a second job?

CONCLUSION

In this chapter, I have presented EFF standards as a way to explore the conditions under which standards-based reform can be a vehicle for focusing educational institutions on achieving higher levels of learning for students. This chapter has argued that three key aspects of standards based reform, the standards, the professional development available, and the institutional environment, determine whether standards-based reforms can help transform educational institutions into the kind of organizations that support such sustained improvements in practice.

The EFF experience to date has demonstrated that standards which focus on results that students and other stakeholders agree are important can be an effective driver for change, in how programs are organized and how material is taught, that can lead to more effective student learning and higher levels of achievement. The EFF field research process has demonstrated that teachers are willing to invest time and energy in learning new instructional approaches that enable them to improve student learning when their programs support these efforts. The field research process also demonstrated that programs are capable of implementing the kind of structural changes that help transform teaching staffs, even with part-time staffs, into communities of practice and programs into learning organizations--if they are given the resources to do so. In both cases, we have seen that one of the conditions for being willing to make these changes is a clear purpose for which to work that everyone agrees is important.

Standards which define results that matter can provide the motivation for change. However, to actually see these results, there needs to be a systemic, long-term investment in the process of standards-based reform. This investment needs to include supports for the kind of intensive program of professional development described here, and, in the case of the adult education system, support for the kind of changes in program structures that enable sustained learning–for students and teachers. With sufficient resources, a supportive institutional environment, and standards that focus on results that matter, standards-based reform can drive changes that really do make a difference in how well adult learners are equipped for meeting the challenges in their daily lives.

REFERENCES

Baldrige National Quality Program. (2004). *Education criteria for performance excellence.* Gaithersburg, MD: National Institute for Standards and Technology.

Bell, B. S., & McGuire, M. (2002). *EFF/NRS data collection project, 2000-2001: An interim report on the development of the EFF assessment framework* (EFF Assessment Report). Washington, DC: National Institute for Literacy.

Bransford, J. D., Brown, A. L. & Cocking, R. R.(Eds.). (1999). *How people learn: Brain, mind, experience, and school.* Washington, DC: National Academy Press.

Deming, W. E. (1982). *Out of the crisis.* Cambridge, MA: MIT Center for Advanced Engineering Study.

Dillon, S. (2004, September 5). Good schools or bad? Conflicting ratings leave parents baffled. *The New York Times,* pp. A1, A31.

EFF/NRS Joint Data Collection Project. (2000-2002). [Quarterly administrator reports]. Unpublished raw data.

Elmore, R. F. (2002) *Bridging the gap between standards and achievement: The imperative for professional development in education.* Washington, DC: Albert Shanker Institute.

Glaser, R. (1991). Expertise and assessment. In M.Wittrock & E. Baker (Eds.), *Cognition and testing* (pp. 17-29). Englewood Cliffs, NJ: Prentice Hall.

Greeno, J. G., Resnick, L. B., & Collins, A. M. (1997). Cognition and learning. In D. Berliner & R. Califee (Eds.) *Handbook of educational psychology* (pp. 15-46). New York: Simon & Schuster Macmillan.

National Commission on Excellence in Education. (1983). *A nation at risk: The imperative for educational reform: A report to the nation and the secretary of education.* Washington DC: U.S. Department of Education.

National Education Goals 2000. Educate America Act, Pub. Law 103-227 (108 stat.125) Title I, Sec 102, Signed into law on March 31, 1994. Retrieved July 14, 2006, from http://www.ed.gov/legislation/GOALS2000/TheAct/index.html

National Research Council. (1999). *Testing, teaching, and learning: A guide for states and school districts* (Committee on Title I Testing and Assessment, Richard F. Elmore & Robert Rothman, Eds.; Board on Testing and Assessment, Commission on Behavioral and Social Sciences and Education). Washington, DC: National Academy Press.

Schimmenti, J., Gamse, B., Giordono, L., Kupfer, A, Smith, W. C., & Weiland, C. (2003). *Evaluation of the Equipped for the Future reading project pilot, final report, September 15, 2003.* Cambridge, MA: Abt Associates Inc.

Scribner, S. (1987, April). *Head and hand: An action approach to thinking.* Paper presented at the annual meeting of the Eastern Psychological Association, Arlington, VA.

Smith, C., Hofer, J., & Gillespie, M. (2001). The working conditions of adult literacy teachers: Preliminary findings from the NCSALL Staff Development Study. *Focus on Basics, 4,* 1-13.

Stein, S. (1995). *Equipped for the Future meeting: Accomplishments and next steps.* Unpublished memo to National Institute for Literacy Director and staff [NIFL EFF program files], Washington, DC.

Stein. S. (2000). *Equipped for the Future content standards: What adults need to know and be able to do in the 21st century.* Washington, DC: National Institute for Literacy.

Wenger, E. (1998). *Communities of practice: Learning, meaning, and identity.* Cambridge, England: Cambridge University Press.

Wurtz, E., & Malcom, S. (1993). *Promises to keep: Creating high standards for American students* (Report to the National Education Goals Panel on behalf of the Goals 3 and 4 Technical Planning Group). Washington, DC: National Education Goals Panel.

Chapter 3

Tales from the Field:
The Struggles and Challenges of Conducting
Ethical and Quality Research
in the Field of Adult Literacy

Daphne Greenberg
Georgia State University

Empirical scientific research using randomized field trials for an experimental or quasi-experimental design is the current "gold standard" for research funded by the federal government and is often referred to as scientifically based. According to the U.S. Department of Education, the federal government is encouraging scientifically based research to increase the effectiveness of instruction. Evidence-based instruction, the desired outcome of scientifically based research, has been described as "the integration of professional wisdom with the best available empirical evidence in making decisions about how to deliver instruction" (Whitehurst, 2002a, p. X).

Although the field of adult literacy suffers from a paucity of scientifically based research (Greenberg, Fredrick, Hughes, & Bunting, 2002; Kruidenier, 2002a), there have been two recent attempts to rectify this deficiency. In 2002, the National Institute for Literacy, along with the National Center for the Study of Adult Learning and Literacy, brought together experts in adult reading research and practice to formulate the Reading Research Working Group. One of the purposes of this group was to provide the field with evidence-based best practices for reading instruction (Kruidenier, 2002b). Because of this effort, the field has a compendium of research-based principles, trends, ideas, and comments for teaching reading to adults with low literacy skills (Krudenier, 2002a). In addition, in 2002, $18.5 million in grants was awarded to six adult literacy researchers by the National Institute of Child Health and Human Development, the National Institute for Literacy, and the Office of Adult and Vocational Education. These funds, to be used over a 5-year period, are focused on studying the efficacy of various approaches for teaching reading to adults who have low literacy skills using experimental and quasi-experimental research designs (more information can be retrieved from http://novel.nifl.gov/nifl/press_releases/02_10 _pr.html).

As more experimental researchers become interested in adult literacy as an area of inquiry, it is important to come to terms with the unique aspects of the field that may challenge these efforts. In this chapter, I articulate some of the challenges that I have experienced as a researcher in a university-based setting who uses experimental research design. Many of the issues that are discussed are important to consider regardless of the researcher's methodological approach, but because my research experience is in the use of experimental methods, challenges in doing this kind of research are highlighted.

My goal in this chapter is not to focus on the strengths and weaknesses of conducting scientifically based educational research. Rather, as a researcher who extols the virtues of conducting scientifically based research, my focus is on the realities and challenges of doing this type of research in the adult literacy field. The purposes for this chapter are multiple. It is hoped that by discussing the challenges that I encountered, other researchers will become aware of the obstacles that they may face while conducting research in the adult literacy field. It is my belief that if the challenges inherent to experimental research in the field of adult literacy are acknowledged and openly shared with the adult literacy community, then the findings from experimental studies in the future will be more grounded in reality, be of higher quality, and have increased potential to improve practice. Finally, it is also hoped that by making the challenges transparent, it will affirm that a broad spectrum of approaches to research are best for studying adult literacy (Belzer & St. Clair, 2005).

A common underlying theme running throughout this chapter is the relationship between university researchers and adult literacy program staff. This relationship is particularly important because of the ways in which the academic researcher status impacts the researcher-practitioner relationship. I have a commitment to making the voices of the research participants--the learners, the teachers, and the program site administrators--heard. We need to hear their voices because they can give us crucial hints about how to conduct ethical and efficacious research so that everyone involved is a "winner"--the researchers, the participants, and the diverse audiences who will read the products of this work. My empirical adult literacy research has always focused on adults who have low word reading skills and their underlying word reading processes, as well as the efficacy of different instructional approaches designed to increase their reading abilities. Issues related to learners, teachers, administrators, and researchers are discussed in the context of this type of research. Specifically, issues focusing on informed consent, measurement, practitioners' perceptions of university-based researchers, logistics, and the realities of adult learners' lives are explored.

INFORMED CONSENT

Before any research can be conducted, gaining informed consent is a critical step that must be negotiated for all researchers-quantitative and qualitative alike. Many researchers and members of Institutional Review Boards (IRBs) realize that it is imperative to write the informed consent in easy-to-read English. However, if adults who read at the third-grade level or below are included in a study, they still may not be able to read the form. Therefore, in my studies, we always read our informed consent forms aloud, with the participants following along with a copy of it in front of them. However, reading the informed consent aloud does not always ensure understanding. As a group, adults who read between the third- and fifth-grade levels have very low oral receptive vocabulary scores (Greenberg, Ehri, & Perin, 1997). For example, Sentell and Ratcliff-Baird (2003) asked their testers to read the Beck Depression Inventory Scale items aloud to their participants and found that low reading adults did not understand many of the items. To further complicate matters, IRBs require that many complex and unfamiliar terms be included in the informed consents. It is a constant negotiation process to make sure that our participants are really giving *informed* consent (i.e., they understand what they are being told), while also making sure that their rights are protected according to the law. For example, my university's IRB recently insisted that all informed consents must include a statement that data will be stored in a password-locked computer. I argued with the IRB that my participants would not know what password-locked meant, and that many of them would barely have the schema to really understand what was meant by data being stored in the computer. We compromised, and my informed consent now includes a statement that all of the participants' information is kept in a computer in a locked office to which only approved research personnel can have access. The best quality data, those most likely to have real implications for improving practice, must be gathered from research participants who truly understand the purposes of research, feel a degree of trust and safety with the researchers, and consent to participate on that basis. Fortunately, IRBs are beginning to be sensitive to the difficulties of accomplishing all of this with the adult literacy population. However, balancing institutional expectations regarding informed consent, and the need for everyday, simple language so that adults who struggle to read can understand it, is an ongoing challenge.

MEASUREMENT

One of the primary challenges facing all researchers and practitioners is how to measure and describe the reading skills of adults who have difficulty reading. Often the controversial grade level construct is used to describe reading skill levels of adult literacy students, although it is based on theories of typical child development (Perin, 1991). Research has shown that even when it appears as if the same word reading processes are similar for both adults and children reading between the third- and fifth-grade levels, the two populations have different strengths and weaknesses (Greenberg et al., 1997; Greenberg, Ehri, & Perin, 2002). However, because the grade equivalency level concept is the one we are most familiar with, is most concrete and easy to grasp, and is also what is readily available, we continue both in practice and in research to describe adult learners by their grade equivalencies. We need to ask the following: how accurate is this description? What are we missing or masking by relying on a construct that is based on children's research? It is important to realize that although we acknowledge this problem (Kruidenier, 2002b; Venezky, 1992), we continue to conduct research and make program decisions based on measurements which yield grade equivalency scores.

Empirical researchers are burdened by the dilemma of deciding which reading test to use that will best describe the population. The Test for Adult Basic Education (TABE) and other tests commonly used by adult literacy practitioners do not break down reading into subcomponents as does the Woodcock-Johnson Psycho-Educational Test Battery (WJ), a test commonly used by empirical reading researchers. However, the WJ is not a test used by practitioners, and it has not been standardized on a large adult literacy population. Ideally, it would make sense to administer both tests as results from such a study would have meaning for both practitioners and researchers. In addition, a comparison could be conducted between performance on popular tests used by researchers and those used by practitioners. However, it is usually not possible to administer both types of tests due to the long duration of many researchers' testing batteries. As a result, researchers usually only administer tests that are relevant to the research question, without administering tests that will also interest practitioners in the field, thereby diminishing the usefulness of the study for many practitioners. This highlights one of the challenges of balancing the researchers' needs and the practitioners' needs, at the same time that it makes clear that there are sometimes competing needs and interests that are not easily resolved.

Another challenge specific to empirical researchers is the decision of how to classify participants. If a researcher decides to use a test that includes subcomponents, which score is best used to describe the learner: word recognition, word attack, reading fluency or reading comprehension? Depending on the nature of the research study, the score that is used can have different implications. For example, if students are screened into a study based on their test scores, does one go by their word reading score, their comprehension score, their word attack score, or their reading fluency score? For many students, their scores are similar across the subtests (with word attack being characteristically lower for many adult learners), and therefore there is not a problem. However, there are students who may have very low individual word reading scores but have very high reading fluency and comprehension scores. For example, recently, a learner with 3.5

word reading and 2.9 word attack grade equivalency scores on the WJ passed the language arts portion of the General Education Development Test (GED). Only when one looked at her reading fluency and comprehension scores (10.4 and 9.8) was one able to make sense of the disparity between her low word reading and word attack scores and her ability to pass the language arts portion of the GED. This example points to the importance of looking at all test scores before decisions are made regarding the classification of learners. The fact that this woman qualified for a study of adults who read individual words at the third- to fifth-grade levels made me assume that she would not have been ready to take the GED. However, her GED teacher, who did not know her word reading and word attack scores, knew that she was ready to take the language arts portion of the GED. This example also illuminates the need for researchers not to act in isolation, but rather to communicate with practitioners about learners involved in their research. It also suggests the importance of researchers not offering instructional advice based on scores from just one or two subcomponents of reading tests.

It is essential to carefully look at all test items before deciding to administer a test to a group of adult learners. For example, in one of the assessments that I have used in a testing battery, an item required participants to repeat the following statement: "Some of the people who live in America are illiterate." Fortunately, this test item was questioned by a research assistant before we administered the test to adult learners. One can only imagine how our learners would feel having to repeat such a statement. Fortunately, this item was not part of a standardized test, and in fact was part of a placement test for a reading program. It was therefore possible to change the sentence to the following: "Some of the people who live in America are political." Another example was not caught in time. One of our tests includes a series of pictures that the participant is expected to verbally label. One of the items is a picture of a noose. Giving this test to African Americans in the South has yielded responses such as the following: "I find that picture offensive." In this particular test, if the participant does not label the picture correctly after a semantic clue ("used for hanging"), the participant is provided with a phonemic cue of /noo/. Before the tester can even say the entire phonemic cue, some participants have said, "Oh you are not going to say the 'n word' are you?" Most of our testers are White, most of our learners are African American, so one can imagine the heightened tension that had been created. We have decided not to administer this particular item. Clearly measurement can be confounded not only by psychometric issues, but also by sociocultural ones as well.

PRACTITIONERS' PERCEPTIONS OF UNIVERSITY-BASED RESEARCHERS

An added challenge unique to university-based researchers is the various said and unsaid perceptions adult literacy program personnel and learners have of university-based research projects. For example, when participants hear that a university is going to administer an experimental program, they may volunteer because they assume that if a university is offering a class, "it must be a good one," or "one that will help in ways no other class can" (direct quotes from learners). Others enroll because they think that they are going to learn to read on a college level. They assume that if a university is offering a reading course, it must focus on university level reading (the learners who have expressed this assumption read between the third- and fifth-grade levels). Clearly, the unspoken assumptions that learners may have about a university-run adult literacy program need to be voiced and clarified as soon as possible. Without such conversations, participants' reasons for consenting to participate may interfere with data collection and interpretation of results.

Adult literacy program staff also have unspoken assumptions and attitudes about university-based research projects. These unspoken thoughts mediate between the participants and the investigator in known and unknown ways. For example, when our research project coordinator goes to adult literacy classes to recruit participants, she goes to classrooms where she has been told that the majority of the students read on at least a second-grade level, but are not quite at the pre-GED level. When she talks to the learners, she does not share the requirement that participants need to read at a specific word reading grade level to qualify. She explains who she is, describes the reading research project, and recruits people who are interested in being screened for participation. Learners are told that classes need to be formed which include individuals who read at about the same level, so regardless of how they perform on the screening tests, they may or may not be included in the class. In one particular class, after the research project coordinator was finished talking, the teacher stated the following: "Folks, her class is for individuals who cannot read well. As far as I am concerned all of you are at least on the 9th grade level." The students were very excited, and one even exclaimed the following: "No one ever told me before that I could read above a 9th grade level." Why the teacher shared this with his students is unclear. We do know that the adult literacy site's administrator forgot to tell him that the research project coordinator was coming. Perhaps he was expressing his anger about this unexpected visit by trying to sabotage the recruitment process. Perhaps he was worried that learners in his class would decide to attend the university reading program and not attend his class. If he did not have enough students in his class, he would not have a class to teach! Perhaps he really believes that his students can read above a ninth-grade level, although he knows that his class is designed for students who are significantly below the pre-

GED level. It is curious that the majority of his learners expressed an interest in being screened despite his statement. Did they know that they could benefit from another reading class despite what he said? Unfortunately, I have not had an opportunity to address my wonders with the teacher. It would be interesting to know more about his perceptions of this incident. Although this incident did not sabotage participant recruitment in this case, it illustrates how practitioners' attitudes regarding university researchers and the ways in which they convey them to learners can potentially influence learners' decisions to take part in the research.

Unspoken attitudes of adult literacy program personnel toward university researchers are often indirectly expressed in the initial negotiation phases. I recently received permission from an executive director to conduct six simultaneous afternoon classes at her program. After meeting with her, I sent her notes listing the various commitments we had made to each other. Unbeknownst to me, she shared this e-mail with her staff members, without providing them with any context. A few weeks later, she invited me to a meeting to finalize our decisions. Once again, unbeknownst to me, she invited her staff to attend this meeting. I ended up walking into a "lions' den" and one by one each staff member fired questions at me: who was I to think that they could provide me with enough students to fill six classes; who was I to think that the students would come in the afternoon; who was I to think that they had space for six additional classes? Although I kept stressing that none of these ideas were mine, that the ideas were the result of the meeting I had with their director, they were extremely agitated. I immediately realized that I needed to start over with the staff members by explaining my research project, how it was a "win-win" situation for all of us (after all, the research project provides free teachers and materials), that it was their decision whether, and to what extent, they wanted to be involved in the research project (one to six classes), and when they wanted the classes to be offered. Based on comments they shared during the meeting, I realized that underneath their resistance, they were angry about the possibility that a university researcher would be telling them what to do, and they were scared that the university would provide a better approach than their program, which might drain students away from their classes. This experience underscores the importance of involving as many people as possible in the initial negotiation stages before conducting research in an adult literacy program. This negotiation is essential so that unclear expectations between program staff and researchers can be discussed, and that perceived threats can be shared, and hopefully, alleviated.

LOGISTICS

Often the day-to-day realities of adult literacy programs do not meet the demands of strictly controlled experimental research projects. The lack of space at program sites is an issue that arises frequently as we try to implement our studies. Quite simply, many adult literacy programs do not have the space to add classes that may be required to implement a research project. For example, in one state-run program where I tried to collect data, the teacher has only one room. This room serves as her office and her classroom. Therefore, while she teaches, she is also interrupted by telephone calls, visitors, and other distractions. She teaches daily from 9 a.m. to 2 p.m. and wanted us to conduct our research class in her room from 2 p.m. to 4 p.m. She offered to stay in the "office" section of her room (in the back of the room) while she completed paperwork, returned phone calls, and met with morning students who needed extra help. Given the nature of our research project, I had to tell her that we could not agree to such an arrangement. It was unfortunate that I had to respond this way to her generous offer, her interest in our project, and her desire to provide an opportunity for students who could only attend afternoon classes. I worried that she heard in my refusal an underlying message that what was "good enough" for her and her students would not be "good enough" for us--the university researchers.

Another example of the mismatch between researchers' needs and adult literacy organizations' realities comes from interactions with a volunteer literacy organization. A director of a volunteer organization, who was extremely excited about the possibility of collaborating on a university-based research project in adult literacy, suggested that evening classes could be provided in her large office space (including a meeting room with tables and chairs). During the day, her staff met in that space, but in the evenings, the space was not utilized. She did not tell us that the space was in an empty building in an isolated part of town, that it would be necessary for the teacher to keep all doors locked while class was in session, and that the teacher would be responsible for turning the security system off and on before and after class. These issues only became apparent on the day we went to screen students for participation in the study. Due to its isolated location, the students had difficulty finding the building. When they did arrive, they told us not to turn our backs to the windows. When I discussed our security concerns with the director, she suggested that late arriving students finding the door locked could knock on the window to be let in. Once again, I was placed in the awkward position of explaining that although she ran her classes in this way, we could not. Part of the research project included measures of time on task, and therefore the teacher could not leave the classroom to open the door. I was also concerned about the safety of my staff in an empty building. Once again, without intending to do so, I may have reinforced the notion that what was good enough for practitioners was not good enough for university researchers and their staff. This experience raised a question about how we can decrease the rifts between researchers and practitioners when researchers, for the sake of research, cannot compromise on issues that practitioners have to contend with on a daily basis.

Sometimes it is the lack of appropriate resources in the area of adult literacy that make it difficult to conduct research, regardless of methodological philosophy or approach. For example, in one study, an instructional approach is being tested which focuses on exposing adult learners to literature. In this class, students read high interest and low vocabulary books. We try to provide a variety of books for a variety of tastes and interests. However, there are not enough books written between the first- and seventh-grade levels that are reflective of all of our students. For example, I have yet to find a book that includes transgendered, gay, or lesbian characters. If the purpose of this approach is to motivate learners to want to read and to relate to the stories that they read, how can this truly be accomplished if there are not enough books published at their reading levels or on topics and with characters that reflect who they are? This lack of resources can compromise the data collection plan for a study.

ADULT LEARNERS' LIVES

Perhaps most compelling and most complex of the research issues I encounter are related to the ways in which the realities of adult learners' lives can sometimes collide with the demands of doing experimental research. For example, if a site is not near public transportation, and most of the participants walk to the site, we cannot blame learners for failing to attend class when there is a torrential storm. This and other issues such as day care, domestic violence, and work demands all prevent learners from attending programs as consistently as program staff and the learners themselves would like. These realities pose serious challenges to empirical researchers, like me, who want to test the efficacy of different instructional approaches. For example, in one of my studies, 100 hr of instruction is specified as the length of class. After the first set of classes for our study ran, it became apparent operationally that planning to give 100 hr of instruction really means providing an opportunity to participate in 100 hr of instruction. It does not mean that every student receives 100 hr of instruction. In fact, many students will receive 50, others 70, and only a few 100. Either an increase in sample size is necessary to increase the number of students who receive 100 hr of instruction, or class meetings need to be flexible so that the class continues until the majority of students have reached 100 hr. Of course, this second option raises many complicated questions. Can a site accommodate a class that runs without a definite end date? How do the learners and teachers feel about a class that does not have a definite end date? How many students in any given class need to reach the 100-hr point? Can students who reach 100 hr of instruction continue to stay in the class until it ends? Does it matter how long it takes to reach 100 hr?

Despite the focus of any study that I have conducted, nonresearch issues that are of critical importance to the teachers and their learners often need to be addressed before instruction can begin. Some of the difficulties I have experienced is the level of demand and stress that distract learners from actively participating, and the need for teachers to deal with learners' emotional states when they come to class, regardless of whether this is part of the research protocol. In fact, several incidents in the field have pitted giving ethical and caring responses to learners against faithfully implementing our stated research methodology. Examples of these demands and stresses include learners not having money for food, transportation, telephone, and child care. For example, nowhere in the research protocol do we have suggestions regarding what a teacher should do if a pregnant student slips a note to the teacher in the middle of class stating that she is hungry and does not have money to buy food. This issue turns into more than an ethical and moral dilemma. The realization dawns on us that if the teacher gives the learner a few dollars, it becomes necessary to ask what is the impact on our results of treating one student differently from the others? How do we know that there aren't other students in the classroom who are also hungry? In other words, how does the kind of help a teacher gives influence motivation, persistence, and attendance? From an empirical researcher's perspective, how should the teacher respond to the student's note? What about from a moral perspective? Are they the same? If they differ, what is the best response for the teacher to make? How can this issue be represented in the data? By working with this population, researchers can be forced to make unfortunate choices between fidelity to their research protocol and responding ethically to learners.

Another issue that we have struggled with is how to react when a student has an unusual response to class activities. For example, in one classroom, a student became upset because she believed the books and the students in the classroom were spreading evil thoughts into her body. Besides the fact that this student needed a referral for psychological help, if being in the class was too upsetting for her, then she should not have been enrolled in the class. Yet counseling students out of programs decreases the sample size. How do we balance our desire and ethical responsibility to encourage her not to attend the class with our need for a large sample size so that we can have sufficient power to answer our empirical research questions? In other words, how strongly do we try to convince her that the class may not be appropriate for her?

What do we do when, in a research study class which is designed to be completely scripted, a student suddenly shares with the class that she is feeling suicidal? From a purely scientific point of view, the answer is the teacher needs to go on with the lesson. However, from a realistic point of view, it is impossible to do so. If the teacher stops what she is doing and lets the student express her thoughts and then lets the other students support that student, the day is ruined from a researcher's perspective. Do we count this as a class that has occurred?

Child care issues are a major concern for many of our participants. What happens in a research project when a student who has been attending classes regularly suddenly brings her 3-year-old to class one day? Do we ask the student to leave and risk losing the student? What if we decide to let the child stay "just this once?" What if the approach used in this classroom involves reading adult-themed books and discussing adult topics? Should the discussion and read-aloud portions of the class be modified to accommodate the presence of a child? Obviously doing so compromises data collection, but protects the child. To further complicate matters, what if it is summertime, and the next day the student comes without the child? When asked who is taking care of the child today, the student replies that her 8-year-old son is watching the child. Do we immediately send the learner home because it is unsafe for an 8-year-old to be watching a 3-year-old? Do we call child protective services because we are concerned about a mother who would do this? What about when, on further discussion, it becomes apparent that the student really wants to come to class, and it is clear that she will either have to bring the 3-year-old to class, or leave the 3-year-old with the 8-year-old? What is the appropriate suggestion here--do not bring your child to class and we will pretend not to know that an 8-year-old is watching your child? Bring your 3-year-old to class, although we may discuss adult topics, and it is hard for her to sit still? Alternatively, do not come to class until your day care situation is resolved? These dilemmas force us to consider how important each individual is for our data collection.

FINAL THOUGHTS

In the field of adult literacy, there is sometimes a rift between researchers and practitioners. Each may perceive the other as having different, noncomplementary agendas. Comings (2003) noted the following: "adult education ... does [not] have a tradition of cooperation between researchers and practitioners" (p. 2). What can be done about this? The first step is for university researchers to recognize that they often have more status, and thus, potentially, more power than do program-based teachers (or are at least perceived that way by some practitioners). After all, researchers are often attached to well-regarded institutions, have prestigious funding sources, and due to having higher academic degrees, may be viewed as more knowledgeable than "typical" adult literacy teachers. In addition, university-based research is sometimes perceived as irrelevant to the day-to-day realities of teachers and learners in adult literacy programs. Because of these differences, the onus of trying to mend the rift is on researchers. Doing so ought to be a priority for researchers because practitioners can be important allies, facilitate implementation of the research project, and provide us with valuable information and feedback that might otherwise be unavailable. The realities of adult literacy practitioners (for example, the applicability of test scores, the lack of adequate space, the lack of appropriate materials, the day-to-day stresses and demands that learners bring to class) need to be voiced and heard. Similarly, researchers also need to hear the learners' voices. Unless their realities are heard, we will not know much about the ways in which the statistical results of a study capture the realities of teachers and learners as they do their work together. Without this information, although statistically significant information may be gained from the research studies, the conclusions may or may not be pertinent to the day-to-day classroom life of an adult literacy learner. If the conclusions are not pertinent, the value of the research project may ultimately be questionable. This has important ramifications for the scientifically based research movement. As Dr. Whitehurst has announced, his goal is that scientifically based research inform practice (Whitehurst, 2002b). Thus, it is of critical importance that researchers ensure that their research is pertinent, useful, and usable to the final consumers--the practitioners and adult learners. One important way to do this is to avoid obscuring the ways in which the day-to-day realities of adult literacy classrooms and programs impinge on, and complicate, the implementation of scientifically based research.

Deshler and Grudens-Schuck (2000) describe four different levels of research: emancipatory, partnership, paternalistic, and extractive. The most participatory level is emancipatory, where stakeholders are involved in all aspects of study construction, implementation, and interpretation. The least participatory level is extractive, where participants consent to providing data (tests, interviews, etc.) to researchers. Evidence-based research usually involves extractive methods. If instruction based on evidence-based research really means "the integration of professional wisdom with the best available empirical evidence" (Whitehurst, 2002a), then all rigorous levels of research (emancipatory, partnership, paternalistic, and extractive) should be equally respected and used, based on their appropriateness for answering specific research questions. Although extractive methods can provide strength in rigor of methodology, and therefore confidence in results that are found, emancipatory methods can provide us with richness and flavor and therefore ensure strong face validity. In addition, other types of research can address findings that cannot be accounted for within the purview of extractive research. For example, in this chapter, issues concerning perceptions of adult literacy practitioners and learners are mentioned. Due to the empirical nature of the research, these perceptions were not explored. In a more open-ended, interpretivist approach, the researcher welcomes unexpected issues and often adapts and modifies the study as new issues are presented by participants. To illustrate this, I would like to conclude with a story about an adult learner who characteristically had good attendance in a class that was part of a research study. One day, without warning, she stopped attending. After many days of trying to contact her, she answered her phone and shared with me that the reason why she stopped attending was because while walking to class one day, she had had a miscarriage. She was so devastated and embarrassed that she did not want to return to class. After she and I talked about it, she felt ready to meet her classmates and teacher again. But how does a conversation like this affect empirical data collection? Obviously, not all students who stop attending class share their experiences. Do we lose some permanently because we are not made aware of their situations? If the research protocol does not include rigorous methods for obtaining this type of information, then we are breaking a fundamental expectation of scientific research that all participants need to be treated equally. What should we do when students reach out to us and tell us their stories? Should we discourage it because it threatens the empiricism of the study? Is this ethical? Would it be moral not to discuss these situations with learners who initiate conversations about them? How do we balance morality and empiricism? Perhaps, qualitative research helps to offer a solution. If we strive toward including and respecting all types of rigorous research methods, we can address all of the relevant factors in the adult literacy field. It is my hope that this chapter is a step in this direction.

REFERENCES

Belzer, A., & St. Clair, R. (2005). Back to the future: Implications of the neo-positivist research agenda for adult basic education. *Teachers College Record, 107,* 1393-1412.

Comings, J. (2003). *Establishing an evidence-based adult education system.* Cambridge, MA: National Center for the Study of Adult Learning and Literacy.

Deshler, D., & Grudens-Schuck, N. (2000). The politics of knowledge construction. In A.L. Wilson & E.R. Hayes (Eds.), *Handbook of adult and continuing education* (pp. 592-611). San Francisco: Jossey Bass.

Greenberg, D., Ehri, L. C., & Perin, D. (1997). Are word-reading processes the same or different in adult literacy students and third-fifth graders matched for reading level? *Journal of Educational Psychology, 89,* 262-275.

Greenberg, D., Ehri, L. C., & Perin, D. (2002). Do adult literacy students make the same word-reading and spelling errors as children matched for word-reading age? *Scientific Studies of Reading, 6,* 221-243.

Greenberg, D., Fredrick, L. D., Hughes, T. A., & Bunting, C. J. (2002). Implementation issues in a reading program for low reading adults. *Journal of Adolescent and Adult Literacy, 45,* 626-632.

Kruidenier, J. (2002a). *Research-based principles for adult basic education: Reading instruction.* Washington, DC: National Institute for Literacy. Retrieved July 6, 2006, from http://www.nifl.gov/partnershipforreading/publications/adult_ed_02.pdf

Kruidenier, J. (2002b). Literacy assessment in adult basic education. In J. Comings, B. Garner, & C. Smith (Eds.), *Annual review of adult learning and literacy, Volume 3* (pp. 84–151). San Francisco: Jossey-Bass.

Perin, D. (1991). Test scores and adult literacy instruction: Relationship of reading test scores to three types of literacy instruction in a worker education program. *Language and Literacy Spectrum, 1,* 46-51.

Sentell, T. L., & Ratcliff-Baird, B. (2003). Literacy and comprehension of Beck Depression Inventory Response Alternatives. *Community Mental Health Journal, 39,* 323-331.

Test of adult basic education. (2002). Monterey, CA: CTB/McGraw-Hill.

Venezky, R. L. (1992) *Matching literacy testing with social policy: What are the alternatives?* Washington, DC: Literacy Policy Forum.

Whitehurst, R. G. (2002a). *Evidence-based education.* Retrieved October 15, 2003, from http://www.ed.gov/nclb/methods/whatworks/eb/edlite-slide003.html

Whitehurst, R. G. (2002b) *Evidence-based education.* Retrieved October 15, 2003, from http://www.ed.gov/nclb/methods/whatworks/eb/edlite-index.html

Woodcock, R. W., & Johnson, M. B. (1990). *Woodcock-Johnson Psycho-Educational Test Battery.* Boston: Teaching Resources.

Chapter 4

Professional Development and Evidence-Based Practice in Adult Education

Mary Beth Bingman
University of Tennessee

Cristine Smith
World Education, Inc.

We will change education to make it an evidence-based field.
> U.S Department of Education Strategic Plan 2002-2007 (March 7, 2002), p. 59. Available at http://www.ed.gov/about/reports/strat/plan2002-07/plan.pdf

Teacher preparation and teacher support are the critical links between theories of evidence-based practice (EBP) and actual practice that leads to student achievement and outcomes. If the field of adult literacy education is to move forward in adopting EBP, we will need well-prepared teachers who are able to use relevant research in providing instructional services to adult students. These teachers will need to work in programs and systems that give them the support they need to make changes in their practice and to stay in the field.

In this chapter, we discuss the meaning of EBP, the importance of professional development as a necessary (but not sufficient) foundation for promoting EBP in adult education programs, and the type of professional development that will adequately prepare teachers to be evidence-based practitioners. We discuss the working and program conditions that form the foundation of support teachers need to do the best job possible and the policies needed to implement adequate teacher preparation and support. We conclude by considering the issues that future research should address to answer critical questions about teacher quality and stability and their role in student achievement.

EVIDENCE-BASED PRACTICE

With the current demand in all fields of education that instruction and services be based on evidence, rather than on intuition, fads, or trial and error, adult literacy programs will feel increasing pressure to demonstrate that their services are evidence-based. Legislation and policy initiatives have offered several definitions of evidence-based or research-based practice. We are using that of the U.S. Department of Education's Institute of Education Sciences, which defines "evidence-based education" as the following: "The integration of professional wisdom with the best available empirical evidence in making decisions about how to deliver instruction" (Whitehurst, 2002a). "Professional wisdom" is defined as "the judgment that individuals acquire through experience" or "consensus views." "Empirical evidence" is defined as "scientifically based research from fields such as psychology, sociology, economics, and neuroscience, and especially from research in educational settings" or "empirical data on performance used to compare, evaluate and monitor progress" (Whitehurst, 2002a). This definition states clearly that both empirical evidence and professional wisdom are necessary for evidence-based education; the definition also focuses on the decisions made by practitioners in designing and implementing instruction.

Before discussing how integration of research evidence and professional wisdom can come about, it is important to point out some assumptions underlying the promotion of EBP: one, that integration of empirical evidence and professional wisdom is not the norm in education today, and two, that such integration would lead to improved practice. Neither assumption, although much discussed in the education field today, has been empirically proven.

Regardless of this lack of evidence about the existence or promise of EBP, the definition does imply that practice is an ongoing process of making decisions about instruction. This is an understanding of evidence-based education that puts the teacher at the center. It is clear that teachers are already making decisions based on their own experience, especially where no empirical evidence exists (which is often the case in adult education), and sometimes they are using the "best available" evidence (Stanovich & Stanovich, 2003). We take the position, for the purposes of getting to the discussion about how evidence-based education can be promoted, that teachers need information to make decisions, that evidence from rigorous and well-designed research of all types is a valuable a source of information, and that, to integrate this evidence and professional wisdom, teachers need to access research, understand how it was conducted, and judge its relevance to their practice. Our purpose in this chapter is to examine how professional development can meet these needs.

One option for "integration" of empirical evidence and professional wisdom involves states adopting models of instruction and services or specific curriculum developed by researchers and experts based on the evidence and their professional wisdom. An example of such a model is the "Success for All" program developed for promoting reading achievement among at-risk children in early grades by the Center for Research on the Education of Students Placed At Risk. In this option, professional development provides training in how to implement the model. In a second option for "integration," individual teachers and program managers become research consumers who *access* the empirical evidence about effective instruction, *understand* the research and *judge* its applicability for their particular learners, and then *use* this evidence in their instruction, adapting it to their specific classroom or program context.

Until we have developed evidence-based models in adult literacy education (and the National Center for the Study of Adult Learning and Literacy [NCSALL] is initiating a process to begin development of just such models; Comings, 2003), our only option is to prepare teachers to be consumers of research: to be aware of new evidence and how it can be integrated into their present practice. Even when evidence-based models of instruction and service or specific curriculum for the various adult learner populations have been developed, we would argue that teachers will still need to know how to understand, judge, and adapt research findings to specific conditions. Even when more systemic models emerge, teachers will need these capacities because no one model or curriculum will work perfectly with 100% of students, and new research will continue to emerge.

To what extent and level should teachers be prepared to use research? We argue that there are several "stances" toward research that teachers might legitimately take as evidence-based practitioners. By "stance" here, we don't mean adopting an unswerving opinion or position; rather, we mean "stance" within its connotation of "perspective" or "way of viewing." *Questioners* adopt a stance that evidence should underlie practice. If they implement an evidence-based model or curriculum, these teachers ask, "Why should I use this technique or strategy and what is the evidence that supports it? Is it based on evidence that I or other teachers have about students' performance (professional wisdom), or on research evidence?" *Consumers* proactively seek research evidence. They adopt the attitude that new evidence is critical to their work and learn enough about research and its findings to integrate what has been found to be effective with their own knowledge of students, and then change their practice accordingly. *Producers* adopt a stance not only as consumers but also as researchers in their own classroom. They generate knowledge that can be shared with others through classroom research, through co-research with university-based researchers, or by documenting how they implemented EBP.

It is our contention that professional development should help teachers acquire the understanding of research and the research process needed to be evidence-based practitioners with whatever "stance" fits their situation, experience, and disposition.

PROFESSIONAL DEVELOPMENT AND THE PROMOTION OF EVIDENCE-BASED PRACTICE IN ADULT EDUCATION

How can we prepare teachers to be evidence-based practitioners, using evidence and professional wisdom together to make decisions about practice in their classrooms and programs? One route is a full teacher preparation package, similar to the education and preparation kindergarten through 12th-grade (K-12) teachers receive. This includes formal coursework and master's degrees or certification and licensure, preservice training and internships, and in-service professional development. In our field, this route is underdeveloped for adult education practitioners in most states. Preservice requirements vary by state and sometimes by program; only 22 states require certification of adult education teachers (although not necessarily in adult education), and only nine states offer adult education-specific preservice training (Tolbert, 2001). Although adult education teachers often are or were former K-12 teachers (Sabatini et al., 2000), this does not mean that they have had any formal preparation about how to teach adults. In a recent study of professional development for adult basic education teachers, over half (53%) of the teachers in the sample ($n = 106$) had taken no adult literacy or adult education-related formal coursework before or after beginning to teach adult education students (Smith, Hofer, Gillespie, Solomon, & Rowe, 2003).

The second route to preparing evidence-based practitioners is through in-service professional development, which for most teachers in our field is the only way to gain formal training in how to teach adults. However, access to professional development is inconsistent and often minimal. With a largely part-time teaching force and lack of resources to support teachers' participation, professional development in adult literacy for teachers is often limited to attendance at annual conferences or the occasional single session workshop (RMC Corporation, 1996; Tibbetts, Kutner, Hemphill, & Jones, 1991; Wilson & Corbett, 2001). Smith and her colleagues (2003) found that of the over 100 teachers in their sample, the average amount of paid release time was 18.9 hr annually, and that 23% received no annual paid staff development release time at all.

Even if our field adopts simultaneous efforts to create masters' degrees and improve salaries and benefits to entice teachers to invest in formal education as K-12 teachers do, in the short-term we have to rely on in-service professional development to prepare and build the professional capacity of teachers.

TYPES OF PROFESSIONAL DEVELOPMENT THAT PREPARE TEACHERS TO BE EVIDENCE-BASED PRACTITIONERS

If we are to depend on professional development to build EBP, we must make good use of the scarce resources that states and teachers can apply to professional development. This has two implications. First, professional development must be designed using the best available evidence about what makes it most effective, that is, we should have evidence-based professional development practice. Second, professional development must include those features and activities that have been shown to increase teachers' access, understanding, judgment, and use of research.

What evidence is there about what makes professional development most effective in helping teachers gain new knowledge and attitudes and improve their practice? There are few studies investigating the effectiveness of professional development in adult education; Smith et al. (2003), in their study of professional development for adult basic education teachers, found that higher quality professional development (characterized by effective facilitation and group dynamics, and by flexible adaptation of the professional development design to the needs of the participants) contributed to more change among teacher participants. Much of the rest of the evidence comes from K-12 research. Overall, a review of the best available empirical evidence indicates that effective professional development should do the following:

- Be longer than an hour or two at a single point in time (Joyce & Showers, 1995; Porter, Garet, Desimone, Yoon, & Birman., 2000; Stein, Smith, & Silver, 1999); Smith et al. (2003) also found that teachers who attended for more hours demonstrated more change (differences in thinking and acting).

- Make a strong connection between what is learned in professional development activities and the teacher's own work context, helping teachers plan for application back in their programs, especially if the professional development (as is the majority in adult education) is organized outside of the school (Fingeret & Cockley, 1992; Ottoson, 1997).

- Include a strong emphasis on analysis and reflection, rather than just demonstrating techniques (Arlin, 1999; Bollough, Kauchak, Crow, Hobbs, & Stoke, et al., 1997; Guskey, 1999; Joyce, 1983; Sparks, 1995).

- Help teachers make their implicit knowledge about teaching explicit, help them articulate their assumptions, and test them against new knowledge (Gardner, 1996; Tibbetts et al., 1991).

- Focus on helping teachers to study their students' thinking, not just listen more to their students or try new techniques (Ancess, 2000; Carpenter & Franke, 1998).

- Include a variety of activities, such as presentation of theory, demonstration, practice, feedback, and classroom application (Elmore, 1996; Joyce & Showers, 1995; Joyce, Wolf, & Calhoun, 1995; Mazzarella, 1980; Stein & Wang, 1988).

- Encourage teachers from the same workplace to participate together (Porter et al., 2000), and wherever possible ensure that what the teachers learn in professional development is supported by program and district priorities (Garet, Porter, Desimone, Birman, &Yoon, 2001).

There is not as much research about the particular features of professional development that help teachers be research consumers. Professional development for adult basic education teachers that used a practitioner research model— where teachers read research and conducted their own classroom research project—contributed to a greater understanding of research in general than did other tested models of professional development (Smith et al., 2003). (However, in this study, the practitioner research model was not significantly different than the other two models of professional development—multisession workshops or mentor teacher groups—in supporting teacher change.) Because research demonstrates that coparticipation and collegiality in programs supports change (Smith et al., 2003), program-based professional development that includes a focus on research consumption may be a promising approach for supporting EBP. We do know that teachers need to talk to each other; reading *Focus on Basics* or other research publications is a way of being aware of new research findings but is not likely to be sufficient for building EBP.

In reviewing the literature on research utilization, Garner, Bingman, Comings, Rowe, and Smith. (2001) found evidence that "sustained interactivity" (Huberman, 1992, p. 8) between teachers and researchers improves research utilization. Zeuli and Tiezzi (1993) identified a range of attitudes teachers have toward research, the most common being the following three:

- Research is useless; it should have a direct impact on my practice but it doesn't.

- Research can be useful; it should have a direct impact on practice and it does if it provides me with practical ideas and strategies.

- Research is useful; it shouldn't necessarily have a direct impact on practice, rather it should expand my understanding of teaching.

They found that teachers' experiences collaborating directly with researchers was a stronger predictor than teachers' level of formal education of a more open attitude regarding the utility of research for practice. Our own experience with adult basic education practitioners seems to affirm and expand this finding. Participants in NCSALL's Practitioner Dissemination and Research Network (PDRN) project indicated that involving practitioners in working on their own research or on university research projects not only improves the research but helps teachers become research consumers (Smith, Bingman, Hofer, & Medina, 2002):

> Prior to PDRN, I was an isolated teacher feeling my way through a new course design. There was little in my experience that encouraged me to check out research findings .... Working in PDRN gave me a new appreciation for the relevance research can have and, more importantly, showed me how I could be a "scientific researcher" myself. Thus, I went from being an empirical, direct experiencer and passive reader of professional research findings to an active researcher.
> --Tom Smith, Practitioner Leader (p. 49)

> Before the PDRN...I was not aware of research done in the adult education area. Now...I don't shy away from research articles but have developed a means of understanding the research process and analyzing results.
> --Pam Meader, Practitioner Leader (p. 49)

The evidence from this project suggests that teachers are better able to use research in their practice if they take part in professional development that uses materials and activities that help them **access, understand, judge, and use research.** Teachers themselves need to grapple with the research—to learn about and critically analyze the research, then plan how to use it. Certain professional development activities primarily provide access to research. These include reading a research article, brief, or report; searching Web sites for research about best practices; or attending one-shot workshops and conference presentations. These approaches may be sufficient to meet the needs of teachers who take a "questioner" stance. Other professional development activities go further in helping teachers to understand, judge, and use research findings and are helpful to teachers who want to be "consumers" of research; examples of such professional development activities include participating in study circles or mentor teacher groups, or using specific teaching materials that involve students in learning about research findings. These activities share common features such as multiple sessions over time, opportunities to discuss and analyze research with other practitioners, and activities that help teachers plan how to adapt research findings to their own practice. Being involved in a research study, either conducting research on a question from one's own practice or as collaborators in research directed by others, supports teachers in being "producers" of research.

SUPPORTING EVIDENCE-BASED PRACTICE

Program Supports

Teachers do not work in a vacuum, and they don't always have the power to implement EBP autonomously. The NCSALL Professional Development study (Smith et al., 2003) demonstrated that teachers were more likely to change as a result of participating in professional development if they worked more hours in their adult basic education job; received benefits, paid professional development release time, and paid preparation time through their adult education[1] job; had more opportunities to share ideas with other teachers in their programs; had the right to make changes to the curriculum; and had a voice in decision making (especially when their program was not otherwise addressing the issue related to the topic of the professional development). Although the study found that individual factors play a role too, teachers need specific supports in their jobs and in their programs to make change as a result of professional development.

Policy Supports

Policies to support EBP must, first of all, support teachers. Programs need sufficient funding to provide teachers with hours, pay, and benefits that are adequate to maintain a stable staff committed to improving practice. How we define *adequate* is a question for research that is discussed later. Teachers need ongoing access to professional development that focuses on research and uses activities that support their abilities to understand, judge, and appropriately use research. Teachers need to be paid to participate in professional development.

States and programs need to emphasize a culture of research consumerism and continuous improvement that includes all program staff in the process. We would hypothesize that program directors and state staff have the same range of attitudes toward research that teachers have, so they also need professional development that helps them be research consumers as well.

---

[1] The term adult education includes English for adult speakers of other languages, adult literacy, high school equivalence, and basic skills programs for adults.

Programs need to be funded and structured to provide mechanisms for teacher decision making in the process of program improvement, to be able to access research that speaks to the issues addressed by the program improvement process, to facilitate a team of peers working together on professional development and program improvement, and to provide time and resources to change practice.

State and federal accountability requirements are a driving force in adult basic education. If teachers are asked to implement EBPs, then program success must be measured by outcomes that follow from these practices. Accountability policies need to be aligned with expectations about practice (Merrifield, 1998).

NEXT STEPS FOR RESEARCH

We know too little about what aspects of teacher preparation and teacher support contribute to teacher quality and teacher stability in the field. This is important because both teacher quality and experience will interact with EBP, in some way, to affect student achievement. Outcomes of teacher preparation and support should include high-quality, stable teachers who actively consume and apply research in their classrooms and programs.

Teacher Quality

Teacher quality has emerged in K-12 literature as the strongest predictor of student achievement. However, what defines teacher quality varies. One line of research in K-12 investigates indicators such as the percentage of certified teachers in a state, degree in subject matter, and knowledge of teaching pedagogy. Focusing on teacher characteristics, these researchers propose that teachers' level of formal education, certification, and a degree in the subject one teaches are all strong predictors of student achievement (Darling-Hammond, 1999, 2000; Darling-Hammond & Youngs, 2002). In a review of available evidence, Darling-Hammond and Ball (1997) cited studies indicating that 40% of variance (the largest percentage of variance) in student test scores is due to teacher qualifications (education, experience, expertise); teacher preparation was more important than parent education level, small class size, and other factors. In another line of research, however, teacher quality is thought to be primarily influenced by "individual differences in … teachers' general cognitive ability, followed by experience and content knowledge," and high-quality teachers are those who adhere to a standards-based curriculum aligned with accountability and school reform (Whitehurst, 2002b).

We do not know what contributes to teacher quality in the field of adult education. One reason for the lack of research on adult education teacher quality is that student achievement measures have been difficult to standardize. Also, teacher certification is not widespread, and needed pedagogy and subject matter knowledge vary relative to the learner population: for low-level and midlevel ABE, the subject matter is reading, writing, and math; for General Educational Development (GED), a range of content subjects; and for English for Speakers of Other Languages (ESOL), oral second language acquisition, plus reading and writing in English.

Research on teachers is desperately needed in our field. Lack of evidence about teacher preparation and support has major policy implications. States and programs do not have the evidence they need to argue for and organize professional development and program structures that promote teachers' use of EBPs. For states to make appropriate decisions with scarce resources, we propose that the following research questions related to teacher preparation and support be prioritized by adult education research funders: (a) What are the relative contributions of working conditions (full time or part time, paid prep time, paid professional development release time, benefits, access to decision making in the program) to teacher quality (as judged by student achievement); that is, do teachers with well-supported jobs have students with higher achievement? (b) What are the predictors of quality in our field (having taught in K-12, certification, adult learning pedagogical preparation, specific subject matter knowledge, professional development consumption, access to colleagues, directors, or information about research, or preparation to teach and adherence to standards-based curriculum); that is, do teachers with specific types of preparation have students with higher achievement?

Teacher Stability

Quality teachers who are prepared to enact EBP are of limited use in a field with a high turnover rate of teachers. In the end, it doesn't matter if teachers are high-quality teachers who use empirical evidence and professional wisdom in their practice if they leave the field after a few years. High teacher turnover makes the best preparation system inefficient and will ultimately defeat the effort to create an "evidence-based field." Again, we know little about teacher turnover rates in adult basic education. There are two types of attrition: "transition attrition," where teachers move from program to program, but stay in the field and continue serving students, even if the program suffers from their loss; and "exit transition," where teachers leave the field of education entirely (Billingsley, 1993). In adult basic education, we are concerned with "exit transition." In the K-12 system, where teachers generally have well-supported (or at least better-supported) jobs, living-wage salaries, benefits, paid prep and professional development time; work in schools that are more stable (funded through tax revenue as opposed to "soft" money grants); and have the opportunity to participate in communities of teachers within the schools, the Schools and Staffing Survey conducted by the National Center on Education Statistics found that nationally only 7% of teachers each year are leaving the field altogether (Ingersoll, 2001). Exact statistics for adult education teachers are nonexistent. Research has either tried to gauge actual turnover among samples of teachers over time, both leaving the field and leaving teaching but staying within the field (Smith & Hofer, 2003), or average years of experience among one-time samples of teachers (Sabatini et al., 2000; Young, Fleischman, Fitzgerald, & Morgan, 1995). Among a sample of 106 adult basic education teachers from New England, 49% had worked in adult education for 4 years or less; this same study found that 12.5% of these teachers left the field during the 18-month period of the study. The most recent national evaluation of adult education programs found that a little more than half of part-time teachers (and the vast majority of adult education teachers are part time) had taught in the field for less than 3 years (Young et al., 1995). Sabatini et al. (2000) found that 43% of part-time teachers had been in the field less than 5 years.

We need research on teacher stability specific to ABE. Although we know from the K-12 research that opportunities for collegiality, strong leadership, good working conditions, and teacher involvement in decision making in the school reduce teacher turnover (Gonzalez, 1995; Ingersoll, 2001; Olson, 2000), there are also a number of working condition factors that only apply in adult basic education, and their relative contribution to teacher turnover is unknown. For example, many adult basic educators receive no paid preparation time or paid professional development release time; and they receive limited salary, no benefits, and most are part time (Smith & Hofer, 2003; Tibbetts et al., 1991; Young et al. 1995).

We propose that the following question be given priority by adult education research funders, to help states make appropriate decisions about how to allocate scarce resources for teacher support: What are the relative contributions of working conditions (full time vs. part time, paid prep time, paid professional development release time, benefits, access to decision making in the program) to teacher stability in adult basic education?

CONCLUSION

The limited research evidence and captured (accessible) professional wisdom in adult basic education poses challenges to developing models of EBP, although we can begin. The limited preparation and support available to many adult education teachers challenge their ability to implement EBP. But our own professional wisdom and research, and the research of others, lead us to conclude that professional development, if it is designed using evidence about the features of effective professional development and if it connects teachers with research and researchers, could make a significant contribution to strengthening the quality of evidence-based adult education.

REFERENCES

Ancess, J. (2000). The reciprocal influence of teacher learning, teaching practice, school restructuring and student learning outcomes. *Teachers College Record, 102,* 590-619.

Arlin, P. K. (1999). The wise teacher: A developmental model of teaching. *Theory Into Practice, 38,* 12-17.

Billingsley, B. S. (1993). Teacher retention and attrition in special and general
education: A critical review of the literature. *Journal of Special Education, 72,* 137-174.

Bollough, R. V., Kauchak, D., Crow, N., Hobbs, S., & Stoke, D. (1997). Professional development schools: Catalysts for teacher and school change.
Teaching and Teacher Education, 13, 153-169.

Carpenter, T. P., & Franke, M. L. (1998). Teachers as learners. *Principled Practice in Mathematics and Science Education, 2,* 1-3.

Comings, J. (2003). *Establishing an evidence-based adult education system.*
Boston: National Center for the Study of Adult Learning and Literacy.

Darling-Hammond, L. (1999). *Teacher quality and student achievement: A review of state policy evidence.* Seattle, WA: Center for the Study of
Teaching and Policy, University of Washington.

Darling-Hammond, L. (2000). Reforming teacher preparation and licensing:
Debating the evidence. *Teachers' College Record, 102,* 28-56.

Darling-Hammond, L., & Ball, D. L. (1997). *Teaching for high standards: What
policymakers need to know and be able to do.* Retrieved from
http://govinfo.library.unt.edu/negp/Reports/highstds.htm.

Darling-Hammond, L., & Youngs, P. (2002) Defining "highly-qualified teachers": What does "scientifically-based research" actually tell us? *Educational Researcher, 31*(9), 13-25.

Elmore, R. F. (1996). Getting to scale with good educational practice. *Harvard
Educational Review, 66,* 1-28.

Fingeret, H. A., & Cockley, S. (1992) *Teachers learning: An evaluation of ABE
staff development in Virginia.* Dayton, VA: Virginia Adult Educator's
Research Network.

Gardner, J. (1996). *Professional development which provides an icing on the
pedagogical cake.* Paper presented at the Annual Meeting of the American Educational Research Association, New York, NY, April 8-12,
1996. (ERIC Document Reproduction Service No. ED 400 589) Retrieved July 7, 2006, from
http://www.eric.ed.gov/ericdocs/data/ericdocs2/content_storage_01/00
00000b/80/23/0

Garet, M. S., Porter, A. C., Desimone, L., Birman, B., & Yoon, K. S. (2001).
What makes professional development effective? Results from a na-

tional sample of teachers. *American Educational Research Journal, 38,* 915-945.

Garner, B., Bingman, B, Comings, J., Rowe, K., & Smith, C. (2001). Connecting research and practice. *Focus on Basics, 4,* 8-12.

Gonzalez, P. (1995). *Factors that influence teacher attrition* (NSTEP Information Brief No. 1-95). Alexandria, VA: National Association of State Directors of Special Education. (ERIC Document Reproduction Service No. ED 389 127)

Guskey, T. R. (1999). Moving from means to ends. *Journal of Staff Development, 20*(2), 48.

Huberman, M. (1992, January). *Linking the practitioner and researcher communities for school improvement.*: Keynote address at the International Congress for School Effectiveness and Improvement. Victoria, British Columbia.

Ingersoll, R. M. (2001, January). Teacher turnover, teacher shortages, and the organization of schools (Document R-01-1). Seattle, WA: Center for the Study of Teaching and Policy. Retrieved July 7, 2006, from http://depts.washington.edu/ctpmall/PDFs/Turnover-Ing-01-2001.pdf

Joyce, B. (1983). Effective staff training for school improvement and staff development as a regular event. In B.R. Joyce, R.H. Hersh, and M. Mckibbin (Eds.), *The structure of school improvement.* New York: Longman.

Joyce, B., & Showers, B. (1995). *Student achievement through staff development: Fundamentals of school renewal* (2nd ed). White Plains, NY: Longman.

Joyce, B., Wolf, J., & Calhoun, E. (1995). *The self-renewing school.* Alexandria, VA: Association for Supervision and Curriculum Development.

Mazzarella, J. A. (1980). Synthesis of research on staff development. *Educational Leadership, 38*(2), 182-185.

Merrifield, J. (1998). *Contested ground: Performance accountability in adult basic education* (NCSALL Report No. 1). Boston: National Center for the Study of Adult Learning and Literacy.

Olson, L. (2000). Finding and keeping competent teachers. *Education Week, 19,* 12-17.

Ottoson, J. M. (1997). After the applause: Exploring multiple influences on application following an adult education program. *Adult Education Quarterly, 47,* 92-107.

Porter, A. C., Garet, M. S., Desimone, L., Yoon, K. S., & Birman, B. F. (2000). *Does professional development change teaching practice? Results from a three-year study: Executive summary.* Washington, DC: U.S. Department of Education, Office of the Under Secretary.

RMC Research Corporation. (1996). *National evaluation of the Section 353 Set-Aside for teacher training and innovation in adult education* (Contract No. EA 93064991). Portsmouth, NH: Author.

Sabatini, J. P., Daniels, M., Ginsburg, L., Limeul, K., Russell, M., & Stites, R. (2000). *Teacher perspectives on the adult education profession: National survey findings about an emerging profession* (Tech. Rep. No. 00-02). Philadelphia: National Center on Adult Literacy.

Smith, C., Bingman, B., Hofer, J., & Medina, P. (2002). *Connecting practitioners and researchers: An evaluation of NCSALL's Practitioner Dissemination and Research Network* (NCSALL Report No. 22). Boston: National Center for the Study of Adult Learning and Literacy.

Smith, C., & Hofer, J. (2003). *The characteristics and concerns of adult basic education teachers* (NCSALL Report No. 27). Boston: National Center for the Study of Adult Learning and Literacy.

Smith, C., Hofer, J., Gillespie, M., Solomon, M., & Rowe, K. (2003). *How teachers change: A study of professional development in adult education* (NCSALL Report No. 26). Boston: National Center for the Study of Adult Learning and Literacy.

Sparks, D. (1995). Focusing staff development on improving student learning. In G. Cawelti (Ed.), *Handbook of research on improving student achievement* (pp. 163-169). Arlington, VA: Educational Research Service.

Stanovich, P., & Stanovich, K. (2003). *Using research and reason in education: How teachers can use scientifically based research to make curricular and instructional decisions.* Washington, DC: National Institute for Literacy.

Stein, M. K., Smith, M. S., & Silver, E. (1999). The development of professional developers: Learning to assist teachers in new settings in new ways. *Harvard Educational Review, 69,* 237-269.

Stein, M. K., & Wang, M. C. (1988). Teacher development and school improvement: the process of teacher change. *Teaching & Teacher Education, 4,* 171-187.

Success for All Foundation. (2006). Summary of research on the Success for All reading programs. Retrieved July 7, 2006, from http://www.successforall.com/_images/PDFs/410055000_SummResearch.pdf

Tibbetts, J., Kutner, M., Hemphill, D., & Jones, E. (1991). *Study of ABE/ESL instructor training approaches: The delivery and content of training for adult education teachers and volunteers.* Washington, DC: Pelavin Research Institute.

Tolbert, M. (2001) *Professional development for adult education instructors: State policy update.* Washington DC: National Institute for Literacy.

U.S. Department of Education Strategic Plan, 2002-2007. (March 7, 2002), p. 59
     Retrieved July 7, 2006, from
     http://www.ed.gov/about/reports/strat/plan2002-07/plan.pdf
Whitehurst, G. J. (2002a). *Evidence-based education.* Retrieved July 7, 2006,
     from http://www.ed.gov/nclb/methods/whatworks/eb/edlite-
     slide003.html
Whitehurst, G. J. (2002b) Research on teacher preparation and professional de-
     velopment. Retrieved February 3, 2005 from
     http://www.ed.gov/admins/tchrqual/learn/preparingteachersconference/
     whitehurst.html
Wilson, B., & Corbett, D. (2001). Adult basic education and professional devel-
     opment: Strangers for too long. *Focus on Basics, 4,* 25-26.
Young, M. B., Fleischman, H., Fitzgerald, N., & Morgan, M. A. (1995). *Na-
     tional evaluation of adult education programs* (Executive Summary,
     Contract No. LC 90065001). Arlington, VA: Development Associates.
Zeuli, J. S., & Tiezzi, L. J. (1993). *Creating contexts to change teachers' beliefs
     about the influence of research* (Report No. RR 93-1). East Lansing,
     Michigan: National Center for Research on Teacher Learning, Michi-
     gan State University. Retrieved July 7, 2006, from
     http://ncrtl.msu.edu/http/rreports/html/pdf/rr931.pdf

PART TWO

PROGRAM STRUCTURES AND INSTRUCTION

Chapter 5

Quality Instruction in Adult Literacy Education

Hal Beder
Rutgers University

What constitutes quality instruction in adult literacy education? The answer has both a values dimension and a measurement dimension. The values dimension has to do with what we, as a society and as literacy professionals, should expect successful participants in adult literacy education to know and to do, whereas the measurement dimension has to do with how we determine whether expected outcomes have been achieved. This chapter argues that although measurement is important, values must be considered before measurement is addressed.

Given the emphasis on accountability in the legislation that funds the federal adult literacy program, the Adult and Family Literacy Act (Title II of the Workforce Investment Act), it is easy to understand why much of the discussion about quality instruction has focused on outcome assessment measurement issues. Adult literacy is underresourced. Most teachers work part time and lack training in measurement methods and procedures. Dropout rates are high and continuous enrollment is the norm (Beder, 1996). Because these factors make accurate outcome assessment extremely difficult, much of the discussion about measurement has been concerned with logistics and the implementation of procedures.

Yet the values dimension—what we expect successful adult literacy education participants to know and do—is ultimately much more important than the measurement issue. This is because measurement decisions should logically follow from decisions about what are the appropriate outcomes of instruction (Condelli, this volume). Clearly, to consider measurement before the kinds of outcomes we want, is putting the cart way before the horse.

There is more than one way to classify the intended outcomes of literacy education. Based on a philosophical orientation, for example, Quigley (1997) classified approaches to literacy as vocational, liberal, humanist, or liberatory. My discussion revolves around conceptions of quality in three approaches to adult literacy education that have been selected because they are practiced in the United States, have been described in the literature, and have a basis in research and theory. For each, instructional quality is defined differently. The approaches are as follows: basic skills literacy, emancipatory literacy, and functional literacy; each has unique strengths and weaknesses.

BASIC SKILLS

Basic skills instruction focuses on teaching a set of reading, writing, and numeracy skills that become progressively more advanced as the learner progresses. These skills are taught as discrete lessons or units of lessons and include such things as phonics, reading comprehension, vocabulary, spelling, and grammar. It is assumed that once these skills have been mastered, learners will be "literate," and that the literacy acquired will generalize across literacy usage contexts (Beder, 1991).

Basic skills is by far the most prevalent approach to instruction in adult literacy education (Beder & Medina, 2001;Collins, 1992; Mezirow, Darkenwald, & Knox, 1975). In a classroom observation study of 20 adult literacy classes in eight states, Beder and Medina (2001) found that a defining characteristic of basic skills instruction was an instructional interaction format which Mehan (1979) termed "initiation-response-evaluation" (IRE) in his observational study of elementary education classrooms. In IRE interactions, the basic unit of instruction is a teacher-prepared and teacher-delivered lesson. Following the lesson, teachers lead an elicitation. Teachers "initiate" the elicitation with a series of questions, to which learners "reply." The replies are then followed by "evaluation" in which the teacher tells the class whether the reply is correct or incorrect. In individualized instruction, IRE is also the norm although the IRE pattern is embodied in the materials rather than in the teacher's lessons.

Mehan (1979) noted four types of elicitations: product, process, choice, and metaprocess. In product elicitations, the teacher elicits correct, factual answers. Beder and Medina (2001) found that product elicitations dominated the IRE sequences in basic skills instruction to the extent that product elicitation was a defining element of basic skills instruction. This is an example of a product elicitation from a class that prepared learners to pass the test of the General Educational Development (GED) class:

> The class begins to work on relief maps. The teacher is sitting on a chair in front of her desk. She asks such questions as, "What is a relief map? How do you know what mountain range is higher on a relief map? What range of mountains are on the West Coast? What mountain range do you find in South America? What continent has few mountains?" Most students provide one word answers, such as shading, cascade, or Africa. All questions are meant to elicit factual answers. Some-

times the teacher calls upon students directly: "Daniel, can you name one Great Lake in the Great Lake area?" (p. 43)

In basic skills instruction, product elicitation serves at least two purposes. Beder and Medina (2001) noted the following:

> First, by gauging correct and incorrect responses, it enabled teachers to evaluate whether learners had understood the lesson. Second, product elicitation often carried the content of the lesson, functioning as a form of instruction. When the teacher or learners provided the correct response, learners who had the incorrect response were "taught" the correct response, and when teachers diagnosed incorrect responses as a need for explanation or elaboration, the mini-lessons that sometimes followed enhanced learners' understanding. (p. 44)

In the second type of elicitation, process elicitation, the teacher elicits learners' opinions or interpretations. The questions posed by the teacher are open-ended, thus providing an opportunity for learner-to-learner interaction. A reading lesson provides an example:

> The teacher begins to ask questions about the story the class was reading. She is in the front of the room. Everyone else is sitting. The teacher says, "What do you think?" A learner answers, "It was cool." Another says, "It was educational." A third says, "What happened to Phyllicia, that do happen." The teacher says, "What happened?" and the learner responds, "The feelings, being judged from the outside not inside. That wasn't right." Another learner says, "It happens a lot. You're judged by the color of your skin." (Beder & Medina, 2001, p. 44)

Process elicitations were rare in the basic skill instruction observed by Beder and Medina (2001).

The third type of elicitation is choice elicitation. In choice elicitation, teachers pose alternatives for responses in their prompts. For example, "Is the answer to this problem 5, 7, or 19?" The fourth type of elicitation is metaprocess elicitation in which learners are asked to reflect on the process of making connections between teachers' questions and their responses, and to formulate and justify their reasoning. Metaprocess elicitation is associated with problem solving and the development of critical thinking. In the basic skills education that Beder and Medina (2001) observed, they did not witness a single episode of either choice or metaprocess elicitation.

Beder and Medina's (2001) analysis of the content and structure of instruction closes with a typology of instruction in adult literacy education. The first type is defined as discrete skills instruction, a type that is nearly synonymous with what I am defining as basic skills instruction in this chapter. Eighty percent of the classes observed fell into this category. The attributes of discrete skills instruction are as follows:

> teacher-prepared and teacher delivered lessons focusing on the convey-ance of factual information and literal recall from learners; a predomi-nance of commercially published materials for reading, writing, math and GED instruction; lessons, each with a clear beginning and end, or-ganized into distinct time periods; a focus on discrete skills that en-compass traditional subject areas. Reading, for example, is divided into comprehension, inference, facts and opinions, etc. Math is divided into addition, subtraction, multiplication and division, and the rules govern-ing mathematical operations are emphasized; a high degree of teacher to learner and learner to teacher interaction and a low degree of learner to learner interaction. (p. 51)

Why Basic Skills Is Prevalent

Why is basic skills instruction so prevalent in adult literacy education? There are several possible explanations. The first has to do with teacher and student so-cialization. The roles of teacher and student are two of the most heavily social-ized roles in Western society. Children begin to learn what constitutes teacher role behavior from the day they enter kindergarten and this socialization contin-ues throughout their education. For those who become kindergarten through 12th-grade (K-12) teachers, there is an additional period of intense socialization as they complete teacher education.

It is probably no accident that the research which identified the IRE-product elicitation pattern that pervades basic skills instruction was conducted in an ele-mentary education setting. Historically, basic skills instruction has been the norm in K-12. Because most adult literacy teachers teach part time (Beder, 1996), and have, or have had, full-time positions as K-12 teachers, there is a tendency for them to carry their K-12 role behavior into their adult literacy teaching. Moreover, because adult learners have also been socialized in a basic skills environment, they are comfortable with it, and may often expect it.

A second reason why basic skills may be prevalent is simply that the "sys-tem" supports and reinforces it. In its definition of adult education, for example, the Adult and Family Literacy Act, which funds the federal adult literacy sys-tem, emphasizes basic skills acquisition by stipulating that the act is for indi-viduals "who have attained 16 years of age, who are not enrolled in secondary school under state law and *who lack sufficient mastery of basic educational skills to function effectively in society* (Adult and Family Literacy Act, Section 203, emphasis added).

The legislation goes on to mandate a series of accountability standards, one of which is tested learning gain. The most common test used to measure leaning gain is the Test of Adult Basic Education (TABE). Indeed, use of the TABE is mandated by many states. The TABE is a paper and pencil, multiple choice, normed exam. It measures reading, mathematics, and language skills. As an option, it also assesses spelling, vocabulary, and language mechanics. The TABE aligns well with basic skills instruction. Thus programs that employ basic skills instruction may well have an advantage in demonstrating that they are meeting legislatively mandated standards measured by the TABE. This is a strong incentive to emphasize basic skills because decisions about funding adult literacy programs are increasingly being made according to programs' success in meeting performance standards.

As noted earlier, teachers who employ basic skills instruction rely to a significant extent on commercially published materials, and most commercially published materials feature basic skills work. For example, in a volume that introduces materials published by Contemporary Books, Fry (2000) described teaching reading to adults as follows:

> The teaching of reading usually begins by presenting the student with a short passage that has simple vocabulary arranged in short, easy sentences. The student is given help and is encouraged to practice the sentences aloud and silently. More words are added to the reading material, and the sentences and pages get longer. Phonics skills, or the relationship between letters and sounds, are taught. Comprehension skills are taught usually by having the student read silently and answer various types of questions. Writing is introduced; the student starts to write and read his or her own short stories or passages. The printed pages, student-written material, phonics lessons, and comprehension activities generally increase in difficulty as the student gains skill and fluency. Usually, a good deal of reading practice and frequent review lessons are necessary. (p. 1)

The materials that constitute the series include exercises targeted at the components of basic skills, tests, and workbooks in which learners enter their answers.

Quality

For adult literacy teachers and learners, quality in the basic skills approach is defined as learning the skills that constitute basic skills as quickly and efficiently as possible. Efficiency is important because most learners, regardless of reading level, have earning high school certification, usually by passing the GED tests, as a goal. Yet at the same time, many receive no more than 6 hr of instruction per week (Beder, 1996). Thus efficiency is important if learners are to reap the benefits of obtaining high school certification in a reasonable amount of time. Teachers are quite aware of this. As Beder and Medina (2001) noted, one reason that there is so little open discussion in basic skills classes is that teachers consider open discussion to be an inefficient deviation from basic skills instruction.

The National Reporting System (NRS) is another factor that may promote efficiency. The NRS was developed by the Department of Education to measure and record accountability data. In the NRS, the tested learning gain accountability requirement mandated by the Adult and Family Literacy Act is measured by the number of levels learners progress in a year. Thus the faster learners progress, the better the program does on accountability measures.

How society defines quality for basic skills instruction (or, for that matter, any form of instruction funded under the act) can be inferred from the Adult and Family Literacy Act accountability standards. A quality program is one that is successful in meeting five standards:

1. The percentage of adult learners enrolled who acquired the basic skills needed to complete the level of instruction in which they were initially enrolled.
2. The percentage of adult learners with a high school completion goal who earned a high school diploma or GED.
3. The percentage of adult learners with a goal to continue their educations who enter postsecondary education or training.
4. The percentage of unemployed adult learners with an employment goal who were employed at the end of the first quarter after they exited the program.
5. The percentage of adult learners with a job retention goal at the time of enrollment, and those adults with an employment goal who obtained work by the end of the first quarter after leaving the program and who were employed at the end of the third quarter after leaving the program.

In 2000 to 2001, 13 states met or exceeded all their performance targets on all five standards (U.S Department of Education, Office of Vocational and Adult Education, 2003)

Few would argue that mastery of basic skills is not necessary for an adult to become literate. Indeed, the other approaches to instruction that I discuss here, functional literacy and emancipatory literacy, include instruction in basic skills. But is basic skills mastery sufficient? Skills such as critical thinking, problem solving, speaking, listening, teamwork, and social awareness are not taught in basic skills instruction. If they are learned, they are learned only as a by-product of other activities. To the extent that these skills are necessary for success in the workplace, family, and continued education, basic skills instruction may be lacking. Furthermore, as Gee (2000) contended, becoming literate has two dimensions. The first dimension Gee termed *school,* the second is *acquisition.* In the school dimension, adults learn the structures associated with reading and writing—the basic skills. Yet according to Gee, school literacy alone does not equip learners to use reading and writing in the contexts of their daily lives at work, in the family, and in the community. Use in context has to be acquired through conscious practice in context. Yet, there is little in basic skills instruction to promote the acquisition process.

EMANCIPATORY LITERACY

As Giroux noted (1987), teaching and learning in basic skills instruction is essentially a technical function. The object of teaching is the individual learner who is expected to use literacy in a utilitarian, instrumental fashion. That is, for example, to gain employment, to increase income, to provide help to one's children, or to continue education. In emancipatory literacy, literacy has a very different function.

The most widely known theoretician and advocate for emancipatory literacy is Brazilian born Paulo Freire. Freire (1970) explained the function of literacy as follows:

> Reading does not consist merely of decoding the written word or language; rather it is preceded by and intertwined with knowledge of the world. Language and reality are dynamically interconnected. The understanding attained by critical reading of a text implies perceiving the relationship between text and context. (p. 29)

In other words, becoming literate enables learners to "name their world." Berthoff (1987) explained as follows:

> Language also assures the power of envisagement: because we can name the world and thus hold it in our mind, we can reflect on its meaning and imagine a changed world. Language is the means to critical consciousness, which in turn, is the means of conceiving change and making choices to bring about further transformations. Thus, naming the world transforms reality from "things" in the present moment to activities in response to situations, processes, to *becoming.* (p. xv)

In *We Make the Road by Walking* (Bell, Gaventa & Peters; 1990), Freire (1970) provided an example of emancipatory literacy practice with nonreaders. The process of teaching reading begins with a codification which, with a picture or photograph, visually depicts something from the learners' daily reality. The second step is a facilitated dialog and collective critical reflection around what the picture shows, and more importantly, what it means and what caused it to be as it is. After this global dialog and collective reflection, the facilitator selects a generative word, a word that summarizes the essence of the dialog and reflection. In Freire's example, the generative word was *favela,* which means "slum" in English. Freire went on to explain the following:

> You have a picture of a *favela* with the word written *favela.* After discussion of the sociological and political dimensions of that—they know very well because they live there—you get the word *favela* and you start a new job which is the job of decodifying the word .... . That is *favela* has three syllables [which are combined to make new words]. Then you have lots of possible combinations. *Favela* makes it possible to create these twenty to thirty words on the first night of the experience. (p. 89)

Although the previous passage is but a short example of emancipatory literacy practice, it demonstrates many of the elements of a form of adult education associated with Freire (1970) and sometimes called critical pedagogy or popular education. Emancipatory literacy is a form of critical pedagogy. It is literacy education conducted using a critical pedagogy format. Emancipatory literacy and critical pedagogy are, therefore, inseparable.

Critical pedagogy rejects what Freire (1970) called banking education, education that inculcates facts in the mind as if they were bank deposits. Rather, the objective of critical pedagogy is conscientization and ultimately social transformation. Conscientization is the process of becoming critically aware of the social, political, economic, and historical forces that shape oppression in an oppressed group. In Freire's previous example, after the codification was presented, through dialog with the participants the facilitator initiated the kind of dialog and collective critical reflection that leads to conscientization. Because the word *favela* was generated though this process, it reinforced conscientization and was "owned" by the participants because it came from their context. This was likewise so for the new words that were generated from *favela's* three syllables—fa,ve,la.

Critical pedagogy posits that not only does social transformation require conscientization—because it is the foundation of an effective change strategy—but that conscientization also motivates social transformation, because once participants understand the roots of their oppression, they will no longer tolerate the status quo.

A central concept in critical pedagogy and emancipatory literacy is praxis. Praxis is the dialectic between reflection and practice which creates new knowledge, knowledge that guides action within a particular context. Praxis begins with collective reflection about the nature and causes of a particular situation or problem. In Freire's (1970) example, the group might have reflected on questions like, "Why do we have slums, why do we live in one, and what cán we do about it?" The knowledge generated from collective reflection is tentative. It represents a theory about reality that does not become "true" until it is tested in practice. Again, through collective critical reflection, group members strategize how to take action to solve the particular problem they have identified. In Freire's example, the group might have planned a sanitation project or a public demonstration. Once action is taken and the results are assessed, again through collective reflection, the initial understanding about the nature of the problem and its causes is modified to account for the results of the action. Because the process is ongoing and cyclical, new knowledge situated in experience is always being created and tested in action. Freire noted the following:

> When a word is deprived of its dimension of action, reflection automatically suffers as well; and the word is changed into idle chatter, into verbalism, into an alienated and alienating "blah." It becomes an empty word, one which cannot denounce the world, for denunciation is impossible without a commitment to transform, and there is no transformation without action.
> On the other hand, if action is emphasized exclusively, to the detriment of reflection, the word is converted into activism. The latter—action for action's sake—negates the true praxis and makes dialogue impossible. (p. 76)

Emancipatory literacy, then, is a collective process in which the ability to code and decode print, conscientization, and social action are inextricably linked. Becoming literate is not a neutral act, it is a political act. Although emancipatory literacy instruction is quite common in developing countries, it is relatively rare in the United States. Part of the reason may be that most adult literacy programs in the United States are publicly funded, and the government is reluctant to fund programs with avowedly political agendas, especially those focused on social change.

Quality

To be of quality, emancipatory literacy must meet three standards. First, obviously, learners must learn to code and decode print. In fact, many of the techniques employed in basic skills instruction are used to meet this standard. Second, the process must be collective and democratic. The problems considered must come from the group. Everyone must have an equal voice in collective reflection, and the group must "own" the process. Finally, conscientization and social action must result. Conscientization and social action are not mere by-products of emancipatory literacy. They are defining elements.

Use

Given the nature of emancipatory literacy, two questions emerge: under what conditions should it be used and by whom? The answer to the first question is that it should be used when conditions of oppression exist. Although the severe oppression that Freire (1970) wrote about may be more common in previously colonized countries, few would argue that we do not have our own share of oppression in the United States. The answer to the question of by whom should emancipatory literacy be used is by the oppressed themselves and the community-based agencies that work with them—not the government. Indeed, funding by the government is nearly anathema. Because many oppressed groups consider the government to be in complicity with oppressive forces, the government is more likely to be the target of emancipatory social action than a source of support. In addition, emancipatory literacy is a process in which the exact outcomes cannot be stipulated before the process commences. Thus, it is very difficult for emancipatory literacy programs to be accountable in ways which the government demands.

FUNCTIONAL LITERACY

Functional literacy broadens the concept of basic skills literacy to include instruction in competencies that are deemed necessary for adult's success in American society. From the early 1970s, there have been three major functional literacy movements in the United States: the Adult Performance Level Project (APL), the Comprehensive Adult Student Assessment System (CASAS), and Equipped for the Future (EFF).

As Beder (1991) noted, in the early days of the federal adult literacy program, functional literacy was broadly defined as survival skills, skills adults needed to perform important life tasks such as reading labels and filling out forms. In the early 1970s, however, the relatively informal approach to functional literacy changed dramatically with the advent of the APL.

Adult Performance Level Project

Between 1966, the year the first federal Adult Education Act was passed and substantial federal funding for adult literacy began, and 1974, when the act was amended, the U.S. Office of Education was authorized to retain up to 20% of the funds allocated under the act for staff training (Sec. 309a) and special projects (Sec. 309b; Rose, 1991). APL was one of the largest and most controversial of the 309b projects. Awarded to University of Texas at Austin's Division of Extension, APL's objectives were "to specify the competencies which are functional to economic and educational success in today's society and to develop devices for assessing those competencies of the adult population of the United States" (Adult Performance Level, 1975, p. 1). To identify the basic requirements for adult living, APL conducted a review of the literature, interviews with 49 representatives of state and federal agencies in 25 states, a series of conferences on adult needs, and semistructured interviews with undereducated and underemployed adults (Adult Performance Level, 1975).

Based on these methods, APL derived a taxonomy of adult needs termed "general knowledge areas." They were consumer economics, occupational knowledge, community resources, health, and government and law. Reanalyzing the data, APL then derived four primary skills: communication skills (reading, writing, speaking, and listening), computational skills, problem-solving skills, and interpersonal relations skills.

For APL, functional competency and success were directly equated with socioeconomic status (SES). It was assumed that higher SES adults achieved and maintained that status by applying a set of competencies. It followed that if low literate adults learned those competencies they too would become "successful." APL also claimed that there was a direct "mathematical" relationship between learning these skills and success in adult life.

Again from the original data, APL then developed performance requirements called objectives. For example, for the knowledge area of community resources and skill area of reading, a performance requirement is "reading a movie schedule" (Adult Performance Level, 1975, p. 2a). Following the development of performance indicators, the indicators were field tested with 3,500 adult learners in 30 states and revised accordingly. Finally, the performance indicators were formatted into a series of interview schedules and the "test" was administered to a sample of 7,500 adults. As a result of these data, the adult population was divided into three groups based on their functional level: APL1, adults who function with difficulty; APL2, functional adults who are not proficient; and APL3, proficient adults. According to APL's findings, 20% of the adult population fell into APL1: 16% of Whites, 44% of Blacks, and 56% of Spanish surname adults (Kazemek, 1983).

APL quickly became the sensation of the 1970s. APL's findings were released to the press and policymakers were shocked that such a high percentage of the population functioned with difficulty. Perhaps because it had invested so much in APL, the Office of Education widely disseminated APL. States were urged to use state-controlled research and development and professional development funds to translate APL into curriculum and an APL competency-based education movement began. With federal leadership, a competency-based adult education network developed and yearly conferences were held at least until 1983 (Shelton, 1983). Through this process, a federally sanctioned definition of competency-based education emerged: "Competency-based adult education is a performance-based process leading to demonstrated mastery of basic and life-skills necessary for the individual to function proficiently in society" (Taylor, 1980, p. 42). It became widely accepted that competency-based adult education had four components: (a) a list of identified and stated outcomes or competencies, (b) a formal assessment system, (c) a functional literacy subject matter integrating both basic and life skills, and (d) certification of mastery of competencies (Miller, 1982).

Advocates of functional literacy and competency-based education extolled its benefits because, in their view, it was a truly "adult" form of adult literacy education that met a much wider range of adult needs than basic literacy. Whole states, most notably California (Tibbetts & Westby-Gibson, 1980), adopted it as orthodoxy. Yet APL had many detractors, mainly in the academic community, who criticized its work both conceptually and methodologically. Criticism focused on the nature of the sample (Kazemek, 1983), the validity and reliability of the test (Griffith & Cervero, 1977), its implicit bias and flawed inferences (Cervero, 1980; Kazemek, 1983), and the impossibility of defining what functionality means (Griffith & Cervero, 1977; Levine, 1982). Given the fact that functionality is only meaningful in specific social contexts, it is impossible to establish functional standards for an entire society (Levine, 1982).

Comprehensive Adult Student Assessment System

As noted earlier, California was one of the states that embraced competency-based instruction early on. Moreover, because of the size of its federal allocation, and because California in turn allocated a very sizeable amount of state funds to adult literacy, the state had a substantial amount of financing available for research and development. The combination of commitment to competency-based instruction and available resources resulted in the development of CASAS.

At the heart of CASAS is a competency-based assessment system which provides the following:

- Effective assessment materials and procedures for all levels of Adult Basic Education (ABE), English as a Second Language (ESL), Adult Secondary Education (ASE) including GED and high school completion, employability programs for learners who are functioning at or below a high school level, and employment training programs.
- Appropriate placement of learners into program and level.

- Monitoring learner progress by group and individually.
- Certification of competency attainment.
- Linkage of assessment to curriculum and instruction.
- Relevant data for learners, instructors and program managers.
- Agency and statewide data to project educational need and access program quality.
- Mechanisms for providing reports at the local, state and federal levels (CASAS, 2004).

The CASAS assessment, commonly known as the CASAS Test, was developed using item response theory methodology. As of 2003, CASAS had developed over 300 competencies. Competencies are reviewed and updated annually by the CASAS National Consortium which represents more than 20 states (CASAS, 2003). Competency-based items fall under nine competency areas: basic communication, consumer economics, community resources, health, employment, government and law, computation, learning to learn, and independent living (CASAS, 2003).

Although CASAS itself does not develop functional literacy curriculum, it supports the development of functional literacy curriculum and instruction in several ways. The CASAS competencies, for example, provide the "raw material" for the development of curriculum and the *Instructional Materials Guide,* which is coded according to CASAS competencies, and lists curriculum materials with significant functional literacy content. In addition, CASAS provides implementation training, professional development, data collection and reporting services, and ongoing test development.

Equipped for the Future

EFF was developed by the National Institute for Literacy (NIFL). EFF is primarily a set of content standards designed to provide the following:

- A common framework that adults can use to assess their own knowledge and skills in relation to their personal career goals so that they can shape a course that will better prepare them for the future.
- A common framework that teachers and programs can use to link curriculum and instruction, as well as assessment and evaluation, to achievement of real world outcomes.
- A common results-oriented language for linking the services provided through the nation's human resource investment system.
- A common standard for demonstrating competence that programs can use to award portable credentials for learning.

- A common definition of important results that public officials and citizens alike can use to assure that public dollars are wisely invested in adult literacy and lifelong learning programs (Stein, 2000, p. 2).

Development of EFF began in 1994 with an open letter from NIFL asking teachers and learners to identify the following: "What is it that adults need to know and be able to do in order to be literate, compete in the global economy and exercise the rights and responsibilities of citizenship" (Stein, 2000, p. 5). A total of 1,500 students from 34 states responded. Content analysis of these responses led to what EFF called the four purposes for learning: access, voice, action, and a bridge to the future. In 1995, NIFL awarded planning grants to eight organizations to acquire feedback about the four purposes from a wide array of stakeholders, including learners, teachers, employers, and policymakers. Feedback was acquired through 114 focus groups, and a series of practitioner inquiry and student writing projects. The result was a recommendation that NIFL should lead a national standards-based reform initiative to help adults achieve the four purposes. NIFL accepted the challenge.

Using the data from the eight planning projects, the next step in the evolution of EFF was the development of "role maps" that defined what adults need to know to be successful in their roles as family members, citizens, and workers. Each role map includes a key purpose, areas of responsibility, and key activities. For example, for the citizen-community key purpose, one of the four areas of responsibility is "to become and stay informed." Some of the key activities for this area of responsibility are as follows: to identify, monitor, and anticipate community needs, strengths, and resources for yourself and others; to recognize and understand human legal and civil rights and responsibilities for yourself and others; and to figure out how the system that affects an issue works. Subsequently, the role maps were refined and validated by a feedback process conducted by three consortia funded by NIFL (Stein, 2000). From the role maps, the EFF content standards were devised through field development in 25 programs and subsequent field testing and refinement.

There are 16 EFF content standards, which, according to EFF, represent what adults need to know to successfully perform adult roles. The standards are organized into four categories: communication skills, decision-making skills, interpersonal skills, and lifelong learning skills. The standards under interpersonal skills, for example, are "guide others, resolve conflict and negotiate, advocate and influence, and cooperate with others" (Stein, 2000, p. 21).

Commonalities and Differences

All three functional literacy systems, APL, CASAS, and EFF, developed from a process of government-funded research and development coupled with efforts to build consensus that functional literacy was the most appropriate approach for adult literacy education. For all three, the collections of competencies (EFF calls them standards) are supposed to guide a wide array of program functions, including assessment, curriculum, instruction, goal setting, and planning. Thus all three are systemic in their orientation.

APL and EFF differ markedly in how they define functional competency. For APL, functional competency meant acquisition of the skills middle class literate adults possessed and poor illiterates did not. Thus APL's definition is essentially a socioeconomic one. In contrast, EFF defines functionality as successful adult role behavior in the areas of work, family, and community. For APL and CASAS, reading, writing, and math instruction align with the basic skills approach. For EFF, however, competency in reading becomes "read with understanding," in writing it becomes "convey ideas in writing," and in math it becomes "use math to solve problems and communicate." Moreover, in EFF, additional communication and problem-solving skills are added to the traditional reading, writing, and math skills, such as speaking, listening, critical observation, problem solving, and planning.

Quality

In functional literacy, standards of quality are expanded beyond acquisition of reading, writing, and math skills to include applied skills and knowledge that adults are presumed to need to function effectively in society. Adult functionality is the ultimate goal rather than the narrower goal of skill development in reading, writing, and math. In functional adult literacy education, the objective is for adult learners to function more effectively *within* society rather than for them to collectively transform society, as is the aim of emancipatory literacy education.

CONCLUSION

In this chapter, I have discussed three approaches to adult literacy instruction: basic skills literacy, emancipatory literacy, and functional literacy. What constitutes quality differs for each and each has its strengths and weaknesses.

For basic literacy, quality is mastery of the skills presumed to constitute basic literacy and gains on the TABE are as good an indicator of this as any. One strength of basic literacy is that teachers know how to do it. This is a considerable advantage given our part-time teaching force and general lack of substantial professional development. Another strength may be that basic literacy is efficient in moving learners ahead on the NRS levels and ultimately toward high school completion. However, such skills as critical thinking and problem solving are not generally included in the basic skills approach, and to the extent to which they are important, basic skills may be too narrow.

For emancipatory literacy, literacy is but a means to conscientization and social transformation. Under conditions of entrenched social oppression, it may be the only approach to literacy that can truly make a difference in improving the lives of learners. Yet because the target of emancipatory literacy is the system, and because the system is not about to embrace it in the United States, it is about as marginal as the marginalized peoples it serves.

For functional literacy, quality is embodied in adult functionality, the ability to successfully function in society. Although functionality includes school-like reading, writing, and math, it also encompasses competence in the ways in which reading, writing, and math are used in everyday adult life. The assumption is that mastery leads to life success. The strength of functional literacy instruction is that it encompasses a broader definition of literacy in its vision, a vision that is decidedly "adult" in orientation. On the negative side, what constitutes functionality is rather fuzzy. Are there a specific set of identifiable functional competencies that do lead to life success? Or is being successful in life an inordinately complex thing that must take into account individual goals, motivations, and the situational context of the learner? Indeed, except for the benefits from learning to read, write, and do math, I am aware of no evidence which demonstrates that functional literacy produces more functional adults.

So what approach to literacy should those who are interested in a quality system of adult literacy education embrace? Although one strategy for addressing the answer might be comprehensive evaluation of the approaches, in my view, evaluation is not a worthwhile strategy. Practically speaking, credible evaluation would entail an expense that is probably beyond the capacity of the adult literacy system. Moreover, I doubt that an evaluation would provide much guidance. This is because for an evaluation of an approach to adult literacy to be fair, it should be based on how well how each approach achieves its own intended outcomes. That would mean three different outcome measures and three different evaluation methodologies. In the end, the differences between the evaluations would make it very difficult to infer whether one approach is more effective than another. We would be left with the proverbial apples, oranges, and bananas problem.

If evaluation is not a realistic strategy for deciding which approach to embrace, then professional judgment is the alternative, but who should do the judging? Currently institutions and individuals with power make the decisions. Congress made decisions in passing the Adult and Family Literacy Act. States make decisions in adopting CASAS or EFF as their model. Local programs make decisions in advocating for emancipatory literacy. Yet despite a wealth of adult education theory that suggests learners should make decisions about their own adult education (Beder, 1991; Brookfield, 1986; Fingeret, 1992; Knowles,

1971), there is little evidence that learners have much of a say in which approach they receive. They take whatever they are given (or they do not stay in the program).

If learners were to have a greater say in which approach to adult literacy they receive, we would need a pluralistic system in which a variety of approaches were available. There would need to be free and easy access to programs that specialize in the various approaches and learners would need clear and accurate information about their options to make informed choices. Although to create such a system might be idealistic, to do so is not impossible.

REFERENCES

Adult and Family Literacy Act, section II of the Workforce Investment Act of 1998, Public Law 105-220.

Adult Performance Level. (1975). *Adult functional competency: A summary.* Austin: University of Texas at Austin, Division of Extension.

Beder, H. (1991). *Adult literacy: Issues for policy and practice.* Malabar, FL: Krieger.

Beder, H. (1996). *The infrastructure of adult literacy education: Implications for policy.* Philadelphia: The National Center for Adult Literacy.

Beder, H., & Medina, P. (2001). *Classroom dynamics in adult literacy education.* Cambridge, MA: National Center for the Study of Adult Learning and Literacy.

Bell, B., Gaventa, J.,& Peters, J. (Eds.). (1990). *We make the road by walking: Conversations on education and social change.* Philadelphia: Temple University Press.

Bertoff, A. E. (1987). Foreword. In P. Freire & D. Macedo (Eds.), *Literacy: Reading the word and the world* (pp. xi-xxiii). South Hadley, MA: Bergin & Garvey.

Brookfield, S. (1986). *Understanding and facilitating adult learning.* San Francisco: Jossey-Bass

Cervero, R. (1980). Does the Texas Adult Performance Level Test measure functional competence? *Adult Education, 30,* 152-165.

Collins. R. (1992). *People programs and politics: Two case studies of Adult literacy classes.* Unpublished doctoral dissertation, Portland State University, Portland, OR.

Comprehensive Adult Student Assessment System. (2003). *CASAS competencies: Essential life skills for youth and adults.* San Diego, CA: Author.

Comprehensive Adult Student Assessment System. (2004). *CASAS technical manual, third edition.* San Diego, CA: Author.

Fingeret, H. (1992). *Adult literacy education: Current and future directions. An update* (Information Series No. 355). Columbus, OH: ERIC Clearinghouse on Adult, Career and Vocational Education. (ERIC Document Reproduction Service No. ED 354 391)

Freire, P. (1970). *Pedagogy of the oppressed.* New York: Seabury Press.

Fry, E. (2000). *How to teach reading to adults.* Chicago: Contemporary.

Gee, J. (2000). *Social linguistics and literacies: Ideology in discourses* (2nd ed.). Philadelphia: Routledge Falmer.

Giroux, H. (1987). Literacy and the pedagogy of political empowerment. In P. Freire & D. Macedo (Eds.), *Literacy: Reading the word and the world* (pp. 1-28). South Hadley, MA: Bergin & Garvey.

Griffith, W., & Cervero, R. (1977). The Adult Performance Level Program: A serious and deliberate examination. *Adult Education, 27,* 209-224.

Instructional Resources (n.d.). Retrieved July 5, 2006, from
    http://www.casas.org/dirctdwnlds.cfm?mfile_id=1692&selected_id=22
    &wtarget=body
Kazemek, F. (1985). An examination of the Adult Performance Level Project
    and its effects upon adult literacy in the United States. *Lifelong Learn-
    ing, 9*(2), 24-28.
Levine, K. (1982). Functional literacy: Fond illusions and false economies. *Har-
    vard Educational Review, 52,* 249-266.
Knowles, M. (1971). *The modern practice of adult education.* New York: Asso-
    ciation Press.
Mehan, H. (1979). *Learning lessons: Social organization in the classroom.*
    Cambridge, MA: Harvard University Press.
Mezirow, J., Darkenwald, G., & Knox, A. (1975). *Last gamble on education.*
    Washington, DC: Adult Education Association of the U.S.A.
Miller, J. (1982). *Competency education for adult literacy* (Overview: ERIC
    Fact Sheet No. 10). Columbus. OH: ERIC Clearinghouse on Adult, Ca-
    reer and Vocational Education. (ERIC Document Reproduction Service
    No. ED 237 798)
Quigley, B. A. (1997). Rethinking adult literacy: The critical need for practice-
    based change. San Francisco: Jossey-Bass.
Rose, A. (1991). *An overview of the history of the Adult Education Act* (Informa-
    tion Series No. 346). Columbus. OH: ERIC Clearinghouse on Adult,
    Career and Vocational Education. (ERIC Document Reproduction Ser-
    vice No. ED 341875)
Shelton, E. (1983, November). *Competency-based adult education: The past,
    present and future.* Paper presented at the Competency-Based Adult
    Education Conference, New York.
Stein, S. (2000). *Equipped for the future content standards: What adults need to
    know and be able to do in the 21st century.* Washington, DC: National
    Institute for Literacy.
Taylor, P. (1980). Competency-based adult education: Toward a functional defi-
    nition. In J. Parker & P. Taylor (Eds.), *The CB reader: A guide to un-
    derstanding the competency-based adult education movement* (pp. 34-
    48). Upper Montclair, NJ: National Adult Education Clearinghouse
    Center of Adult Continuing Education, Montclair State College.
Tibbetts, J., & Westby-Gibson, D. (1980). Process approaches to CBAE staff
    and program development. In J. Parker & P. Taylor (Eds.), *The CB
    reader: A guide to understanding the competency-based adult educa-
    tion movement* (pp. 49-60). Upper Montclair, NJ: National Adult Edu-
    cation Clearinghouse Center of Adult Continuing Education, Montclair
    State College.

United States Department of Education, Office of Vocational and Adult Education. (2003). *Adult and Family Literacy Act report to Congress on state performance: Program year 2000-2001*. Washington, DC: Author.

Chapter 6

Volunteer One-to-One Tutoring: Critical Factors in Providing Quality Instruction

Alisa Belzer
Rutgers University

Since the 1960s, when federal funding for adult basic education (ABE) was first legislated, programs have been staffed, in part, by paid instructors (sometimes, but not necessarily, teachers certified in some area of kindergarten through 12th-grade education). However, volunteer tutors in the field predate this development and continue to play an extremely significant instructional role. Nationally, 42% of the personnel in programs that receive federal funding are volunteer (U.S. Department of Education Division of Adult Education and Literacy, 2000), although an indeterminate number of these are one-on-one tutors, as opposed to support staff of some kind. When literacy councils and community-based organizations that do not receive federal funding are included, it is evident that volunteers make up the majority of the ABE workforce. Yet, there is little research on the nature of teaching and learning transactions between volunteer tutors and adult literacy learners, and what constitutes quality one-to-one tutoring in ABE. As with all questions related to quality in ABE, a definition of what constitutes best practice is needed before quality can be supported, improved, or ensured. This chapter lays out basic areas of focus that research on volunteer tutoring in ABE will need to consider to begin to define quality in this sector of the field. It is based on an analysis of tutor training and actual tutoring in four diverse, volunteer, tutor-based programs. Although the concept of one best practice is problematic given the diversity of learners, volunteer tutors, and programs, a close examination of practice can begin to uncover critical gaps, areas of important concern, and existing strengths within a wide range of potential instructional approaches.

It is clear from the conceptual and descriptive literature on adult literacy programs generally that there are a wide range of approaches to service provision in volunteer-based programs. For example, Fingeret (1984) identified two kinds of ABE organizational structures: individual and community oriented. Quigley (1997) identified four philosophies of adult education: liberal, humanistic, vocational, and libratory. Lytle and Wolfe (1989) identified four different conceptions of literacy: skills, tasks, practices, and critical. These three conceptual frames illustrate some of the ways that have been used to theorize the many differences in ABE programs. Researchers, practitioners, and policymakers debate the relative merits of various approaches on philosophical and empirical grounds. Yet, these conversations have not been influenced so far by detailed knowledge of what tutors and learners actually do when they work together, a key ingredient in the success of any approach. Descriptive data on program contexts and on tutors and students working together in a range of programs can help us understand important distinctions that emerge, and can provide a meaningful impetus for research on quality in this sector of the field. The research described in this chapter begins this task.

RESEARCH ON ONE-TO-ONE TUTORING

During the late 1980s and 1990s, a popular genre of adult literacy research emerged which used case descriptions of adult literacy learning in one-to-one tutoring situations (Forester, 1998; Greenberg, 1997/1998; Jenkins, 1995; Meyer, 1991; Purcell-Gates, 1993; Rigg, 1985; Sharpe & Ganschow, 1982). Typically, these descriptive studies advocated for a particular instructional approach based on the accomplishments of individual learners, or made assertions about the nature of adult learning or adult literacy learners. In almost every case, the researchers typically were reading experts and university-based researchers. Although helpful in many ways, this research did not focus on volunteers and was not contextualized within the culture of specific programs. Additionally, none of them compared cases across contexts.

The only known study in which an external (not the tutor) researcher analyzed this instructional format by looking deeply and descriptively at what goes on between multiple student-tutor pairs was completed by Anita Pomerance in 1990. In her study, she investigated how literacy tutoring is constructed by analyzing the instructional strategies and relational aspects of the interaction between five student-tutor pairs in one program with regard to their theories of literacy, reading and writing instruction, adult learning, and tutoring.

Sandlin and St. Clair (2005) provided a helpful synthesis of the little research that has been done on the quality of instruction when volunteers tutor adult literacy learners. Although largely dated, this research suggests that their motivation to help is beyond doubt. Even those who tutor for a relatively short time do so because they want to make a difference in learners' lives. However, questions about tutors' efficacy surface frequently, and typically revolve around the adequacy of training (Ceprano, 1995; Kazemek, 1988; Meyer, 1985). Although conducted under highly artificial circumstances with predetermined categories of "best practices," Ceprano (1995) argued that volunteers often fall short in selecting appropriate materials, responding to reading errors, and developing comprehension strategies. She did not provide evidence to suggest that professional staff are any more effective than volunteers; Bell, Ziegler, and McCallum (2004), in fact, suggested that many paid teachers lack both training and expertise in evidence-based reading instruction. However, Ceprano's research clearly suggests that the volunteer sector is failing to reach its potentiality. She implicated tutor training in her analysis. Others also suggest that training is both the culprit and the potential answer to the problematic practice of volunteer tutors.

Current research interest in tutoring has been spurred on by the America Reads initiative and other volunteer-based efforts to help children read at grade level. This work identifies effective tutoring practices (Baker, Gersten, & Keating, 2000; Fitzgerald, 2001; Juel, 1996; Wasik, 1998a, 1998b), or compares models of instruction (Morrow & Woo, 2001). Most discusses the outcomes of various approaches with regard to children's reading scores and grade level achievement. Although some of these studies briefly describe tutor training, none document what tutors actually do while they tutor. Therefore, there is little information on the relationship between tutoring training and reading achievement (Baker et al., 2000). Although there are many similarities among the models described in this research, their application to adult literacy learners is difficult to ascertain because the tutoring context is so different. For example, many of these models are school-based and are meant to supplement classroom instruction. They are designed to bring children up to the average level of their grade level peers; adult literacy volunteers do not typically work within these kinds of structures or supports which could assist them in their work. This body of research, along with that more focused specifically on adult learners, indicates significant gaps in the knowledge base regarding one-to-one tutoring between volunteers and adult developing readers. The data discussed here begin to fill in the gaps by identifying significant differences among programs, and the relationship between program contexts (as exemplified in tutor training) and what actually gets done in the instructional setting. The relationship between instructional moves and learner achievement await further research.

DATA COLLECTION METHODS AND THE PROGRAM SITES

The larger study from which the data here are drawn was designed to answer the following questions: (a) What is the nature of teaching-learning transactions in tutor-based adult literacy instruction? (b) What is the relationship between the instructional context and instruction in one-to-one adult literacy tutoring? (c) What can looking across diverse program contexts tell us about the influence of context on the teaching-learning transaction in tutor-based adult literacy instruction? To address these questions, four diverse programs that depend exclusively, or to a significant extent, on volunteer tutors for one-on-one instruction were selected as focal sites. At each program, participant observations were conducted throughout a complete volunteer tutor training series, key program staff (e.g., the program coordinator or education director) were interviewed, and three student-tutor pairs were selected at random from a pool that met the selection criteria (the pair had to have been meeting for at least 3 months, and had to be focusing on basic literacy instruction) to participate. Student-tutor pairs audiotaped three consecutive tutoring sessions (36 sessions total). Once these tapes were transcribed, separate interviews were conducted with each student and tutor which focused on his or her perceptions of the tutoring sessions, influences on their work, and also provided an opportunity to get clarification and explanation of activities captured on the tapes. At this writing, 36 sessions have been audiotaped, 23 sessions have been transcribed, and interviews with 7 pairs have been conducted.

Program selection was based on attaining diversity, and identifying programs with distinctive tutor training approaches. The Polkville Literacy Council (PLC),[2] a Laubach (LLA) affiliated program, and The Essex County Literacy Volunteers (ECLV), a Literacy Volunteers of America (LVA) affiliated program, were sites for this study. Given their convenient location and their affiliations with the two (now merged into one) national literacy organizations that champion the one-to-one volunteer tutor instructional format, these seemed like obvious choices. A third program, the Center for Lifelong Learning (CLL) was selected because of its unique student-tutor orientation training format: tutors participate in an initial orientation session, are matched with their students, and then participate as a pair in the rest of the training. The program has taken this approach on the assumption that the meaning-based, holistic approach to literacy instruction advocated there requires a paradigm shift for many students and tutors; it might more likely be carried out if students were clued in about it from the beginning, just as are tutors. The fourth program, Lincoln County Library Literacy (LCLL), was selected because it had integrated the Equipped for the Future content standards into its program—including it as part of tutor training and required in-service sessions. It is one of a very few volunteer-based, one-to-one programs that has done so. Although there are many similarities among the four programs, they do represent distinctively different assumptions about reading and writing, teaching and learning.

---

2 All program names have been changed.

PROGRAM FEATURES

Adult literacy programs have significant latitude in how they are organized and in their instructional approach to teaching reading and writing. Although this autonomy, and the resultant variability in service provision, could be decreasing as a result of the Workforce Investment Act of 1998, programs still vary widely based on their theories of literacy, beliefs about reading and writing instruction, adult education, and assumptions about how these theories should be put into practice in the tutoring context. In particular, analysis of the data indicate that the four programs varied in the ways the programs supported their student-tutor pairs through their tutor training procedures, tutor training content, and access to staff and information over time (see Table 6-1).

TABLE 6–1
Program Training Features

	LCLL (EFF)	ECLV (LVA)	PLC (LLA)	CLL (STO)
Program size (students)	68 active, 182 total;	123 active	90 active	40 active, 65 total
Training hours	2.5 hours orientation, 1-1 ½ hrs one-to-one (post match)	20 hours (5 sessions)	15 hours (5 sessions; 4 + 1 4-5 weeks later)	9 hours (3 sessions)
Training focus	Orientation	ESL & BL (0-4)	BL (0-4)	BL (3-6)
Matching procedure	After orientation	After training and final exam	After 4th session	After 1st session
Primary training materials	Functional strategies handbook	Tutor handbook Hand-outs *Challenger* Series Real life materials	*Voyager* Series *Laubach Way To Read Reading & Spelling via Phonics Focus on Phonics*	Tutor handbook Goal oriented functional materials

Tutor Training Procedures

The amount and focus of training reflects the potential depth and breadth of knowledge that can be conveyed to volunteers. This varied significantly. Across the four programs, the tutor training lasts from 2.5 hr (an introductory orientation) at LCLL, to one that lasts 20 hr (ECLV). The focus of training is another area of difference. Two trainings focus on basic literacy instruction only, at PLC it is explicitly aimed at adults who read at the "0 to 4" level, at CLL at the 3rd- to 6th-grade levels. ECLV combines English as a Second Language (ESL) and Basic Literacy training (not surprisingly then, the training there is the longest). LCLL provides a general orientation as an initial training and informational session for volunteers to help them decide whether they want to tutor. If they decide they do, they meet once with program staff, one-on-one, after they have been matched with a student to receive guidance specific to the student with which they will work.

The point at which students and tutors are matched varies in each program as well. Although ECLV matches students only after training has been completed and participants have successfully carried out a final assignment, PLC holds a mandatory follow-up session 4 to 5 weeks after the match. It is designed to give tutors an opportunity to ask questions and share experiences with each other and a trainer after they have actually begun to tutor. CLL attempts (but actually does not always succeed) to match tutors and students after an initial tutor-only orientation. Then the pair attends the remainder of the orientation together. In this way, they gain access to the same information about what they should be doing together, and can practice what they are learning with the help of a staff person. The timing of the match at each program seems to reflect different assumptions about learning. Although matching after completion may imply that learning can occur in the abstract and then be applied in actuality, the other matching plans seem to assume, to varying degrees, the importance of experiential learning opportunities by engaging volunteers in trying out what they learn with their students, reflecting and questioning, and then revising their practice. LCLL's approach is customized; it enables staff to tailor a brief training for tutors to the particular learner with whom they will work.

The materials that are provided to tutors during training seem to be telling artifacts of program beliefs about teaching and learning and reading and writing. The principal printed materials used in trainings range from introductions to highly prescriptive, commercially produced instructional materials which take a subskills approach to reading and writing instruction at PLC, to a handbook that focuses on general strategies for teaching reading which can be applied to a wide range of tasks and activities at LCLL.

TABLE 6–2. Program Training Topics
Training Topics

	LCLL	ECLV	PLC	CLL
Learner goals	●	●	○	●
Adult learning	●	●	●	●
Student perspective	● (student testimonial)	● (Case descriptions used as examples)	○ (role play student)	● (students participate)
Lang. exp. (LEA)		●	●	●
Phonics		○	●	○
Sight words		●	●	●
Word patterns		○	○	○
Why low literacy			○	●
Reading process			●	●
Writing			○	●
Good tutor		●		●
Comprehension			○	●
Authentic material		●		●
Oral reading		○	○	●
Learning styles		●	●	
EFF	●	○		
Lrning log/portfol				●
ESL activities		●		
First meeting		●		
LWTR/voyager (how to use)			●	
Problem solving			●	
Definition of Literacy	●			
Lesson planning		●		●
Avail. materials		○	●	○
Sensitivity exper.			●	●

• = Topic is covered extensively
○= Topic is covered briefly

Tutor Training Content

Literacy definitions and teaching reading and writing

Only one program explicitly talked about the definition of literacy—and this program took a sociocultural approach. The other three did not make explicit the purposes and roles of literacy in our culture. Rather, the emphasis was simply on teaching strategies for improving reading and writing. All four programs used

some of the discourse of the whole language approach (e.g., reading as meaning-based, writing as a process), but there were vast differences in emphasis among these concepts. Similarly, there were considerable differences in emphasis and in suggested strategies for implementing ways to help adults improve their reading and writing abilities—from scripted phonics lessons and programmed work-books, to teaching phonics only when needed within the context of reading authentic texts.

Describing the distinctions in tutor training among the four programs is difficult because some of the differences were subtle, a matter of emphasis. There were several key topics that every program touched on, to a greater or lesser extent. These included the importance of focusing on learner goals, what it means to be an adult learner, the adult learners who come to the program, and the Language Experience Approach. The three programs that have an extended training approach also all covered phonics and sight words. It is interesting to note what is not consistently covered in training—some programs cover them, others do not. These include why some adults do not learn to read, the writing process, the qualities of a good tutor, comprehension, using authentic materials, oral reading strategies, learning logs and portfolios, what to do at the first meeting, and problem solving. Examples of areas not covered at any of the programs are math, using technology for instruction, and what to do when students encounter words they do not recognize or can not spell (see Table 6-2).

Adult learners, learning, and tutoring

Obviously, choices about what to cover are driven by program staff beliefs and assumptions about how adults learn, the purposes of literacy, how adults get better at reading and writing, and best practices for one-to-one instruction. Although there seem to be many similarities in assumptions, there are key differences. For example, three out of four programs demonstrated a similar stance on the adults who come for instruction. They characterized them as intelligent but having missed out on learning to read and write for one reason or another, as resourceful, as bringing valuable and usable knowledge, experiences, and skills to their literacy learning, and as able survivors. However, at the fourth program, the trainer seemed to pathologize the learners by taking a deficit approach, stating that they are mostly learning disabled, make very little improvement, and are helpless, scared, frustrated, and isolated. For example, she said of the learners, "they need help to lead productive lives" and "they have huge gaps in their knowledge."

With regard to adult learning, three programs emphasized the importance of focusing on learners' goals, but PLC's training was more focused on the development of academic skills. Two programs explicitly stated that there is no "recipe" for lesson formats and planning. However, ECLV placed a heavy emphasis on lesson planning and requires volunteers to write a detailed lesson plan before tutor training is considered completed. A third strong distinction among the programs was that two of them found it important to talk about finding a balance between friendly helpfulness and personal involvement in the learner's life. All four programs emphasized that the tutoring relationship should be a partnership with the student taking an active role and equal responsibility for learning. Also the importance of patience, affirmation, and confidence building were ideas presented in all four programs' tutor training.

Although we do not know what program features, training procedures, and content achieve the best outcomes for which students under what circumstances, the differences among these four programs do make clear that programs can and do make very different choices about what they hope tutors will do with students and how they will support them as they attempt to do so. Analyzing the impact of these differences highlights significant areas for program reflection and further inquiry.

Access to Staff, Information, and other Resources

The ratio of staff to students served varied significantly among the four programs. The smallest program (CLL) reported 40 active students (65 total) with one full-time and one part-time staff person. The largest program (ECLV) had 123 active students with one full-time and two part-time staff people. Although the number of part-time staff hours is unknown, and the range of staff responsibilities and areas of expertise vary from program to program, taken simply as a ratio of staff to active students, the programs range from a 1 staff person to 27 students (CLL) to a 1 to 61.5 ratio (ECLV). In other words, the staff to student ratio is more than double in the program with the highest ratio compared to that in the lowest. These differences raise questions about the number of student-tutor pairs that staff can be expected to adequately monitor, supervise, and support. Given that this aspect of their job is often only one of several for which staff members are responsible, the number of students and tutors that staff work with could directly influence the nature of interactions, from only leaving them time for quick monthly "check-ins" that may simply consist of the tutor reporting on the number of contact hours with the student, to having the time for extensive contact regarding instructional and personal issues for both the student and the tutor.

The nature of support can be described in many ways. In addition to how much time staff have to talk to tutors about their challenges, another aspect of support can be provided by access to information. One specific way in which this plays out is in the location of staff people in relation to where students and tutors meet. PLC and CLL have their staff offices at the primary or only tutoring site, the ECLV office is off site, and LCLL is located at one of three primary tutoring sites. Being physically located where tutors and students meet enables quick informal contact and help that can be very timely, as well as easy access to instructional materials. Being off site can impede or discourage impromptu communication and access to materials and other resources between students, tutors, and staff.

A further support issue is the availability of in-service professional development for tutors. All but one program (LCLL) makes these sessions available, but optional. They are offered very rarely and the program does not seem to use them as a major opportunity to support and improve instruction. LCLL offers in-service sessions on a range of topics every 6 weeks and requires that tutors participate in three per year.

Again, as with differences in training procedures and content, the differences in tutor support among the four programs are distinctive. Although we cannot know what difference these differences make with regard to learner outcomes, these distinctions provide information that can inform further research and reflection on why programs do what they do and how it influences opportunities to learn.

WHAT ACTUALLY GETS DONE

In looking across the activities of all the pairs, there are some generalizations that can be made. The good news is that almost all of the pairs used at least part of their instructional time to read connected prose texts (as opposed to completing worksheets and workbooks). The text was generally, but not always, chosen by the tutor. However, the tutors almost always were able to state a purposeful reason for the selection that related to the interests and needs of their students. Types of texts that the students read included young adult fiction, children's books, high interest-low level vocabulary nonfiction for adults, newspapers, and the Bible. Students read aloud to their tutors (and two tutors read aloud to their students, as well). They were not only developing their reading fluency, they were also getting practice in word recognition and word attack in the context of actual reading. Although students never read silently during tutoring sessions, one did so extensively at home and a few others did so to a lesser extent. There was little isolated skills practice on word attack and recognition (but those who did it, did it extensively). There was almost no work done on comprehension before, during, or after this reading took place. In fact, there was little discussion at all. When comprehension work was done, it was usually because they had come to a workbook exercise that required it. Two students did talk about what they were reading as they read, indicating their comprehension, but the tutors generally did not do anything to encourage or teach about comprehension.

Very little writing was going on in or outside of tutoring sessions. Only one student was working on an extended narrative, revising and editing over several weeks. Another pair reported that they do so periodically and almost always get these efforts published in the program's newsletter. Two students were asked to copy text, a few others circled or wrote brief responses to workbook questions, one student was asked to take notes. Likewise, there was almost no math instruction. Only one pair worked on math. They did so using a workbook. There was little technology use. Word processing and the Internet were used by just one pair. The only other evidence of technology was a learner who uses a "reading pen" which can scan a printed word, pronounce it, break it into syllables, and define it. Although workbooks were in evidence, they were not used exclusively, even in the case of a student who was a fairly low level reader in the program with the most prescriptive approach to using workbooks. Workbooks were not used as a predominant teaching technology among any of the pairs.

Three of the four programs covered word identification strategies in general (using the context, phonics, word families, and sight words), and two discussed ways to increase fluency by actually reading (tutor reads and student listens, echo reading, duet reading, oral assisted reading, silent reading; see Table 6-2), but there was never any guidance on how to integrate these two activities. In other words, none of the trainings specifically addressed the question of what to do when a student is reading aloud and gets stuck on a word. Yet every student encountered word level difficulty while reading, and either misread or waited for their tutors to help. As a result, the tutors used a wide range of strategies to assist them as they read. These included supplying the word, spelling out the first syllable or the entire word, saying the initial consonant or consonant blend or syllable, giving the definition of the word, having the student spell the word, calling attention to the error to prompt student self-correction, prompting rereading, or encouraging students to make multiple attempts to identify the word while providing constant feedback during the process, or simply supplying the word. There was not necessarily a strong relationship between the word, the nature of the error, and the type of assistance the tutors provided. Tutors tended to depend consistently on one or two of these strategies, only occasionally trying others.

Tutors could sometimes give a rationale for the word identification strategies they encouraged their students to use, but also admitted that their choices were not always conscious and could not necessarily identify what factors were involved in encouraging one strategy over another. Tutors from the same programs did not necessarily rely on similar strategies, suggesting that tutor training did not have a strong impact on instructional strategies.

A detailed look at the work of a few pairs helps illustrate further the relationship between tutor training and instruction. At ECLV, two of the three students were reading at a considerably higher level than those the program aims to serve. According to their tutors, these students began in the program at the target level, but they had both exceeded the profile of the program's typical student. Because both these pairs were working at a considerably higher level than that assumed by the training, the tutors were left to improvise instructional plans. Also interestingly, there is no overlap in activities or materials used between these two pairs. This seems to indicate that the pairs were drawing on their perceptions of what was needed rather than anything specific that they learned in the training.

CLL advocates what it calls an eclectic approach to literacy instruction and suggests that tutors should "do whatever works." Although nonprescriptive, the training does offer a fairly wide array of strategies for teaching reading and writing (see Table 6-2). The two students who serve as examples from this program are both at a more beginning level than those at ECLV. One pair spent almost all its time together reading sight words from flash cards. The other pair had a much greater range of activities. They read passages from the Bible (a student goal), a children's book which the tutor had selected, tutor generated sentences, (which the student also copied), and the student wrote out (spelled) numbers and filled out a form that he wanted to complete to order something. This tutor, interviewed several months after their sessions were taped, reported that they had switched to an intensive effort to improve the student's sight word recognition of the 300 most frequently used words (Fry, 1980). Again, there were few similarities between the two pairs, despite the fact that the students seemed to be at a fairly similar reading level, and the two tutors participated in the same tutor training.

Both students seem very weak in their phonetic awareness and ability to decode words using phonetic clues (phonemes) or larger chunks. Their tutors refer to various phonetic clues and rules, as difficulties arise in word recognition, but neither took any kind of systematic approach to teaching them phonics. They did not offer the students any other strategies for identifying unknown words either. Whereas one placed a great deal of emphasis on reading fluency and student goals (as advocated in the training), the other did almost nothing to address either of these areas (although by working on sight word recognition she may well believe that she was addressing the fluency challenge).

Overall, the data do not indicate any clear, strong relationship between the program context as exemplified by the tutor training and what the students and tutors actually did at any of the programs. The examples from ECLV make clear that at least one explanation for this may be a mismatch between instructional strategies presented in training and learners' actual needs. However, the cause of the gap between training and instruction at CLL is less clear. When interviewed, few tutors from any of the programs mentioned their training as an important influence on their work. Instead, it was more common for tutors to identify their students as the primary influence on their work. Following the lead of the learner was very much in keeping with messages that were conveyed in every program's tutor training; this is one idea that did transfer well from training to practice. Volunteers were admonished to address student goals and be relevant, to work as a team with learners by approaching the tasks as equals, and to build on student interests. Yet within this broad instructional approach, there is a huge range of implementation strategies for actually helping adults acquire better literacy skills. To do this, the tutors assessed their students' needs (no tutors referred to any information they had received about their students from program staff) and then depended on their own ideas, their contacts with teachers in their lives, their educational backgrounds, their own experiences as learners, and, to a much lesser extent, strategies they had learned in tutor training to try to help their students progress and meet their goals.

CONCLUSION

The data presented here helps focus our attention on salient context features of programs and tutor training which can help us define and work toward quality in volunteer-based instruction. They also indicate that tutor training may not be accomplishing what we hope. The distinctive features of tutor training that were highlighted by comparing the four programs relate to the focus of training (level of students, basic literacy, and ESL), the length of the training (this is potentially but not necessarily linked to the breadth of focus), the timing of the student-tutor match relative to completion of training, and the instructional materials and the messages they convey about literacy, learning, and adults. At the program level, the quantity, quality, and access of staff support varied considerably from program to program based on the ratio of staff to students, the range of job responsibilities staff had to fulfill (in addition to supporting instruction), the physical location of staff in relationship to where students and tutors meet, and the amount of training, topics covered, and expectations regarding participation in ongoing training. These are all important differences among the programs, which point to relevant issues of quality in tutor-based instruction.

An analysis of topics covered by the tutor training yields interesting and telling differences among programs, but based on the findings detailed earlier, it seems important to ask how much difference the topics covered actually make in instruction. When they actually began working with their students, the tutors seemed to rely on a variety of resources and strategies regardless of the training they received. The data cannot fully explain this, but suggest that, at least in part, the problem may be that the training does not fit their needs, interests, and beliefs, or those of their students. It is also likely that a few short hours of tutor training cannot successfully train tutors to adopt an unfamiliar philosophy and complex instructional strategies. If the former is the case, then trainings should be far shorter and should focus on a few general topics such as how to access materials and support, appropriate ways to involve learners in their own learning, and the importance of responding to learner goals—ideas that do seem to "stick" with volunteers. If the latter is true, there are many possible topics that the data indicate should be included but are not: what to do when students encounter unknown words while reading, more specific strategies for understanding and improving comprehension, how to integrate technology with instruction, and how to make math instruction relevant to adult life, just to name a few. At any rate, training ought to help tutors be able to generalize from what they are learning then to the specifics of their students' needs later. It is probably very hard to do this after the fact. This would suggest the importance of matching students and tutors during the training process so that tutors can relate what they are learning and ask questions about it with a concrete, real person in mind.

It seems likely that both a lack of fit between tutor training and actual learners, and the impossibility of covering everything a literacy tutor should know to meet the needs of his or her students in the 9, 12, or even 20 hr commonly required of volunteers for training, are indicated by the data and by the reality of tutor-based programs. On the one hand, it seems that by trying to cover many topics (albeit briefly), almost no one's specific needs are addressed. On the other hand, it seems unrealistic to ask volunteers to participate in the numbers of hours it would potentially take to train them adequately.

What then is the answer? Some might suggest that the findings here argue against the possibility of ever adequately preparing volunteer tutors to effectively meet the needs of the learners they teach. Yet, this instructional format does meet the needs of many learners. Interviews with the students and tutors indicate a high level of satisfaction and significant progress. However, it must also be acknowledged that tutor-based instruction does not meet the needs of many others. A significant number of adults never even begin the process, many drop out after a few hours, and still others fail to progress despite their best efforts and their tutors' best intentions. In the end, the data presented here illustrates great successes among students and tutors who have minimal training or experience, raises significant potential implications for improving practice in the one-to-one volunteer sector of the field, and confirms some of our serious concerns about the feasibility of effective volunteer-based instruction. Further research is needed to untangle the knotty issues raised here. However, the data can be used to begin meaningful conversations about defining and improving quality in volunteer, tutor-based, literacy instruction.

REFERENCES

Baker, S., Gersten, R., & Keating, T. (2000). When less may be more: A 2-year longitudinal evaluation of a volunteer tutoring program requiring minimal training. *Reading Research Quarterly, 35,* 494-519.

Bell, S. M., Ziegler, M., & McCallum, R. S. (2004). What adult educators know compared with what they say they know about providing research-based reading instruction. *Journal of Adolescent and Adult Literacy, 47,* 542-563.

Ceprano, M. A. (1995). Strategies and practices of individuals who tutor adult illiterates voluntarily. *Journal of Adolescent and Adult Literacy, 39,* 56-64.

Fingeret, A. (1984). *Adult literacy education: Current and future directions* (Information Series No. 284). Columbus, OH: ERIC Clearinghouse on Adult, Career, and Vocational Education, Ohio State University. (ERIC Document Reproduction Service No. ED 246 308)

Fitzgerald, J. (2001). Can minimally trained college student volunteers help young at-risk children to read better? *Reading Research Quarterly, 36,* 28-47.

Forester, A. D. (1998). Learning to read and write at 26. *Journal of Reading, 31,* 604-613.

Fry, E. (1980). The new instant word list. *Reading Teacher, 34*(3), 284-289.

Greenberg, D. (1997/1998). Betsy: Lessons learned from working with an adult nonreader. *Journal of Adolescent and Adult Literacy, 41,* 252-261.

Jenkins, C. (1995). Reflective practice: Blurring the boundaries. *Adult Basic Education, 5,* 63-81.

Juel, C. (1996). What makes literacy tutoring effective? *Reading Research Quarterly, 31,* 268-289.

Kazemek, F. (1988). Necessary changes: Professional involvement in adult literacy programs. *Harvard Educational Review, 58,* 464-487.

Lytle, S., & Wolfe, M. (1989). *Adult literacy education: Program evaluation and learner assessment* (Information Series No. 338.). Columbus, OH: ERIC Clearinghouse on Adult, Career, and Vocational Education, Ohio State University. (ERIC Document Reproduction Service No. ED 315 665)

Meyer, V. (1985). The adult literacy initiative in the U.S.: A concern and a challenge. *Journal of Reading, 28,* 706-708.

Meyer, V. (1991). Case study--Norman: Literate at age 44. *Journal of Reading, 35,* 38-42.

Morrow, L. M., & Woo, D. G. (2001). The effects of an America Reads work study tutoring program on reading achievement of young children. In L. M. Morrow & D. G. Woo (Eds.), *Tutoring programs for struggling readers* (pp. 117-139). New York: Guilford.

Purcell-Gates, V. (1993). I ain't never read my own words before. *Journal of Reading, 37,* 210-219.

Quigley, B. A. (1997). *Rethinking literacy education: The critical need for practice-based change.* San Francisco: Jossey-Bass.

Rigg, P. (1985). Petra: Learning to read at 45. *Journal of Education, 167,* 129-139.

Sandlin, J., & St. Clair, R. (2005). Volunteers in adult literacy education. In J. Coming, B. Garner, & C. Smith (Eds.), *Review of adult learning and literacy* (Vol. 5, pp. 125-154). Mahwah, NJ: Lawrence Erlbaum Associates, Inc.

Sharpe, C., & Ganschow, L. (1982). Teaching an adult to read: A case study. *Journal of Developmental and Remedial Education, 5,* 22-23, 26.

U.S. Department of Education Division of Adult Education and Literacy. (2000). *State administered adult education program 2000 adult education personnel.* Retrieved July 12, 2006, from http://www.ed.gov/about/offices/list/ovae/pi/AdultEd/datatables/2000-2001pers.xls

Wasik, B. (1998a). Using volunteers as reading tutors: Guidelines for successful practices. *Reading Teacher, 51*(7), 562-570.

Wasik, B. (1998b). Volunteer tutoring programs in reading: A review. *Reading Research Quarterly, 33,* 266-292.

Chapter 7

Supporting the Persistence of Adult Basic Education Students

John P. Comings
Harvard Graduate School of Education

Sondra Cuban
Seattle University

A key difference in learning between adults and children is that adults choose to participate in educational programs whereas children participate because of legal mandates and strong social and cultural forces. Adults must make an active decision to participate in each class or tutoring session and often must overcome significant barriers to do so. Although some adults come to adult basic education programs with very limited goals, most come with goals that require hundreds if not thousands of hours of instruction to achieve. Every adult basic education program, therefore, should help its students persist in their learning so that they can reach their educational goals.

Persistence is the amount of time (measured in hours and months) of participation in learning. Adult basic education programs usually refer to persistence as retention and measure it by recording participation in formal classes or tutoring sessions. Comings, Parella, and Soricone (1999) proposed the term persistence after they found that adults often persist in learning through self-study or distance education after they stop attending program services and sometimes return to a program (not necessarily the one they dropped out of) after a lapse in attendance. The term retention defines this phenomenon from a program's point of view; the program wants to retain its students. Comings et al. (1999) preferred the term persistence because it defines this phenomenon from the point of view of students who persist in learning inside and outside of a program until they have achieved their goals. This chapter defines persistence as the following: Adults staying in programs for as long as they can, engaging in self-study or distance education when they must stop attending program services, and returning to program services as soon as the demands of their lives allow. Persistence is a continuous learning process that could start through self-study before a first episode of program participation, and lasts until an adult student meets his or her educational goals.

The relationship between persistence and learning is supported by two studies that identified approximately 100 hr of instruction as the minimum needed by adults to achieve an increase of one grade-level equivalent on a standardized test of reading comprehension (Darkenwald, 1986; Sticht, 1982). Comings, Sum, and Uvin (2000) found that, at 150 hr of instruction, adult students in Massachusetts had a 75% probability of having made a one (or greater) grade-level equivalent increase in reading comprehension or English language fluency. Unfortunately, most adult students are not participating in a program for 100 hr. The average time that an adult spends in a program is less than 70 hr in a 12-month period (U. S. Department of Education, 2001). These figures do not include adults who drop out before they complete 12 hr of instruction, which would lower the average significantly. Seventy hours of instruction is less than one tenth of the time that a kindergarten through 12th-grade student spends in class during a year. Adult students who enter adult literacy programs with a specific goal may need relatively few hours of instruction, but most adult students have instructional needs that require a long-term effort. Program participation of 100 or even 150 hr, therefore, is probably inadequate for most adult students to reach their learning goals. A high student persistence rate is both a support to and an indicator of quality programming.

This chapter first summarizes the findings of four literature reviews and then describes the lessons learned in two connected studies.

LITERATURE REVIEW

Much of the literature on adult student persistence draws on research with adults who have sufficient literacy skills, speak English, and have high school diplomas. Although this research is informative, it may not be directly applicable to adult basic education students, who have low literacy and math skills, do not speak English, or do not have a high school diploma. In addition, most adult education persistence research takes place in short-term courses with defined, limited goals, such as vocational classes and certificate programs. In contrast, adult basic education students usually face a long-term commitment that may involve many different goals that change over time. Finally, most studies look at participation, the decision to join a program, rather than persistence, the decision to continue in a program. These two decisions are similar, and so the participation literature is useful to understanding persistence. In addition, most studies help define the problem but do not necessarily provide insights into how to help adult basic education students persist in learning. Even with these limitations, this research is the best available evidence for understanding persistence and identifying ways to improve it.

Four literature reviews analyze the participation, retention, and persistence literature in ways that are particularly relevant to our work (Beder, 1991; Quigley, 1997; Tracy-Mumford, 1994; Wikelund, Reder, & Hart-Landsberg, 1992). All of these reviews have authors who have experience with adult basic education programs, and this experience helps them adapt research on other populations to adult basic education students.

Beder (1991) explored motivation as the force that helps adults overcome barriers to participation and then focuses more closely on those barriers. Beder suggested that adult education programs must change their recruitment and instruction practices to be congruent with the motivations and life contexts of adult students. If they did, more adults would enter programs, and they would persist longer. Beder also suggested that adults are weighing the perceived benefits and costs of participation and making decisions based on that analysis. In many cases, a decision to drop out may be justified if the costs outweigh the benefits.

The Beder (1991) review concluded by asserting that the system, at this time, probably only has enough resources to serve those who are eager to enter classes. Although education can never be easy, this review suggests that the effort could be more manageable for students if programs had the resources to fit instruction to the needs and learning styles of adults and if programs looked less like school and more like an activity in which adults would want to participate.

Drawing on the same sources as Beder (1991), Wikelund et al. (1992) critiqued the reductionism of this research and suggested that a useful theory of participation would incorporate the complexity of this phenomenon. The report called for broadening the definition of participation to acknowledge that adults engage in education in many ways, not only coming to formal classes. The Wikelund et al. review criticized the concept of "nonparticipant" because it implied that every adult who has low literacy skills needs to enter a program, an unproven assumption. The review ended with the conclusion that research and theory, as well as practice, should break out of the framework of schooling. A new definition of participation would acknowledge that learning, even improvements in literacy skills, could take place outside of formal programs. With this new definition, programs could increase persistence by continuing to support learning at times when students cannot attend classes or participate in other formal arrangements.

In her review, Tracy-Mumford (1994) called for programs to develop a commitment to and a plan for increasing persistence, which she suggested would send a strong message to students that the program is there to help them reach their goals. Because student goals can change, the program must be willing to make changes to accommodate new goals as they arise. For the commitment to be meaningful, the program should have a set of criteria for measuring persistence and a set of strategies that reduce dropout, increase student hours of attendance, improve achievement, increase personal goal attainment, and improve completion rates.

Tracy-Mumford (1994) defined an effective persistence plan as one that both provides support to students and improves instruction. The review summarized the findings of a large number of studies and descriptions of practice to provide a list of elements of a student persistence plan that weaves persistence strategies into all aspects of the program structure. These elements are as follows:

- Recruitment methods that provide enough information for potential students to make an informed decision about enrolling.

- Intake and orientation procedures that help students understand the program, set realistic expectations, build a working relationship with program staff, and establish learning goals.

- Initial assessment tools that provide students and teachers with information on both cognitive and affective needs, and are integrated with instruction, and should form the foundation for measuring progress.

- Programs and teachers that establish strategies for formally recognizing student achievement.

- Counseling services that identify students at risk of dropping out early.

- Referral services that coordinate with social service agencies to ensure that all students are connected to the support services they need.

- A system for contact and follow-up that helps students who drop out return to the program and solicits information on ways to improve program services.

- Noninstructional activities that help form a bond between the program and its students and their families.

- Program evaluation that involves students in assessing, and offering advice on, each aspect of the program.

- Child care and transportation assistance is provided.

- Instruction and instructional staff that is of sufficient quality to support effective learning.

- A student persistence team that coordinates dropout prevention activities, collects data on student persistence, and involves students and teachers in addressing this issue.

Tracy-Mumford's (1994) list is comprehensive, and it is useful to program staff because it translates theory into practical advice. Unfortunately, most adult basic education programs lack the funding required to implement all of these elements, but implementing some of them may contribute to increased persistence.

Quigley (1997) viewed persistence as significantly affected by the negative schooling experiences adult students had when they were younger and suggests the need to change programs so that they are different from those schools. Quigley saw three major constellations of factors that contribute to dropout, which he referred to as situational (influences of the adult's life circumstances), institutional (influences of systems), and dispositional (influences of experience). He suggested that situational influences are largely beyond the control of adult education programs, although they receive most of the attention in the literature on dropouts. Institutional factors are areas that practitioners could affect and should work on continuously. However, he suggested that dispositional factors provide a focus for program reform that might affect persistence.

According to Quigley (1997), intake and orientation processes and the first 3 weeks of instruction are critical to improving persistence. He suggested that intake should begin with goal setting and planning for success. Students then need to be matched to classes and teachers that can meet their goals and learning needs. Because students are adults, they can take charge of this process, but they may need help in the form of careful questions and the provision of useful information for making these decisions.

PERSISTENCE STUDY

In 1996, the National Center for the Study of Adult Learning and Literacy (NCSALL) began a three-phase study of the factors that support and inhibit persistence. The first phase interviewed and tracked the persistence of 150 adults in pre-General Education Development (pre-GED) classes (Comings et al., 1999). Of the total, 100 students persisted for the 4 months of the study and 50 dropped out. The second phase studied the efforts of five library literacy programs as they attempted to increase student persistence over a 3-year period (Porter, Cuban, & Comings, 2005). The third phase will undertake an experiment to test whether a model of persistence support developed during the first two phases does, in fact, have an impact on persistence in programs. This section summarizes what has been learned in the first two phases of this research.

Phase One

The first phase of the study employed a force-field analysis, which places an individual in a field of forces that are supporting or inhibiting action along a particular path (Jones, 1998; Lewin, 1999), as its theoretical model. This model expands the motivation-barriers and cost-benefit models to include a large number of forces on each side of the persistence equation. Understanding the forces, identifying which are strongest, and deciding which are most amenable to manipulation provides an indication of how to help someone move in a desired direction, such as reaching an educational goal.

This study found that the many ways in which we can classify adult students (by gender, ethnicity, employment status, number of children, and educational background of parents or guardians) do not have a strong influence on persistence. The study does suggest that immigrants, those over the age of 30, and parents of teenage or grown children, are more likely to persist than others in the study. The greater likelihood of persistence by immigrant students in English for Speakers of Other Languages (ESOL) classes is well documented (Young, Fleischman, Fitzgerald, & Morgan, 1994), and the findings of this study suggest that this effect continues as immigrants learn English and move on to pre-GED programs. Adults who are over 30 are more likely to have teenage or grown children than those under 30. Their children may encourage their parents to join and persist in a program. These findings suggest that older students persist longer because they benefit from the maturity that comes with age, and they no longer have the responsibilities of caring for small children.

The study found that previous school experience (among U.S.-schooled students) does not appear to be associated with persistence. Of course, those potential students who are significantly affected by negative school experience may never enter a program or may have dropped out before the research team arrived. However, many of the study's participants did describe negative school experiences, with most of the comments centered on high school. Respondents reported being ridiculed and even struck by teachers, bullied or intimidated by other students, told that they were stupid, and asked to leave school by administrators. Issues of class, race, and sexual orientation contributed to the negative school experience for some. Entering an adult basic education program may signal that a student has overcome the influences of negative school experiences and is ready to restart his or her education.

Prior nonschool learning experiences, particularly self-study focused on improving basic skills or studying for the GED, may be related to persistence. Attempts at self-study may be an indication of strong motivation, or some people may need several attempts at learning before they are ready to persist. Research that explores these attempts might uncover factors that lead to later persistence or to permanent nonparticipation. Another line of inquiry might look at making self-study outside of class a part of instruction so that adult dropouts are ready to continue their learning when they do leave class. This self-study might make a return to classes more likely and the development of ways to document that self-study could provide a more realistic account of persistence.

Both the students who persisted and those who dropped out talked about the forces supporting and inhibiting persistence in the same way. Students mentioned four types of positive forces: relationships, goals, their teacher and fellow students, and self- Both the students who persisted and those who dropped out talked about the forces supporting and inhibiting persistence in the same way. Students mentioned four types of positive forces: relationships, goals, their teacher and fellow students, and self-determination. Relationships incorporate the support noted by participants derived from their families, friends, or colleagues, God or their church community, support groups, community workers, mentors or bosses, and their children. Goals included helping one's children, getting a better job, self-improvement, moving ahead in life, attending college or some other academic institution, proving wrong someone's assessment of the student's abilities, or obtaining citizenship. The support provided by the people involved in their classes and their own determination to succeed were also important positive forces to which students pointed.

Students mentioned three types of negative forces: life demands, relationships, and poor self-determination. Life demands included special child care needs, work demands, transportation difficulties, the student's own or his or her family's health issues, age, lack of time, fatigue, bad weather, welfare and other official rules, unfavorable conditions at home, moving, and lack of income. Relationships included family members, friends, colleagues, community or welfare workers, and religious beliefs that were not in support of persistence, as well as fears about letting other people down by failing in a program. Lack of determination was indicated by comments such as "thinking negative thoughts," "my own laziness," and statements indicating a lack of confidence in students' ability to succeed.

How adults describe the positive and negative forces that affect them did not predict persistence, but this information is still valuable in that it gives practitioners input from adult students on what might be important. Adults in this study had much more to say about positive forces than about negative forces. Adding this information to the finding that negative school experience was not associated with persistence points to a conclusion that building positive supports may be more critical to increasing persistence than is the removal of barriers. If this is so, then understanding which positive forces are most important is essential to a model that supports persistence. The study team summarized the implications of its findings by identifying four supports to persistence:

The first support to persistence is the establishment of a goal by the student

The process of goal development begins before an adult enters a program. An adult who could be classified as a potential adult basic education student experiences an event in his or her life that motivates entry into an educational program. That event might be something dramatic; for example, a well-paid worker might lose his or her job and find that he or she does not have the basic skills needed to qualify for a new job at a similar pay scale. That event might be less dramatic; for example, a parent may decide he or she needs more education when a first child begins school. That event might be subtle; for example, a school dropout might have always felt the desire to study for the GED but when his or her children are older and need less attention, there is finally some free time available for education. The event provides potential adult students with goals they hope to accomplish by entering an adult basic education program. The staff of the educational program should help the potential adult student articulate his or her goal and understand the many instructional objectives that must be accomplished on the road to meeting that goal. Teachers should then use those student goals as the basis for instruction. The effort to identify goals must be continual as instruction proceeds because they may change over time.

The second support is to increase a sense of self-efficacy

The self-determination mentioned by students must build on a foundation of self-efficacy, a feeling that they can reach their goals. The term self-confidence is quite often used in adult education literature, but self-efficacy has a different definition. Self-confidence is a global feeling of being able to accomplish most tasks. Self-efficacy is focused on a specific set of tasks and represents the feeling of being able to accomplish that set of tasks.

The third support is management of the positive and negative forces that help and hinder persistence

Programs should help students develop an understanding of the negative and positive forces that affect their persistence. Building on that understanding, each student could then make plans to manage these forces so that persistence is more likely. The plans that come out of such an exercise should include strategies for persistence when the forces that affect peoples' lives cause them to drop out. These plans must be revised as adults persist in their studies and these forces change.

The fourth support is ensuring progress toward reaching a goal

Assuming the goal is important, then adult students must make progress toward reaching that goal, and they must be able to measure that progress. Programs should provide services of sufficient quality that students make progress, and programs need assessment procedures that allow students to measure their own progress.

Phase Two

The second phase of the project observed 10 library literacy programs in California, New York, and North Carolina that were attempting to increase student persistence and interviewed 30 of their students about their history of participation and supports and barriers to their persistence. The study found that the persistence of most students was affected by factors that were personal (related to the student) or environmental (related to the student's life situation). Adult basic education programs do not have the resources to address these personal and environmental factors.

This study also identified five persistence "pathways" that are determined by these personal and environmental factors and ways that programs might support students on each pathway. Each pathway describes a pattern of persistence. However, any one student might begin a program on one pathway and change to another. In addition, these pathways might be arbitrary points on a continuum. These pathways, therefore, provide guidelines that can help programs broaden the ways they help students persist rather than student types that could allow programs to identify the specific needs of an individual student. The five pathways are as follows: long-term, mandatory, short-term, try-out, and intermittent.

Long-term students participate regularly over a long period. Long-term students usually do not express specific goals, but rather, talk of education as an end in itself. Long-term students have managed the personal and environmental factors that support and inhibit their persistence. Presumably, they will persist in a program that helps them meet their needs, is convenient for them, and provides an enjoyable experience. In fact, this is the story told to the study team by long-term students. Most long-term students viewed their program as a comfortable and supportive community and talked about it as a family, a club, or a home base for learning. They referred to the program staff as friends or family members. Long-term students expressed a strong personal commitment to their programs and to their goal of becoming more educated.

Most of the long-term students identified through interviews were over the age of 30. Adults over the age of 30 may no longer have child care responsibilities and may have a stable income, housing situation, and set of relationships, whereas younger students may not be as stable. The long-term persistence of older students may appear to be supported by their emotional maturity, but, in fact, it may be supported by stable personal and environmental factors related to children, partners, and employment.

For students who are able to travel the long-term pathway, an intake and orientation process that clearly sets out steps, with measurable objectives along the path to reaching their often ambitious goals, might help support their persistence. This study found that improving formal instruction (through training of teachers and volunteers, improving curriculum, and other program development inputs) and offering many different types of informal instruction, appeared to increase hours of instruction for these students.

Mandatory students must attend a program because they are required to do so by a public assistance or law enforcement agency. Their participation is usually regular and long term, but their goals are often those of the agency that is mandating their attendance. They look like long-term students while they are under the requirement to participate, but usually leave abruptly once attendance is no longer mandatory and sometimes even while it still is a requirement.

Mandatory students overcome personal and environmental factors that constrain their persistence because they are required to do so. Because factors outside the program support their participation, programmatic improvements may not help these students to stay longer. However, if the program changes its services (making them more convenient, more useful, or more enjoyable), mandatory students might choose to participate for more hours or become long-term students. Counseling during intake, orientation, and throughout instruction that focuses on helping mandatory students commit to learning as a way to improve their lives, understand how they learn best, find ways to enjoy learning, and build a support system to sustain their learning, might help mandatory students persist after the mandate has ended. Additional hours of participation and persistence after legal mandates for participation have ended are probably good measures of impact for innovations meant to address the needs of mandatory students.

For students who are on the mandatory pathway, program intake and orientation must help them move past the required goals of attendance and begin to see learning as something they would choose to do. This building of motivation probably requires identifying goals that are personal and an instructional process that helps students see that they can learn and that learning can be enjoyable. Literacy learning focused on family, work, personal interests, or even the problems that led to their legal or social service status might be a focus of instruction that supports persistence for adults on this pathway. An instructional process that involves discussions among a group of adults might provide a social network that supports persistence for mandatory students, and referral to support services (such as counseling, day care, and employment) might be necessary for these students to persist, even while they are under a mandate.

Short-term students enroll in a program and participate intensively for a short period to accomplish a specific goal. For some of these students, short-term participation in a particular program meets their needs, but for others, this participation leads to enrollment in another more suitable program. Although students on a short-term pathway may leave their programs after only a few weeks of instruction, some may persist in another program that more closely meets their needs. Because personal goals determine their length of participation, programmatic innovations may have little impact on the persistence of students on a short-term pathway. Transition into another program or accomplishment of a specific, limited goal are probably good measures of the impact of innovations meant to address the needs of short-term students.

For students who are on the short-term pathway, programs should be careful during intake and orientation to identify their specific goal. When transfer to another program is appropriate for reaching that goal, the program might be able to provide some learning opportunities that prepare these students to be successful in a more appropriate program. When new students have a specific short-term goal, programs should try to focus on it, possibly with an individual tutor, or make that goal the focus of their instruction in a more general learning environment.

Try-out students have barriers to persistence that are insurmountable and have goals that are not yet clear enough to sustain their motivation. These students end an episode of program participation quickly with neither goal achievement, nor transfer to another program. Students on the try-out pathway are motivated to learn, and their decision to initiate participation is a positive step. However, they are not ready to make a commitment to it.

Program staff members believe that every new student can succeed and are usually opposed to counseling students to defer participation. However, admitting students who are likely to fail, particularly because most of these students have failed in education before, is probably not helpful to the student. Students on the try-out pathway who leave a program with a plan on how to address the personal and environmental barriers constraining their participation so that they can return at sometime in the future is probably a good measure of impact for innovations meant to address the needs of try-out students.

Helping try-out students during intake could improve program persistence rates by both lowering the number of students who drop out after very little participation and by providing more program resources to students who are on a different pathway. To do this, programs would have to design intake processes that identify try-out students, counsel them to delay entry, and help them design a program that would lead to successful participation some time in the future.

Intermittent students move in and out of program services. During the time that they are not attending program services, intermittent students may stay in contact with their programs, and their episodes of participation and nonparticipation may reoccur several times and take place in more than one program. Belzer (1998) found that students identified as dropouts in adult education programs often see themselves as still connected but temporarily unable to attend.

These students may have broad goals (such as improving language or basic skills ability) or specific ones (such as passing a citizenship test), but either way their goals require a long period of engagement to reach them. However, personal and environmental factors limit their ability to attend on a regular basis. Programmatic changes probably cannot have an impact on the persistence of these students unless program services change to fit a pattern of episodes of participation over a long period.

These program changes would redefine participation as connection to the program rather than hours of attendance in program services. This connection would have to be meaningful, not just a name in a database. An example of a meaningful connection could be monthly discussions between a program staff member and a student in which they review progress on a self-study plan. Programs would define any form of learning activity that serves the goals of the program and the student as participation. These activities would include classroom instruction or tutoring, but might also include guided self-study at home or at the program venue. Length of continuous connection to the program and cumulative hours of engagement in learning might be good measures of impact for innovations meant to address the needs of intermittent students, regardless of whether they are formally participating in program activities.

The intermittent pathway may be the only one open to most students. Personal and environmental factors are always going to present barriers to long-term persistence, and most students have goals that require a good deal of study to achieve. Programs should accept this reality and look at ways to redesign their services to provide connected episodes of participation that use a multiplicity of learning resources. Program staff also need ways to help students maintain contact with the program and to continue to think of themselves as students.

IMPLICATIONS FOR PRACTICE

These five pathways provide a way to think about the kinds of program changes that might be useful to different types of students. Practitioners know that a single approach to services will not help all students persist and learn, but programs generally do not have the resources to provide an individual approach for each student. A middle ground is for programs to provide supports based on an understanding of these five pathways and help students identify which one most closely fits their circumstances.

The second phase of the NCSALL study describes the implications of its findings by making suggestions for how programs could support persistence for three chronological phases of program participation: entrance into services, participation in services, and reengagement in learning.

Entrance into Services

Entrance into services includes recruitment, intake, and orientation. This is the time when programs prepare students to be successful in learning. Rather than trying to identify a student's pathway when he or she enters a program, program staff might just assume that all students are intermittent. That is, that students are prepared to participate in an episode of learning that, if it is short, might lead to additional episodes of learning that continue until they reach their goal.

The first step in this phase would be to help students express clear goals that represent their motivation for participation. The second step would be to develop a learning plan that includes both instruction and the support services a student needs to persist in learning to reach those goals. For try-out students, this phase would lead to their postponement of participation, but they would leave the program with a plan on how to prepare to enter services later. The program would identify this student as successful, because the program provided the student with the best possible outcome. For other students, intake and orientation would lead to a plan for participation in the program. That plan would assume that students would engage in episodes of participation that lead to accomplishment of a specific goal, transfer to another program, or departure from the program followed by another episode of participation. Of course, students on a long-term pathway may only have a single long episode of participation.

The plan would be a written document that sets out the goals each student is trying to reach, the skills and knowledge the student needs to learn to meet those goals, and the services the student needs to successfully complete that learning. These services would include both instruction, self-study, and support services. The plan would also include a process that would allow the student to judge progress.

Participation in Program Services

Participation in program services includes both instruction and support services. General improvements in instruction and expansion of support services probably help support learning and persistence, but most students need more than just good services. They need instruction that fits their patterns of participation and support services that help them address their particular persistence needs.

A multiplicity of instructional modes (such as classes, tutoring, peer learning groups, technology, and print and media materials) provides students with ways to participate that do not always demand adherence to a regular schedule. However, these different modes would be more effective if they fit into a plan that is followed by both the student and the tutor or teacher. Helping students and instructional staff follow a plan that uses several modes of instruction and that builds toward the attainment of specific goals is not easy. This chapter can only point out this problem, not provide a solution.

The individual plan would allow a student, who must stop instruction, to continue learning (either at home or at the library) through self-study. When that student is ready to return to regular attendance, any tutor or teacher should be able to look at how far the student has been able to progress on his or her plan and start instruction there. Program services should include regular counseling that helps students meet their need for support services and identify the times when they will not be able to meet the instructional schedule and so begin the self-study part of their plan.

Reengagement in Learning

Most students do not tell their program or tutor that they are stopping participation. Most just stop attending. Interviews with students uncovered that many of them believe that once they stop attending they cannot return (Porter et al., 2005). Programs should have a procedure for staying in contact with students who are not attending and for reengaging them in services, and this procedure should be explained during orientation. Former or even current students might do this best, because they may have addressed many of the same personal and environmental factors as the students who have dropped out. These new procedures require resources that are now being used to support instruction. However, if these procedures were successful, program services would improve as students who have had a single episode of instruction return to continue learning.

CONCLUSION

The literature reviews defined persistence as supported by motivation and constrained by barriers. The NCSALL persistence study broadened this equation to include a wide range of supports and barriers, but it also identified the limits on how much programs can do to address the barriers that students bring to programs. Most programs could make their services more convenient, enjoyable, and useful, but they may not have sufficient resources to directly address the personal and environmental factors that constrain persistence. Programs that add supports to persistence would be more expensive than those that do not, and additional resources are not easy to find. The first step in implementation, therefore, would require programs to limit enrollment as a way to increase per student spending. Once persistence and achievement rates increase, programs could more effectively argue for funds to expand services.

Although the course set out here is based on empirical studies, no research has tested whether these recommendations would indeed have an impact on persistence and help more students reach their learning goals. Although further study into the nature of persistence and the forces that support and inhibit it would add valuable knowledge, now may be the time to test program models that incorporate the existing research. If these models prove to be sound, practitioners and policymakers could feel assured in making changes based on them, and further research could begin to build on this foundation.

REFERENCES

Beder, H. (1991). *Adult literacy: Issues for policy and practice*. Malabar, FL: Krieger.

Belzer, A. (1998). Stopping out, not dropping out. *Focus on Basics*, 2, 15-17.

Comings, J., Parrella, A., & Soricone, L. (1999). *Persistence among adult basic education students in pre-GED classes* (NCSALL Report No. 12). Cambridge, MA: National Center for the Study of Adult Learning and Literacy.

Comings, J., Sum, A., & Uvin, J. (2000). *New skills for a new economy: Adult education's key role in sustaining economic growth and expanding opportunity*. Boston: Massachusetts Institute for a New Commonwealth.

Darkenwald, G. (1986). *Adult literacy education: A review of the research and priorities for future inquiry*. New York: Literacy Assistance Center.

Jones, E. E. (1998). Major developments in five decades of social psychology. In D. Gilbert, S. Fisk, & G. Lindzey (Eds.), *Handbook of social psychology volume I* (4th ed., pp. 21-22). Oxford, England: Oxford University Press.

Lewin, K. (1999). *The complete social scientist: A Kurt Lewin reader* (M. Gold, Ed.). Washington, DC: American Psychological Association.

Porter, K., Cuban, S., & Comings, J. (2005). *One day I will make it: A study of adult student persistence in library literacy programs*. New York: MDRC.

Quigley, B. (1997). *Rethinking literacy education: The critical need for practice-based change*. San Francisco: Jossey-Bass.

Sticht, T. (1982). *Evaluation of the reading potential concept for marginally illiterate adults*. Alexandria, VA: Human Resources Research Organization.

Tracy-Mumford, F. (1994). *Student retention: Creating student success* (NAEPDC Monograph No. 2). Washington, DC: National Adult Education Professional Development Consortium.

U.S. Department of Education. (2001). *1999-2000 report on adult education*. Washington, DC: U.S. Department of Education.

Wikelund, K., Reder, S., & Hart-Landsberg, S. (1992). *Expanding theories of adult literacy participation: A literature review* (NCAL Tech. Rep. No. TR 92-1). Philadelphia: National Center on Adult Literacy, University of Pennsylvania.

Young, M., Fleischman, H., Fitzgerald, N., & Morgan, M. (1994). *National evaluation of adult education programs: Patterns and predictors of client attendance*. Arlington, VA: Development Associates.

Chapter 8

Learning To Read As a Cultural Process

James Paul Gee
University of Wisconsin-Madison

We are, again, in an era of controversy over reading (Kruidenier, 2002; National Institute of Child Health and Human Development, 2000a, 2000b). I argue in this chapter that this controversy is as relevant to adult literacy as it is to child literacy, although I start from the latter and eventually move to the former.

LEARNING PROCESSES

Traditionalists advocate a sequential, skills-based approach to reading instruction (Carnine, Silbert, & Kameenui, 1996; Lyon, 1998; National Institute of Child Health and Human Development, 2000a, 2000b): first, instruction on phonemic awareness, then on phonics (decoding), then practice with fluent oral reading, then work on comprehension skills training. Mastery of each stage is supposed to guarantee readiness for the next. Traditionalists argue that learning to read requires overt instruction. For them, reading is what I call an instructed process.

Nontraditionalists, on the other hand, stress meaning-making (e.g., Edelsky, 1994). They believe that people learn to read best when they pick up skills as part and parcel of attempting to give meaning to written texts, rather than by directly concentrating on skills out of the context of meaning-making activities. There have been many different nontraditionalist approaches, although Whole Language has been the best known of these after the 1950s (Goodman, 1998).

Advocates of Whole Language have argued that learning to read is a "natural" process in the same way in which the acquisition of one's native language is a natural process (Goodman, 1998). Every human child, barring quite severe disorders, acquires his or her native language through immersion in talk and activity. No instruction is needed or helpful. Many linguists, following the work of Noam Chomsky (e.g., 1965, 1968, 1986, 1995; see also, Pinker, 1994), argue that the acquisition of one's native language happens in this "natural" way be-

141

cause acquiring a first language is biologically supported in human beings. Much as some species of birds know innately how to build their species-specific nest or sing their species-specific song, human children know innately what a human language can be like (including the parameters of possible variation across human languages), and how to go about "building" one. This is to say, in a sense, that for human beings, acquiring a native language is a type of instinct.

Today's reading traditionalists, supported by many linguists, myself included (Gee, 2001; Rayner, Foorman, Perfetti, Pesetsky, & Seidenberg, 2001; Rayner, Foorman, Perfetti, Pesetsky, & Seidenberg, 2002), argue that the process of learning to read, unlike the process of acquiring one's first oral language, cannot be a biologically supported process, and thus, is not "natural." Literacy (written language) is too new a process historically to have had the evolutionary time required to have become "wired" into the human genetic structure. Written language is, at the very best, 6,000 to 10,000 years old, too short a time to have gained biological support. Furthermore, written language was invented by only a few cultures and only a few times, unlike oral language, which has existed for all human cultures for long enough to have become part of our human biological inheritance.

I agree with the traditionalists that learning to read is not a natural process like acquiring a first language, or for that matter, learning to walk. Such natural processes simply happen when a child is exposed to the right sorts of inputs and environments (e.g., speaking with others, moving around a three-dimensional world). They "unfold." So, does this mean that, as the traditionalists argue, reading is an instructed process, that is, the sort of learning that requires overt instruction? Not necessarily.

There are actually three major learning processes in human development, not just two (natural and instructed). When humans acquire something by a natural process supported by their biological inheritance, like their first language or walking, we find that everyone, barring serious disorders, succeeds and succeeds well. This is the hallmark of biologically supported acquisition.

There are many things that for most human beings are acquired, more or less, by overt instruction. This is how most people acquire knowledge of physics, social studies, and mathematics. In such cases, we humans have no support from our biological inheritance. Even when instruction is good, we find a pattern in such cases where a small number of people succeed quite well and a far greater number succeed much less well. Every human is built to learn a native language well; not everyone is built to learn physics well.

We can construe the traditionalists' argument that learning to read is an instructed process as a claim that learning to read is more like learning physics than learning one's native language. We can construe the Whole Language argument that learning to read is a natural process as a claim that learning to read is more like learning one's native language than learning physics. They are both wrong or right, depending on how one looks at the matter, because learning to read is neither like learning one's native language nor like learning physics.

Besides natural and instructed learning processes, there are also what I call "cultural processes." There are some things that are so important to a cultural group that the group ensures that everyone who needs to learn them does (Lave & Wenger, 1991; Rogoff, 1990). Take cooking, for example. Human cultures have always ensured that some group of people (different in different cultures) learns how to cook, and cook well enough to keep themselves and others alive and well. Here we see a pattern where a few people really excel (as in physics); but nearly everyone who needs to, learns "well enough," a relatively small percentage has some difficulty, but no apparent disorder otherwise (for cooking and other cultural achievements, the standard of excellence need not be as high as for speaking a native language).

So the pattern of acquisition for reading is different from both acquiring one's native language and from learning things like physics. If most people learned to cook as well as they learn physics, whole cultures would starve. If everyone learned to read at the level they have mastered their native-language grammar, everyone would be an equally expert reader. Neither condition is true. About 80% of people learn to read well, about 20% have difficulties, either because they have a genuine disorder or they simply find learning to read difficult, something that rarely happens in the case of first language acquisition (Snow, Burns, & Griffin, 1998). That 80% figure is high for things like learning physics and low for acquiring one's native language.

How, for the most part, have people learned to cook in human cultures? This usually is not done via cooking classes. The process involves "masters" (adults, more masterful peers) creating an environment rich in support for learners. Learners observe masters at work. Masters model the behavior with talk that keys learners in on what to pay attention to. Learners collaborate in their initial efforts with the masters who do most of the work and scaffold the learner's efforts. Texts or other artifacts (e.g., recipes, cookbooks) that carry useful information, although usually of the sort that can be used "on demand" or "just in time" when needed, are often made available. Learners are continually given verbal and behavioral feedback for their efforts. And, finally, learners are aware that masters have a certain socially significant identity (here, "cook") that they wish to acquire as part and parcel of membership in a larger cultural group.

Now here is a problem with what I have just said: Cultural learning processes, like learning to cook (or tell stories, give and get gifts, set up a household), undoubtedly have their origin in the basic workings of human culture. However, long ago, specific groups of human beings learned how to engage in this learning process even when they were not really "cultures" or were cultures only in some extended sense. To take a contemporary example, consider that what I have called a cultural learning process is how the vast majority of young people today learn to play computer and video games (and the vast majority of them do play such games). People who play video games do not really constitute a "culture" in any classic anthropological sense, although we can certainly use the word in an extended sense here if we want. Such people constitute what I have elsewhere called a "Discourse" with a capital "D" (Gee, 1996, 1999, 2005). Thus, I would prefer to replace the term *cultural learning process* with *Discourse learning process*. However, given space restrictions here, I avoid explicating the term *Discourse* and simply stick with the term *cultural*.

DEEP CAUSE OF READING FAILURE

So, the argument so far is this: although you can turn learning to read into an instructed process, it works best as a cultural process (for the full argument, see Gee, 2004). Traditionalists would have us believe that poor readers, young and old, failed to learn to read well because they received poor skills instruction early on in school. There is, however, good reason to believe that in general, this traditionalist claim is not true, at least for people who do not have a genuine neurologically based reading disorder.

One skill that the contemporary traditionalists have focused on is phonemic awareness, the conscious awareness that words are composed of individual phonemes or "sounds." They see this as a crucial prerequisite skill for learning to read (National Institute of Child Health and Human Development, 2000a). They advocate explicit training in phonemic awareness as the foundation for later explicit and intensive phonics instruction. However, research on reading undermines the central significance traditionalists place on phonemic awareness training. Even the traditionalists' own current reading reports, ironically, indicate this. Consider, for example, the remarks that follow from the National Academy of Sciences' report *Preventing Reading Difficulties in Young Children* (Snow et al., 1998; in the quotes that follow, the term *phonological awareness* is used for phonemic awareness and other aspects of knowledge about how sounds work in oral language):

> ... studies indicate that training in phonological awareness, particularly in association with instruction in letters and letter-sound relationships, make a contribution to assisting at risk children in learning to read. The effects of training, although quite consistent, are only moderate in strength, and have so far not been shown to extend to comprehension. Typically a majority of the trained children narrow the gap between themselves and initially more advanced students in phonological awareness and word reading skills, but few are brought completely up to speed through training, and a few fail to show any gains at all. (p. 251)

When classificatory analyses are conducted, phonological awareness in kindergarten appears to have the tendency to be a more successful predictor of future superior reading than of future reading problems
(Wagner, 1997; Scarborough, 1998). That is, among children who have
recently begun or will soon begin kindergarten, few of those with
strong phonological awareness skills will stumble in learning to read,
but many of those with weak phonological sensitivity will go on to become adequate readers ...
   In sum, despite the theoretical importance of phonological awareness for learning to read, its predictive power is somewhat muted, because, at about the time of the onset of schooling, so many children
who will go on to become normally achieving readers have not yet attained much, if any, appreciation of the phonological structure of oral
language, making them nearly indistinguishable in this regard from
children who will indeed encounter reading difficulties down the road.
(p. 112)

Tests of early phonological awareness (or lack thereof) do not fruitfully
select those students who will later have problems in learning to read. Furthermore, although a stress on phonological awareness and overt phonics instruction
does initially help "at risk" students, it does not bring them up to par with more
advantaged students, and they tend to eventually fall back, fueling the phenomenon known as the "fourth-grade slump" (this fact is amply documented in the
report; Snow, Burns, & Griffin, 1998, pp. 216, 228, 232, 248-249, 251, 257).
The "fourth-grade slump" (Chall, Jacobs, & Baldwin, 1990) is the phenomenon
where children seem to acquire reading (i.e., pass reading tests) fine in the early
grades, but fail to be able to using reading to learn school content in the later
grades, when the language demands of that content (e.g., science) become more
and more complex.
   From remarks like those shown earlier, it would certainly seem that the
problems children, particularly poor and minority children, have with reading
must lay, for the most part, someplace other than in just a lack of early phonemic awareness or other "basic skills." The fourth-grade drop-off tells us this
much, as well. Although much of *Preventing Reading Difficulties in Young
Children* (Snow et al., 1998) is driven by the correlation between early phonological awareness and later success in learning to read, the report does readily
acknowledge that such a correlation does not prove that phonological awareness
causes success in reading. And, indeed, remarks from the report like those cited
earlier, and the fourth-grade drop-off problem itself, would seem to indicate that
something else causes both reading success (or failure) and early phonemic
awareness (or lack of it).
   The authors of the report are, ironically, aware of just what this something
else might be. They readily acknowledge (but then go on to ignore the fact) that

another correlation is just as significant (if not more so) as that between early phonological awareness and learning to read. This is the correlation between what the report calls "early language abilities" and later success in learning to read. And, as one might suspect, early language abilities and early phonological awareness are themselves correlated:

> Chaney (1992) also observed that performance on phonological aware-
> ness tasks by preschoolers was highly correlated with general language
> ability. Moreover it was measures of semantic and syntactic skills,
> rather than speech discrimination and articulation, that predicted pho-
> nological awareness differences (p. 53).

> What is most striking about the results of the preceding studies is the
> power of early preschool language to predict reading three to five years
> later (pp. 107-108).

> On average, phonological awareness (r. = .46) has been about as strong
> a predictor of future reading as memory for sentences and stories, con-
> frontation naming, and general language measures (p. 112).

So what are these early language abilities that seem so important for later success in school? According to the report, they are things like vocabulary—receptive vocabulary, but more especially expressive vocabulary (p. 107)—the ability to recall and comprehend sentences and stories, and the ability to engage in extended, semantically connected verbal interactions. Furthermore, I think that research has made it fairly clear what causes such verbal abilities. What appears to cause enhanced verbal abilities are family, community, and school language environments in which children interact intensively with adults and more advanced peers and experience cognitively challenging talk and texts on sustained topics and in different genres of oral and written language (see pp. 106-108).

However, the correlation between language abilities and success in learning to read (and in school generally) hides an important reality. Almost all chil-dren—including poor children—have impressive language abilities used to en-gage in conversation, language play, and learning within their cultures. The vast majority of children enter school with vocabularies fully fit for everyday life, complex grammar, and deep understandings of experiences and stories. It has been decades since anyone believed that poor and minority children entered school with "no language" (Gee, 1996; Labov, 1972).

The verbal abilities that children who fail in school lack are not just some general set of such abilities, but rather *specific verbal abilities tied to specific school-based practices and school-based genres of oral and written language.* Many children who have trouble learning to read well in school, or who later fuel the fourth-grade slump, are children who have not had lots of home-based practice with school-based forms of language, the sorts of language used in talk and writing in school. Today, schools tend to douse these kids in phonics, but do little to enhance their school-based language development.

With our equation of verbal abilities in the *Preventing Reading Difficulties in Young Children* report (Snow et al., 1998) to school-based language skills, we have hit a crucial point that needs to be stressed. The term *school-based language skills* is not quite right here. Broadly speaking, people acquire two different major styles of language throughout their lives. Everyone, early in life, acquires a vernacular style of their native language. This style is used for face-to-face conversation and for "everyday" purposes. Each human being learns a vernacular variety of his or her native language that constitutes a specific dialect connected to the person's family and community. Thus, a person's vernacular dialect is closely connected to his or her initial sense of self and belonging in life.

People, sometimes early on, sometimes later on, also acquire various non-vernacular specialist styles of language used for special purposes and activities. For example, they may acquire a way of talking (and writing) about fundamentalist Christian theology, video games, or bird watching. One category of specialist styles of language is what we can call academic styles of language, that is, the styles of language connected to learning and using information from academic or school-based content areas (Gee, 2002; Schleppegrell, 2004; Schleppegrell & Cecilia Colombi, 2002). The styles of language used in (different branches) of biology, physics, law, or literary criticism fall into this category.

Some texts are, of course, written in vernacular styles of language, for example, some letters, e-mail, and children's books. But the vast majority of texts in the modern world are not written in the vernacular, but in some specialist style of language. People who learn to read the vernacular often have great trouble reading texts written in specialist styles of language. Of course, there are some texts written in specialist styles of language (e.g., nuclear physics) that many very good readers cannot read.

It is obvious that once we talk about learning to read specialist forms of language, it is hard to separate learning to read and learning the sorts of content or information that the specialist language is typically used to convey. That content is only really accessible through the specialist form of language, and, in turn, that content is what gives meaning to that form of language. The two—content and language—are married.

Of course, one key area where specialist styles of language differ from vernacular styles is in vocabulary. But they also offer differences in syntax and discourse features, as well. For example, suppose someone is studying the development of hornworms (green caterpillars with little yellow horns). Contrast the vernacular sentence, "Hornworms sure vary a lot in how well they grow" to the specialist sentence, "Hornworm growth exhibits a significant amount of variation."

The specialist version differs from the vernacular version in vocabulary (e.g., "exhibits"), but it also differs in syntactic structure, as well. What are verbs naming dynamic processes in the vernacular version (e.g., "vary," "grow") show up as nouns naming abstract things in the specialist version ("variation," "growth"). The vernacular sentence makes the hornworms (cute little caterpillars) the subject or topic of the sentence, but the specialist sentence makes "hornworm growth" (a measurable trait for hornworms) the subject or topic. A verb adverb pair in the vernacular version ("vary a lot") turns into a verb plus a complex noun phrase in the specialist version ("exhibits a significant amount of variation").

Although I do not have space to pursue the matter here, vernacular styles of language also differ from specialist styles at the discourse level. We can see this even with our two sentences. Note that the specialist version does not allow an emotional marker like the "sure" that occurs in the vernacular version. At the cross-sentential level, specialist languages use many devices to connect, contrast, and integrate sentences across stretches of text that are not used as frequently, or exactly in the same ways, in vernacular styles of language (like the phrase "at the cross-sentential level," which starts this sentence in what Halliday [1985] called the "Theme" position).

Failing to know that these sorts of syntactic and discourse devices are used and used together in this sort of specialist language, and failing to know why they are used and what their functions are in this sort of specialist language, means a person cannot effectively write, read, or speak this sort of language. Many academic specialist languages share some of these features, although each of them also has its own distinctive features. And, of course, nonacademic specialist languages, like the language of computer or video gamers, have their own characteristics.

So, I have argued that poor readers fare poorly in school not because they received poor skills training (although, of course, they may have, and, of course, that poor skills training could have been too much overt phonics). They fared poorly because they did not get a good induction (at home or at school) into the sorts of practices that allow people to acquire specialist forms of language, especially academic or school-based forms of specialist language. Even many good early readers fail at the specialist language task, and, thereby, fueled the fourth-grade slump.

LEARNING TO READ

The current controversies over reading, focused on phonics instruction, as they are, have ignored a much more important problem with learning to read, one crucial for children and adults who did not learn to read well early in life. It turns out that people with poor vocabularies—especially poor vocabularies in regard to academic varieties of language—are poor readers. This is, of course, especially true for reading texts written in specialist styles of language. Research shows that the only way that poor readers can catch up in vocabulary is by doing lots of reading, especially because teaching vocabulary out of the context of reading is not very effective. This is already a paradox because these readers cannot read well, and thus, are unlikely to do lots of reading, especially of texts filled with words they do not know. But the bigger paradox here is that reading is, in fact, not an especially good way to learn vocabulary. Consider, then, the two quotes that follow:

> … the variety of contexts in which words can appropriately be used is so extensive, and the crucial nuances in meaning so constrained by context, that teaching word meanings in an abstract and decontextualized manner is essentially futile and potentially misleading. (Baker, Simmons, & Kameenui, n.d.)

> … The only realistic chance students with poor vocabularies have to catch up to their peers with rich vocabularies requires that they engage in extraordinary amounts of independent reading. Furthermore, research finding are increasingly clear that opportunities for developing adequate reading skills are limited. In fact, the status quo in beginning reading instruction may be entirely insufficient to meet the reading and vocabulary needs of many diverse learners (Adams, 1990; Liberman & Liberman, 1990). (Baker, Simmons, & Kameenui, n.d.)

> It may be somewhat surprising to learn that most researchers agree that although students do learn word meanings in the course of reading connected text, the process seems to be fairly inefficient and not especially effective (Beck & McKeown, 1991). Beck and McKeown (1991) stated that "research spanning several decades has failed to uncover strong evidence that word meanings are routinely acquired from context" (Gersten, Fuchs, Williams, & Baker, 2001, p. 799).

So, poor readers cannot become good ones unless they improve their vocabularies. They cannot improve their vocabularies unless they read a lot, but reading a lot is not a particularly effective way to increase one's vocabulary. So what, for heaven's sake, can be done? Are poor readers just fated to stay poor readers?

But, then, think a minute what the aforementioned quotes imply about good readers. They have large vocabularies, especially for the specialist texts they can read, but they didn't get these large vocabularies by reading alone, because even reading a lot is not an effective way to grow a large vocabulary. So how, then, did they get these vocabularies? The answer, I assert, is that they got these large vocabularies by learning to read, not as an instructed sequential skills-based process, but as a cultural process. So we need now to look at how people learn to read when learning to read is a cultural process.

LEARNING TO READ AS A CULTURAL PROCESS

One problem with learning vocabulary, which the quotes I offered earlier make clear, is that words do not have just one general dictionary-like meaning. They have quite different and quite specific meanings in different situations where they are used and in different specialist domains that recruit them. This is true of the most mundane cases. For instance, notice the change in meaning in the word "coffee" in the following sentences which refer to different situations: "The coffee spilled, go get the mop" (coffee as liquid); "The coffee spilled, go get a broom" (coffee as grains); "The coffee spilled, stack it again" (coffee in cans).

Consider all the different meanings of "work" in the following sentences: "I'm going to work;" "Relationships take work;" "Joe is really working the system;" "Bush's plan won't work;" "I managed to work my point in;" "I never dreamed I would work past the age of 65;" "It was the work of God, not man;" "Let's work this out before a fight starts." Many more could be added. Furthermore, these are all everyday (vernacular) uses of the word. The word "work" has a different meaning in the specialist domain of physics.

In the specialist domain of playing computer and video games, the term *power up* (as in "I just found a power up") has a general meaning—namely any device that increases the player's character's health or powers. Knowing this general meaning is almost worthless unless you know how they look and function in different games, and you can recognize and use power ups in specific games. So, too, with any word: knowing the general meaning is worthless unless you can recognize the word's applications in specific cases.

But, then, too, here is our key: How does a gamer learn the specific meanings of a word like "power up?" Obviously, this is done by playing games. How does any reader learn the specific meanings of any word? This is done by playing the "games" in which the words are used. Reading lots of texts may not be an effective way to learn what words mean specifically, but playing the games in which they are used is an effective way. The games in which they are used are what give them specific meanings and these games cannot be played if you do not know what the word means (or, at least, know the specific concept to which the word refers). For humans, "playing the game" is a form of cultural learning.

So let's look a moment at how gamers learn vocabulary about games and how they learn to read texts about games (Gee, 2003). What we learn here should be applicable to vocabulary and reading in other specialist domains. Computer and video games often contain lots of print and they come with manuals. It is notorious that young people do not read the manuals, but just play the game. Although older people bemoan this fact as just one more indication that young people today do not read, these young people are making a very wise decision when they start by playing and not reading. The texts that come with games are very hard to understand unless or until one has some experience playing the game, experience which, then, will give specific situated meanings to the language in the text.

Let me take the small booklet that comes with *Deus Ex,* to use as an example of what I mean by saying that texts associated with video games are not lucid unless and until one has played the game. The book contains 20 small-sized pages, printed in double columns on each page. In these 20 pages, there are 199 bolded references that represent headings and subheadings, including: "Passive Readouts," "Damage Monitor," "Active Augmentation & Device Icons," "Items-at-Hand," "Information Screens," "Note," "Inventory," "Inventory Management," "Stacks," "Nanokey Ring," and "Ammunition." Each of these 199 headings and subheadings is followed by text that gives information relevant to the topic and relates it to other information throughout the booklet. In addition, the booklet gives 53 keys on the computer keyboard an assignment to some function in the game, and these 53 keys are mentioned 82 times in the booklet in relation to the information contained in the 199 headings and subheadings. So, although the booklet is small, it is just packed with concise and relatively technical information.

Here is a typical piece of language from this booklet:

> Your internal nano-processors keep a very detailed record of your condition, equipment and recent history. You can access this data at any time during play by hitting F1 to get to the Inventory screen or F2 to get to the Goals/Notes screen. Once you have accessed your information screens, you can move between the screens by clicking on the tabs at the top of the screen. You can map other information screens to hotkeys using Settings, Keyboard/Mouse.

This makes perfect sense at a literal level, but that just goes to show how worthless is the literal level. When you understand this sort of passage at only a literal level, you have only an illusion of understanding, one that quickly disappears as you try to relate the information in this passage to the hundreds of other important details in the booklet. Such literal understandings are precisely what kids who fuel the fourth-grade slump have. First of all, this passage means nothing real to you if you have no situated idea about what "nano-processors," "condition," "equipment," "history," "F1," "Inventory screen," "F2," "Goals/Notes screen" (and, of course, "Goals" and "Notes"), "information screens," "clicking," "tabs," "map," "hotkeys," and "Settings, Keyboard/Mouse" mean in and for playing games like *Deus Ex.*

Second, although you know literally what the sentences mean, they raise a plethora of questions if you have no situated understandings of this game or games like it. For instance, is the same data (condition, equipment, and history) on both the Inventory screen and the Goals/Notes screen? If so, why is it on two different screens? If not, which type of information is on which screen and why? The fact that I can move between the screens by clicking on the tabs (but what do these tabs look like, will I recognize them?) suggests that some of this information is on one screen and some on the other. But, then, is my "condition" part of my Inventory or my Goals/Notes—doesn't seem to be either, but, then, what is my "condition" anyway? If I can map other information screens (and what are these?) to hotkeys using "Setting, Keyboard/Mouse," does this mean there is no other way to access them? How will I access them in the first place to assign them to my own chosen hotkeys? Can I click between them and the Inventory screen and the Goals/Notes screens by pressing on "tabs?" And so on and so forth—20 pages is beginning to seem like a lot—remember there are 199 different headings under which information like this is given a brisk pace through the booklet.

All these terms and questions can be defined and answered if you closely check and cross-check information over and over again through the little booklet. You can constantly turn the pages backwards and forwards. But once you have one set of links relating various items and actions in mind, another drops out just as you need it and you are back to turning pages. Is the booklet poorly written? Not at all. It is written just as well or poorly as any of a myriad of school-based texts in the content areas. It is, outside the practices in the domain from which it comes, just as meaningless, however much one could garner literal meanings from it with which to verbally repeat things or pass tests.

Of course, you can utter something like, "Oh, yea, you click on F1 (function key 1) to get to the Inventory screen and F2 to get to the Goals/Notes screen" and sound like you know something. The trouble is this: in the actual game, you can click on F2 and meditate on the screen what you see at your leisure. Nothing bad will happen to you. However, you very often have to click on F1 and do something quickly in the midst of a heated battle. There's no "at your leisure" here. The two commands really do not function the same way in the game—they actually mean different things in terms of embodied and situated action—and they never really *just* mean "click F1, get screen." That's their general meaning, the one with which you cannot really do anything useful until you know how to spell it out further in situation-specific terms in the game.

When you can spell out such information in situation-specific terms in the game, then the relationships of this information to the other hundreds of pieces of information in the booklet become clear and meaningful. And, of course, it is these relationships that are what really count if you are to understand the game as a system, and thus, play it at all well. *Now* you can read the book if you need to piece in missing bits of information, check on your understandings, solve a particular problem, or answer a particular question.

As I discussed earlier, school requires, both in respect to oral and written language, forms or styles of language that are different from, and, in some respects, more complex than, everyday vernacular oral language used in informal face-to-face conversations. These forms of language are the kind used in texts and discussions in science, math, social studies, and other content areas.

Academic language, like the language in the *Deus Ex* booklet, is not really lucid or meaningful if one has no embodied experiences within which to situate its meanings in specific ways. For example, consider the academic language here: "The destruction of a land surface by the combined effects of abrasion and removal of weathered material by transporting agents is called erosion...The production of rock waste by mechanical processes and chemical changes is called weathering" (Martin, 1990, p. 93).

Again, one can certainly understand this in some literal, word by word, sentence by sentence way. However, this is not "everyday" language. No one usually speaks this way at home around the table or at a bar having drinks with friends. But understanding this language is filled with all the same problems for me as the language in the *Deus Ex* booklet before I had lived through any experiences that could help me situate its meanings. Without embodied experiences with which to cash out its meanings, all the aforementioned academic text will do—like the *Deus Ex* booklet did to me initially—is fill one with questions, confusion, and, perhaps, anger. The argument is this then: learning to read in a way that allows people more than a literal understanding, that does not fuel the fourth-grade slump and create poor readers, requires that people "play" in a domain in such a way that they can give specific situated meanings to the styles of language associated with that domain.

Schools very often fail to facilitate academic language development (i.e., learning the specialist languages of the content areas) for those children who have not come from homes that have already given them a head start in this process and which continue to support them in the process. It is an important question why this is so and more important is the question of how schools could do a better job in this respect. I do not have the space here to take up these issues beyond the brief ways in which I have touched on them in the previous discussion. I deal with these issues at greater length in other texts (Gee, 2003, 2004).

CHILDREN AND ADULTS

Our whole discussion so far has implications for the issue of adults learning to read, as well as children. Learning to read works best as a cultural process for everyone, children and adults alike. In that sense, everything I have said here applies to people who come to reading later in life. However, there is a problem. When people learn anything, whether this be cooking or video games, as a cultural process, they learn skills and content as part and parcel of picking up a new identity. The video game learner becomes a game player of a certain sort affiliated with other players in different ways. In our culture, learning to read is widely connected to the identity of children being socialized into their families (if these families are literate) and into their identities as students in early schooling. This obviously won't work for nonliterate or poorly literate adults.

The solution is easy in theory, hard in practice. When adults learn to read, the learning process must be connected to some literate culture of which they want or need to become a member, just as literate children want and need to become members of their literacy-affiliated families and school communities. The adult must value this culture, must be allowed true access to it, and must firmly believe, even if at an unconscious level, that he or she will gain membership in the culture and will function well within it for the fulfillment of his or her own interests and desires.

Of course, in typical adult education programs, adults often do value the culture that they want or need to enter, but the programs sever these identities from class work. Programs often try to teach adults to read in isolation from the discourses in which they wish to join. At the same time, for many other adults, programs need to make clear what are the values and meaning of the new cultures they are trying to enter, beyond mere content and skills.

Learning to read cannot be a generic process—"learning to read"—it must be a cultural process—"learning to use literacy to become and be a certain type of person with other people." This is as true for adults as it is for children. It is just a lot harder to find the requisite culture for adults, cultures that they really can enter, want to enter, and that will truly function for them. In the end, this is what Paulo Freire's work was all about. Learning to read the word is integrally linked not just to learning to read the world, as Friere argued, but it is also integrally linked, as Freire so well knew, to becoming a new type of person. When we teach reading in ways that sever the link to identities and cultures, we cut off the engine that drives learning.

REFERENCES

Adams, M. J. (1990). *Beginning to read: Thinking and learning about print.* Cambridge, MA: MIT Press.

Baker, S. K., Simmons, D. C., & Kameenui, E. J. (n.d.). *Vocabulary acquisition: Synthesis of the research.* Retrieved March 2, 2003, from http://idea.uoregon.edu/~ncite/documents/techrep/tech13.html

Beck, I., & McKeown, M. (1991). Conditions of vocabulary acquisition. In R. Barr, M. Kamil, P. Mosenthal, & P. D. Pearson (Eds.), *Handbook of reading research* (Vol. 2, pp. 789-814). New York: Longman.

Carnine, D. W., Silbert, J., & Kameenui, E. J. (1996). *Direct instruction reading* (3rd ed.). Englewood Cliffs, NJ: Prentice Hall.

Chall, J. S., Jacobs, V., & Baldwin, L. (1990). *The reading crisis: Why poor children fall behind.* Cambridge, MA: Harvard University Press.

Chaney, C. (1992). Language development, metalinguistic skills, and print awareness in 3-year-old children. *Applied Psycholinguistics, 13,* 485-299.

Chomksy, N. (1965). *Cartesian linguistics. A chapter in the history of Rationalist thought.* New York: Harper & Row.

Chomksy, N. (1968). *Language and mind.* New York: Harcourt Brace & World, Inc.

Chomsky, N. (1986). *Knowledge of language: Its nature, origin, and use.* New York: Praeger.

Chomsky, N. (1995). *The minimalist program.* Cambridge, MA: MIT Press.

Edelsky. C. (1994). *With literacy and justice for all: Rethinking the social in language and education* (2nd ed.). London: Taylor & Francis.

Gee, J. P. (1996). *Social linguistics and literacies: Ideology in discourses* (2nd ed.). London: Routledge/Taylor & Francis.

Gee, J. P. (1999). *An introduction to discourse analysis: Theory and method.* London: Routledge.

Gee, J. P. (2001). Progressivism, critique, and socially situated minds. In C. Dudley-Marling & C. Edelsky (Eds.), *The fate of progressive language policies and practices* (pp. 31-58). Urbana, IL: NCTE.

Gee, J. P. (2002). Literacies, identities, and discourses. In M. Schleppegrel & M. Cecilia Colombi (Eds.), *Developing advanced literacy in first and second languages: Meaning with power* (pp. 159-175). Mahwah, NJ: Lawrence Erlbaum Associates, Inc.

Gee, J. P. (2003). *What video games have to teach us about learning and literacy.* New York: Palgrave/Macmillan.

Gee, J. P. (2004). *Situated language and learning: A critique of traditional schooling.* London: Routledge.

Gee, J. P. (2005). *An introduction to discourse analysis: Theory and method* (2nd ed.). London: Routledge.

Gersten, R., Fuchs, L. S., Williams, J. P., & Baker, S. (2001). Teaching reading comprehension strategies to students with learning disabilities: A review of research. *Review of Educational Research, 71,* 279-320.

Goodman, K. (1998). *In defense of good teaching: What teachers need to know about the "reading wars."* Portland, ME: Stenhouse.

Halliday, M. A. K. (1985). *An introduction to functional grammar.* London : Edward Arnold.

Kruidenier, J. (2002). *Research-based principles for adult basic education reading instruction.* Jessup, MD: The National Institute for Literacy.

Labov, W. (1972). *Language in the inner city.* Philadelphia.: University of Pennsylvania Press.

Lave, J., & Wenger, E. (1991). *Situated learning: Legitimate peripheral participation.* New York: Cambridge University Press.

Liberman, I., & Liberman, A. (1990). Whole language vs. code emphasis: Underlying assumptions and their implications for reading instruction. *Annals of Dyslexia, 40,* 51-76.

Lyon, G. R. (1998). Overview of reading and literacy research. In S. Patton & M. Holmes (Eds.), *The keys to literacy* (pp. 1-15). Washington, DC: Council for Basic Education.

Martin, J. R. (1990). Literacy in science: Learning to handle text as technology. In F. Christe (Ed.), *Literacy for a changing world* (pp. 79-117). Melbourne: Australian Council for Educational Research.

National Institute of Child Health and Human Development. (2000a). *Report of the National Reading Panel. Teaching children to read: An evidence-based assessment of the scientific research literature on reading and its implications for reading instruction* (NIH Publication No. 00-4769). Washington, DC: U.S. Government Printing Office.

National Institute of Child Health and Human Development. (2000b). *Report of the National Reading Panel. Teaching children to read: An evidence-based assessment of the scientific research literature on reading and its implications for reading instruction: Reports of the subgroups* (NIH Publication No. 00-4754). Washington, DC: U.S. Government Printing Office.

Pinker, S. (1994). *The language instinct: How the mind creates language.* New York: William Morrow.

Rayner, K., Foorman, B. R., Perfetti, C. A., Pesetsky, D., & Seidenberg, M. S. (2002). How should reading be taught? *Scientific American, 286,* 84-91.

Rayner, K., Foorman, B. R., Perfetti, C. A., Pesetsky, D., & Seidenberg, M. S. (2001). How psychological science informs the teaching of reading. *Psychological Science in the Public Interest Monograph, 2,* 31-74.

Rogoff, B. (1990). *Apprenticeship in thinking: Cognitive development in social context.* New York: Oxford University Press.

Scarborough, H. S. (1998). Early identification of children at risk for reading disabilities: Phonological awareness and some other promising predictors. In B. K. Shapiro, P. J. Accardo, & A. J. Capute (Eds.), *Specific reading disability: A view of the spectrum* (pp. 77-121). Timonium, MD: York Press.

Schleppegrell, M., & Cecilia Colombi, M. (Eds.). (2002). *Developing advanced literacy in first and second languages: Meaning with power.* Mahwah, NJ: Lawrence Erlbaum Associates, Inc.

Schleppegrell, M. (2004). *Language of schooling: A functional linguistics perspective.* Mahwah, NJ: Lawrence Erlbaum Associates, Inc.

Snow, C. E., Burns, M. S., & Griffin, P. (Eds.). (1998). *Preventing reading difficulties in young children.* Washington, DC: National Academy Press.

Wagner, R. K. (1997, April). *Phonological awareness training and reading.* Paper presented at the conference of the American Educational Research Association, Chicago.

Chapter 9

The Forgotten R:
Why Adult Educators Should Care About
Writing Instruction

Marilyn K. Gillespie
SRI International

Within the literacy research community, writing has sometimes been described as "the forgotten of the three R's" (Freedman, Flower, Hull, & Hayes, 1995, p. 1). This has become even more true in recent years, as the focus on reading has intensified. Writing has been subsumed under the general category of "literacy" and thereby rendered much less visible. Although the teaching of writing has not been neglected entirely in classrooms, it receives less attention and research funding than reading. We still do not know enough about how to use the full potential of writing as a tool for learning, how writing can be most effectively learned under varied conditions, and how to help adult educators teach it. This is especially true in the context of adult education, where there is very little research and few resources for teachers who might want to apply research-based knowledge to writing instruction. The aim of this chapter is to discuss why the adult education system should pay more attention to the teaching of writing, and what we might do to improve the quality of writing instruction within the adult education system.

WHY TEACH WRITING?

Why should we care about writing instruction in adult education? With the limited time adult learners have to study and our limited resources, *shouldn't* our focus be on reading? Do the adults who come to our classes really need to know how to write, beyond filling out forms and writing simple letters? In this chapter, I argue that writing (that is, writing that extends beyond language arts exercises and the production of very short pieces of text) is, in fact, one of the most important things we should teach adult literacy learners.

One of the most obvious arguments supporting the teaching of writing is that it is an important tool for learning to read. Writing has been shown to support the development of many of the "basic" skills advocated by recent reading panels, including phonemic awareness, the understanding of phonics, and, in particular, vocabulary development (see Tierney & Readance, 2000). Connecting reading with writing also supports reading comprehension by providing learners with a stronger understanding of literacy as a meaning-making process. Reading supported by writing about what was read has been found to foster better text-based learning and aid in comprehending and recalling text (see Langer & Applebee, 1987). As students become older, writing also becomes a tool for enhancing many other kinds of learning. High school students use it as part of even the most basic research processes, for planning, and as a tool to solve problems in many school-related subject areas.

Langer and Applebee (1987) reminded us that the power of writing is that it possesses so many qualities that make it a particularly good tool for the kinds of "higher order thinking" advocated by reading specialists, and, in the case of adult learners, for lifelong learning. The permanence of written text allows writers to step back as they reread their ideas and to rethink and revise them over time. The act of writing itself can often help the writer to discover ideas that would otherwise not have been discovered. Even at a beginning literacy level, adult education teachers have found that many adults can benefit from writing. Writing short narratives about their reasons for coming back to school, for example, often helps new adult learners to put into words, examine, and affirm their goals. Even learners with limited literacy or English language skills can use writing about what they have read to connect what they are learning with their prior experiences. Writing can function as a bridge between what they already know and what they hope to learn, thus helping them engage with the literacy process. For teachers who involve beginning adult literacy students in writing from the start, rather than waiting until they have what might be called the "prerequisite language arts skills," it readily becomes apparent that "a beginning writer is not a beginning thinker" (Opening Time, 1987).

The relatively limited amount of research on writing outside of school contexts has obscured the fact that writing is a tool we use in everyday life much more than we might realize. Peter Elbow (who, for the past three decades, has played a leading role in helping English teachers understand more about teaching writing) recently observed that when he asks people to talk about their history as writers, most refer only to the writing they do in school or on the job. "It's as though they don't notice or remember any other writing they've done" (2002, p. 218). Some people, he said, even say, "I never write"—when in fact they do write" (2001, p. 218). Recent studies of writing in the community (see Barton & Hamilton, 1998) have documented the fact that people actually write a remarkable amount. People write lists of all kinds (and often spend quite a lot of time doing it), sketch out plans and brainstorm ideas on paper, and write all kinds of letters, notes, and increasingly, e-mail. They write with family members, at church, on the Internet, and in the community. More people than we might expect also write poetry and keep journals off and on, as evidenced by the rows of blank books that fill the shelves of the local Barnes & Noble. When we hear people say that adult literacy learners do not need or want to write, they may be thinking about "school" writing, associated with essays and extended compositions rather than these kinds of everyday writing. In preliminary findings from a longitudinal study of adults participating in adult education and a cohort of nonparticipants, Stephen Reder (this volume) found that for these two groups combined, 65% engaged in some kind of self-study outside the classroom and 30% said they engaged in some form of creative writing.

The technological revolution has also led not to fewer but to more demands for writing. New and easier technology-based ways of generating, organizing, and editing text, and the availability of multimedia forms of expression, have created more immediate and much larger audiences for all kinds of writing. E-mail is becoming a form of communication as ubiquitous as the telephone, both in and outside the workplace. The Internet is rapidly allowing us to become a global community, where we can share our special interests and needs with others from around the world. Consider our immigrant learners in classes for English language learners who now can keep in touch with relatives and friends in their native countries in ways previous generations of immigrants never could have imagined. Electronic communication, some writing experts speculate, is even introducing a new textual component to human relationships (Sperling & Freedman, 2001).

Another set of reasons why writing is important has to do with its importance for success in postsecondary education. Recently, the National Commission on Writing in America's Schools and Colleges (2003), a blue ribbon panel formed by the National College Board, expressed concern that "writing today is not a frill for the few, but an essential skill for the many." The commission cited recent results of the 2002 National Assessment of Education Progress, which found that most high school students perform at a writing proficiency level deemed by its developers to be inadequate to succeed in today's world. Without better writing abilities, it was observed, students currently entering postsecondary education will not have the skills to succeed—at college or on the job. This concern has resulted in the addition of a writing assessment as part of the new Scholastic Assessment Test (SAT) taken by most college applicants, and to recommendations to increase the attention given to writing at the high school level.

This issue is of crucial importance to adult literacy educators because it has been shown that if adults do not get at least some postsecondary education, they cannot expect to qualify for jobs that pay a living wage. Reder (1999) has brought this point home to us, citing economic analyses which show that the mean annual earnings of U.S. adults age 18 and older rise dramatically with education. Given this reality, thinking about the skills that facilitate the transition between adult education and higher education is becoming increasingly important.

Reder's (1999) study also found that although 65% of the General Educational Development (GED) examinees in 1999 indicated that they were obtaining the credential to pursue further education, only 30% to 35% of those GED holders actually enrolled in any postsecondary education. Only 5% to 10% attained at least a year of postsecondary education. We do not know nearly enough about the challenges GED graduates face when they enter postsecondary education, or the best ways to prepare them to meet the demands they face. There are multiple reasons why GED examinees are not entering and succeeding in postsecondary education, but we can speculate that being underprepared for the writing demands of college may be one of them.

One indication of this possibility is a body of qualitative research conducted during the 1980s. A number of writing researchers working with novice writers at the university level began to uncover the role that cultural learning processes play in preparing students to enter academic life. For example, when David Bartholomae (1985) looked closely at the nontraditional students he taught, he came to recognize that, to enter the world of academia, basic writers had to "invent the university," a world and a discourse with which they often had little familiarity. He observed that his students had to find ways both to imagine and write from a position of privilege and to imagine for themselves the privilege of being insiders—"that is, of being both inside of an established and powerful discourse, and of being granted a special right to speak" (p. 277). In *Lives on the Boundaries: The Struggles and Achievements of America's Underprepared* (1989), Mike Rose recounted the stories of adults who were trying to "cross the boundaries" and enter into the academic world:

> Through all my experiences with people struggling to learn, the one thing that strikes me most is the ease with which we misperceive failed performance and the degree to which this misperception both reflects and reinforces the social order. Class and culture erect boundaries that hinder our vision—blind us to the logic of error and the ever-present stirring of language—and encourage the designation of otherness, difference, deficiency. (p. 205)

Since the 1980s when this research took place, budgets for remedial education at the college level have been reduced in many states, leaving adult literacy educators to take more responsibility for helping adults "cross the boundaries" and be successful participants in academic life.

Once adults are on the job, functional writing skills are often required to move up to better jobs. A frequent reason given by practitioners for neglecting writing (beyond filling out forms and such) is the perception that most adults do not need to write for their jobs. Although this may be true for some entry-level jobs, preparing adults only for these kinds of jobs is not enough. Even moving up one rung on the employment ladder, such as from an entry-level housekeeping job to floor supervisor, often requires being able to effectively write up staff schedules, accident reports, and short memos.

When Larry Mikulecky (1998) conducted a study of writing at work, he found that in nearly all job categories, significant percentages of workers, including employees without a college education, wrote regularly as part of their jobs. They most frequently wrote memos and reports and filled in forms. Only 24% of workers he surveyed reported that they never write memos, and 36% reported that they never write reports. The misperception of many educators and the public at large, that writing is not required for most jobs, is of growing concern. As the National Council of Teachers of English (2003) pointed out, we need more research about the kinds and nature of writing required on the job, as well as research on how best to get this information into the hands of teachers.

Another important dimension of writing is its potential to promote personal growth. For countless adult learners, writing and sharing what they have written has played an immeasurable role in their process of shaping new identities for themselves as actors in the world and as lifelong learners. It helps them develop what Jerome Bruner (1986) called a sense of "agency," to individuate themselves as well as locate themselves within their families, communities, and indirectly, their cultures. Writing can be a tool for helping adults to move toward developing what Robert Kegan and his colleagues (2002) called a "self-authoring" way of knowing. This "self-authoring" stance allows them to begin to converse with others as part of a cultural learning process, what James Gee (this volume) called a "discourse process."

Lidia Nubile, an adult beginning reader in a writing class I taught several years ago, described what she learned about herself by writing about her life:

> I learned that I matter. I learned that no matter what happened as a child, you live through it. If you go through those trials and tribulations that is an education in itself that you wouldn't understand if you didn't go through it....It wasn't just the ability to write....It was the image of myself. I'm not just a little grain anymore. You know that grain went down inside the ground and died but there is a plant that came out and is sprouting again, is going through branches. It's as if I've know all along and I thought, "Why did I think I was just a seed when I'd done so much in life without reading and writing?"...You have to break free to form yourself and say... Hey, I matter. My voice matters. (Gillespie, 1991, p. 96)

Not only does the development of writing skills accrue many benefits, but failure to attain those skills can exact a toll. This is conveyed perhaps most poignantly by Victoria Purcell-Gates (1995) in her case study of Jenny in *Other People's Words: The Cycle of Low Literacy*. Before working with Purcell-Gates, Jenny had spent over 4 years in adult literacy classrooms. Most of her time was spent using workbooks. "She had never written anything on her own, for her own purposes besides her name, a few notations on the calendar and her address on the few occasions when she had been required to do so" (Purcell-Gates, 1993, p. 213). When Purcell-Gates (1993) suggested to Jenny that she write in a journal and then read her own writing, "She looked at me with an expression of stunned awareness. 'Why I ain't never read my *own* words before!' she exclaimed softly ... 'That's all I ever really did was copy stuff, you know, from a book.'" Purcell-Gates remarked as follows: "It is hard to believe that Jenny had *never*—in 7 years of school, 4 years of adult school, and 31 years of life—*never* written or read her own words at the text level" (p. 218).

The sense of oneself as someone who shapes one's own history is not an outcome that is easily measured, but is at the heart of what many adult educators feel is most significant about literacy learning in adulthood. Writing is not the only tool in helping learners to move from seeing themselves as consumers of "other people's words" to producers of their own knowledge, but it is an important one that is too often overlooked if we focus solely on teaching reading skills.

Throughout history, in large and small ways, writing has also played a powerful role in shaping our political lives and in giving voice to movements for social justice and social change.

> At its best, writing has helped transform the world. Revolutions have been started by it. Oppression has been toppled by it. And it has enlightened the human condition. American life has been richer because people like Rachel Carson, César Chavez, Thomas Jefferson and Martin Luther King Jr., have given voice to the aspirations of the nation and its people. (National Commission on Writing in America's Schools and Colleges, 2003, p. 10)

Within our field, there are many examples of how literacy teachers and students have used writing as a vehicle for the analysis of the broader economic and political inequalities they have experienced in their lives, and of how their publications have become part of a social change process. Peyton (1993) described many kinds of learner- and worker-generated writing projects that flourished in the United States, Canada, and Great Britain during the late 1970s and into the 1980s. Learner-written articles and descriptions of classroom activities related to social justice and social action topics can also be found in *The Change Agent,* a journal for the adult literacy education community published by the

New England Literacy Resource Center. The availability of multimedia and Internet communication provides new ways to share writing with larger audiences. For example, Glynda Hull (this volume) describes her work in a community technology center in West Oakland where community members create multimedia productions that allow them to represent their lives as a counterpoint to the negative stereotypes of inner-city life portrayed in the dominant media. For many adults, the writing they do in adult literacy classes becomes the beginning of a process of moving toward more active participation in the civic arena and the political process.

WRITING INSTRUCTION IN ADULT EDUCATION CLASSROOMS

Unfortunately, we know little about the kinds of writing instruction that currently occur in adult literacy classrooms. Over the years, a few teachers have written about their experiences implementing innovative teaching approaches including dialog journals, personal diaries, student newsletters, project-based learning, and other kinds of computer-based writing projects (Gillespie, 2001). When the GED writing test first required, in the mid-1980s, that test-takers write an essay, there was a small flurry of articles written which described how to help students prepare for the essay test. To date, however, no large-scale systematic studies of writing in adult literacy education have been conducted. We have no reliable evidence of the kinds of writing instruction that take place in classrooms, or even the extent to which writing is taught at all.

Two small-scale studies in Michigan reveal that, in at least some classrooms, writing instruction focuses primarily on "language arts" skills such as grammar, punctuation, and spelling. When Padak and Padak (1988) studied writing at five adult education sites in Michigan, for example, they found that the vast majority of interactions related to writing involved the teacher and a single student, and were focused on mechanics. The primary goal of the teachers was to help students learn the skills required to pass the GED test. Teachers used commercial workbooks to model the five-paragraph essay but did not teach students to do any other kinds of writing. "I may be in a rut," one teacher said, "but I know how to get them through. I know what books to use so they can pass the test" (p. 6). When Young (1997) observed how computers were used in another group of classrooms in Michigan, she found that participants primarily worked alone using drill and practice software for language arts. Students engaged in word processing solely to type in their own previously handwritten texts as corrected by teachers. These findings are consistent with more recent research by Beder and Medina (2001) who found that a skills-based approach to instruction predominated in most of the classrooms they studied, and that students had limited interactions with one another related to the subject matter. Clearly more research is needed if we are to make any kind of valid and reliable characterization of the state of writing instruction in adult education classrooms.

IMPROVING THE QUALITY OF WRITING INSTRUCTION IN ADULT LITERACY EDUCATION

Recommendations for expanding and improving writing instruction in adult literacy education contexts must be tempered with the recognition that many adult literacy teachers work in environments that do not allow them to implement instructional improvements they might optimally like to make. Poor working conditions, limited attendance hours, open enrollment, high dropout rates, and scarce opportunities for professional development present ongoing challenges to improving practice (Smith, Hofer, Gillespie, Soloman, & Rowe, 2003). Some of these issues are discussed in the recommendations that follow, which focus on policies at the state and national level that can support improvement in writing instruction.

Support Research-Based Approaches to the Teaching of Writing

Although very little systematic research on writing has been conducted with the populations we serve in adult basic education, there is a fairly substantial body of general research on the cognitive processes of writing and a growing number of studies of the sociocultural dimensions of writing. Some of this research has been conducted with populations similar enough to adult literacy learners (such as learners enrolled in "basic" or remedial writing courses at the college level) to be useful as a point of departure.

We now know, for example, that there are essentially three cognitive writing processes: planning (deciding what to say and how to say it), text generation (turning plans into written text), and revision (improving existing text). Sperling and Freedman (2001) and Freedman, Flower, Hull, and Hayes (1995) have useful summaries of the research that led to these findings. Writers do not progress through these processes in linear, ordered stages. Rather, they work recursively back and forth between one process and another. At one moment writers might be writing, moving their ideas and their discourse forward; at the next, they are backtracking, rereading, and digesting what they have written. The discovery during the 1970s and 1980s that these processes are recursive, with subprocesses such as planning and editing often interrupting each other, represented an important shift in understanding the writing process. Most proficient writers do not "get it right" the first time, but rather revise and rerevise their work multiple times. In fact, the most expert writers often revise the most.

In kindergarten through 12th-grade (K-12) settings and in many colleges, these research findings have been applied to a growing literature on how best to use the classroom as a "writing workshop" that includes collaborative "prewriting" activities, the production of multiple drafts, and peer review processes. Because research shows that students learn grammar, punctuation, spelling, and other writing conventions best when they apply the rules they learn to their own writing, these skills are often taught in the context of having students edit their own work.

Writing research also led to a consolidation of findings on the differences between novice and expert writers, and on how novices develop expertise. This research was part of a broader movement on the part of cognitive researchers to examine how experts perform in a growing number of fields (especially math and science). Strong evidence was developed that experts do not just know *more* facts. Rather, they have developed a more complex, richly structured knowledge base related to their field (National Academy Press, Donovan, et al., 1999). With respect to writing, researchers found that experts and novices take on different problems when they write, as described in Table 9-1.

The differences between novice and more proficient writers have been confirmed in studies of students enrolled in basic writing programs at the college or precollege level. Researchers found that adult students often make errors that "make sense" from the point of view of someone not familiar with written discourse, and use an intermediate grammar somewhere between speech and writing. Basic writers follow a more rigid set of rules than their more proficient peers, become blocked when they interrupt their train of thought to attend to more mechanical concerns, and solve problems simply by rewriting, without analyzing the problems with their text. Less proficient English language learners at the university level were also found to reread less frequently, to focus on grammar rules, and to fall back on spoken English strategies when they write in English.

Adult educators need to find ways to apply these findings in our adult literacy classrooms. We need to model the process of writing and focus more on teaching students the kinds of planning and revision strategies that experts use. Instead of teaching "language arts" skills (such as grammar, punctuation and spelling) out of context through the use of workbooks, we need to build on research which shows that students learn these skills best through short minilessons and just-in-time conferences where students apply them within their emerging writing. A number of good resources for teaching these kinds of writing strategies now exist (e.g., Pressley & Woloshyn, 1995).

TABLE 9–1   Differences between proficient and less proficient writers

Less Proficient Writers	Proficient Writers
Focus on correct spelling, word choice, and syntax.	Focus on the generation and elaboration of ideas.
Monitor what is written primarily for correct spelling, word choice, and syntax.	Monitor what is written primarily for sense and coherence.
Utilize a limited range of strategies when meaning breaks down, such as sounding out, seeking assistance, or stopping.	Utilize a variety of strategies when meaning breaks down, such as rereading, rethinking, rewriting, writing on and returning if necessary, substituting, and seeking assistance.
View writing as a "think it – say it" process.	View writing as a process for generating, exploring, discovering, and revising meaning.
Write all texts in a similar manner, regardless of purpose.	Vary the manner in which texts are written, based on purpose.
Focus on surface-level revisions and begin editing before much writing has been generated.	Focus on meaning and organization first and focus on surface-level revising only after the generation of a substantial amount of writing.
Focus on one letter or word at a time, resulting in "tunnel vision."	"Chunk" ideas for writing.

Note. This table was adapted from Kucer (2001).

Build Curriculum Around Learners' Real-World Purposes and Uses for Writing

Research on learning transfer has shown that unless students are explicitly taught how to apply what they have learned to real-life contexts, we cannot assume that they will automatically know how to do so (National Academy Press, 1999). This means that instead of teaching language arts skills separated from their context first, and hoping that learners will *end up* knowing how to transfer what they have learned to life outside the classroom, we need to *start* with classroom activities that are as close as possible to real-life writing tasks, and embed skills instruction within them.

Part of the reason this is important is because writing in real life requires not only learning discrete skills but also strategies for knowing when and how to apply the skills, and what to do when difficulties arise in performing a task. Heide Wrigley (1999) provided a good example of this concept in a paper entitled *Live by the Form, Die by the Form.* She described the qualitative difference between ESL writing instruction aimed simply at developing the skill of filling in forms, and instruction grounded in real-life tasks that require the applied use of forms:

Instead of having our students practice form filling until they can give address, phone number and social security number in their sleep, might we not spend some time talking about what the access points are that they are trying to get beyond and then treat forms as one way of negotiating the system, along with strategies such as asking others for help, finding out what translators are available, or sharing tips and information with others who have been in similar circumstances?

Some programs are applying this approach by beginning an instructional cycle with a carefully planned goal setting stage. In programs based on Equipped for the Future (EFF), for example, students are guided to look first at their immediate goals and then to decide on one or more content standards to work on to develop the skills and knowledge they need to reach those goals (Gillespie, 2003; Stein, 2000). If they name learning to write memos at work as a goal, they are encouraged to examine why, to whom, and in what contexts they need to send memos, before moving on to decide on a learning activity that will allow them to practice the skills associated with memo writing. Together with their teachers, they may look at the EFF developmental performance continuum based on the content standard *Convey Ideas in Writing* (Equipped for the Future Assessment Resource Collection, 2004), and use it to develop checklists or rubrics to help them self-assess what "good memo writing" looks like. Once the activity is completed, learners may be asked to investigate how what they have learned might transfer to other roles they play in life, such as within their families or in their community life.

Research in writing has also revealed that many of the skills required to write in one genre may not transfer to the ability to write well in another genre (Freedman et al., 1995). Of course, we know that someone who has expert proficiency at writing technical reports on the job may not have the same level of skill for writing fiction. Even the writing of academic essays may require a somewhat different set of skills than those the expert technical writer possesses. In our field, we need to consider whether a student who is able to write a good five-paragraph essay has also mastered skills required to write for other purposes, such as being able to do the kinds of writing he or she needs to do at work, at home, or in postsecondary education. This further supports the need to match the kinds of writing taught in the adult literacy classroom to the kinds of writing-related tasks students need to perform in their lives.

Encourage Students to Collaborate As They Write

Studies of writers in natural settings have also revealed that for most expert writers, writing is less a solitary process than a collaborative one, involving frequent interaction with others, especially during the planning and revision stages (Sperling & Freedman , 2001). At work, for example, a team may meet together to share ideas for a new project. One or two team members may work on a first draft and then send it to the rest of the team for revision. A supervisor might make further changes before handing the work over to an in-house editor. An administrative assistance might then input the changes and format the final version.

Because writing is a nonlinear, recursive process, many expert writing teachers describe their classrooms as "messy" places where groups of students may be working together at various stages of the writing process. Teachers can help students to mirror the kinds of things expert writers do by teaching them methods for rehearsing what they will write in small groups, and strategies for offering feedback to peers during the revision process. This approach can capitalize on the fact that students at varied ability levels and levels of understanding of the issues reflected in the content can help one another. Glynda Hull (this volume) describes how this works in a community technology center in Oakland, CA. Novice writers and computer users learn to write and develop multimedia projects together, with younger participants often teaching older adults how to use the computer and older adults sharing their life experiences. Seeing the "digital stories" of students who have been in the program longer gives students who have joined the class more recently models for how to represent "discourses, identities, and practices" in ways that more closely resemble their world as they live it than the portrayals they see in the dominant media. In this example, learning is influenced in fundamental ways by the cultural context of the learning environment.

Adult educators can find many good examples of how to plan and organize peer collaboration in the K-12 writing literature. We need to analyze and share how these can be adapted to encourage more student-to-student interactions in the adult education classroom.

Encourage Ongoing Classroom-Based Assessment That Allows Students, As Well As Teachers, to Monitor and Evaluate Progress

By observing experts as they work in a variety of fields, we now know that they spend a great deal of their time monitoring their progress, adjusting the cognitive strategies they use, and "thinking" about their own thinking, a process known as metacognition (National Research Council, 1999). For many experts, these processes are mostly unconscious. By interviewing them as they work, researchers have been able to identify and make explicit the kinds of thinking processes they use. These findings have been the basis for considerable progress in our understanding of the importance of ongoing classroom-based assessment, for the development of new strategies for collecting evidence of student learning, and for ways to involve students in assessing their own thinking and learning processes.

One key finding is that experts often begin a new task by actively considering the work at hand in light of their prior knowledge. This has led to a new awareness of the importance of beginning a formative assessment process by helping students to identify and "activate" their prior knowledge of a given topic. The fact that this is true in the case of writing with adult literacy learners was clearly demonstrated in a study by Mary Russell (1999). She found that although the adult education teachers she observed encouraged students not to worry about form, and to focus on content during the drafting stage of writing, the students (like many novice writers) were mostly concerned with avoiding mistakes and writing the "right" way. Interviews with students revealed that they believed a "good" writer to be someone who knows how to use correct punctuation and write a perfect first draft. Without more explicit instruction, they could not conceive of strategies that put themselves in the role of revising or correcting their own work. In effect, she observed, "teachers and learners appear to be speaking two different languages, perhaps different dialects of the language of writing instruction" (p. 20). Russell's work highlights the fact that it may not be enough just to encourage students to use a new approach to writing. They must first be helped to think about what writing is for, to analyze their preconceptions about what good writers actually do, and to learn, try out, and reflect on the cognitive and metacognitive strategies that help them improve their writing.

Many programs are beginning to develop self-assessment tools to help students evaluate and reflect on what they are learning. As part of this process, they develop their own learning checklists and rubrics so they can plan and monitor their understanding as they practice new skills. Writing portfolios are also used to help learners identify patterns in their writing development over time and across different kinds of writing activities. This kind of approach provides essential feedback not only to students, but to their teachers as well.

Develop Adult Literacy Education Content Standards for Writing

Within K-12 education, content standards developed at the state level with help from experienced practitioners are now seen as key to aligning instruction, assessment, and staff development. Within adult education, there is now a similar movement underway, with a particular focus on the development of content standards for reading and math. If we are to promote strong research-based approaches to the teaching of writing in adult literacy education, policymakers need to provide support for the development of state-level content standards in writing. The standards development process itself can build capacity for improving writing instruction by focusing on understanding how expertise develops in writing, and identifying the kinds of knowledge and skills that are associated with different levels of performance. The development of standards can draw on states' K-12 writing standards, as well as standards and writing benchmarks developed by the Canadian Language Benchmarks (2000), the Core Curriculum guides developed by the Adult Literacy and Basic Skills Unit in Great Britain (2001), and writing standards for adults that have been developed in a few states. Within this process, special attention needs to be given to the differences between how native speakers of English and how English language learners develop and progress as writers.

Develop Better Assessments of Writing for Accountability Purposes

If writing is to "count" within our system, and if teachers are to be guided toward the kinds of standards-based and research-based writing instruction described earlier, it is clear that we need to develop better large-scale assessments of writing. This is of particular importance within our current climate because state agencies, programs, and teachers often feel compelled to choose content and materials that are aligned with the skills and knowledge measured by existing tests. Most widely used standardized tests include indirect measures of writing ability (i.e., multiple-choice questions about language usage, punctuation, and grammar). In the early 1980s, the addition of a required essay on the GED test was an important innovation as the first direct measure of writing for adult literacy learners. As discussed earlier, however, too often teachers may use preparation for the five-paragraph essay as the only kind of writing instruction they offer, and, in the process, may overlook important skills students need to prepare for the writing demands of postsecondary education, writing on the job, and other adult roles.

Developing valid, reliable, and content-appropriate large-scale assessments of writing is not easy, as efforts to develop direct assessments of writing for K-12 and as part of the new SAT test and the Test of English as a Foreign Language (TOEFL) test for non-native speakers at the college level can demonstrate (see Council of Chief State School Officers, 2004). Although some preliminary findings suggest that direct writing assessments appear to measure a more diverse set of skills (Crislip & Heck, 2001), many issues related to the design, implementation, and costs of writing tests remain. The issue of training raters and assuring interrater reliability, for example, is an ongoing concern in many states. Even when raters are extensively and carefully trained and given anchor papers to improve consistency, results can still sometimes be unreliable (Hill, 2000). A recent study of the score dependability of the writing section of the new TOEFL test indicates that one way to maximize score reliability is to increase the number of tasks, rather than the number of ratings per task (Lee, Kantor, & Mollaun, 2002). The fact that multiple pieces of writing should be assessed has been echoed by advocacy groups such as the National Commission on Writing in America's Schools and Colleges (2003) that pointed out the following: "no single piece of writing, even generated under ideal conditions, can serve as an adequate indicator of overall proficiency" (pp. 21-22).

Although the tasks associated with developing new kinds of writing assessments may be considerable, by pooling the resources among states, making use of technology-based resources, and drawing on the expertise of K-12 writing assessors, we can begin to find creative solutions to these challenges.

Begin an Initiative to Provide Teachers With Professional Development on the Teaching of Writing

Research on the impact of state-mandated large-scale assessment policies has shown that the implementation of new standards and assessments must be accompanied by teacher training and the development of effective support materials for teachers (Lumley & Yan, 2001). In designing professional development in writing, we should look closely at the model developed by the National Writing Project (NWP). Initiated in 1973, it began as a collaborative university-school partnership to incorporate research-based findings on writing into classroom practice. The NWP model identifies successful teachers of writing, brings these teachers together in invitational summer institutes, and prepares them to teach other teachers in workshops in schools during the school year. Thousands of teachers have been trained through the NWP. Today a network of 175 local writing project sites exist in all 50 states. This research-to-practice model has, without question, had a major impact on the dissemination of information on research on writing and can be a key resource in our own efforts to get research on writing into the hands of adult education teachers. One hallmark of the approach is that the professional development activities themselves mirror the kind of writing workshop approach advocated for the classroom. Teachers brainstorm ideas for writing, produce draft materials (often curriculum materials), and share and revise their work as part of the training. Particular attention should be paid to designing professional development for adult educators which provides them with examples of what good writing instruction might look like in the kinds of varied contexts in which they teach.

Some professional development models support the integration of the development of standards and professional development. To develop the continuum of performance for the EFF standard *Convey Ideas in Writing* (Equipped for the Future Assessment Resource Collection, 2004), for example, teachers from programs in five field development states (Tennessee, Ohio, Maine, Washington, and Oregon) participated in national meetings to help them learn about how to develop a continuum of performance for writing and writing-related performance tasks. Teachers' expertise in using the standard grew over time as they participated in successive rounds of national and state meetings to review the work in progress. In some cases, these same teachers are now working within their states on committees to develop standards that are adapted to the particular needs of their statewide system.

Fund Research on How Writing Develops in Adulthood Both Inside and Outside the Classroom

Although we can learn a great deal from the research that has been conducted with other populations, more research is needed to better understand how the writing development of adult literacy education learners is both similar to and different from the writing development of children, of college level learners, and of native and non-native speakers of English. We need to support the development of model programs for teaching writing that allow us to track the writing development of learners over time, and compare the efficacy of different approaches. Models that appear to hold promise for improving the writing-related development of adult learners need to be replicated in other contexts so we can learn what works under the varied kinds of conditions within which we teach. Producing videotapes of classroom writing activities would be useful in enabling teachers to see what the components of good writing instruction look like in practice. We also need to learn more about the kinds of writing-related challenges faced by adult learners who move from our programs into various kinds of postsecondary education and how to develop effective programs which prepare our students to meet them. In studying how writing can be taught in the classroom, university and teacher researcher partnerships can play a key role in developing model programs, and have the added benefit of providing professional development in writing instruction for the teachers.

More research is also needed outside the classroom. We do not yet know enough about the writing-related demands our learners face in the workplace, and about whether or how the development of writing abilities facilitates the move from entry level to higher levels of employment. We also need to learn more about other kinds of writing demands outside of work and school which our learners face as they fulfill their roles as parents, family members, and members of the community, and about the impact of computers and multimedia technology on the writing demands they face outside the classroom.

THE POWER OF WRITING

Even in our modern, multimedia saturated world, writing remains one of the greatest of all human tools—for thinking, for creating new ideas, for dreaming, and for sharing what we dream. We need to make sure it does not continue to be the "forgotten r" in adult literacy education for many functional reasons, including its role in learning to read, succeeding in the workplace, and transitioning into postsecondary training. But we also need to recognize its role in enabling the adults we work with to be *producers* as well as *consumers* of knowledge; to research, solve problems, and express ideas *they* define as important in their lives. As adult educators, we need to join with the National Commission on Writing in America's Schools and Colleges to propose our own action agenda for the improvement of writing in adult education.

REFERENCES

Adult Literacy and Basic Skills. (2001). *Adult Literacy Core Curriculum* and *Adult ESOL Core Curriculum.* Retrieved October 3, 2003, from http://www.basic-skills.co.uk

Bartholomae, D. (1985). Inventing the university. In E. R. Kintget, B. M. Kroll, & M. Rose (Eds.), *Perspectives on literacy* (pp. 273-285). Carbondale: Southern Illinois University Press.

Barton, D., & Hamilton, M. (1998). *Local literacies.* London: Routledge.

Beder, H., & Medina, P. (2001). *Classroom dynamics and adult education* (Report No. 18). Boston: National Center for the Study of Adult Literacy and Learning. Retrieved October 3, 2003, from http://www.ncsall. org

Bruner, J. (1986). *Actual minds, possible worlds.* Cambridge, MA: Harvard University Press.

Canadian language benchmarks. (2000). Retrieved October 3, 2003, from http://www.language.ca

Crislip, M., & Heck, R. (2001, April). *Accountability, writing assessment and equity: Testing a multilevel model.* Paper presented at the annual meeting of the American Educational Research Association, Seattle, WA.

Elbow, P. (2001). Toward a more spacious view of writing. In T. Enos, K. D. Miller, & J. McCracken (Eds.), *Beyond postprocess and postmodernism: Essays on the spaciousness* (pp. 217-234). Mahwah, NJ: Lawrence Erlbaum Associates, Inc.

Equipped for the Future Assessment Resource Collection (2004). *Guide to using the convey ideas in writing performance continuum.* Retrieved August 4, 2004, from http://www.eff.cls.utk.edu/assessment

Freedman, S. W., Flower, L., Hull, G. l., & Hayes, J. R. (1995). *Ten years of research: Achievements of the National Center for the Study of Writing and Literacy.* Berkeley, CA: National Center for the Study of Writing.

Gillespie, M. (1991). *Becoming authors: The social context of literacy for adult beginning writers.* Unpublished doctoral dissertation, University of Massachusetts, Amherst.

Gillespie, M. (2001). Research on writing: Implications for adult education. In J. Comings, B. Garner, & C. Smith (Eds.), *Annual review of adult learning and literacy, volume 2* (pp. 63-110). San Francisco: Jossey-Bass.

Gillespie, M. (2003). EFF research to practice notes 1-3. Retrieved October 3, 2003, from http://www.nifl.gov/lincs/collections/eff/eff_publications.html

Hill, R. (2000, June). *A success story from Kentucky.* Paper presented at the annual national conference of the Council of Chief State School Officers on Large Scale Assessment, Snowbird, UT.

Kegan, R., Broderick, M., Drago-Severson, P., Helsing, D., Popp, N., & Portnow, K. (2002). *Toward a new pluralism in ABE/ESOL classrooms:*

Teaching to multiple "cultures of mind" (NCSALL Report No. 19). Boston: National Center for the Study of Adult Learning and Literacy.

Kucer, S. B. (2001). *Dimensions of literacy: A conceptual base for teaching reading and writing in school settings.* Mahwah, NJ: Lawrence Erlbaum Associates, Inc.

Langer, J., & Applebee, A. N. (1987). *How writing shapes thinking: A study of teaching and learning.* Urbana, IL: National Council of Teachers of English.

Lee, Y., Kantor, R., & Mollaun, P. (2002, April). *Score dependability of the writing and speaking sections of the new TOEFL.* Paper presented at the annual meeting of the National Council on Measurement in Education, New Orleans, LA.

Lumley, D.R., & Yan, W. (2001, April). *The impact of state mandated, large-scale writing assessment policies in Pennsylvania.* Paper presented at the annual meeting of the American Educational Research Association, Seattle, WA.

Mikulecky, L. (1998). Adjusting school writing curricula to reflect extended workplace writing. In M. S. Garay & S. A. Bernhardt (Eds.), *Expanding literacies: English teaching and the workplace* (pp. 201-223). Albany: State University of New York Press.

National Academy Press, Bransford, J. D., Brown, A. L., & Cocking, R. R. (Eds.). (1999). *How people learn: Brain, mind, experience and school.* Retrieved from http://www.nap.edu/html/howpeople.html*

National Academy Press, Donovan, M. S., Bransford, J. D., & Pellegrino, J. W. (Eds.). (1999). *How people learn: Bridging research and practice.* Retrieved October 3, 2003, from http://books.nap.edu/books/0309065364/html/index.html*

National Assessment of Educational Progress. (2002). *NAEP report card on writing.* Retrieved January 8, 2004, from http://nces.ed.gov/pubsearch/pubsinfo

National Commission on Writing in America's Schools and Colleges. (2003, April). *The neglected "R": The need for a writing revolution, a report of the National Commission on Writing in America's Schools and College.* Retrieved November 21, 2004 from http://www.writingcommission.org/

National Council of Teachers of English. (2003). *Writing assessment: A position statement.* Retrieved October 10, 2003, from http://ncte.org/about/over/positions

Opening Time. (1987). *Gatehouse project.* Manchester, England: Manchester Free Press. Federation of Worker Writers and Community Publishers.

Padak, G., & Padak, N. (1988). Writing instruction for adults: Present practice and future directions. *Lifelong Learning, 12,* 4-7.

Peyton, J. K. (1993). Listening to students' voices: Publishing students' writing for other students to read. In J. Crandall & J. K. Peyton (Eds.), *Approaches to adult ESL literacy instruction* (pp. 59-74). McHenry, IL: Delta Systems and the Center for Applied Linguistics.

Pressley, M., & Woloshyn, V. (1995). *Cognitive strategy instruction that really works.* Cambridge, MA: Brookline Books.

Purcell-Gates, V. (1993). I ain't never read my own words before. *Journal of Reading, 37*(3), 210-219.

Purcell-Gates, V. (1995). *Other people's words: The cycle of low literacy.* Cambridge, MA: Harvard University Press.

Reder, S. (1999). Adult literacy and postsecondary education students: Overlapping populations and learning trajectories. In J. Comings, B. Garner, & C. Smith (Eds.), *The annual review of adult learning and literacy, volume 1* (pp. 139-172). San Francisco: Jossey-Bass.

Rose, M. (1989). *Lives on the boundaries: The struggles and achievements of America's underprepared.* New York: Macmillan.

Russell, M. (1999). The assumptions we make: How learners and teachers understand writing. *Focus on Basics, 3,* 20-23.

Smith, C., Hofer, J., Gillespie, M., Soloman, M., & Rowe, K. (2003). *How teachers change: A study of professional development in adult education* (NCSALL Report No. 25). Cambridge, MA: National Center for the Study of Adult Learning and Literacy.

Sperling, M., & Freedman, S. W. (2001). Research on writing. In V. Richardson (Ed.), *Handbook of research on teaching* (pp. 370-389). Washington, DC: American Educational Research Association.

Stein, S. G. (2000). *Equipped for the future content standards.* Washington, DC: National Institute for Literacy.

Wrigley, H. (1999, April). *Live by the form, die by the form.* Paper presented at the International Conference for Teachers of English to Speakers of Other Languages, New York.

Young, D. (1997). *Adult basic education: Literacy, learning, and instruction.* Unpublished doctoral dissertation, University of Michigan, Ann Arbor.

* Note: National Academy Press recommends using their name as the author (see their Web site http://www.nap.edu/).

Chapter 10

The *EMPower* Project: Connecting Curriculum Development and Research

Mary Jane Schmitt and **Martha Merson**
TERC (Technical Education Research Centers)

The story of improving mathematics instruction in the late 20th century owes a debt to the National Council of Teachers of Mathematics (NCTM). Its principles and standards (NCTM, 1989, 2000) shaped a movement, and although these documents have attracted criticism, they also are responsible for shifting the emphasis in mathematics instruction to problem solving, communication, reasoning, and connections between mathematics and other disciplines, making possible great strides in young people's abilities not only to solve problems, but to articulate their mathematical thinking as well. In the world of adult basic education, the NCTM standards remain a bit obscure but are known to those who have sought out professional development in mathematics from the Adult Numeracy Network or opportunities designed for kindergarten through 12th-grade (K-12) teachers. However, in 2000, the National Science Foundation (NSF) funded the development of a curriculum that would extend the principles and practices of the NCTM standards to adults and young adults enrolled in adult basic education or alternative high school diploma programs.

The stated intent of the Extending Mathematical Power to Adults (*EMPower*) project is to transform mathematics instruction in the adult education context, to offer participants mathematics instruction of high quality similar to that made possible by K-12 reform programs such as *Investigations in Number, Data, and Space*® (Russell, Tierney, Mokros, & Economopoulos, 2004; Russell et al., 1995), *the Connected Mathematics Project*™ (Lappan, Fey, Fitzgerald, Friel, & Phillips, 1991-1997), or the *Interactive Mathematics Program*™ (Fendel, Resek, Alpert, & Fraser, 1998). Over the course of four years (2000-2004), a collaborative group of teachers and researchers with expertise in adult numeracy education[3] and K-12 mathematics reform has developed and piloted curriculum units for teachers and students organized around the topic areas of number sense; patterns, functions, and relations; geometry and measurement; and data and graphs.

Although state and federal departments of education and the National Institute for Literacy focused on standards that encouraged educators to define levels and criteria for students' placement, and articulated definitions of progress, NSF allocated resources for *EMPower* to develop curriculum. The need for improved mathematics instruction in adult basic education motivated these initiatives.

This chapter reviews the reasons why a transformation is needed in adult basic education's typical approach to mathematics, outlines how *EMPower* addresses this need by differing from the traditional approach, and describes three investigations from one unit that it developed: *Seeking Patterns, Building Rules: Algebraic Thinking* (Schmitt, Steinback, Donovan & Merson, in press), to show how the curriculum has both benefited from, and suggested new directions for, research about the development of adults' mathematical thinking. The three investigations described bring to life the mathematical understandings and misunderstandings that learners bring to the adult basic education classroom. They show not only what tools students have at their disposal for predicting, generalizing, and making sense of a situation, but they also show how research and professional development can make a difference in the provision of quality math instruction for adult learners.

THE NEED FOR TRANSFORMATIVE MATHEMATICS CURRICULUM

One presumes that the "second chance" system—adult basic education—would see as its primary mission the need to address the numeracy skills of U.S. adults. After all, over 40% of the nation's population is estimated to have quantitative literacy skills inadequate to meet the demands of today's society (Kirsch, Jungeblut, Jenkins, & Kolstad, 2002). However, the adult basic education system that serves over 3 million of this subpopulation has, to date, focused primarily on literacy and language skills, although participant goals such as obtaining a high school equivalency diploma (GED), improving workforce skills, and pursuing further education require mathematical proficiency. Poor mathematical skills

---

3 In adult basic education, the term numeracy is sometimes used instead of mathematics as a way to point to the broad range of contexts in which adults face the mathematical demands of the real world. Numeracy, like the term literacy (as opposed to reading), puts the emphasis on contextualized and broad use of a set of skills.

impede adults' potential to reach all three goals. The mathematics portion of the GED has the lowest passing rate of the test's five sections (Auchter, 2004); in workforce studies, mathematical literacy has been shown to be more predictive of economic success than prose literacy (Murnane, Willet, & Levy,1995), and in some states, Massachusetts, for example, up to 80% of the incoming community college students are ineligible for credit-bearing mathematics courses (Massachusetts Community College Executive Office, 2002). For them, mathematics, but algebra, in particular, often serves as a "gatekeeper," preventing them from matriculating and ultimately graduating.

Although the need for including high quality mathematics instruction in the adult basic education curriculum is evident, the field has never reached a research-based consensus on what is quality instruction. At issue are the mathematical topics most deserving of attention, as well as how these topics are best taught. Prior to such discussions, practitioners, policymakers, and funders need to recognize in concrete ways that mathematics is more than a set of skills that can be taught in a proscribed way. Learning from "drill-and-kill" workbooks is analogous to learning a language only by studying its grammar. Precision in solving closed problems with paper and pencil algorithms (for example, long division) is useful, but not representative of the mathematical tasks many adults face that can be solved using mental math, estimation, calculators, or spreadsheets. Although mathematics is generally recognized as a way to describe situations, sets of procedures that can be used together or in isolation to approach problems that can shift in their complexity, and a number system that lends itself to solutions through patterns, adult basic education texts and tests reduce mathematics to a set of rules by which to manipulate numbers (for example, Howett, 2000).

In spite of growing awareness that their students need more math, teachers and administrators acknowledge that the current staffing patterns within adult basic education have strengths in teaching literacy and language that are not equaled in the area of mathematics. Improving mathematics instruction for adults depends on a teaching force that is well-versed both in mathematical content and pedagogy. Yet, several researchers have pointed to the lack of preparation on both accounts in the teaching force (Gal & Schuh, 1994; Mullinix, 1994; Ward, 2000).

EMPOWER: A TRANSFORMATIVE MATHEMATICS CURRICULUM

EMPower calls for a change in the classroom structure, in the content covered, and proposes that teachers become co-learners and researchers. Most math classes in adult education centers are places of silence. Students often work individually on instructional packets or in workbooks. Although there may be good reasons for this structure (such as erratic attendance and multileveled classes), the dominant practice of using routine procedures outlined in workbooks (Kloosterman, Hassan, & Wiest, 2000) often "discourages intuitive approaches and promotes a mathematics that comes from an outside authority rather than a personal mathematics that can be applied in many situations" (Tout & Schmitt, 2002, p. 162). The *EMPower* curriculum requires a shift in the classroom culture from individualized silence to collaborative "math talk," that is communication about problem solving and strategies.

EMPower organizes each lesson around an investigation with the following characteristics: a context that engages adult learners, mathematical concepts and skills that are important for adults to know, opportunities for learners to strengthen math language by communicating their thinking, various ways of entering and solving the problem, and a puzzling force, whereby the problem draws students in and provides enough interest to motivate learners to seek a solution.

The curriculum asks teachers to create classroom environments where students work in small groups, interacting, puzzling over problems, strategizing about solutions, sharing these solutions with other groups in the class, and listening to others' solutions and strategies. As they collaborate, students "talk math." Their discourse includes mathematical vocabulary and explanations of how they have solved a problem and why the solution makes sense. The teacher acts as a facilitator to guide the learning and to make the mathematics explicit (Steinback, Schmitt, Merson, & Leonelli, 2003). Another change for teachers is that skills in geometry, measurement, data, and algebra are infused in all the *EMPower* units and are meant to be taught to students at all skill levels. In other words, topics such as "interpreting data" are developed at the adult basic education (ABE), pre-GED, and GED levels.

Adult basic education programs typically stick to a popular instructional sequence: the four basic operations (addition, subtraction, multiplication and division) with whole numbers and money, followed by fractions, decimals, and percentages. Although this content stood workers in good stead in the early and mid-20th century, the emphasis on these skills to the exclusion of data analysis, geometry, and algebraic thinking works against adults in the 21st century. The numeracy demands on adults now include massive amounts of data consumption for the purposes of purchasing health and life insurance, choosing loans, or making voting decisions. For those interested in college degrees, avoiding algebra only intensifies the burden on them to catch up later. To determine the content for the *EMPower* series, the development team consulted with leaders in mathematics education, adult numeracy teachers, and K-12 mathematics consultants regarding the most important mathematics topics for adults to know and be able to use in their lives. All groups included the expected fractions, decimals, and percentages; but they also highlighted number sense, interpreting data, estimation, ability to see patterns, proportional reasoning, and quantitative reasoning-algebra.

Professional development is a key component of change, whether the change is in content, pedagogy, or assessment practices. In-depth and sustained professional development has been essential for the successful implementation of NSF-funded elementary curricula (Senk &Thompson, 2003). The successful implementation of the NSF-funded basic mathematics curricula for adults and out-of-school youth will depend on in-depth professional development as well, because the mathematics background of the teachers is more like elementary school teachers than secondary school teachers who have specific content area knowledge and training. Adult basic education teachers often lack both content and pedagogical knowledge. Therefore, the *EMPower* curriculum is also designed to be a vehicle for professional development. This is yet another key departure from business as usual. Writing a curriculum that embeds staff development within it is unique for adult education. The authors of Technical Education Research Centers' (TERC's) kindergarten through 5th-grade curriculum, *Investigations in Number, Data, and Space®* (Russell,1998), are advocates for this fusion. These authors take the stance that teachers form a kind of partnership with the curriculum. When curriculum supports teacher development, it assumes that teachers will benefit from ideas for how to lead mathematics discussions, how to respond to learners' questions, and what to look for when students are working in small groups on investigations.

The texts marketed to adult educators often claim that they use adult appropriate problems, but their development of math concepts mirrors sequences designed for children prior to the recent mathematics reform movement. *EMPower's* goal was to write a curriculum for adults that built on their strengths and had a strong foundation in adult learning. Unfortunately, the research base for adults learning mathematics is distressingly shallow. Safford-Ramus (2000) pointed out that most research studies focus on achievement or emotion, rather than on insight into the nature of adults' mathematical understandings. To address this gap as best they could, the authors drew from research on children's mathematical thinking, studies on adults' everyday cognition, and learned everything they could from the adults who piloted the curriculum.

The following section of the chapter describes in more depth the research on algebraic thinking, its influence on one *EMPower* unit, three mathematical investigations in which adult learners participated, and their responses to them. Each investigation raises questions for further research into the development of adults' mathematical thinking.

PILOTING A UNIT ON ALGEBRAIC THINKING

EMPower's pre-GED unit on algebraic thinking focuses students' attention on seeking patterns and building rules. This is a very different starting point than the usual launch of algebra in GED books, which typically begin with signed number computation and balancing equations. The emphasis on structural elements and symbol manipulation reflects students' and teachers' perceptions of algebra. When we ask adults in our classrooms what "algebra" brings to mind, they tend to reply, "it's x's and y's," or "it's solving equations." No one ever says, "it's finding patterns," or, "it's looking at relationships between quantities." But it is systematically looking for patterns and articulating the relationships between quantities that bring meaning and life to the algebraic symbols and the unspecified numbers those symbols represent. It is identifying and translating patterns to a mathematical language that make algebra a powerful tool for predicting and problem solving. Furthermore, adults who can find patterns easily might apply this skill to solve a range of fraction and percentage problems, as well as problems involving measurement or geometry contexts. Although some of the power of algebra lies ultimately in the efficiency with which one can manipulate symbols, for example, transform $x(x+4)$ to $x^2 + 4x$, without attention to the meaning behind the symbols, this is just one more trick to perform. It is important that symbol manipulation is robustly grounded in the meaning behind those symbols.

Influence of the Research on EMPower's Approach to Algebraic Thinking

The extensive body of research on the development of algebraic thinking with children and adolescents has informed *EMPower's* approach to algebra. Overall, the research categorizes algebraic reasoning activity as the following: (a) patterns and functions, (b) modeling, (c) language and representation, and (d) structure and syntax (Bednarz, Kieran, & Lee, 1996; National Research Council, 1997; Usiskin,1988). These four areas are interrelated yet have distinctive aspects. Patterns point to the need to generalize as a way of establishing how two or more quantities (variables) are related. Modeling examines features of a particular physical or social situation and relates those through an arithmetic or algebraic expression or graph. Language and representation can be about the use of pictures, words, tables, graphs, and literal symbols with which to think and communicate. The term "representation" refers to both the process of capturing a mathematical relationship in some form and to the form itself (NCTM, 2000). Although the first three algebraic thinking categories connect to the situation or context, structure and syntax ask algebraic thinkers to step away from context and attend to transformational rules. One way this dichotomy has been described in the literature is that the former requires a person to look through symbols, and the other to look at symbols (Kaput, 1998).

These four aspects of algebraic thinking are developed in the *EMPower* curriculum. Three are the focus of a unit called *Seeking Patterns, Building Rules* in which students are asked to build and interpret mathematical models of situations such as pricing schemes for phone plans, job offers, and heart rates. In doing so, students use a variety of representations to express a generalized pattern, usually a linear function. In this particular unit, structure and syntax play a secondary role and are brought to bear when the situation or context calls for their use. Structure is developed throughout *EMPower's* five number and operation sense units where an emphasis on flexible mental math strategies encourages students to break apart and recombine numbers in various ways. Such strategies make frequent use of algebraic properties such as commutativity, associativity, distributivity, inverse operations, and identities. *EMPower's* approach to helping students strengthen their computational skills relies on this "algebrafying" of arithmetic.

The K-12 research has not only expanded our understanding of what algebra is, but also when it should be introduced. Because of NCTM's "Algebra for Everyone" campaign (Edwards, 1990), algebra is now often integrated into young children's arithmetic instruction, anticipating what it is that children should know and be able to do for formal high school Algebra I courses and beyond. Researchers are now studying the development of algebraic thinking in children in second and third grades (National Research Council, 2001; Schliemann et al., 2003).

Adult education programs tend to reserve algebra for GED preparation classes where learners are assumed to have arithmetic down cold and be familiar with fractions, decimals, and percentages. However, algebraic ideas can and should be developed much earlier, so that when abstract notation and equation manipulation are introduced, learners are able to make meaning of them. The *EMPower* unit encourages learners to develop a sense of the quantitative and numerical patterns and relationships that underlie equations and formulas, thus demystifying algebra and its symbols. The goal is to help learners understand that the symbols are not magic; they make sense. The *EMPower* unit assumes that they can be understood if given the proper introduction and development.

Applying the Research Literature on Algebraic Thinking to the ABE Curriculum

The research review influenced the authors' decision to approach algebra from a contextual perspective (Schmitt, 2003). An important thread woven throughout this research and an assumption of the *EMPower* project is that a contextualized approach is more motivating for students of all ages when compared to a decontextualized approach. Figure 10-1 displays a thematic icon for the unit which is intended to convey that the situation is central, and one derives and communicates meaning about that situation via the use of and connections between various representational tools. A variety of representational tools magnifies understanding of the situation. Depicting a situation with diagrams, rules, tables, or graphs enables the problem solver to predict and generalize.

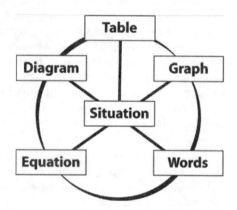

Figure 10.1. Icon for seeking patterns, building rules: algebraic thinking.

Examples of Algebraic Thinking

During early 2002, the developers piloted a unit (12 lessons) in three Massachusetts pre-GED classes: at a university workplace education program for custodial and food service workers, an urban program for young high school dropouts, and a basic skills (predevelopmental) program in a rural community college. Its intent was to teach students to do the following: (a) recognize different patterns and relationships; (b) represent patterns and relationships in various ways (with a picture or diagram, in words, in literal symbols, with a table, or with a graph); (c) use either a pattern to predict or a relationship to solve; and (d) strengthen their personal command of algebraic notation. The lessons always began with a situation such as deciding on job offers or comparing calories burned and heart rates during physical exercise.

Investigation 1, "Personal Patterns."

In the unit's first lesson, students were asked to describe a pattern in their own lives in sentences and then to show the same pattern using a diagram, table, graph, or some other representation. In the final lesson, we presented to the class some statements that students had made earlier about their personal patterns and again asked for multiple representations. Both times students were asked to think about using the representations to predict the future. Because the unit was designed to develop students' ability to use the tools or representations to describe and predict patterns, this task served as part of the pre-assessments and post-assessments as a means to understand what tools were already at students' disposal and as a means to assess the change in students' use of those tools.

In the first lesson, sets of representations were often unconstrained by convention and were quite creative. Many of the early alternative representations were iconic drawings of people eating food, working, or in the case of S. (see Figure 10-2), a drawing of the workplace and a clock. Students did choose to represent their patterns with bar graphs and line graphs, but they often invented nonstandard conventions such as the labeling of the axes in Figure 10-3. In this opening lesson, no one used a table or an equation.

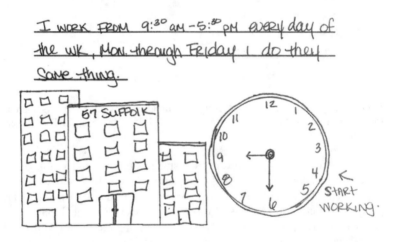

Figure 10.2. Representation for "I work from 9:30-5:50pm everyday of the week, Monday through Friday I do they (sic) same thing" (Lesson 1).

Instead of sentences, use a diagram, table, graph, or some other representation to show the same pattern you just described. Try to make it so someone can use this representation to predict your future behavior.

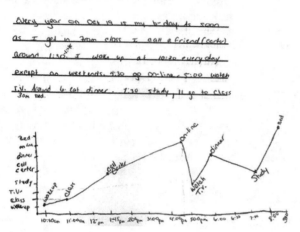

Figure 10.3. Representation for "Every year on Oct. 19 is my b-day. As soon as I get in from class I call a friend (Carter) around 1:30-1:45. I wake up at 10:30 everyday &" (Lesson 1).

In the final lesson, however, most students constructed a table and a graph, wrote a statement, and attempted an equation. Figure 10.4 is an example of how one student (T.) came to use these tools more naturally to describe a classmate's (Caleb's) pattern. An analysis of this learners' work indicated that he had a tendency to use language imprecisely when describing the rule in words or labeling axes ("cups of coffee each day" instead of "total cups of coffee" over a number of days), made meaningful attempts at describing the relationship between two variables (8 x d = Total cig), and used a mixture of conventional and personal representations. We saw similar patterns of development among the other students.

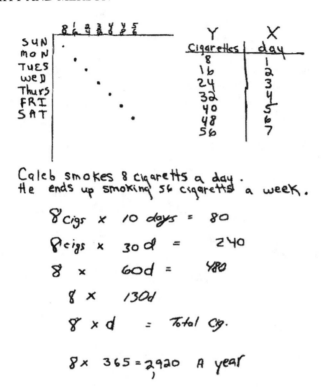

Figure 10.4. T.'s four representations of Caleb's personal pattern (Lesson 12).

These data from the pilot informed a subsequent wave of lessons as the authors considered how explicit to make the instruction and how much freedom to allow students to explore on their own. On the one hand, the primary goals are being met as long as there is internal and consistent logic and strong communicative value in students' representations. T.'s final set of representations of "Caleb smokes 8 cigarettes a day," in Figure 10–4, is a case in point. Pointing out choices such as the graph's origin in the upper left-hand corner, and the mathematically unnecessary use of d in her equations, seems petty given the strong connection between her four highly communicative representations. On the other hand, adults need to know standard conventions. This is only one of the many tensions that arise when looking carefully at students' work.

The pilot of "Personal Patterns" confirmed for the development team that open-ended questions can and must be used in the curriculum to uncover students' understandings. Although many adults have seen graphs in their day-to-day lives, and many felt comfortable enough to use them to communicate, students' work frequently did not conform to conventions. The development team assumed that if students used graphs, they would use graph conventions such as putting the origin on the lower left-hand corner or using a well-spaced number scale on the axis. When the first question simply asked students to generate tools to communicate, it tapped into a set of understandings that would never have surfaced if the question implied or presupposed a set of conventions. A possible direction for further research is then to look at students' choices as they persist in or adopt conventional ways of conveying ideas with graphs.

By the 100th example, some people continued to draw every table in a literal graphic representation of the problem.

Others produced a more abstract picture.

$$1 \boxed{} 1 \Rightarrow 201.$$

However, some students were able to utilize symbols by the time they were thinking about the 100th arrangement of tables.

$$202 \quad 100 \times 2 + 2 = 202$$

First attempts to formulate rules also revealed various levels of generalization.

Some students held on to specific numbers.

Take the # of people (100) subtract 2. Which give me 98 then I divide by 2.

Some began to communicate a more generalized view of the pattern that would work regardless of the numbers involved.

Add each sides of tables plus 2 in each small sides.

Figure 10.5. Student responses.

Investigation 2, "Growing Banquet Tables."

This "Growing Banquet Tables" investigation set the stage for further development of pattern-seeking and rule-building habits. Pre-GED students readily engaged with the problem. In the question that is about 100 tables (see Figure 10-5 for student responses), some people drew every table in a literal representation of the problem. Others produced a more abstract picture, labeling with numbers how many people would fit along the side. However, some were able to employ symbols without the use of a sketch as a support.

When students were asked to write a rule either to find the number of tables needed to seat any number of people or the number of people who could be seated at any number of tables, some students held on to specific numbers. Others began to communicate a more generalized view of the pattern that would work regardless of the numbers involved. Still others wrote an algebraic rule as well as a verbal rule.

This lesson, when presented to students in pre-GED classes and teachers in *EMPower* Teacher Institutes, yielded work that helped *EMPower* authors begin to see a range and variation in strategies and use of representational tools. Because each problem posed revealed multiple strategies for solving it, the multi-level nature of the group was impossible to ignore. Pilot teachers and observers watched for learners' ability to do the following: continue a visual pattern, connect the visual representation to numbers, generalize the pattern in words, and generalize in literal symbols. The banquet table problem made visible problem solvers' handling of the pattern through a picture and the transition to predicting based on a rule. Students' responses yielded a rubric useful for teachers assessing students' work.

The development team analyzed responses to create a rubric. For example, authors recommended that teachers look closely at their student work, noting how students handled extending a visual pattern and how they handled making generalizations. The authors identified three "levels" for extending a visual pattern: (a) student needs to draw every example, (b) student comes to a general rule by the 100th table arrangement, and (c) student comes to the general rule by the 10th table; and three "levels" for using algebraic notation: (a) student uses specific numbers when asked for a generalization, (b) student is comfortable generalizing in words, and (c) student writes accurate equation with literal symbols (variables).

However, the day-to-day realities of assessing students' understandings are complex. For example, how does a teacher rate and then address a strategy that simultaneously leads to an incorrect answer but reveals a sophisticated set of skills? There were several instances of 220 as the answer to how many people could be seated at 100 tables, although 202 is the correct response. This error appears to have resulted from an overapplication of proportion. One student reasoned that because 10 tables seat 22 people, 100 tables (10 times as many) would seat 10 times as many people or 220. Some teachers set up a proportion and performed a cross-multiplication for 10/22 = 100/x, arriving at x = 200. That strategy provided an opportunity for the group to reflect on why setting up a proportion failed to yield a correct answer. Wrestling with a mathematical error such as the overapplication of proportion, has implications for professional development, research, and curriculum development. The overapplication of proportion confirms what the literature on proportional reasoning states: cross products distance problem solvers from the meaning of the problem and its solution (Smith, 2002; Weinberg, 2002). The curriculum must find ways to deepen teachers' understanding of the math so that they too look for ways to check the results of their tried and true algorithms against the sense of the problem. The tension here surrounds the sketch. Although the curriculum urges teachers to prompt students to show their reasoning using a picture, if students feel they must draw a literal picture each time, drawing will interfere with their efficiency. Proving one's thinking is often the quickest route to self-correction, but sending a message that the pictures do not need to be a literal drawing of 100 tables, is equally important.

The significant questions raised here relate to developmental stages. If the touch points identified mark the range of abilities in the classes, do individuals have to go through all these levels as stages before reaching the most abstract level of understanding?

The Problem:

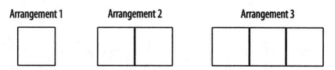

Consider a pattern. Think of the first picture as a small square table that four people can sit around. The second picture is of two of the square tables pushed together to make a bigger banquet table. And the third arrangement shows three tables pushed together to make an even larger banquet table. How many people would fit around each of those banquet tables? Draw the next table arrangement in this pattern. Show how many people could be seated. How many people could sit around the 10th table arrangement? Show your work. Explain how you would figure out the number of people who could fit around the 100th table arrangement.

Fig 10. 2 Problem

Investigation 3, "Flying Cs and Ds."

In another lesson, students were told that the distance around the earth's equator had been measured, but the distance through the center of the earth could not be experientially determined. Through an exploration of the circumferences and diameters of a variety of circular objects, students were asked to explain the relationship of the circumference to the diameter. Small groups measured lids, the round tables in the classroom, plates, oranges, and other objects, recorded the data in a table, and were asked what patterns they noticed. In several pilot classes, the discussions were lively.

During one group discussion, several students articulated what the general relationship is between the circumference and the diameter. There is a point in the tape, however, where one student who was previously on target begins to struggle. This moment occurs when the teacher asks how to write the rule expressed in English as a mathematical equation.

> Teacher: Okay, looking at these (the tabulated data), is there any pattern or relationship that jumps out at anybody?
> Student 3: Yup, the diameter is three times (muffled) the circumference.
> Teacher: One more time?
> Student 3: The diameter is three times smaller than the circumference.
> Teacher: Okay, does anybody else see any relationships or patterns that are going on here? (Silence) ...
> Teacher: Okay, can we say a sentence turning this around? The circumference is what, if I started with the diameter?
> Student 3: Three times ...
> Teacher: The circumference is about three times bigger?
> Student 3: About three times the size of the diameter.
> Teacher: About three times the size of the diameter. (Teacher writes this on board). Okay, so how would we say that in maybe a more algebra type sentence?
> Student 3: C ...
> Student 3: With the sign, you know, it's bigger than ...
> Teacher: Okay, so C ... Actually, come draw it up here ...
> Student 3: Which one's bigger? (makes the < sign with her fingers)
> Teacher: Which one do you think?
> (Student chooses one and writes on board $C > D^3$)
> Student 3: Do I do that?
> Teacher: Is that three times larger?
> Student 3: No.
> Teacher: What would three times larger be?
> Student 3: C times ... C plus C plus C

Teacher: C times 3?
Class: 3 ... 3C ... (laughter). .. how many times is that?
Teacher: Three times diameter or three times circumference?
Student 5: Diameter.
Teacher: Okay, so how do I show three times diameter? What would I do up here?
Class: Times 3 ... 3 times.
Teacher: 3 times, okay.

Watching the video of the class, the sense of confusion is striking when the student approaches the board. The confident responses about the relationship of circumference and diameter fall to pieces when the relationship needs to be transcribed in algebraic notation. In some classes, the students' lost their grasp on the relationship between the circumference and the diameter. They reverted to thinking of the diameter as half the circumference in spite of their recent concrete experiences measuring, the data in the table, and the class discussion. This persistent misconception is at least understandable because the diameter cuts the circle in half. However, losing track of the "three-ness" was not the problem for Student 3. How to transcribe it was the problem (as an exponent, as a repetition of the diameter or circumference, or as a constant in front of a variable). Some of the difficulty with notation can be attributed to the expectations typical of math classes. For the most part, the literal symbols in equations are treated as missing elements, rather than as variables. Moreover, until algebra, students often do not have to generate an equation of their own, particularly one that draws on signs such as greater than ($>$) or not equal to ($\neq$). Shifting from a passive to an active use of mathematical notation may take more time than most teachers or books provide. In this case, the discussion points out that students still have to take a big leap between articulating an observation based on an investigation and writing a mathematical statement.

The transcript prompted interesting questions for further research. These include the following: Do students frequently find themselves lost when the concrete disappears? What analogous examples could math curriculum draw on to build more success for students in this area? Further research into the development of algebraic thinking in adults could track the connections between abbreviations and their referents. Are all symbols equally likely to create stumbling blocks or are the more familiar symbols (+ and -) less likely to cause difficulty? And finally, how does the concept of variable develop?

CONCLUSION

Investigations like those described in this chapter make students' understanding audible and visible. They also teach math a whole new way. Although standardized tests cannot immediately validate the importance of this approach, without classroom time spent in this way, teachers can easily miss where the breaks in understanding occur. Ultimately, what teachers and researchers learn from such investigations is not limited to helping individual students. Collecting and examining students' work adds to the scant knowledge base on the development of adults' mathematical thinking. Close examination of students' work on every mathematical topic should inform directions for further research. Only by gathering and sharing such information will adult educators improve the quality of instruction.

Interventions at the classroom, professional development, research, and policy levels could compel the field to change the face of mathematics instruction from one of remedial isolation to collaborative inquiry community, from classrooms where school-based arithmetic algorithms reign to places where adults begin to mathematize their world.

At the policy level, several changes could make a difference for students' experiences of math instruction. Literacy campaigns in the United States have opted to subsume numeracy under literacy, making it invisible. Leaders could bring numeracy to the forefront in legislation and include numeracy in policy discussions on what is needed for adults to succeed. This acknowledgment would pave the way for broader policy definitions of what counts as progress, which is informed by the needs of adults in their workplaces, communities, homes, and in higher education settings. It is an anomaly that the adult basic education system does not see as part of its central mission improving numeracy in the same way it sees improving literacy and spoken English. In contrast to literacy campaigns in the United States that have omitted numeracy, similar campaigns for adult access to basic education in other English-speaking countries have integrated mathematics into their efforts. For example, in New Zealand, people refer to the adult basic education system as the "LNL system," meaning literacy, numeracy, and language; in Australia and the UK, they consistently refer to literacy and numeracy when talking about adult basic skills. The implications for policy go beyond the name change; the United States might do well to emulate these models.

Research agendas in adult basic education need to be updated. The body of knowledge in children's mathematics development is extensive in topic areas such as algebra, geometry, rational numbers, and proportional reasoning. The insights from these studies ought to inform research at the adult level, with research confirming or helping to identify a different model for how adults learn mathematical concepts. The *EMPower* project has begun to mine the research to inform the further development of its units. The work remains to distill what works and does not work as new approaches to math topic areas are tested.

Historically the gap between research and practice is a wide one. Research on mathematics must be undertaken at the same time as curriculum is developed and implemented by classroom teachers. This structure allows teachers to enter into the research process as partners, assuming the role of in-class observer, looking and listening for students' understanding. The written curriculum can serve as a tool for sharing research among teachers.

Professional development is essential, but is especially crucial for reform curricula such as *EMPower* because the instruction calls for deep changes that challenge what math is taught as well as when and how it is taught. Learners come to adult basic education classes with hopes of passing tests, but teachers know the mathematical demands on adults do not stop with the GED. This has motivated groups of teachers to begin to collaborate to develop new knowledge, curriculum, and professional development. The Massachusetts ABE Math Team, the Adult Numeracy Network, and the *EMPower* team are examples of groups of teachers and researchers who have come together out of an interest in improving math education for adults. They fuel domestic and international searches, looking to educators in Australia, the Netherlands, and the United Kingdom, and the Adults Learning Maths—A Research Forum, for new approaches and solutions.

Clearly, those who want to see high quality education available for adults need to be catalysts for change with stamina to face tremendous obstacles. Given numeracy's stepchild status within an already marginalized field, the need to be creative and multidimensional and maximize existing resources leads us to consider new ways to combine practice, research, theory, and policy. A multidimensional research program centered on insight, as well as impact, would inform practice and policy and build theory about adults' numerate thinking in and out of classroom settings.

ACKNOWLEDGMENTS

We wish to thank the *EMPower* team at TERC: Myriam Steinback (Principal Investigator), Juania Ashley, Donna Curry, Tricia Donovan, Marlene Kliman, Valerie Martin, and Jill Pellarin for their unflagging commitment to improving learning opportunities for adults. We are grateful to the adult students and their teachers who have generously joined with us in developing the curriculum. We are all teaching. We are all learning.

Extending Mathematical Power (*EMPower*) was funded in part by the National Science Foundation under Grant Number ESI-9911410. Any opinions, findings, and conclusions or recommendations expressed in this publication are those of the authors and do not necessarily reflect the views of the National Science Foundation (the Web site is http://*EMPower*.terc.edu). TERC is a not-for-profit education research and development organization dedicated to improving mathematics, science, and technology teaching and learning.

REFERENCES

Auchter, J. (2004, April). *Discover who passed the GED tests and the best route for passage.* Presentation at the COABE Conference, Columbus, OH.

Bednarz, N., Kieran, C., & Lee, L. (Eds.). (1996). *Approaches to algebra: Perspectives for research and teaching.* Dordrecht, The Netherlands: Kluwer.

Edwards, E. (Ed.). (1990). *Algebra for everyone.* Reston, VA: National Council of Teachers of Mathematics.

Fendel, D., Resek, D., Alpert, L., & Fraser, S. (1998). *Interactive mathematics program.* Berkeley, CA: Key Curriculum Press.

Gal, I., & Schuh, A. (1994). Who counts in adult literacy programs? A national survey of numeracy education (Tech. Rep. No. TR94-09). Philadelphia: University of Pennsylvania, National Center on Adult Literacy.

Howett, J. (2000). *Contemporary's number power 2: Decimals and percents.* Chicago: McGraw-Hill/Contemporary.

Kaput, J. (1998). Transforming algebra from an engine of inequity to an engine of mathematical power by "algebrafying" the K-12 curriculum. In National Research Council (Ed.), *The nature and role of algebra in the K-14 curriculum: Proceedings of a national symposium, May 28 & 29, 1997* (pp. 25–26). Washington, DC: National Academy Press.

Kirsch, I. S., Jungeblut, A., Jenkins, L., & Kolstad, A. (2002). *Adult literacy in America: A first look at the findings of the National Adult Literacy Survey* (3rd ed.). Washington, DC: U.S. Department of Education.

Kloosterman, P., Hassan, M., & Wiest, L. (2000). Building a problem-solving environment for teaching mathematics. In I. Gal (Ed.), *Adult numeracy development: Theory, research, practice* (pp. 51-72). Cresskill, NJ: Hampton.

Lappan, G., Fey, J., Fitzgerald, W., Friel, S., & Phillips, E. (1998). *Connected mathematics.* Palo Alto, CA: Dale Seymour Publications.

Massachusetts Community College Executive Office. (2002). *100% mathematics: A Massachusetts Community College System initiative funded by the U.S. Department of Education.* Boston: Author.

Mullinix, B. (1994). *Exploring what counts: Mathematics instruction in adult basic education.* Boston: World Education.

Murnane, R., Willet, J., & Levy, F. (1995). The growing importance of cognitive skills in wage determination (Working Paper No. 50-76). Cambridge, MA: National Bureau of Economic Research.

National Council of Teachers of Mathematics. (1989). *Curriculum and evaluation standards for school mathematics.* Reston, VA: Author.

National Council of Teachers of Mathematics. (2000). *Principles and standards for school mathematics.* Reston, VA: Author.

National Research Council. (1997). *The nature and role of algebra in the K-14 curriculum: Proceedings of a national symposium, May 28 & 29, 1997.* Washington, DC: National Academy Press.

National Research Council. (2001). *Adding it up: Helping children learn mathematics.* In J. Kilpatrick, J. Swafford, & B. Findell (Eds.), *Mathematics Learning Study Committee, Center for Education, Division of Behavioral and Social Sciences and Education.* Washington, DC: National Academy Press.

Russell, S. J. Tierney, C., Mokros, J., & Economopoulos, K. (2004). *Investigations in number, data, and space.* Glenview, IL: Pearson Scott Foresman.

Russell, S. J., Tierney, C., Mokros, J., & Economopoulos, K. (2004). *Investigations in number data, and space.* Glenview, IL: Pearson Scott Foresman.

Safford-Ramus, K. (2000, August). *A review and summary of research on adult mathematics education in North America (1980-2000).* Paper presented at the 9th International Congress on Mathematical Education (ICME 9), Japan.

Schliemann, A. D., Carraher, D., Brizuela, B., Earnest, D., Goodrow, D., Lara-Roth, S., et al. (2003). Algebra in elementary school. *Proceedings of the 2003 Joint Meeting of PME and PME-NA,* Eds. N.A. Pateman, B.J. Zilliox, *4,* 127–134.

Schmitt, M. J. (2003). *Perspectives on algebraic thinking and its development: From studies on children and adolescents to adult education* (Qualifying paper). Cambridge, MA: Harvard University Graduate School of Education.

Schmitt, M. J., Steinback, M., Donovan, T., & Merson, M. (2007). *Extending mathematical power (EMPower).* Emeryville, CA: Key Curriculum Press.

Senk, D., & Thompson, D. (2003). *Standards-based mathematics curricula: What are they? What do students learn?* Mahwah, NJ: Lawrence Erlbaum Associates, Inc.

Smith, J. P. (2002). The development of students' knowledge of fractions and ratios. In B. Litiller (Ed.), *2002 yearbook of the National Council of Teachers of Mathematics* (pp. 3-14). Reston, VA: National Council of Teachers of Mathematics.

Steinback, M., Schmitt, M. J., Merson, M., & Leonelli, E. (2003). Measurement in adult education: Starting with students' understandings. In D. Clements & G. Bright (Eds.), *2003 yearbook of the National Council of Teachers of Mathematics* (pp. 318-331). Reston, VA: National Council of Teachers of Mathematics.

Tout, D., & Schmitt, M. J. (2002). The inclusion of numeracy in adult basic education. In J. Comings, B. Garner, & C. Smith (Eds.), *Annual review of adult learning and literacy, Volume 3* (pp. 152-202). San Francisco: Jossey-Bass.

Usiskin, Z. (1988). Conceptions of school algebra and uses of variables. In A.F. Coxford, and A.P. Shulte (Ed.), *The ideas of algebra, K-12, 1988 yearbook* (pp. 8-19). Reston, VA: National Council of Teachers of Mathematics.

Ward, J. E. (2000). Arkansas GED mathematics instruction: History repeating itself. In M. J. Schmitt & K. Safford-Ramus (Eds.), *A conversation between researchers and practitioners. Proceedings of ALM-7, the 7th international conference of adult learning mathematics--a research forum* (pp. 54–58). Cambridge, MA: National Center for the Study of Adult Learning and Literacy.

Weinberg, S. (2002). Proportional reasoning: One problem, many solutions. In B. Litiller (Ed.), *2002 yearbook of the National Council of Teachers of Mathematics* (pp. 138-144). Reston, VA: National Council of Teachers of Mathematics.

PART THREE

RETHINKING OUR ASSUMPTIONS AND CONCEPTS

Chapter 11

Reconceptualizing Adult Basic Education and the Digital Divide

Elisabeth Hayes
University of Wisconsin-Madison

The use of computer-based, or digital technologies in adult basic education (ABE) is increasingly widespread, along with the proliferation of instructional software designed specifically for adult literacy learners. Some advocates claim that computer-based instruction offers learners a wider range of engaging, motivating, and presumably more effective learning opportunities. More significantly, another argument for incorporating such technologies into ABE is that the mastery of what are commonly now called "digital literacies" can be crucial to adults' success in accessing information important in their daily lives, obtaining better jobs, helping their children succeed in school, and generally improving the quality of their lives.

The rhetoric surrounding the use of such technologies, most commonly the Internet but also other computer-based tools, suggests that those who do not have access to such technologies are becoming increasingly disadvantaged in this "Information Age." The so-called digital divide has been linked with economic disadvantage, low levels of educational attainment, and other indicators of social disadvantage and quality of life. For example, the types of jobs with higher economic and social rewards now tend to be those that provide "symbolic-analytic services" requiring the use of multiple forms of oral and visual representations, problem posing as well as problem solving (Reich, 1992), typically associated with the use of new technologies. Social disadvantage has been characterized as a cause as well as a consequence of digital "illiteracy." National survey data indicates that only 22% of children in households with incomes of less than $20,000 have access to home computers (and the resulting opportunities to acquire knowledge and skills related to digital technologies), compared to 91% of those in families with annual incomes of more than $75,000 (Becker, 2000, p. 44).

Simply introducing digital technologies into ABE will not ensure that those technologies are used in meaningful or empowering ways, however. In education as a whole, new technologies tend to be assimilated into traditional classroom practices, rather than making any significant impact on the goals or organization of instruction (Hodas, 1993). Howard Becker (2000) criticized the tendency in schools of using information communication technologies (ICT) for drill and skill instruction among low achieving children:

> Certainly, lower-performing students and students from economically poorer backgrounds can profit from greater competency in arithmetic and literacy. Targeting computer opportunities to those limited domains, however, will exacerbate these students' disadvantage compared to more advantaged students who use their computer access to gain mastery of higher-order skills and competencies. (p. 69)

Similarly, ABE typically does not go beyond addressing the most limited forms of digital literacies. For the most part, the impact of new technologies is limited to the incorporation of computer-mediated instruction (often no more than a "workbook on a screen") and instruction in "computer literacy," which is typically defined as the use of word-processing or spreadsheet applications, e-mail, and searching the World Wide Web. This limited curricular focus suggests that current instructional practices in ABE are more likely to reinforce a digital divide rather than reduce it (Ginsburg, 2004; Hopey, Harvey-Morgan, & Rethemeyer, 1996; Levesque, 2000).

In this chapter, I argue that literacy educators should begin to think more expansively about the nature of new technologies, the kinds of literacies inherent in such technologies, and their implications for literacy learning and teaching. Such literacies should not be considered within the purview only of an elite; they can and should be incorporated even into our conceptions of "basic" education for adults. Although talk of constructivist and even emancipatory views of literacy and literacy education are common, the majority of ABE instruction rests on assumptions about literacy as a set of basic skills (Beder, this volume). Improving the quality of digital literacy education requires different ways of conceptualizing literacies in general, and digital literacies in particular.

SOCIOCULTURAL PERSPECTIVES ON DIGITAL LITERACIES

A growing number of scholars argue that common approaches to "computer literacy" instruction are based on conventional conceptions of literacy that are inadequate and obsolete (e.g., Cope & Kalantzis, 2000; Lankshear, 1997; Perelman, 1992). The rise of new technologies has provided impetus and focus for the work of theorists associated with what has been variously described as the

New Literacy Studies, multiliteracies, and sociocultural perspectives on literacy (e.g., Cope & Kalantzis, 2000; Gee, 1996; Lankshear, 1997; New London Group, 1996). Rather than viewing literacy as a set of cognitive abilities or skills, these scholars share the belief that literacy concerns "social practices – something to do with social, institutional, and cultural relationships" (Gee, 1996, p. 1). How people construct meaning from texts is central to conceptions of literacies from this perspective. The term *multiliteracies* signifies the assumption that understanding literacy as meaning-making must include broadening our definition of "texts" to encompass multiple forms of representation, including those that involve not only language but also visual images, such as pictures and diagrams, and auditory and spatial modalities (Cope & Kalantzis, 2000). Multiliteracies also refers to the increasing blurring of cultural and linguistic boundaries, and the corresponding need for people to interact with multiple languages and discourses (Cope & Kalantzis, 2000).

Sociocultural perspectives on literacies can be applied to more traditional print-based texts and educational contexts, as well as texts created with new technologies; indeed they form the basis of a radical rethinking of our conceptions of literacy in general. My purpose here is more narrow; to provide detailed examples of several key concepts, or ways of understanding digital literacies from a sociocultural perspective, and to suggest implications for digital literacy learning in ABE. I have chosen to use one particular manifestation of digital technologies, video gaming, as a primary source of examples for this discussion. Video gaming might seem an unlikely focus for an analysis of digital literacies for educationally disadvantaged adults; however, as I argue later, such games are of interest precisely because they challenge our current beliefs about literacies.

THE SIGNIFICANCE OF VIDEO GAMING

Video gaming (I use this term as inclusive of both computer and console games) has become a mainstream activity in the United States and elsewhere around the world. Video gaming has grown to be an $8.9 billion dollar industry in the United States, generating far more revenue than movie box-office receipts or video rentals (Poole, 2000, p. 6). For many children, video gaming is their first and most powerful introduction to digital technologies. The appeal of these games extends to a growing number of adult gamers. According to a gaming industry trends survey, 42% of frequent video-game players in 2002 were over the age of 36 (Interactive Digital Software Association [IDSA], 2003, p. 2). According to the same survey, in the United States, women now comprise 43% of frequent computer gamers (IDSA, 2003). A trend in many games is toward reducing or even eliminating violence while increasing the emphasis on problem solving, plot development, and character interaction (Poole, 2000). Gaming is often quite social; the majority of people who play games do so with friends and family (IDSA, 2003).

In addition to the rampant popularity of video gaming as a form of popular entertainment, gaming is being adopted for a variety of more "serious" purposes, such as patient education, psychotherapy, training in a variety of occupations, second language learning, and museum education (see the Serious Games Initiative site at http://www.seriousgames.org/). Scholars in a variety of academic disciplines have begun to take an interest in video gaming as an object of theoretical and cultural significance. There are now entire journals devoted to research on video gaming, such as *Game Studies*, with publications on topics ranging from the nature of narrative in games, virtual economies, and forms of interaction and communication in multiplayer games (see http://www.gamestudies. org/).

RISE OF NATIONS: "THE ENTIRE SPAN OF HUMAN HISTORY IS IN YOUR HANDS"

The source of examples for my discussion is the widely praised game *Rise of Nations*^{TM} *(RoN)*. In *RoN,* players build civilizations, advancing in size and sophistication by accumulating resources, researching new technologies, and expanding their territories. Battles with civilizations controlled by other players, human or virtual, are an important, although not essential, aspect of game play. *RoN* is what gamers describe as a real-time strategy (RTS) game; as a genre, these games share several key attributes. As the name suggests, game play takes place in "real-time;" the players, human or virtual, are simultaneously building their civilizations, and battles can take place at any time, at the players' discretion. RTS games involve the constant manipulation of a wide variety of elements, such as creating villagers and soldiers; directing villagers to gather resources such as food, gold, or wood necessary to maintain and expand a civilization; constructing houses, military buildings, storehouses, and other essential buildings; and researching technologies to upgrade capacities and progress to more advanced levels of civilization. The goals of these games are quite broad, including overcoming an enemy, or gaining the most resources in a particular time period. Game play itself is nonlinear and presents the players with an indefinite number of choices about how to proceed. One player, for example, might spend a lot of time initially accumulating resources and building a civilization, whereas another more intent on combat might seek to attack another civilization early in the game, relying on battle strategy more than resources. RTS games, like many games of other genres, have multiplayer options, in which human players can play each other by connecting through a local area network or on a Web site. A written description is sorely inadequate as a means to capture the nature of any computer game, and I encourage interested readers to investigate Microsoft Game Studios[TM] *Rise of Nations* Web site (http://www.microsoft.com/games/riseofnations/).

THE NATURE OF DIGITAL LITERACIES

In this section, I describe four key concepts that I have drawn from literature associated with sociocultural perspectives on digital literacies: (a) multimodal textuality, (b) semiotic domains and designs, (c) critical literacies, and (d) identities and affinity groups (e.g., Cope & Kalantzis, 2000; Gee, 1996, 2003; Lankshear, 1997; New London Group, 1996). Gee's (2003) work is particularly relevant to my analysis, as it represents one of the first attempts to move beyond exclusively cognitive psychological approaches to the study of learning in the context of video gaming. I draw selectively from Gee's work as well as the work of literacy scholars more broadly in my discussion of these concepts. These concepts can serve as a foundation for reconceptualizing digital literacy education.

Multimodal Textuality: Not Just Words on a Page

The picture in Figure 11–1 is a screen from the middle of a *RoN* game. Someone unfamiliar with the game might identify certain images as buildings or forests,

Figure 11.1. Game screen (screen shot reprinted by permission from Microsoft Game Studios™).

and might recognize numbers and phrases, but overall the screen is likely to be meaningless, similar to how a page in a textbook might appear to a new reader. How does a gamer make meaning of or "read" this screen? Unlike a textbook, however, the task obviously is not one of finding the main idea or supporting details, and it is not a matter of following step-by-step instructions as in a manual.

The New London Group (1996) pointed out that all meaning-making involves *multimodality,* or a combination of modes; for example, a written text involves both linguistic (how sentences are structured, for example) and visual design (how the text is laid out on the page, font style, and so forth). Different modes of meaning offer different potentials for meaning-making; a picture, for example, can communicate meaning that language cannot, and vice versa (Kress & van Leeuwen, 1996). Digital technologies, due to their new affordances, make new combinations of modes more possible, apparent, and valued. This juxtaposition of modes creates the potential for the creation of new meanings or representations through innovative and creative designs.

The *RoN* screen offers an example of how different modalities of meaning, such as images, texts, icons, and numbers, can be integrated in ways that take advantage of the affordances of digital technologies, rather than repeating the formats and patterns of traditional texts. One key attribute of multimodal texts in games such as *RoN* is their reliance on icons and images to convey information in a form useful for immediate action. Unlike texts composed primarily of words, meanings are presented in a condensed form and their meaning is not dependent on surrounding texts. Figure 11–2 shows just how much information is represented in a typical game interface.

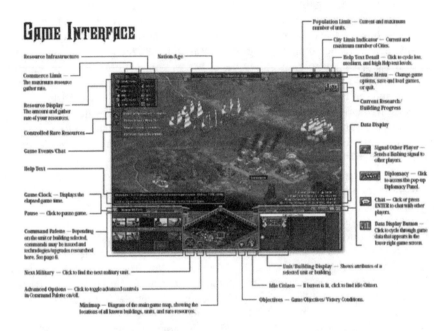

Figure 11.2. Game interface (screen shot reprinted by permission from Microsoft Game Studios™).

Unlike texts in which pictures are used to illustrate ideas or concepts from written passages, words and phrases on the *RoN* screen primarily are used to illustrate or clarify the central image. Furthermore, images such as icons are used to illustrate other images. For example, the chart in the lower left-hand corner of the screen consists of a set of icons representing commands that can be executed in the central game map.

Written and numeric texts are important in digital contexts such as *RoN,* although they are not the main sources of information. Lengthy written texts, such as game manuals, descriptions of game elements that can be accessed within the game, and strategy guides prepared by other players, are available.

However, the role of such texts is more comparable to the ways in which words and numbers are embedded in a context of use in daily life outside of school rather than to how they are used in textbooks. For example, signs and labels are juxtaposed with what they describe, long narrative texts are used as a reference for action rather than for memorization and restating, and information is continually changing as the "world" changes rather than remaining static and fixed.

Games such as *RoN* are designed to give the player considerable freedom to pursue various goals. The player is presented with a wide range of information and potential choices at all times. To make meaning of a text such as a book, the reader must learn the conventions of how a book or other type of text is organized, and once those conventions are understood, the reader is provided with considerable guidance in navigating the text. In contrast, the gamer has to take a much more proactive role in finding his or her way through the text of a game, which includes identifying the overall pattern of how information is organized. For example, in *RoN,* the gamer learns that information provided in charts at the edges of the map illustrates the civilization; he or she also learns that this information does not necessarily relate to what is currently at the center of the screen. The organization of information is paradigmatic rather than linear (Kress & van Leeuwen, 1996).

These examples indicate that making meaning of digital texts can require very different kinds of skills and knowledge than those that are commonly taught in ABE. The ability to identify patterns and relationships among modes of meaning, to move back and forth in a nonlinear way within and across texts, and to understand the strengths and limitations of diverse modes of meaning, are just a few examples of abilities that learners might need to recruit to become more adept at using digital texts. In some cases, these may be abilities that learners already use in "real-world" literacy practices such as those that I described earlier, that can be adapted and expanded to include digital texts. However, it is not simply a matter of transferring "generic" skills; learners must marry those skills to an understanding of the broader semiotic domains and designs of digital worlds.

Semiotic Domains and Designs: Reading the World

To read the world you must understand the world, not just its parts, and the same can be said of texts. Any text is more than the sum of its parts. Texts, including the digital texts of computer games, make sense only if you understand the text in relation to a wider social context, which includes their role in specific social practices and their association with particular social groups. The nature of texts, in whatever modes, and our interactions with them must be understood in these contexts. As Gee (2003) pointed out, one cannot be literate, even in the most traditional sense of making meaning through reading, if one is not familiar with the broader *semiotic domain* that gives words their meaning.

Gee (2003) defined a semiotic domain as "any set of practices that recruits one or more modalities (e.g., oral or written language, images, equations, symbols, sounds, gestures, graphs, artifacts, etc.) to communicate distinctive types of meaning" (p. 18). Semiotic domains are pervasive in our daily lives; examples vary from domains associated with occupations and professions to domains related to entertainment or everyday tasks. As an example, think of the practices and meanings associated with driving a motor vehicle, including understanding different indicators on the dashboard, and interpreting traffic signs, turn signals on other cars, and sometimes the gestures of other drivers. Of particular importance is the distinctive nature of meanings ascribed to symbols and practices within a domain. A few light taps on a car horn can signal a friendly greeting, whereas a long loud blare can be a warning of an impending crash.

A semiotic domain is defined by an *internal design grammar* that specifies what particular kind of content is appropriate and valued within the domain. Grammar, in this sense, refers not to the set of rules for correctness in writing or speech, but to "a means of representing patterns of experience … . It enables human beings to build a mental picture of reality, to make sense of their experience of what goes on around them and inside them" (Halliday, 1985, p. 101, cited in Kress & van Leeuwen, 1996, p. 2). A design grammar related to driving a car in the United States is locating the driver's seat on the left-hand side of the vehicle, and driving on the right-hand side of the road. Think of the confusion that drivers from the United States experience when they go to another country such as England where people drive on the "wrong" side of the road!

Digital texts and tools are also embedded in distinctive practices and domains that affect their meanings and uses. There are different genres of computer games, for example, that are based on different design principles and conventions. The importance of this design knowledge is reflected in *RoN's* manual (Rymaszewski, 2003). In the manual's *Foreword,* one of the game designers explains how the design team attempted to integrate features of another type of game, turn-taking games, into the RTS mode of *RoN.* The first chapter of the manual includes a detailed discussion of key elements of RTS games, as well as how *RoN* differs from other games of this genre. The digital tutorial for the game embeds instruction in "basic skills" essential for game play within simplified scenarios that also introduce players to the overall game domain and its design features, such as how civilizations and their capacities change over time or the importance of strategies like targeting military barracks for attack. The player learns to "read" the digital *RoN* world with attention to a range of features, including location and prevalence of resources (which might affect the best location for buildings and towns), the expansion rate of other civilizations (indicating their choice of conquest strategy), and their own nation's rate of resource consumption (suggesting how labor should be allocated).

In schools, including ABE, instruction often focuses on isolated, supposedly "generic" skills or content without much connection to wider domains and practices. However, a generic lesson on Web sites, for instance, may be of little value to learners without an understanding of specific practices and features associated with different types of sites. Learning activities must be tied to the conventions of relevant domains to be meaningful and useful. For example, learning to use Web sites as a *RoN* gamer requires making distinctions among the different kinds of information that might be found on another gamer's blog as compared to a fan site, or to Microsoft Game Studios^{TM} (the game producer) *RoN* site. I would likely use each site for different purposes, and engage in different practices at each site. Even within each site there are different rules and conventions for various social practices that must be learned. For instance, in an online discussion thread, I need to know what kinds of questions might be considered "stupid" to avoid insults.

Critical Literacies: Redesigning Worlds

All domains incorporate beliefs and ways of judging desirable designs. Returning to motor vehicles, we make judgments about cars based on beliefs and values related to functionality and economics as well as aesthetics and other values such as environmental impact. Identifying and thinking about design principles within the context of a domain opens up possibilities for critique and creativity, including what we commonly think of as critical literacies. Although critical literacy practices are often equated with critical thinking as a cognitive skill, from a sociocultural perspective, engaging in critical literacy practices requires an understanding of the broader domain and its assumptions, the ability to question those assumptions, and often the ability to redesign aspects of the domain.

In *RoN,* players are encouraged to think about design principles in several ways. The game manual brings design elements to the player's attention through an initial discussion of how *RoN* is similar and different to other real-time strategy games. Strategies for game play are presented in relationship to the overall design and goals of the game. The player is given many different options for playing the game; in a limited way, he or she is designing game play, through choosing civilizations to play and with which to compete, the levels of difficulty and speed, the particular map as a context for the game, and the criteria for victory, such as accumulating the most territory. Setting the game parameters encourages the player to reflect on design principles and how he or she relates to game play. Player participation in game design is taken a step further through the provision of an editing tool that allows players to create their own landscapes, prompting reflection on the effects of geography on game play.

Critical literacy abilities are also recruited and developed as players engage in reflection and discussion of the values and assumptions underlying game design. A good example is a debate that arose among gamers over the nationalities that were selected for inclusion in *RoN.* A focal point for the debate among U.S. gamers was the decision not to include the United States. As summarized on a gamer's Web site (Rise of Nations: The Great Debates, 2003), the arguments for and against this decision reflected a wide range of values and perspectives. Some players argued in favor of including the United States based on their perception of its influence as a "superpower" in global affairs. Others, taking the perspective of the game manufacturer and audience, argued that the United States should be included because it would be a major market for the game, and presumably players would want the ability to command (or perhaps compete with) their own nation. Those against the inclusion of the United States presented a similarly wide range of arguments. These included, "Having American Hoplites, longbow men, and war galleys in RoN would create significant historical dissonance," "America is a nation of immigrants, and this is beyond the reasonable modeling capabilities of the game engine," and "Leaving America for an expansion pack makes good business sense." The debates extended to questioning the underlying assumptions of the game, in particular the assumption that more technologically advanced civilizations had inherently superior intelligence or other attributes.

The aforementioned examples suggest ways through which critical literacy abilities might be recruited in other domains of digital literacy learning. Making design principles explicit, engaging in discussion of the assumptions underlying design decisions, and ultimately acting as designers, not just consumers of digital texts, can contribute to critical literacies. In ABE, learners might identify and critique the assumptions underlying Web sites, video games, and other media, as well as create their own digital "texts." *Tropical America* is a relevant example of one such media literacy project, in which high school students created a video game to bring attention to little recognized but significant events and people in the history of Central America (see http://www.tropicalamerica.com/). Learners also begin to take on identities within the context of the domain, as they align themselves with certain sets of values and beliefs, and with other people who share similar interests and affiliations within the domain.

Identities and Affinity Groups: New Selves in New Social Worlds

From a sociocultural perspective, identities and affinity groups are key elements of literacies within a domain. Becoming "literate" in a particular domain is not simply about making meaning of texts. It involves participating in certain kinds of social practices and acquiring identities associated with those social practices, as well as perhaps modifying or even abandoning old identities. For example, the goals of ABE typically are not characterized solely as reading, writing, or math skills improvement. We hope that ABE learners will become *certain kinds* of workers, parents, or citizens as a result of acquiring new knowledge and skills. These identities, in turn, are often what motivate learners; one person might want to be a "better" parent, another might seek the status (as well as income) of a more highly skilled occupation. To achieve such goals, learners and educators must gain a deeper understanding of the social practices and identities associated with specific domains.

Within the video gaming community, players construct identities as fans of a particular game genre or a particular game. If this seems far removed from everyday technology use, think of how people identify themselves as Mac versus PC users, or members of particular online chat rooms or listservs. Solitary game play, playing multiplayer games, sharing strategies, troubleshooting, and just discussing experiences with other gamers, often on the Internet, are important social practices associated with gaming. By participating in such practices, gamers learn about the beliefs, behaviors, and values of other *RoN* gamers. In turn, these beliefs, behaviors, and values can shape (and are shaped by) players' gaming practices and the kinds of identities that they find desirable. Certain identities are limited to individuals with specific skills and knowledge, such as expertise in gaming, the ability to create a fan site, or the detailed experience required to write a walkthrough. Even if a player does not actively participate on a site or directly interact with others, he or she can gain a sense of identity as a particular kind of gamer by comparing his or her own gaming preferences and abilities to those made public on Web sites or in gaming magazines.

Participation in affinity groups can lose value if it is forced or if groups are not supportive. In most naturally occurring affinity groups, such as those associated with *RoN,* people have choices about their level of involvement and the kinds of identities they wish to attain. Such groups also vary in the extent to which they support and invite potential participants and provide opportunities for varied levels of involvement. Interestingly, gaming listservs can be simultaneously supportive, offering tips for very beginning players, while tolerating if not encouraging participants to swap insulting comments about their skills and questions.

In ABE, social support for literacy learning, digital or otherwise, is sometimes provided through small group learning in which learners can share ideas and information as well as provide emotional support. However, such groups are typically transitory and offer learners few opportunities to develop meaningful identities in relationship to relevant social practices that extend beyond the classroom. How might ABE programs take into account the role of identities and affinity groups in digital literacy learning? A first step could be recognizing identities that learners find compelling and motivating, connecting technology skills and knowledge to these identities and participation in these social practices and groups. For example, a parent of a bilingual child might be motivated to take a more active role in supporting her child's success in school. She could learn to use the Internet to locate information about bilingual education, share information with other parents on listservs or face-to-face, use e-mail to communicate with her child's teachers, and even work with other parents to create a Web site with information about bilingual education that can inform other parents.

LOOKING FORWARD: CHANGING PERSPECTIVES AND PRACTICES

How might ABE programs move toward incorporating instructional practices based on this reconceptualization of digital literacies? I can suggest a few broad strategies. Policymakers can take the lead by developing more expansive goals for digital literacy learning, both policymakers and program administrators should consider a reallocation of resources to staff development and reduce reliance on expensive and readily outdated software, and teachers can adopt instructional activities that emphasize learning through engagement in social practices.

More Expansive Goals

A major challenge is the current policy emphasis on narrow definitions of functional and workplace skills as the goals of ABE. The federal National Reporting System (NRS) for ABE reflects this emphasis in how benchmarks for assessing student progress are described. For example, NRS benchmarks for high intermediate basic education (reading grade level 6-8.9; United States Department of Education, n.d.) include the following: "The individual can learn or work with most basic computer software, such as using a word processor to produce own texts, and can follow simple instructions for using technology." Compare these to two of ten benchmarks for students in Grades 3 to 5 proposed by the National Educational Technology Standards Project (International Society for Technology in Education [ISTE], n.d.):

Prior to completion of Grade 5, students will ...

- Use technology tools (e.g., multimedia authoring, presentation, Web tools, digital cameras, scanners) for individual and collaborative writing, communication, and publishing activities to create knowledge products for audiences inside and outside the classroom

- Evaluate the accuracy, relevance, appropriateness, comprehensiveness, and bias of electronic information sources.

These standards are much more compatible with the perspectives on literacies advocated in this chapter, which emphasize engagement in social practices associated with digital technologies. Because the NRS benchmarks are used as a program accountability measure, standards such as those proposed by ISTE might be viewed as a threat to program funding and reputation. However, such benchmarks often become translated into what is deemed possible and desirable on a program level, and clearly present a barrier to more sophisticated views of digital literacies. Local ABE programs can and should establish their own conceptions of digital literacies that more adequately reflect sociocultural perspectives on literacies.

Reallocation of Resources

At the most fundamental level, the actual hardware and software available in programs is often outdated and nonfunctional (e.g., Levesque, 2000), perhaps more so than in kindergarten through 12th-grade schools, which have benefited more from public and private technology funding initiatives. However, a persistent problem is that teachers often are not prepared to use such technologies even when they are available. Teachers' limited expertise and experience with digital technologies contribute to overreliance on commercial educational software, particularly software that fits most easily into existing curricula and instructional formats. Lack of familiarity with technology also leads to assumptions that the cost of developing more innovative software and instructional methods are prohibitive.

More resources should be devoted to staff development rather than to purchasing expensive software. Teachers who are more familiar with digital technologies are more likely to identify and use existing resources in creative and sophisticated ways. Yasmin Kafai (2001)) wrote about children, but his comments apply to teachers as well:

> Just as fluency in language means much more than knowing facts about the language, technological fluency involves not only knowing how to use new technological tools, but also knowing how to make things of significance with those tools, and (most important) develop new ways of thinking based on the use of those tools. (p. 5)

It seems unreasonable to expect teachers to assist learners in developing such technological fluency, if they do not have opportunities to develop such fluency themselves.

The National Technology Laboratory for Literacy and Adult Education (n.d.) at the University of Pennsylvania is sponsoring a number of staff development initiatives related to improving teachers' use of technologies for instruction, including study circles and documentation of promising practices. The project "Connecting Communities" sponsored by the national agency Learning and Teaching Scotland (n.d.) is an example of a training program designed to enhance the use of ICT and communication in community learning agencies.

Learning by Engagement in Social Practices, In and Out of School

Another issue in ABE, related in some ways to the lack of resources, is the pre-dominant reliance on individualized instruction directed toward goals such as passing the General Educational Development (GED) test or enhancing func-tional skills assumed to be necessary for success in the workplace and other adult roles and contexts. As a result, instructional software is often designed as a substitute for workbooks or other individualized curricula. Clearly, a skill and drill, individualized instructional format is not compatible with a sociocultural perspective on literacy learning, digital or otherwise. There are a small but growing number of instructional resources that reflect some of the assumptions associated with a sociocultural perspective on digital literacy learning. For ex-ample, the National Educational Technology Standards Web site (ISTE, n.d.) offers a helpful description of strategies for more sophisticated integration of technologies into classroom teaching. The Captured Wisdom on Adult Literacy Web site, sponsored by North Central Regional Laboratory, describes seven innovative activities for ABE and English as a Second Language (ESL) adult learners. For instance, in one activity, "The Restaurant Problem," students act as consultants hired to save a failing restaurant. They use technology to deal with irate customers, schedule work hours, and design new menus (North Central Regional Laboratory, n.d.).

Changes are needed not only in classroom instruction, but also in the con-nections made to literacy learning and social practices beyond the classroom. Many ABE teachers and most ABE students are likely to be "digital immi-grants." Unlike middle class children and young adults, they have not grown up with computers and other digital technologies as an integral part of their lives, and they are less likely to have peers with such experiences. Most middle class children and adults have access to much more sophisticated technologies than are currently found in ABE programs or even in most public schools. ABE stu-dents, like disadvantaged children, are much less likely to have access to such technologies outside of the classroom. They are also less likely to have family or peers who can be recruited for assistance with learning social practices associ-ated with digital technologies. Warschauer (2003a) pointed out the following:

> People access digital information in a wide variety of ways and usually as part of social networks involving relatives, friends, and co-workers ... people become literate not just through physical access to books but through education, communication, work connections, family support, and assistance from social networks. (p. 47)

As I discussed previously, learning the "cultures" or semiotic domains in which digital technologies are embedded is just as important as learning basic skills. Some of this learning must occur outside the classroom as learners use digital technologies to engage in actual social practices that help them achieve meaningful goals.

RETHINKING THE DIGITAL DIVIDE

Perhaps most important, however, is the effort on the part of some scholars and educators to rethink the overall purpose of digital literacy education. Mark Warschauer (2003b) argued for an emphasis on social inclusion:

> The goal of using ICT (information communications technology) with marginalized groups is not to overcome a digital divide, but rather to further a process of social inclusion ... the extent that individuals, families, and communities are able to fully participate in society and control their own destinies .... (p. 5)

The goal of social inclusion suggests that the focus of digital literacy education should go beyond the acquisition of technical skills to address how digital technologies enable people and groups to engage in particular social practices. Ultimately, digital literacy education must be integrated with broader community development projects in which technology is used to attain broader social, political, and economic aims. In this regard, we can learn from successful and unsuccessful efforts to use technology for community development in other countries (e.g., Digital Divide Network, n.d.; Warschauer, 2003a, 2003b). As Warschauer suggested, adult educators should move from technicist considerations about the role of technology in ABE to more social and political considerations about the role of ABE in a technologically driven society. This can lead to some difficult questions, because viewing technology as a means, not an end of instruction, prompts us to ask what is it that our current and potential uses of technology support? Do we contribute, albeit unintentionally to a widening of the digital divide? Or can adult educators, together with learners, find creative ways to use digital technologies as tools in an effort to promote greater social inclusion of all people in our society? Rethinking our conceptions of digital literacies may be a starting point.

REFERENCES

Becker, H. J. (2000). Who's wired and who's not: Children's access to and use of computer technology. *Children And Computer Technology, 10,* 44-75. Retrieved December 19, 2003, from http://www.futureofchildren.org

Cope, B., & Kalantzis, M. (2000). *Multiliteracies: Literacy learning and the design of social futures.* London: Routledge.

Digital Divide Network. (n.d.). *Economic development.* Retrieved December 12, 2003, from http://www.digitaldividenetwork.org/content/sections/index.cfm?key=6

Gee, J. P. (1996). *Social linguistics and literacies: Ideologies in discourses* (2nd ed.). London: Taylor & Francis.

Gee, J. (2003). *What videogames have to teach us about learning and literacy.* New York: Palgrave MacMillan.

Ginsburg, L. (2004). *Adult literacy practitioners' readiness to use technology in the classroom: A five state survey in 2002-2003* (TECH21-NCAL Policy Report). Retrieved December 2, 2003, from http://www.literacy.org/products/T21SurveyRpt-jcs14-feb13.pdf

Halliday, M. A. K. (1985). *An introduction to functional grammar.* London: Edward Arnold.

Hodas, S. (1993). Technology refusal and the organizational culture of schools. *Education Policy Analysis Archives, 1,* 1-19.

Hopey, C. E., Harvey-Morgan, J., R., & Rethemeyer, R. K. (1996). *Technology and adult literacy: Findings from a survey on technology use in adult literacy programs* (NCAL Tech. Rep. No. TR96-12). Retrieved September 20, 2003, from http://www.literacyonline.org/products/ncal/pdf/TR9612.pdf

Interactive Digital Software Association. (2003). *The essential facts about the computer and video game industry.* Retrieved November 11, 2003, from http://www.idsa.com/pressroom.html

International Society for Technology in Education National Educational Technology Standards Project. (n.d.). *Profiles for technology-literate students: Grades 3-5.* Retrieved December 29, 2003, from http://cnets.iste.org/students.s_profiles.html

Kafai, Y. B. (2001). *The educational potential of electronic games: From games-to-teach to games-to-learn.* Chicago: University of Chicago Cultural Policy Center.

Kress, G., & van Leeuwen, T. (1996). *Reading images: The grammar of visual design.* New York: Routledge.

Lankshear, C. (Ed.). (1997). *Changing literacies.* Buckingham, UK: Open University Press.

Learning and Teaching Scotland. (n.d.). *Connecting communities*. Retrieved
    December 30, 2003, from
    http://www.ltscotland.org.uk/connectingcommunities/index.asp
Levesque, J. (2000). Across the great divide. *Focus on Basics, 4,* article no. 1.
    Retrieved December 29, 2003, from
    http://ncsall.gse.harvard.edu/fob/2000/fobv4ic.htm
National Technology Laboratory for Literacy and Adult Education. (n.d.).
    TECH21. Retrieved December 30, 2003, from www.tech21.org
New London Group. (1996). A pedagogy of multiliteracies: Designing social
    futures. *Harvard Educational Review, 66,* 60-92.
North Central Regional Educational Laboratory. (n.d.). *Captured wisdom on
    adult literacy*. Retrieved December 15, 2003, from
    http://www.ncrtec.org/pd/cw/adultlit.htm
Perelman, L. (1992). *School's out: The new technology and the end of educa-
    tion*. New York: Morrow.
Poole, S. (2000). *Trigger happy: Videogames and the entertainment revolution.*
    New York: Arcade Publishing.
Reich, R. (1992). *The work of nations*. New York: Vintage.
Rise of Nations: The great debates. (2003, November 1). Retrieved December
    20, 2003, from http://www.geocities.com/rohag3/RoNDebates.html
Rymaszewski, M. (2003). *Rise of Nations: Official strategies and secrets*. Ala-
    meda, CA: Sybex.
United States Department of Education. (n.d.). *Educational functioning levels.
    National Reporting System Online*. Retrieved December 29, 2003, from
    http://www.oei-
    tech.com/nrs/reference/m_and_m/methods/direct_program/3c_six_leve
    ls_abe_esl.html
Warschauer, M. (2003a). Demystifying the digital divide. *Scientific American,
    289,* 42-47.
Warschauer, M. (2003b). *Technology and social inclusion: Rethinking the digi-
    tal divide*. Cambridge, MA: MIT Press.

Chapter 12

Beyond the Life Boat:
Improving Language, Citizenship, and Training
Services for Immigrants and Refugees[4]

Heide Spruck Wrigley
Literacy Work International

Providing English language and literacy services for adults who are not yet proficient in English continues to be both a growing need and a growing concern in the United States. A high quality immigrant education system is critically important for millions of immigrants whose success in the new country depends in large part on their ability to communicate in English, manage the ins and outs of a new system, and integrate into the larger society. An effective immigrant education system is no less important for receiving communities and society at large as they are more likely to absorb newcomers and to benefit from the knowledge, skills, and resources that immigrants bring with them once English proficiency is no longer a major barrier.

English as a Second Language (ESL), now often referred to as language services for English language learners (ELLs), is a key component of the adult education system. In fact, ESL is the fastest growing segment of the program, comprising 40% to 50% of the total enrollment. Adult ESL is the place where research and practice can meet up with policies on immigrant integration, job training, employment, and community development to build collaborations

---

4 Some of the information in the demographic section has been adapted from an earlier paper by Wrigley, Richter, Martinson, Kubo and Strawn (2003), *The language of opportunity: Expanding employment opportunities for adults with limited English proficiency.* Washington, D.C. Center for Law and Social Policy.

across agencies and interest groups; English language and literacy skills are central to all of these endeavors.

For the immigrants and refugees themselves, control--if not mastery--of English represents the key to the Golden Door behind which lie the benefits of American society: educational opportunities, jobs that pay a living wage, social mobility, and a better life for oneself and one's children. For thousands, the adult education and training system offers the best hope for getting through the Golden Door. Adult immigrants often dream of a time when they no longer have to depend on their children to translate and their intelligence and accomplishments are no longer judged by their ability to speak English. For those with higher levels of education or professional experience, mastering English means recognition as professionals and attaining access to positions (social and economical) that afford them the respect--often denied those not yet able to--express sophisticated ideas in a new language. Adult education, serving as an entry point for low literate as well as educated adults needing English, can play an important role in helping these immigrants advance.

Providing language and literacy services to a wide variety of adult immigrants and refugees is a multifaceted process that deserves closer attention if the system is to be effective. This chapter argues for differentiating services based on the needs of various subgroups of adult ELLs, including those with only a few years of schooling in the home country, those hoping to naturalize, and immigrants seeking English to improve their job prospects. Many adults have broad overlapping goals; others are looking not for general, all-purpose ESL classes, but rather for focused, single-purpose classes that move them quickly toward their goals.

Currently, we do not have a system of adult immigrant education and training in the United States that is highly effective and efficient, although most participants do come away with some gains in language proficiency and many who participate do find jobs (many others also find jobs without having taken part in programs). On the policy side, the system serving immigrants with English language needs is highly fragmented. There is a patchwork of services provided by a variety of departments, including the Department of Education, the Department of Labor, along with the Department of Health and Human Services, along with various state initiatives. Little guidance is provided by the federal government on how ELLs should be served, or how program structures and programs funded by different federal departments might be integrated (Chisman, Wrigley, & Ewen 1993; Wrigley, Richter, Martinson, Kubo, & Strawn, 2003). On the state level, the guidance given by the federal government and the states tends to ignore regional differences such as the lack of appropriate infrastructure in the new immigrant states like North Carolina and Georgia, and the need for new models that take into account the strictly bilingual nature of many linguistically isolated areas where Spanish is now the *lingua franca* of everyday communication, including communication in many workplaces.

This chapter makes the case that the current system does a fine job serving as a "life boat" for newcomers who need English skills to go shopping, talk about family, understand our currency, or make a doctor's appointment. Although this emphasis meets the needs of beginning language learners and new entrants to the country, it tends to fall short of meeting the goals of those who no longer need survival English to help them function day-to-day. A largely generalized curriculum emphasizing a broad set of life skills (including general pre-employment skills and civic activities) is not sufficiently focused on the specific demands of different contexts for English learning to make a significant difference in the lives of participants. Given the broad spectrum of backgrounds and needs among the immigrant population, a system that is more highly differentiated, although perhaps more expensive in the short run, (classes are likely to be smaller), is a worthwhile investment.

The chapter starts by providing an overview of recent demographics and the implications for communities as well as for adult literacy programs and then highlights the diverse linguistic, cultural, and educational backgrounds of adult immigrants, along with the differences in status that exist among legal immigrants, refugees, and students without legal papers. It then focuses on two current policy challenges: the recent changes in citizenship testing, and the relationships between language services and workforce development. Policy recommendations conclude the chapter.

DEFINING THE NEED—DEMOGRAPHICS OF ADULT ESL

More people came to the United States in the 1990s than in any other decade in the nation's history. As a result, all across the country, agencies and schools serving adult learners are seeing more and more language minorities come to their doors. Currently, among the 264.4 million people ages 5 and over who live in the United States, 47 million (18%) speak a language other than English at home, a number that has doubled over the last 20 years (Schmidley, 2001). Many of these families are recent arrivals, and a significant number are settling in different states than did earlier immigrants. Both legal and silent immigration are likely to continue across the United States as many new immigrants and refugees enter the country, either to live on their own or to join families already in the United States. We can expect many of these newcomers to have very low levels of literacy in the native language (Fix, Passel, & Sucher, 2003; Wrigley et al., 2003). Given these changes, providing services for new entrants constitutes a major challenge for programs which, in the past, could assume that learners had sufficient reading skills in their native language to make an easy transition from literacy in the first language to English literacy while developing their oral English skills.

Diverse Education Levels

Adult ESL learners have a much wider range of educational backgrounds than do ABE (Adult Basic Education) students who, as a rule, share the common characteristic of not having a high school diploma. In fact, educational backgrounds among all foreign-born individuals show a bimodal distribution: one third lack a high school education, a proportion twice as large as among native born adults. Educational needs are even greater for immigrants from Mexico where two thirds have not completed high school (Wrigley et al., 2003). At the same time, however, the immigrant population has the same proportion of educated adults as their native-born counterparts; roughly one quarter of the foreign-born have a bachelor's degree or higher (Schmidley, 2001). This disparity in education levels makes it clear that a one size fits all system is not likely to be the most effective or the most efficient way to advance skills. Rather, we must conceive of a system that takes educational backgrounds into account and provides different kinds of services for professionals new to English but with higher levels of education than for those who not only need English but who look to adult education as a way to fill educational gaps and build their literacy skills.

A National Issue with Local Impact

Although providing quality educational services to adults who speak a language other than English is concern in all U.S. states, the impact of immigration on ABE and ESL services varies by region. According to the 2000 Census report on language use, more than one quarter of the population in seven states spoke a language other than English at home. California has the largest percentage (39%), followed by New Mexico (37%), and Texas (31%), Arizona and New Jersey (each had about 26%). Cities are differentially affected as well. For example, the metropolitan areas of Los Angeles and New York City are home to one third of all immigrants in the United States (Schmidley, 2001). In these cities, large majorities, from two thirds to three quarters of immigrant adults report not speaking English well (Capps et al., 2002). This then is the very population likely to come for services under the ABE system and other programs funded under the Workforce Investment Act.

Increasingly, immigrants settle in areas that are not in the traditional immigrant states. Within the last 10 years, 40% of all immigrants who have come to the United States have settled in Iowa, Georgia, Kentucky, and North Carolina, for example. Other states, like Arkansas and Idaho, have seen their immigrant populations rise by over 150% within that time, a trend that presents new challenges for communities and schools (Passel & Zimmerman, 2001). To offset the burden on local districts, state ABE directors from the key immigration states have started to advocate for Federal Impact Aid Funds to mitigate the cost of serving adult ESL students.

Lacking the history, and thus infrastructure to serve immigrants, these new immigrant states and their educational systems are not always well-prepared to assist newcomers in their quest to enter and advance in the workforce and gain financial stability. Federal funding and technical assistance is needed to help them build a system that can meet the language and job development needs of immigrants and of the local employers who need skilled workers. Such a system should include infrastructure that can train teachers and provide resources to implement effective instructional models and structures, as well as disseminate research which can be linked to practice. These new immigrant states will also need help setting up collaborations between educational entities such as adult schools or community colleges, immigrant assistance groups that provide support services, job training providers, and employers. Although such partnerships are mandated under the Workforce Investment Act, in reality there is very little collaboration between the One Stop Centers providing services under Title I of the Workforce Investment Act and adult literacy providers funded under Title II of the Workforce Investment Act. (Strawn & Martinson, 2002; Wrigley et al., 2003). The challenge lies in building different kinds of collaborations in which adult education providers play a key role in service provision for immigrants, and can draw monies from different funding sources such as the Department of Labor, which funds training for low skilled immigrant workers, and the Department of Health and Human Services, which funds welfare to work services, as well as language and employment services for refugees.

Language Distribution

The countries of origin and languages spoken at home of non-native speakers help shape the nature of ESL literacy services that a community provides. For example, throughout the adult ESL system, Spanish speakers predominate, reflecting the overall immigrant population that shows 43% of immigrants coming from Spanish speaking countries, the vast majority from Mexico. According to the 2000 Census, 19,594,395 people in the United States are Spanish speakers and half of these report speaking English less than very well, making up a significant group of adults and families who could benefit from language and literacy services. The West and the South combined had about 3 times the number of Spanish speakers (21 million) as the Northeast and Midwest combined (7.1 million). This pattern highlights the need for services that reflect the bilingual, bicultural nature of life and work that exist in many of the traditional receiving communities for immigrants from Puerto Rico, Mexico, and other parts of Central America[5].

---

[5] Adult language learners from South America and Spain tend to have much higher levels of education and are generally not a target group for ABE/ESL

Speakers of languages associated with Asia and the Pacific Islands make up the second largest language group but constitute a much smaller percentage (26%) of the immigrant population. Among the latter, Chinese is the most common language spoken at home, with a range of other languages taking second place. In areas where there is a high proportion of one Asian language group, bilingual staff, particularly counselors and outreach workers, may be necessary to provide meaningful access and advisement along with other resources that are available in both English and the language of the community.

Differences in Immigration Status

A wide range of language and literacy skills is not the only characteristic that sets immigrants apart from their U.S.-born counterparts in adult literacy education. Differences in immigration status play a significant role as well, both in terms of educational needs and in access to services. The most significant features to consider deal with legal immigration, refugee status, U.S.-born status, and denial of access to federally funded educational programs.

Lawful Immigrants

By far the largest group of ESL learners was born in another country and are classified by the U.S. Citizenship and Immigration Service (USCIS) as "immigrants," meaning "legal immigrants," although immigrant households often include individuals without legal status. In some families, only the children are legal immigrants, a status they acquired by being born in the United States, whereas the rest of the family, including the parents, lack authorization to live, work, or study in the United States. The vast majority of students served in adult ESL programs are lawful, sometimes called legal immigrants.

Refugees

The category of legal immigrants includes a subcategory of refugees who came to the United States under special circumstances. Typically they have suffered hardships related to persecution, civil strife, and war. Refugees are the only group whose arrival and education is guided by explicit policies which guarantee assistance, including English language education linked to employment, resettlement assistance, and mental health counseling. Although they have been the smallest group of immigrants since the end of the Vietnam War, refugees are a population of special concern because of the hardships they have endured, the gap between their old way of life and U.S. circumstances, their relative poverty, and their need for English and cultural services. In fact, only 8% of refugees reported speaking English well at the time of their arrival in the United States. Although thousands of refugees are languishing in overseas camps waiting to be resettled, entry into the United States has become far more difficult since the attacks on the United States in September 2001. The U.S. Committee on Refugees reports that although 70,000 refugees were authorized to come to the United States in fiscal year 2002, only about 50,000 were admitted by the U.S. State Department. Once restrictions are eased, adult ESL programs can expect thousands more to enter classes, because participation in a formal English language program with a focus on employment preparation is mandatory for refugees to receive cash assistance as part of their resettlement.

Their numbers are small, but refugees deserve special consideration as part of the adult ESL system, not only because the United States has made a promise to shelter and educate them, but because of the hardships they have endured. A significant percentage of refugees have experienced trauma related to war or civil strife. Most refugees are women and many face serious emotional challenges as they seek to adjust to U.S. society (Isserlis, 2001). Uprooted and forced to leave family behind, they now must negotiate a new culture, find work, and often switch from living in a rural area dependent on agriculture, to an industrialized and technology-driven society. Often with little school experience, these refugees must struggle with a strange language while finding their way in a country that is different in almost every way from what they knew back home. Two groups of refugees illustrate these points. The Hmong, displaced as a result of the Vietnam War, were expected to enter the United States in 2004 and 2005 after having lived in Thailand as refugees for over 20 years. In addition, since 2003, 12, 007 Somali Bantu have been resettled in the U.S. (The Refugee Council USA, 2006). For these refugee families, ESL literacy classes are the entry point into U.S. civic life that allows them to gain cultural competence, and to acquire the English they need to be successful in American society. For many, these classes are also the first and sometimes the only chance to learn to read and write.

Native Born

Although most ESL program participants are foreign-born, a small portion of students were born in the United States, but have not acquired full proficiency in English. Both the oral language and writing of these students may show traces of non-native language interference, and learners may still have difficulties creating the kind of writing expected in college. This group includes young people who did not complete high school. Their profiles in many ways are similar to those of ABE students who communicate quite well but speak and write a nonstandard variation of English. It also includes residents of Puerto Rico, who grew up speaking Spanish, and residents of Guam, who may speak Chamorro, Palauan, or Tagalog as a first language. English learners in this group also include speakers of native American languages. In some areas in Alaska (Bethel, for example), 66% of the population speak a language other than English and

97% of those speak a native North American language. A similar situation exists in the Navajo Indian reservation, spanning several counties throughout Arizona, New Mexico, and Utah. Currently, the needs of U.S.-born adults who are not fully English proficient don't receive a great deal of attention in the adult ESL literacy field. However, some community colleges, particularly in California and Texas, are paying attention to a group of students with similar needs, known as Generation 1.5 (see Crandall & Sheppard, 2004; Thonus, 2003). These students may have been born in the United States, or may have come to the United States as young children, and have grown up in households where a language other than English is spoken. Generation 1.5 students share characteristics of both first- and second-generation immigrants. They fit neither the traditional profile of academically underprepared literacy students who grew up speaking English, nor that of foreign-born immigrant students who are trying to acquire English language skills. The insights gained by college teachers working with these students might help inform adult literacy programs as to the kind of support that ESL learners who have transitioned to ABE or GED (General Educational Development) might need.

Undocumented Immigrants

Under the Workforce Investment Act, which governs services for both ABE and adult ESL, only students with legal status in the United States may be served in federally funded programs. However, exceptions are common as local districts find ways to circumvent federal legislation. As a result, quite a few students without legal documentation find their way into adult ESL programs. Not surprisingly, serving unauthorized immigrants with federal monies is a highly contentious issue in adult ESL. In many areas with high proportions of families without legal status, programs struggle to serve these students in ways that fall within the law, but at the same time do not turn the program into an enforcement arm of the Homeland Security Office. Strategies for straddling the issue include asking students for official identity numbers, recording whatever number is given in the official database, and then simply notifying the student that he or she may have made a mistake if a number given is already in the system. Most programs do not ask for official documentation such as green cards or Social Security numbers because these kinds of documentation are not required for registration in kindergarten through 12th-grade (K-12) schools. Other programs, committed to providing services to all adults who need ESL and literacy, go one step further. When an adult student signs up for classes, staff members simply assign an available identification number, often generated by computer. All in all, there is a great deal of "fudging" within the system to provide services to all who need and want them. Some advocacy groups point out that denying services based on legal status often means allowing some family members to participate in English classes while denying access to others. The practice seems especially harsh in cases where parents with U.S.-born children may not participate in federally funded family literacy programs although their children attend publicly funded schools, and they and their children would greatly benefit from these services.

It is not necessarily a given that immigrants without legal status will forever be denied educational services funded by the federal government. Although the Immigration Control and Reform Act is clear in its intent to deny federally funded ABE and ESL services to undocumented adults, the act could be amended, particularly at a time when "amnesty" for those living in the United States without official documentation is being discussed in Washington. Although full amnesty may be a long way away, advocacy efforts geared toward regularizing the status of "illegals" in adult ESL classes certainly deserves consideration in the meantime. Amendment of the law would allow both adult English learners and the programs that serve them to come out of the shadows. Because the U.S. Supreme Court has already given the right to an education to undocumented children (Plyler v. Doe, 1982), similar arguments can be made to allow parents and other adults to learn English and increase their literacy skills. From a broader perspective, the more adults that are educated and literate, the more that individuals, families, and societies will benefit. If we do indeed want to move toward a quality education system for adult immigrants who still struggle with English, the need to serve individuals who lack proper documentation will need to be broached.

Linguistically Isolated and Multilingual Environments

Demographics, educational backgrounds, and immigrant status are only some of the factors that shape curriculum and instruction for immigrants. The language environment in which students live and study plays an important role as well. Various regions and cities within the United States differ significantly in the composition of their population, and (among other individual factors) the language mix within a particular area greatly influences how much opportunity immigrants have to hear English and use English. Local demographics, in particular, tend to determine the composition of a class and sometimes of an entire program. This has significant implications for curriculum and instruction. For example, in El Paso, TX, in East Harlem, NY, and in the *barrios* of Los Angeles and Chicago, classes are made up almost exclusively of students who share a single language background–Spanish. In the West, the Spanish language group may also include speakers of Maya who struggle with Spanish as a second language as well as with English. In these areas, Spanish is invariably used by teachers and students, particularly in beginning ESL classes, where translation is often the quickest and surest way to ensure directions and tasks are understood. Classes composed of a single language group are also common in various Chinatowns across the United States and are found in other ethnic communities, such as Somali neighborhoods in Seattle, Haitian-Creole in Boston, or Hmong neighborhoods in Fresno and Minneapolis/St.Paul.

Serving students in communities where one language predominates in classes as well as in the neighborhood presents a special challenge to programs. To help immigrants become bilingual and bicultural, teachers must find ways to acknowledge the monolingual nature of day-to-day interactions while providing opportunities for students to develop their English and not depend on continuous translation in class. Unlike their K-12 counterparts, few adult ESL teachers have been trained in how to implement an approach that takes into account bilingual realities. If these students are to be served well, curriculum, instruction, and staff development need to take on the challenge of helping them develop their English skills in ways that offer maximum exposure to and use of English. To succeed in that endeavor, models that look at effective ways of teaching English as a foreign (rather than a second) language may provide some insights because teachers overseas also struggle with using the native language just enough to facilitate learning but not so much to create overdependence on translation.

Language diversity looks quite different in cities such as Seattle, Brooklyn, or Las Vegas, where multiple language groups are learning English together. Because immigrants from different countries live, work, and study together there, English tends to be the *lingua franca,* and there are many more occasions inside and outside of class that demand the use of English. Because they cannot rely on the home language outside a small neighborhood, students in these situations are used to hearing different variations of English and tend to be much less hesitant to use imperfect English to get their point across or accomplish a task. For programs that serve this group, one of the ongoing challenges is to encourage students to keep learning and refining their English so that their language does not become "fossilized"–as is the case when a student's "interlanguage" (English influenced by the native language) becomes permanent and errors persist although fluency may continue to develop. As a result of fossilization, nonstandard language forms become fixed, and interlanguage stabilizes at a point well short of native speaker proficiency. If adults are to be prepared for employment or academic work where grammatical accuracy matters, programs serving adult immigrants will need to find an appropriate place for instruction that addresses the special needs of those who speak English quite fluently but nevertheless make errors that are distinctive from those within a larger population focused on communicative competence.

SYSTEMS AND PROGRAM CHALLENGES

In recent years, several major developments have challenged the adult ESL programs to think beyond typical survival English instruction, and respond to new opportunities, while confronting policy that seems shortsighted or ill conceived.

These opportunities and challenges come in the form of the fairly recent inclusion of EL (English literacy) Civics to the federally funded ESL program, the prospect of a new test for citizenship that could adversely effect low literate immigrants, and the need to respond to the needs of low literate immigrants who are in the workforce and require both English language services and skills training as well.

Civics Education

Adult ESL encompasses a broad charge that includes not only language teaching but services related to the civic integration of newcomers to the United States. As such, adult ESL is influenced by federal policies that determine what kind of service can be provided to whom and what should be the nature of these services. At times, these federal policies are shortsighted and regulations contradictory and not necessarily in the best interest of the students and their families. If we truly want to have a quality system of education, it becomes important not only to implement policy in the best possible way but also to challenge policies that appear unreasonable or unfair. Recent discussions in Congress focused on what it should take for immigrants to become naturalized citizens is a case in point.

The notion of an adult education system that prepares immigrants for community engagement and citizenship is not new and a number of countries offer classes designed to help newcomers acculturate, integrate, and if they wish to do so, naturalize and become citizens. In the United States, funding specifically designated for civics and citizenship has been available since 1999, when the federal government, on urging of the Congressional Hispanic Caucus, created a separate funding stream, called EL Civics, designed specifically for those born in another country who speak no or little English. According to the federal regulations, EL Civics is an education program that emphasizes contextual instruction on the rights and responsibilities of citizenship, naturalization procedures, civic participation, and U.S. history and government to help students acquire the skills and knowledge to become active and informed parents, workers and community members. (Federal Register, 1999)

The EL Civics funding stream and its requirements challenge programs to develop classes for immigrants and refugees who either plan to become citizens or simply need English to communicate with others, function in daily life, or gain a better sense of how the United States works. Teachers in EL Civics classes are expected to develop or deliver curriculum that connect immigrants and refugees with the wider community, help them understand local services, and engage them in dialogue around community issues. There is also an expectation that programs teach the civic values on which the United States is built: tolerance for diversity, democracy, freedom of expression, and a legal system that promises due process. Teaching might also include civic rights and responsibilities, including the right to challenge the system and advocate for change. Although it seems extremely worthwhile for ESL programs to offer a window to understanding "what it means to be American," civic values and concepts are difficult to teach, particularly for ESL instructors, whose training and education generally do not include the teaching of subjects related to immigrant integration. The challenge is particularly great for programs serving students who understand only minimal English and do not have a deep knowledge of the principles and values associated with living in a Western democracy.

The Redesign of the U.S. Citizenship Test

Because funding for EL Civics encompasses both the teaching of civics and the knowledge and skills associated with naturalization, ESL programs must grapple with the dual nature of the program: on the one hand, they are expected to increase the civic engagement of immigrants and refugees (whether or not they are citizens), on the other, they are expected to prepare students who are interested in naturalization to pass the federally mandated national citizenship exam. Although the civics and literacy component is conceptualized fairly broadly and provides quite a bit of leeway in terms of educational outcomes--it may include life skills related to commerce, transportation, or health related issues--preparation for citizenship is rather specific and is driven by the requirements of the United States Office of Immigration and Citizenship Services (USCIS, formerly known as the Immigration and Naturalization Service). Because many students who plan to become citizens look to adult ESL programs to teach them the skills required to pass the exam, programs are now faced with additional challenges that go beyond the teaching of communication, grammar, pronunciation, and life skills--the mainstay of most regular ESL programs.

Preparing adult ESL students for naturalization is made particularly difficult by the fact that most students coming to classes have language skills well below the level needed to pass the citizenship test (Fix et al., 2003), and these conditions are not likely to change quickly. As is true for the adult population of immigrants and refugees overall, the profile of those eligible for naturalization is changing, creating additional challenges for programs and classrooms. Currently 7.5 million foreign-born immigrants are eligible to naturalize with 2 million additional legal immigrants likely to become eligible (Fix et al., 2003). When compared with groups who have already become citizens, individuals in the newly eligible group, most of whom are from Mexico, have more limited English skills and have lower educational levels. Among the 8 million adults in this category, many will not be able to pass the citizenship test because of the lack of English proficiency. These demographics highlight the need for programs to establish services for low literate Spanish speaking applicants who have few years of education in their home countries, minimal literacy in the native language, and who may not have the academic preparation that would help them understand complex concepts and sophisticated vocabulary that appear in most citizenship textbooks, including those being developed by USCIS.

In the next few years, adult educators will be directly confronted with policy in action. Citizenship preparation is likely to be a contentious issue, as the Office of Citizenship and Immigration moves toward redesigning the naturalization test in ways that may put additional burdens on non-English speaking immigrants. USCIS, in response to Congress's desire to have a test that is both more fair and more meaningful, is planning to make several changes to the test that have the potential of making it more demanding both linguistically and cognitively. Proposed changes relate to the two basic requirements in the immigration act: to show an understanding of the fundamentals of U.S. history and government, and to speak and respond to ordinary English.

The implications of the proposed changes are far-reaching. Whereas in the past, citizenship teachers could focus on strategies for memorizing and recalling key information from a set of predetermined questions, they may now be confronted with the task of helping students gain deeper knowledge of U.S. history content, learn difficult and uncommon vocabulary related to U.S. government structures, and become familiar with complex concepts such as the separation of church and state. Language and literacy skills that could be required may be assessed in new and more difficult ways as well.

The test currently in place assesses the language requirements for citizenship through a one-on-one interview in which the examiner may ask applicants about their families or their work histories. For the most part, the interviewer tries to gauge English proficiency by engaging the person in a conversation that revolves around topics with which individuals are likely to be familiar. Under the proposed model, applicants no longer would hold a conversation on everyday topics but would be asked to describe one or more pictures instead–orally and in writing. Clearly, this type of task requires a different kind of English (descriptive and narrative, rather than interactive). Early USCIS proposals also indicated that portions of the exam may be administered via computer. If the English portion of the exam changes from an assessment administered person to person and focusing on everyday topics to a pencil and paper or technology-mediated test, applicants will need to develop a set of skills different from those required in the past and will look to adult ESL programs for help. If the adult education system is to be responsive to emergent needs, pedagogies will be needed that focus on the acquisition of content knowledge and test-taking skills.

The debate over the proposed changes in the citizenship test highlights another feature of quality programs for immigrants and refugees: the motivation to keep current on proposed legislation and advocate for changes in policies that are not educationally sound or potentially discriminate against certain groups. Advocating for sound policies and providing students with quality education geared toward naturalization deserves special consideration because the citizenship test carries serious consequences. The stakes are high. Passing the test confers special advantages tied to access to public benefits, the right to vote and serve on a jury, and the opportunity to sponsor family members who will be eligible to enter the United States and live here legally. It also allows immigrants to obtain citizenship for children born abroad. Conversely, failing the test means being potentially subject to deportation, not being able to live overseas for extended periods of time, and limited political participation. If we are to build a quality education system, monitoring, and responding to policies that affect the lives of millions of immigrants and refugees, must be in integral part of our mission.

Community-based organizations, associations of ESL teachers (TESL), and immigrant rights groups have followed the proposed changes closely and have submitted strongly worded commentary regarding both the content and the format of the new test. The Illinois Coalition of Immigrant Rights, for example, has voiced its concerns that the proposed citizenship test will discriminate against applicants with limited formal education if one-on-one conversations focused on everyday conversational skills are replaced by more academic content (da Mota, 2003). The board of TESL, the International Organization for those Teaching English to Speakers of Other Languages, had expressed concerns as well and recommends that both the test and the proposed study guide focus on "practical civics knowledge" related to civic participation, rather than on academic content related to history and government. The organization is so concerned about both the content and the potential impact of the proposed redesign, that it established a special committee in 2005 to work on citizenship issues. The strongest critique of the test comes from the National Research Council of the National Academies, which, in its Letter Report (December 2004), questioned the scientific basis for the redesign of the test (now under development) and suggested that the process for developing a citizenship test be systematic rather than ad hoc, based on established principles of test development (which were largely ignored in the USCIS design), and transparent to the public. The Research Council also strongly recommended that sufficient classes and appropriate materials be made available, stressing the importance of providing immigrants with the "opportunity to learn" a key principle in high stakes testing.

Workforce Education

The needs of ELLs who are either working or looking for work deserve special consideration. This is true in terms of both educational policy and program design. English for work, either to find a job, succeed in a job, or advance beyond current employment, is consistently named the number one reason why immigrants attend ESL classes. Yet, for the most part, most ESL programs focus on teaching general life survival skills such as shopping, accessing community services, health, or family. Although topics related to work, such as filling out an application or answering questions in an interview, may be included, such generalized skills may not be sufficient to help immigrants gain access to jobs that pay a living wage. The following section highlights the economic situation of immigrants in the workforce and suggests a new model that integrates language teaching and occupational skills training so that adults with limited English skills can attain the knowledge, skills, and strategies needed for the kind of employment that helps families move out of poverty.

How well adult education helps prepare undereducated adults for jobs that pay a living wage is of utmost concern to both individuals and communities and may be one of the indicators of a quality system. In terms of immigration, statistics tell the story: Immigrants supplied half of the workforce growth in 1990 and will account for all of the net growth over the next 20 years (Wrigley, Chisman, & Ewen, 1993). However, immigrants will only be able to fill skilled jobs if they have access to both skills training and language education. Adult ESL can play a significant role in linking immigrants to employment and in helping them move out of poverty because English fluency is directly linked to both employment opportunities and to economic independence. For example, a 1999 report on refugees in the United States found that only 26% of those who did not speak English were employed, compared with 77% of those who spoke English well or fluently (Office of Refugee Resettlement, 1999). In addition, English fluency increases immigrants' earnings by 17%, far more than increases attributed to additional years of work experience (Fremstad, 2003).

Why should the adult ESL system be concerned with teaching the kinds of English that prepare students for jobs? Adult education does not exist in isolation and can often be most effective if it is tied to other efforts to improve the lives of learners (Auerbach, 2004; Freire, 1972). In the case of immigrants, language and literacy learning tied to employment prospects offers such an opportunity. Research has shown that immigrants constitute a high percentage of the "working poor" and are likely to remain so unless the system makes a full out effort to provide language and literacy skills that speak to workforce needs (Wrigley et al., 2003). Currently, immigrants have higher rates of employment than their U.S.-born counterparts, but at the same time, they earn lower wages than native-born workers. As a result, over 20% of immigrant families live below the poverty rate, a proportion twice as high as that of the native-born population (Wrigley et al., 2003). That means that many of the clients who come to ESL programs need support services to help them deal with the issues and concerns associated with poverty: limited access to quality child care, transportation, health care services, and advice on how to negotiate the social service system. Comprehensive service models that integrate language and literacy education with skills training and are offered within a larger system of social services show a great deal of promise in addressing multiple needs (Cave, Bos, Doolittle, & Toussaint, 1993).

To advance in the labor market, individuals with limited English skills clearly need both to improve their English language abilities and acquire job-specific skills. Research shows that the most effective programs for moving low-income individuals into work combine job training with basic skills instruction or provide a mix of services, including job search, education, and job training (Strawn & Martinson, 2002). These programs produced larger and longer-lasting effects on employment and earnings than programs in which the primary program activity was job search or basic education.

To make this model work for immigrants with limited English, language instruction will need to be tied to training in particular occupations and should incorporate key instructional elements, including general workplace communication skills, job-specific language needed for training, certification and testing, and soft skills to help navigate U.S. workplace culture.

Integrated approaches—models that combine language education with skills training—show a great deal of promise for immigrants and refugees. They offer a number of potential benefits: (a) participants gain important job skills while developing the communication skills needed to obtain jobs, (b) the language and cultural skills needed for job search and job retention are more easily integrated into training, (c) learning is both focused and contextualized and therefore more easily absorbed by participants who have little experience with formal schooling, and (d) motivation to learn remains high as participants see a clear end goal (Cave et al, 1993; Orr et al, 1996; Strawn & Martinson, 2002, Wrigley et al., 2003).

In some areas of the United States—for example along the U.S.-Mexico border and in large ethnic enclaves in Chicago or Los Angeles—English proficiency is not necessarily a requirement for entry-level jobs. This is particularly true for jobs in the ethnic economy where immigrants work for other immigrants, although both advancement and lateral movement are often severely limited in these circumstances. In communities where two languages are commonly spoken, some service providers have started delivering job skills training in the native language concurrently with ESL classes. This model, sometimes referred to as bilingual-vocational training, has distinct advantages for adults who find learning English difficult. Older adults may benefit the most—particularly displaced workers who possess only marginal literacy in the native language and speak little English, in spite of having worked for many years before job loss occurred (Wrigley & Powrie, 2003). Continued access to ESL services after the completion of the bilingual training program is important, however, to ensure that limited English skills do not hurt participants' prospects later on when English is required for advancement.

Although the One Stop System in the United States was meant to build such a model, it has not been effective for those most in need: individuals who speak little English, have no levels of literacy, and need access not just to ESL but to technical programs that offer the kinds of knowledge and skills that translate into jobs likely to move a family out of poverty (Wrigley & Powrie, 2003). As manufacturing jobs move overseas, adults with low levels of skills, immigrants and U.S.-born, run the danger of being ghettoized in service jobs unless technical training, in areas such as health care, construction, and transportation, is made available.

Because the integration of adult ESL and job training is both a hot issue and a relatively new notion for both policymakers and educational providers, studies into "what works" in this area are very much needed. The educational community could greatly benefit from research and development efforts that investigate what it takes to successfully combine English instruction, literacy education, and job training for a diverse population group.

CONCLUSION

Given the large numbers and diverse needs of immigrants in general, and the large numbers of adults seeking language services, the United States would be well served by a language policy that spans federal departments (e.g., Departments of Labor, Education, and Health and Human Services), and specifically addresses the needs of adult immigrants and refugees. The nation would benefit from a quality system of educational services that looks at adult ESL as part of a comprehensive effort toward immigrant integration. Such a system could help states and programs address a number of challenges, including those discussed here. These include creating an infrastructure for newcomer services in new immigrant states, and providing differentiated services for various subgroups of immigrants and refugees. It also means monitoring federal policies and advocating for fair assessments, especially in areas such as naturalization where people's futures are at stake. Finally, a quality system should be concerned with collaboration among federally funded services, with a special emphasis on programmatic innovations such as integrated language and job skills training where research has shown significant success.

As immigration to the United States is ever-increasing, demand for English language services is likely to remain high. Adult ESL can play a critical role in enhancing the opportunities of those who have left their countries to seek new lives, as well as those who have been uprooted by war or civil strife. A well thought out, well articulated adult ESL system that takes into account different subgroups and their goals, as well as different contexts for language learning, can make an important contribution not only to the adults who seek services but also to the social good and the well-being of our communities.

REFERENCES

Auerbach, E. (2004). Connecting the local and the global: A pedagogy of not literacy. In J. Anderson, M. Kendrick, T. Rogers, & S. Smythe (Eds.), *Portraits of literacy across families, communities, and schools: Intersections and tensions* (pp. 363-379). Mahwah, NJ: Lawrence Erlbaum Associates, Inc.

Cave, G., Bos, H., Doolittle, F., & Toussaint, C. (1993). *JobStart: Final report on a program for school drop-outs.* New York: Manpower Demonstration Research Corporation.

Capps, R., Ku, L., Fix, M., Furgiuele, C., Passel, J., Ramchand, R., et al. (2002). *How are immigrants faring after welfare reform? Preliminary evidence from Los Angeles and New York City - Final Report.* Washington, DC: Urban Institute.

Chisman, F., Wrigley, H., & Ewen, D. (1993). *ESL and the American dream: Report on an investigation of English as a second language service for adults.* Washington, DC: Southport Institute for Policy Analysis. (ERIC Document Reproduction Service No. ED 373 585)

Crandall, J., & Sheppard, K. (2004). *Adult ESL and the community college* (Working Paper 7, CAAL Community College Series). New York: Council for Advancement of Adult Literacy.

da Mota, L. (2003). *Denying the dream: How the proposed changes to the US naturalization test would prevent immigrants from becoming citizens.* Chicago: Illinois Coalition for Immigrant and Refugee Rights.

Federal Register: November 17, 1999, Volume 64, Number 221 (pp. 62919–62941). U.S. Government Printing Office.

Fix, M., Passel, J., & Sucher, K. (2003). *Trends in naturalization* (Brief No. 3, Immigrant Families and Workers: Facts and Perspectives). Washington, DC: Urban Institute.

Freire, P. (1972). *Pedagogy of the oppressed.* London: Penguin.

Fremstad, S. (2003). *Immigrants, persons with limited proficiency in English, and the TANF program: What do we know?* Washington, DC: Center on Budget and Policy Priorities.

Isserlis, J. (2001). *On the screen: Bringing women's barriers to literacy, learning, and employment to light.* Washington, DC: National Institute for Literacy.

National Research Council of the National Academies (2004). *Redesigning the U.S. naturalization tests: Letter report.* Washington, DC: The National Academies Press.

Office of Refugee Settlement. (1999). *Annual report to Congress, 1999.* Washington, DC: Department of Human Services.

Orr, L., Bloom, H., Bell, S., Doolittle, F., Lin, W, & Cave, G. (1996). *Does training for the disadvantaged work? Evidence from the national JTPA study.* Washington, DC: Urban Institute Press.

Passel, J., & Zimmermann, W. (2001). *Are immigrants leaving California? Settlement patterns of immigrants in the late 1990's.* Washington, DC: Urban Institute.

Plyler v. Doe (1982). Supreme Court 457 U.S. 202, Docket Number 80-1538.

Refugee Council USA (2005). Opening NGO statement, UNHCR annual tripartite consultations on resettlement. Retrieved July 27, 2006, from http://www.refugeecouncilusa.org/atc-2006ngostate20060622.pdf

Schmidley A. (2001, December). *Profile of the foreign-born population in the United States: 2000.* Washington, DC: U.S. Census Bureau, Current Population Reports, Series P23-206, U.S. Government Printing Office.

Strawn, J., & Martinson, K. (2002). *Built to last: Why skills matter for long-run success in welfare reform.* Washington, DC: Center for Law and Social Policy.

Thonus, T. (2003). Serving generation 1.5 learners in the university writing center. *TESL Journal, 12,* 17-24.

Wrigley, H. S., Chisman, F. P., & Ewen, D. T. (1993). *Sparks of excellence: Program realities and promising practices in adult ESL.* Washington, DC: The Southport Institute for Policy Analysis. (ERIC Document Reproduction Service No. ED 373 586).

Wrigley, H., & Powrie, J. (2003). *Meeting the challenge on the border: A report on language and literacy on the U.S. Mexico border.* Washington, DC: U.S. Department. of Labor

Wrigley, H., Richter, E., Martinson, K., Kubo, H., & Strawn, J. (2003). *Expanding employment prospects for adults with limited English skills.* Washington, DC: Center for Law and Social Policy, the National Institute for Literacy, and the National Adult Education Professional Development Consortium.

Chapter 13

Filling in the "Black Box" of Family Literacy: Implications of Research for Practice and Policy

Eunice N. Askov, Cathy Kassab, Elisabeth L. Grinder
Ladislaus M. Semali, Drucilla Weirauch, Eugenio Longoria Saenz, Barbara Van Horn
Goodling Institute for Research in Family Literacy
Institute for the Study of Adult Literacy
The Pennsylvania State University

Family literacy has been described as a "black box" because research-based exemplary practices for each component of family literacy do not, for the most part, exist (Askov, 2002). Family literacy programs are as varied as the communities in which they reside; thus no true model exists. However, most family literacy programs, funded by the William F. Goodling Even Start Act, have adopted a four-component model comprised of adult literacy (adult basic and secondary-level education, called ABE, or instruction for English language learners, called ESL), early childhood education (birth to age 8), parenting education, and structured interactive literacy education between parents and children (Elementary and Secondary Education Act, Title I, as reauthorized by the No Child Left Behind Act of 2001 [2002]). Although adult educators in family literacy are informed by the research in adult education, and early childhood education has been the most researched of the four components of family literacy, the remaining two components of family literacy–parenting education and parent-child interactive literacy (also known as Parent and Child Together or PACT time)–are the least investigated aspects of family literacy. Yet they provide the "value-added" of family literacy in an integrated four-component system of intergenerational programming because these two components provide learning opportunities to parents and children that go beyond the traditional adult education or early childhood education programs. The Goodling Institute for Research in Family Literacy at The Pennsylvania State University–in an effort to move beyond a "default" approach to instruction to a research-based best practices model for family literacy–is conducting research that can improve the quality of family literacy programs in all four components of family literacy.

This chapter, written by a team of faculty, staff, and students funded by the Goodling Institute, addresses the challenges of determining research-based best practices to improve the quality of programming for the family literacy components that involve adults. It also identifies research in progress which seems to hold promise for improving our understanding of practices in these areas. When possible, implications for practice are discussed.

The first challenge that is being investigated concerns best practices in the adult education component. Adult education is an important component in the family literacy model, recognizing that low-literate parents, as their child's "first teacher," must improve their own literacy competence to foster literacy in their children. However, participation in the adult education component, and in adult education programs in general, has been identified as a major research issue (Comings, Parrella, & Soricone, 1999) affecting the quality of services and long-term impact (Young, Fleischman, Fitzgerald, & Morgan 1994). What are the best practices in the adult education component that might increase participation?

The second challenge in determining best practices is identifying the literacy-related activities that occur during the Adult and Parenting Education components. Are programs offering appropriate and relevant instruction that keeps adults engaged in the family literacy program? What tools could be used to analyze instruction?

The third challenge concerns the parent-child interactive literacy time. Although this component is essential in developing the parents' abilities to foster their children's literacy development, little is known about what is actually occurring during this component of family literacy. What are the types of literacy-related activities that are occurring with the goal of developing an observational instrument for self-assessment?

The fourth challenge relates to determining best practices in family literacy more broadly, particularly studying effective practices that integrate the four components of family literacy and that tie family literacy programs to the local communities. Evaluation studies have indicated that the Family and Children Education (FACE) family literacy programs (funded by the Bureau of Indian Affairs for American Indian adults and children) are highly successful. What are the exemplary practices of these programs that may be transferred to other non-FACE programs to improve quality of programming?

ADULT EDUCATION PARTICIPATION AND IMPACT

The first challenge that we addressed is determining best practices that might increase retention in the adult education component. As reported elsewhere (Askov, Kassab, & Weirauch, 2005; Kassab, Askov, Weirauch, Grinder, & Van

Horn, 2004), we analyzed the database created by the Pennsylvania Statewide Evaluation of Family Literacy to study how various measures of persistence of participation related to outcomes of parents. We discovered that adults who participated with greater intensity in the adult education component had more positive outcomes in terms of standardized test scores. This study led us to inquire about best practices that might increase participation in the adult education component. In other words, what are some key learner characteristics that lead to greater participation in the adult education component of family literacy programs? What impact does parental participation in adult education have on the achievement of both the adults and their children?

Using adult student data since the 1998-1999 program year, persistence in adult education was defined as two measures of intensity of instruction (whether the participant obtained at least 50 hr of adult education instruction during the most recent program year, and the average number of hours of participation per week in adult education since entering the program), as well as by duration (also using the average number of hours of participation per week). We also studied participation in parenting education. We included ABE and ESL women who participated in some adult education and parenting education during the 2001-2002 program year, and who were not missing data on any of the other variables included in the analyses (men were not included in the participation studies because few of them participate in family literacy programs in Pennsylvania). The multilevel modeling analyses were conducted using the Hierarchical Linear Modeling software. Two sets of analyses were conducted: with women who exited the program during the 2001-2002 program year, and with women who continued their participation into the next program year (that is, an exit date was not indicated). These two independent samples provided an opportunity to verify results that are similar in the two samples, and to critically examine those results that differ. A total of 167 women from 36 family literacy programs had pretest and posttest Tests of Adult Basic Education (TABE) reading data, 149 women from 33 programs had TABE mathematics pretest and posttest data, and 115 women from 11 programs had pretest and posttest Basic English Skills Test (BEST) total literacy scores.

The results from these analyses indicate that participating in the adult education component does result in better adult literacy skills, as measured by the TABE and BEST (Kassab et al., 2004). However, the results also indicate that gains are greater if instruction is more intense. Total amount of instruction in adult education was not related to posttest scores when intensity of instruction was controlled. In addition, ABE women who continued their participation to the next program year performed better on the posttest when they participated in the program for a shorter period of time, with the negative effect growing smaller over time. In contrast, continuing ESL women performed better on the BEST the longer they participated in the program, although the positive impact grew smaller over time. Although the number of parenting education hours was not related to TABE posttest scores, it was related to BEST literacy skills scores, but only among ESL women who were continuing their participation to the next program year. The direction of the effect was unexpected, however, because the amount of parenting education was negatively related to BEST total literacy scores.

The results from these analyses of the statewide evaluation data of family literacy programs indicate that adult learners who accumulate between 50 and 99 hr of adult education within a single 12-month period perform better on the TABE reading, whereas at least 75 hr are needed to perform better on the TABE mathematics posttest. At least 50 hr of adult education instruction appear to be needed for ESL participants before they perform better on the BEST test, especially for those who are continuing their participation to the next program year. Intensity of instruction was consistently more important than total number of hours accumulated in adult education. This implies that practitioners should focus on strategies for increasing the participation of adults in adult education each week for both ABE and ESL learners.

We also wanted to learn about the persistence of subgroups of adult students within the database as a way to advise practitioners about which groups were most vulnerable in their efforts to persist (Askov, Kassab, Weirauch, & Van Horn, 2004; Askov, Kassab, & Weirauch, 2005). Results indicated that being employed hinders participation. Employed participants had fewer hours of instruction and participated with less intensity in the adult education component than unemployed participants. Employment status, however, was not related to time in the program (duration). Being a single-head of a household also appears to hinder participation. Furthermore, the number of actively participating children is negatively related to duration and intensity of participation in the adult education component. These results indicate that alternative approaches, such as distance education, are needed to increase the duration and intensity of participation for groups with competing demands, such as those who are employed or are single parents or who have a greater number of children in the program.

Women in ESL programs participated to a greater extent with both duration and intensity in family literacy programs than other students. Population size of the city or town in which participants lived on entry into the program was positively related to participation in the adult education component, in terms of both number of hours and intensity. This finding may indicate only that larger communities are able to offer more extensive service hours. Also, as the parents' age increased, they were more likely to participate intensely during a program year, and to a greater extent in the entire family literacy program.

Impact on Children

We were also interested in seeing if parental participation in adult education relates to children's outcomes in early childhood education because the model adopted by Even Start programs assumes that children will benefit academically from their parents' increased education. The next set of analyses concerned the impact of parents' participation in adult education, parenting education, and interactive literacy on gains between the pretest and posttest in children's developmental skills, as measured by the Child Observation Record, Learning Accomplishment Profile-Revised (LAP-R), and Early Learning Accomplishment Profile (ELAP). Results indicate that intensity of participation in adult education had a significant effect on most of the developmental skills measured by the ELAP for children less than 3 years of age (Askov, Grinder, & Kassab, 2005). For the LAP-R (for ages 3-6), there was a tendency for children in families with more interactive literacy hours to have higher posttest scores on the cognitive domain. The results indicate that family literacy program participation is associated with improvements in participating children's developmental skills. The study affirms the assumption that at-risk children will be more ready for school with parental participation in adult education.

ADULT AND PARENTING EDUCATION OBSERVATIONAL RESEARCH

Retaining families with sufficient duration and intensity of participation is critical to adults reaching their literacy goals as demonstrated by our and others' research. Our second research challenge is to develop a better understanding of the dynamics in the classroom that might maximize the impact of participation and encourage persistence.

An ongoing study involves analyzing the reading instruction in family literacy adult education. It is based on a typology of adult education classrooms developed by Beder and Medina (2001). Their study, *Classroom Dynamics in Adult Literacy Education,* was the first major study since 1975 to investigate classroom behavior in adult literacy classes. It looked at the content and structure of instruction, social processes in the classroom, and shaping factors (class composition, enrollment turbulence, funding fears). The implications of their findings for family literacy participants were based on the following question: "How do classroom dynamics in family literacy adult education classes impact participation and learning?" A study currently underway has adapted Beder and Medina's analytic categories to be used as an observation tool for studying family literacy classrooms.

Beder and Medina's (2001) typology, based on a study of 20 adult education classrooms, classifies classroom instruction into two basic types: Discrete Skills and Making-Meaning. Discrete Skills classrooms were subdivided into three categories: Decontextualized (teacher-led use of commercial materials), Contextualized (teacher-selected thematic materials relating to learners' lives), and Disjointed (unfocused content, goals, or objectives).

At issue is the definition and purpose of literacy. At one end of the spectrum it means acquiring factual knowledge to pass standardized tests; at the other end of the spectrum, it means developing, in addition to basic skills, "...critical thinking, problem-solving ability, oral as well as writing proficiency, creativity and an understanding of how society works..." (Beder & Medina, 2001, p. iii). Beder and Medina's (2001) typology provided a valuable theoretical framework on which to build an observation instrument of adult and parenting education classes in family literacy programs. The ultimate purpose of using the observation tool is to be able to categorize types of family literacy adult classes as a way to compare persistence results among a range of classroom styles, and to explore the educational outcomes (in terms of educational gains and rate of participation) of different types of instruction. Development of this observational tool will assist family literacy providers in evaluating the types and qualities of classroom instruction with the intent of making instruction more meaningful to the adult students, and hopefully maximizing their participation and their ability to meet academic and family goals.

PARENT-CHILD INTERACTIVE LITERACY

The third challenge in our research involves the parent-child interactive literacy component of family literacy. This component is considered the "heart and soul" of family literacy programs because it provides a unique opportunity for parents and children to learn and play together, rather than individually. While participating in this component, parents can apply to themselves and their children, under teacher supervision and guidance, the knowledge they have gained in other components, especially parenting education. Parents are thus supported in their efforts to make positive changes in their lives and in the lives of their children.

Although federal legislation states that Even Start programs must "use instructional programs based on scientifically-based reading research for children and adults, to the extent such research is available" (U.S. Department of Education, 2003, p.21), interactive literacy time is difficult to define and describe because each family literacy program determines how to design and implement that component based on the population they serve. Because each program has local control, it is unclear what activities programs are conducting and how much the activities and curriculum are based on currently available research on language and literacy development of children.

As a first step in determining best practices in interactive literacy, a research study was conducted which examined what occurs during the process of planning and implementing this component in family literacy programs across Pennsylvania (Grinder, Longoria Saenz, Askov, & Aldemir, 2005). In particular, the study focused on the extent to which language and literacy development is explicitly or implicitly taught during this time. To determine how programs administer it and what actually occurs during interactive literacy time, a qualitative study was conducted in 24 sites from 19 of the 73 family literacy programs in Pennsylvania. Data were derived from individual phone interviews of family literacy administrators and staff members who administered interactive literacy time, and a written description of the activities from the programs. The phone interview consisted of a series of questions that focused on defining, administering, and assessing interactive literacy. Data collected from program sites included a list of activities with explanations of how each activity is related to children's literacy development.

We found a number of interesting issues that programs face as they develop these activities for their families. First, when programs were asked to define the purpose of interactive literacy, the majority of comments from programs focused on enhancing parenting skills--especially as they relate to building bonds between parents and children, increasing parents' understanding of child development and how children learn, and modeling appropriate behavior for their children. Fewer comments were related to children's literacy and language development. In contrast, most programs were able to connect activities with areas of literacy development (e.g., vocabulary development, comprehension, print knowledge), especially with regard to activities designed for children who were 3 to 5 years of age.

A second finding from our analyses was that programs primarily used two sources of information to develop activities: (a) programmatic implementation issues, such as family's schedules, the structure and setting of where interactive literacy time occurs, and how it relates to what is occurring in the early childhood classroom; and (b) participant issues and characteristics. When planning for interactive literacy, staff members considered needs expressed by parents for themselves and for their children as well as assessments of children and families. The legislation, however, states that the primary focus of the parent-child interactive literacy component is to be on the development of literacy and language skills.

Another interesting point, derived from an interview probe, pertained to scientifically based reading research. Program staff were asked about the sources of information they use to develop interactive literacy activities. No one reported that they use scientifically based reading research as a resource. After being probed, a minority of practitioners stated that they actually did use scientifically based reading research as a resource, but were not specific regarding the information. In fact, many programs may be implementing scientifically based reading research, as defined by the National Reading Panel (National Institute of Child Health and Human Development, 2000), in interactive literacy activities, but they may not be using research in their planning. The data revealed that family literacy personnel need a clearer understanding of what scientifically based reading research is and how to apply it in their family literacy programs.

The fourth finding focused on who meets to plan and prepare for interactive literacy time in the family literacy programs. Most programs reported that they have a team of staff members that meets to discuss interactive literacy time, including an early childhood educator, parenting educator, adult educator, home visitor, and, sometimes, parents. On the other hand, some programs commented that staff members plan for this time independently. In these programs, there was little or no collaboration among the four family literacy components in planning for interactive literacy.

Collaborators were also mentioned as another group that met with family literacy staff to plan and prepare for interactive literacy (collaborators included programs such as Head Start, Family Centers, and elementary schools). Although a few programs mentioned collaborating with elementary school staff members, the majority of programs commented about the difficulty they had collaborating with schools to meet the needs of interactive literacy for school-age children. Elementary school teachers were viewed as being both too overwhelmed to become involved, and as not understanding family literacy programs. To family literacy staff members, school staff seemed reluctant to commit to a relationship with family literacy programs. Assuming the importance of this relationship, this suggests that family literacy programs need to work to increase elementary teachers' understanding of the value of family literacy programs to school-age children and to be seen as a support system for elementary school teachers and for participating children.

These findings from the interactive literacy research study reveal several challenges to quality that programs encounter as they implement this component of family literacy. Conceptually, this portion of the program should focus on language and literacy development of children through interactions with parents, but programs are defining interactive literacy as a time for parents to work on their parenting skills. As with scientifically based reading research, programs are integrating language and literacy into many of the activities, but they are not valuing their importance in the overall definition of interactive literacy. If programs had a universal definition for interactive literacy and were provided with examples of research-based exemplary practices, as the Goodling Institute is planning, the integration of language and literacy would likely be improved.

Finally, family literacy programs need to improve their collaborations with elementary schools to address better the interactive literacy needs of school-age children. This age group is often overlooked because of the difficulty programs have making connections with elementary school teachers. However, children may need the most support from their parents when they begin school. When schools begin to understand that the goals of family literacy programs are similar to theirs, then the working relationship may be improved.

FACE RESEARCH

The fourth challenge to our research involves identifying and describing key features of exemplary family literacy programs. To do so, we investigated the FACE program, as an example, to study family literacy programs holistically in our efforts to determine best practices for family literacy programs (Bureau of Indian Affairs, 2001; Semali, 2004). FACE offered the ideal context for this inquiry. Initiated in 1990 by the Bureau of Indian Affairs (BIA) and the Office of Indian Education Programs (OIEP), FACE is presently implemented at 39 sites in 14 states. The humble beginnings of FACE with just five sites has grown to a network of reputable programs that have been evaluated and found to be effective. Since the inception of FACE, 15,000 individuals representing 5,000 families have received program services. More than 400 adults have received their GED (high school equivalency exam) and over 1,500 adults have obtained employment.

FACE was chosen for this case study because it has been referenced frequently as a successful program in the integration of services for parents and children (e.g., U.S. Department of Education, 2002). The task was to identify key features of an exemplary program which support successful coordination of the components of family literacy, and the transition of parents and children to the world of work and elementary school, respectively. The overarching purpose of the study was to examine the indicators in the FACE implementation process that show a composite (profile) of success with the assumption that educators and policymakers will then be able to replicate the successes of FACE in non-FACE family literacy programs.

First, the perceptions of stakeholders on program implementation at the local level were examined. Stakeholders included school personnel, parents, families, program and other school staff members, and representatives from the local communities. The rationale for studying program implementation was based on the assumption that participant outcomes depend on program variables and the faithful implementation of this model of family literacy.

The data collection methods used in this study included on-site visits, class observations, expert interviews, and content analysis of trainers' manuals and program evaluation reports (1991-2001). In the first analysis, the researcher identified the critical program features based on FACE evaluation reports. Then, he derived from these program features principles of successful implementation using Porter's framework (Porter, 1994; Porter, Floden, Freeman, Schmidt, & Schwille, 1988) and Thompson's critical success factors analysis (Thompson, 2003). Porter's framework consisted of five components: specificity, consistency, authority, power, and stability. Thompson's critical success factors analysis targeted reform changes that encompass standards, school climate, accountability, professional development, system resources, collecting and using data effectively, and effective communication.

By applying Porter's theoretical framework of successful policy implementation and Thompson's critical success factors analysis to evaluate the components of the FACE program, five key program features were identified that could be predictors of high performance. They are as follows: (a) having an established curriculum (e.g., Born to Learn, Equipped for the Future), (b) following a well-known implementation structure (e.g., FACE guidelines based on Even Start legislation, Reading First, and Early Reading First), (c) establishing quality control measures (e.g., collaboration among partners who provide technical support to ensure that family literacy is implemented with integrity, intelligence, and sensitivity to local needs and circumstances; taking control of regular on-site training and national training sessions), (d) providing strong funding support (e.g., maintaining an annual budget, providing equipment and transportation), and (e) having efficient organizational communication (e.g., maintaining regular communication among the BIA, administrators, collaborating partners, and coordinators; holding on-site weekly and annual meetings; having an effective school principal or coordinator; maintaining school-community relationships). Collectively, these factors are critical to the successful implementation of FACE as a family literacy program. These factors need to be tested further in a field experimental study to see whether they qualify empirically as predictors of critical success factors of high performance in family literacy programs. Next, these critical success factors will be used to build an empirical model that can be replicated or expanded to other non-FACE programs.

In summary, this case study revealed that FACE is a well-implemented family literacy program. Our observations in center-based classrooms confirmed that the FACE staff's pedagogical methods are student-centered and based on problem-solving strategies in a constructivist environment. Classrooms are print rich and reflect the language, history, and culture of the students and the community. The curriculum includes the four components of family literacy. For each component, clear statements prescribe what needs to happen in the classrooms. For example, in the adult education component, participants have to spend a minimum of 2 1/2 hr in educational instruction each day, focusing on adult basic education, technology skill development, high school classes, basic life skills, and job training. Thus, this prescription for adult education addresses the need for sufficient intensity of services so that participants can make meaningful differences in their academic and life skills and their children's academic achievement.

Our analysis of FACE documents revealed that FACE has a rigorous policy which ensures that there is stability in the programs at all of its 39 sites. Each FACE site actively participates in strengths-based technical assistance provided by the OIEP to ensure fidelity to the model. The collaborating partners—National Center for Family Literacy, Parents as Teachers, and Engage Learning consultants—provide technical assistance at national meetings and on site. Administratively, FACE programs are located in the local BIA schools. The coordinator of the program is usually the elementary school principal or the early childhood teacher or the adult education teacher. The teacher or coordinator must have teacher certification and have experience working with children, adults, and families. It was also evident to stakeholders that the principal playing an active role at each site was significant to the successful implementation of FACE.

Collectively, these qualities affirm Porter's and Thompson's conceptual frameworks and show that the collaboration among the three partners with BIA and OIEP produce the synergy of both consistency and stability that fuels the success of FACE. In sum, Porter's (1994) policy attributes theory and Thompson's (2003) critical success factors provide useful perspectives to examine family literacy efforts and move toward a better understanding of how to foster successful implementation. As noted by Porter, without consistency, for example, a program is too unreliable to be of value in the large-scale context. However, consistency does not mean that the family literacy program will work in all cases. Rather, it means that the model is highly robust and will work powerfully in the vast majority of cases with a variety of measures (Pogrow, 1998).

CONCLUSIONS FROM THIS MODEL-BUILDING RESEARCH AGENDA FOR FAMILY LITERACY

Our focus on the challenges of identifying best practices for family literacy looked primarily at the adult components of the widely practiced four-component model, in addition to studying the integration of the components and the coordination with other organizations. The purpose of these efforts is to identify and use research that can improve the quality of family literacy programs. Specifically, the Goodling Institute for Research in Family Literacy has studied the participation of adults and linked it to literacy outcomes in Pennsylvania family literacy programs. Our research revealed that intensity of services is the most important of the participation variables. We are beginning to build on others' research to study instructional quality in adult and parenting education classrooms to ensure that adults will not only want to stay in their programs but also participate more intensely.

The Goodling Institute is also attempting, through its research, to identify exemplary practices for the two components of family literacy that are the least defined, namely parenting education and parent-child interaction. Doing so can help programs evaluate themselves to improve the quality of instruction in family literacy programs.

Finally, the research on the FACE program has enabled us to define the key ingredients for each component by explicitly identifying exemplary practices. The OIEP has retained the services of three partners to provide technical assistance in implementation of the components. Equally important, it has mandated that the principal of the elementary school, at least initially, serve as director of each FACE program, ensuring the connection of the family literacy program to the schools. This mandate also ensures the coordination of the components and integration of services. Non-FACE family literacy programs can use these findings to improve the quality of their services.

Our goal is to advance the field of family literacy so that it is less ad hoc and more defined. Providers must indeed be sensitive to the needs of their communities, for context is critically important. However, they also need implementation guideposts and research-based best practices to deliver high quality programs. Policymakers likewise can benefit from our research in creating regulations that encourage quality through research-based best practices in family literacy.

REFERENCES

Askov, E. N. (2002). *Family literacy: A research agenda to build the future.* Retrieved July 4, 2006, from www.ed.psu.edu/goodlinginstitute/research.htm

Askov, E. N., Grinder, E. L., & Kassab, C. (2005). Impact of family literacy on children (Update section). *Family Literacy Forum, 4,* 38-39.

Askov, E. N., Kassab, C., & Weirauch, D. (2005). Women in Pennsylvania's family literacy programs: Effects of participant characteristics on extent of participation. *Adult Basic Education, 15,* 131-149.

Askov, E. N., Kassab, C., Weirauch, D., & Van Horn, B. (2004, April). *Women in Pennsylvania's family literacy programs: Effects of participant characteristics on extent of participation.* Paper presented at the annual meeting of the American Educational Research Association, San Diego, CA.

Beder, H., & Medina, P. (2001). *Classroom dynamics in adult literacy education.* Cambridge, MA: National Center for the Study of Adult Learning and Literacy, Harvard University.

Bureau of Indian Affairs, Office of Indian Education Programs. (2001). *Keep the circle strong – Family and Child Education (FACE) Guidelines 2001.* Washington, DC: Author.

Comings, J., Parella, A., & Soricone, L. (1999). *Persistence among adult basic education students in pre-GED classes.* Cambridge, MA: National Center for the Study of Adult Learning and Literacy, Harvard University.

Grinder, E. L., Longoria Saenz, E., Askov, E. N., & Aldemir, J. (2005). What's really happening during parent-child interactive literacy in family literacy programs? *Family Literacy Forum, 4,* 38-39.

Kassab, C., Askov, E. N., Weirauch, D., Grinder, E. L., & Van Horn, B. (2004). Adult participation related to outcomes in family literacy programs. *Family Literacy Forum, 3,* 23-29.

National Institute of Child Health and Human Development. (2000). *Report of the National Reading Panel. Teaching children to read – an evidence based assessment of the scientific research literature on reading and its implications for reading instruction* (NIH Publication No. 00-4769). Washington, DC: U.S. Government Printing Office.

No Child Left Behind Act of 2001, Pub. L. No. 107-110, 115 Stat. 1425 (2002).

Pogrow, S. (1998). What is an exemplary program and why should anyone care: A reaction to Slavin & Klein. *Educational Researcher, 27*(7), 22-29.

Porter, A. (1994). National standards and school improvement in the 1990s: Issues and promise. *American Journal of Education, 102,* 421-449.

Porter, A. C., Floden, R., Freeman, D., Schmidt, W., & Schwille, J. (1988). Content determinants in elementary mathematics. In D. Grouws & T. Cooney (Eds.), *Perspectives on research on effective mathematics teaching* (pp. 96-113). Hillsdale, NJ: Lawrence Erlbaum Associates, Inc.

Semali, L. M. (2004). *Mapping success: Family and child education program.* Retrieved July 4, 2006, from http://www.ed.psu.edu/goodlinginstitute/ongoingresearch.htm

Thompson, S. (2003). Creating a high-performance school system. *Phi Delta Kappan, 84,* 489-495.

Young, M., Fleischman, H., Fitzgerald, N., & Morgan, M. (1994). *National evaluation of adult education programs: Learner outcomes and program results.* Arlington, VA: Development Associates.

U.S. Department of Education. (2002, January/February). *Community update* (No. 94). Washington, DC: Author.

U.S. Department of Education (2003, September). Policy guidance for the William F. Goodling Even Start Family Literacy Programs, Part B, Subpart 3 of Title I of the Elementary and Secondary Education Act. Retrieved July 4, 2006, from http://www.ed.gov/policy/elsec/guid/evenstartguidance02.doc

Chapter 14

Giving Literacy Away, Again:
New Concepts of Promising Practice

Stephen Reder
Portland State University

Adult literacy programs commonly aim to help adults increase their literacy proficiency through improving their skills and knowledge or through increasing their utilization of written language and engagement in literacy practices. Broadly speaking, this programmatic support of adult literacy development may occur in two ways: bringing people to literacy and bringing literacy to people. More programmatic attention has been given to the former. New directions for program development are needed for implementing the latter.

This chapter presents some results from an ongoing longitudinal study of adult learners that suggest some promising new directions for bringing literacy to people, a process that Reder and Green (1985) called "Giving Literacy Away." As we see, adults regularly engage in self-directed efforts to improve their basic reading, writing, and math skills and prepare for the high school equivalency General Educational Development (GED) tests. Such self-study is widespread both among adults who participate in adult literacy programs and those who do not. In considering the implications of these findings for adult literacy education, the chapter suggests some new program designs that have the potential to significantly expand and deepen participation in adult literacy education. The chapter ends with a description of an ongoing effort to implement a research-driven prototype of such a program, called the *Learner Web*.

TWO APPROACHES TO SUPPORTING ADULT LITERACY DEVELOPMENT

In most societies, literacy education has involved much more than merely teaching individuals to read and write. Whole systems of values and institutions have become historically associated with the use of writing in most societies (Goody,

1968; Goody & Watt, 1963). These contextual features of literacy are so deeply entrenched in cultural practices that it is conceptually and practically difficult for us to separate the *technical* dimensions of literacy (i.e., the information processing involved in reading or writing activities) from the *functional* dimensions of literacy practices (i.e., the social uses made of written materials) or the *social meanings* engendered in particular literacy practices (Reder & Green, 1983). In most Western societies, it is indeed difficult to "unpack" literacy from its social and cultural contexts (Barton, Hamilton, & Ivanic, 2000; Scribner & Cole, 1981).

Bringing People to Literacy

The deeply contextualized nature of literacy practices has had profound implications for literacy education. In Western societies, literacy has been socialized within contexts of powerful institutions, especially organized religions and schools (Goody & Watt, 1963; Olson, 1977). Individuals typically acquired basic reading and writing skills as participants in these institutions. Access to literacy entailed access to these powerful institutions. It is thus not surprising that early efforts to teach literacy to adults were based on a conception of bringing people to literacy, of inculcating in the adult learners not only the technical skills required to read and write, but also the system of values and practices associated with the institutional sponsor of literacy. Over time, the number and types of these sponsors has increased in Western societies, including the United States (Brandt, 2001).

   This approach to facilitating adult literacy development is based on engaging adults in basic skills programs or other new social practices that involve the use of writing. This involves recruiting adults to participate in those basic skills programs or other new social practices and retaining them sufficiently long to develop new skills and knowledge. Such efforts often entail large differences between the settings, materials, and literacy practices of the program and those of the learner. These contextual differences may create logistical or cultural barriers to participation for many learners. These contextual differences sometimes engender conflicts between the goals, needs, and assumptions of program providers and those of the learners they seek to serve (Brandt, 2001; Purcell-Gates, Degener, Jacobson,& Soler, 2000; Reder & Green, 1985; Street, 1995).

Bringing Literacy to People

Another approach to facilitating adult literacy development is based on embedding or expanding the use of writing in existing social practices. "Giving Literacy Away" is the name Reder and Green (1985) gave to such literacy development strategies based on bringing literacy to people. This approach attempts to support literacy development directly within the settings and contexts and with the materials of the learners as opposed to the settings, contexts, and materials of program providers or "sponsors." We see that giving literacy away can offer new modes of supporting adult literacy development as well as new ways to expand and increase the quality of existing programs.

SELF-STUDY AS AN ETHNOPEDAGOGY OF ADULT LITERACY

Much more is known about adult learning among participants in education and training programs than among adults who do not participate in such formal programs. Research in general tends to focus on adults in institutional settings if only because they are more readily accessible for study. This leaves us relatively uncertain about the characteristics of learning that take place outside of these formal programs. Reder and Green (1985), in their original formulation of giving literacy away, explored how informal social networks of "literacy helpers" (i.e., individuals who assist or collaborate with individuals to perform everyday literacy tasks) function as contexts for adult literacy development. The more recent notion of a "community of practice" (Wenger, 1998) significantly broadens the theoretical framework available for understanding adult learning as a socially constructed process. Application of this framework to adult literacy development is beginning to occur (e.g., D'Amico & Capehart, 2001).

Adults' participation in literacy programs and other activities associated with literacy development reflect their beliefs and practices about how individuals acquire or improve their literacy abilities. I have termed these beliefs and practices about adult literacy learning as the *ethnopedagogy* of adult literacy (Reder, 1992). Ethnopedagogy refers to cultural beliefs and practices about teaching and learning in the same way that *ethnobotany* refers to cultural beliefs and practices about plants. We see that adults' self-directed learning practices to improve their literacy proficiencies reflect their ethnopedagogy for literacy development. Although self-directed learning has been a heavily researched topic within the field of adult education (e.g., Brookfield, 1985; Candy, 1991; Garrison, 1992; Hammond & Collins, 1991; Johnstone & Rivera, 1965; Knowles, 1975; Long, 1993; Oddi, 1987; Penland, 1979, 1977; Tough, 1971), very little of it has considered the self-directed learning of basic literacy proficiencies. Some large-scale surveys of self-directed learning (Johnstone & Rivera, 1965; Penland, 1977) found ample evidence that "self-initiated" or "self-planned" learning and "learning projects" are undertaken by large segments of the American adult population, including adults with relatively little formal education. But these seminal studies–that generated many secondary analyses and theories of the self-directed learner–did not differentiate the content of such independent learning in ways that enable us to examine self-directed efforts to improve basic literacy skills. Nevertheless, the prevalence of self-directed learning activities in

general among adults with relatively little schooling certainly suggests considering the possibility of self-directed learning in adult literacy development. For
clarity, we designate adults' independent study activities specifically to improve
their basic skills as *self-study*.

There are many indications that adults engage in self-study to improve their
basic skills. The National Center for the Study of Adult Learning and Literacy
(NCSALL) Persistence Study (Comings, Parrella, & Soricone, 1999), for example, found such self-study to be one learning strategy used by some participants
they interviewed from adult literacy programs. The extent to which such self-
study occurs among nonparticipants has not been examined in previous research.
The learning outcomes attributable to self-study have not been investigated, either. An ongoing research project, the Longitudinal Study of Adult Learning
(LSAL), can provide some new information about adults' self-study to develop
their literacy skills. LSAL includes both adult literacy program participants and
nonparticipants from the target population for adult literacy education. Information that LSAL provides about self-study in the target population will help us
better understand the ethnopedagogy of adult literacy.

THE LONGITUDINAL STUDY OF ADULT LEARNING

The Longitudinal Study of Adult Learning has been described in detail elsewhere (Reder & Strawn, 2001a, 2001b).[6] LSAL addresses four major research
questions about adult literacy:

- To what extent do adults' literacy abilities continue to develop after
  they are out of school?

- What are adult learners' patterns of participation over time in literacy
  training and education, and in other learning contexts?

---

6 Thanks to Clare Strawn, my esteemed colleague and collaborator on the Longitudinal Study of Adult Learning (LSAL), for her many contributions to my
own learning and understanding about these issues. Thanks to Erik Simensen
and Cynthia Lopez for their leadership and management of the LSAL interviewers and trackers too numerous to mention individually, without all of whose tire-
less efforts this work would not be possible. All of us who work on the LSAL
project are humbled by the enormous contributions of the nearly 1,000 LSAL
respondents who have given so generously to the project by opening up their
lives, their homes, and in many cases, their hearts. Our hope is that the project
will be not only *about* them but also *for* them. Thanks also to Meg Young, Executive Director of Oregon Literacy, Inc., for her early partnership, collegiality,
and vision in developing the Learner Web.

- What life experiences are associated with adult literacy development? How do formally organized basic skills programs contribute to these learning trajectories, workplace training, and other contexts and activities?
- What are the impacts of adult literacy development on social and economic outcomes?

The LSAL was designed as a panel study, representative of a local (rather than a national) target population for adult literacy education. This target population was defined as residents of the Portland, OR, metropolitan area, ages 18 to 44, proficient but not necessarily native English speakers, high school dropouts (i.e., did not receive a high school diploma and were no longer enrolled in school), and had not received a GED or other high school equivalency credential, although their status may change during the study period. A statistically representative sample of this population was drawn from a combination of random-digit-dialing and enrollment forms provided by the three major adult education programs serving the Portland metropolitan area. Sampled households were called and screened for members in the defined target population. The resulting LSAL sample contained 940 individuals and was weighted so that population statistics could be estimated from the sample data.

The LSAL conducted a series of five periodic interviews and skills assessments in respondents' homes. Respondents are paid for each of these sessions, which take an average of about 1.5 hr to complete. The five sessions or "waves" of data collection were conducted according to the following schedule:

Wave 1: 1998-1999
Wave 2: 1999-2000
Wave 3: 2000-2001
Wave 4: 2002-2003
Wave 5: 2004-2005

Individuals were interviewed at about the same time in each wave so that there is approximately constant spacing among individuals' successive interviews and assessments (e.g., a respondent interviewed in February 1999 in Wave 1 is interviewed during February 2000 in Wave 2, February 2001 in Wave 3, etc.) Data from Waves 1 to 3 are included in this chapter.

Characteristics of the LSAL population have been described elsewhere (Reder & Strawn, 2001a). Table 14–1 shows some features of this target population at Wave 1. The population had an average age of 28, was evenly divided among men and women, approximately one third were members of minority groups, about one in ten were born outside of the United States, about one third describe themselves as having a learning disability, and one in three reports having taken special education classes while they were in school.

TABLE 14–1 Some Characteristics of LSAL Population at Wave 1.

Average age	*28 years*
Female	50%
Minority	35%
Foreign born	9%
Live in poverty	34%
Have a learning disability	29%
Took special education classes	34%

Self-Study in LSAL

There are several reasons why LSAL initially decided to include a few questions about respondents studying on their own to improve their basic skills. To begin with, some adult education students anecdotally report that they have studied by themselves before starting classes. Comings et al. (1999) reported that some of the adult education students interviewed in NCSALL's Persistence Study included self-study as one of their learning strategies. Some individuals taking the GED tests similarly report preparing for the tests by studying on their own (Baldwin, Kirsch, Rock, & Yamamoto, 1995). There were thus converging indications that self-study could be an important learning process for adults striving to improve their basic skills or prepare for the GED, although this had not been examined systematically among education students let alone among those in the target population who never participate in programs or take the GED tests.

LSAL operationalized self-study as "studying on your own to improve your reading, writing or math skills or prepare for the GED." In Wave 1, only a few questions were included about self-study, asking individuals who indicated they had self-studied to provide further details about the recency and intensity of their self-directed efforts to improve basic skills.

Initial Snapshot of Self-Study

Results from the Wave 1 interviews are shown in Figure 14–1. Among the LSAL population who had at some time participated in a formal adult education class, nearly half (46%) had also engaged in self-study to improve their reading, writing, or math skills or prepare for the GED. Even more interesting is the finding that among those in the target population who had never participated in an adult education program, one in three (34%) had engaged in self-directed efforts to improve their basic skills. This represents a large group of adults who do not turn up in programs, but who nevertheless are engaged in activities to improve their basic skills or prepare for the GED. It is possible of course that some of the individuals who have self-studied but have not attended a basic skills class will later enroll in a program. Although we will have the opportunity to observe such transitions as we follow the LSAL population over time, there are already some indications of such transitions within the Wave 1 data. When we look at data about recency of participation in formal programs and in self-study among individuals who report at Wave 1 having previously done both, we find individuals who clearly did self-study before they had ever attended a program as well as individuals who attended a program before their first period of self-study. Although the temporal precision of many of the retrospective reports at Wave 1 is limited, we will be able to track such transitions more accurately in later interviews because subsequent transitions will be reported as relatively recent events.

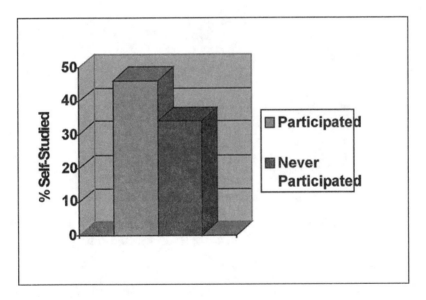

Figure 14.1. Percentage of adults in the target population who have self-studied to improve their basic skills, shown for those who have previously participated and those who have never participated in an adult basic skills program adults in target population.

Literacy Level and Self-Study

Because self-study may not be a viable strategy for adults with relatively poor basic skills (e.g., because there may not be appropriate materials available), it is important to examine the relationship between literacy proficiency in the target population and the tendency to engage in self-study. In particular, we can examine the extent to which there is a literacy threshold affecting the tendency of LSAL's adult population to engage in self-study.

Figure 14–2 displays the proportion of adults who had self-studied to improve their basic skills or prepare for the GED as a function of their assessed literacy proficiency at Wave 1. The literacy measure is the Test of Adult Literacy Skills (TALS) developed by the Educational Testing Service. The TALS measures adults' proficiencies at performing simulated everyday functional literacy tasks such as filling out forms, locating information in charts and maps, extracting key information from written materials, and so forth. The TALS assesses literacy proficiencies on three 0 to 500 point scales: Prose, Document, and Quantitative. These scales have been widely used in national and international studies of adult literacy.

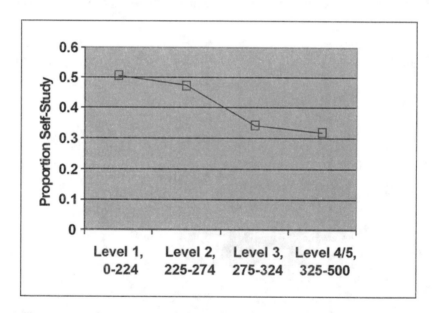

Figure 14.2. Proportion of adults who have engaged in self-study (Wave 1) to improve their reading, writing, or math skills or prepare for the GED, as a function of their assessed level of literacy proficiency.

Figure 14–2 displays the proportion of adults who had self-studied prior to Wave 1 in relation to their assessed Document proficiency levels. If there were indeed a literacy threshold below which such self-study became infeasible, or if weak skills generally made it difficult for adults to engage in self-study, then we might expect adults to show an increasing tendency to engage in self-study with increasing proficiency. The LSAL data, in fact, show exactly the opposite trend:

as literacy proficiencies rise, adults become less likely to engage in self-study to improve their basic skills. About half of the adults performing at the lowest proficiency level (Level 1 in Figure 14–2) have engaged in self-study, with progressively declining proportions as the skill level increases. At relatively higher levels of proficiency, of course, we might well expect adults' felt needs for improved basic skills to diminish along with their tendency to self-study to improve those skills. The fact that a substantial proportion (more than 30%) of adults at even the highest levels of proficiency have engaged in self-study may indicate that adults seek to improve their skills even when they are well above the levels needed to pass the GED tests (Baldwin et al., 1995, and Kirsch, Jungeblut, Jenkins, & Kolstad, 1993, have found that those passing the GED have an average proficiency of about 275 on the NALS, the threshold between Levels 2 and 3). Although additional analyses are needed to interpret the relationship between literacy proficiency and self-study shown in Figure 14–2, one finding seems already clear: a broad spectrum of the target population engages in self-study, including adults with relatively weak basic skills.

Self-Study Over Time

The field interviewers, debriefed at the end of Wave 1, were certain that respondents were reporting only their self-study activities intended to improve their basic skills or prepare for the GED. Knowing the significance of such self-study for the field of adult literacy education, we wanted to probe further to learn more about the nature of these activities.

In Wave 3, we asked respondents about self-study activities they might have undertaken during the 2-year period since their first (Wave 1) interview. Self-study was defined in Wave 3 and beyond in exactly the same way as it was in Wave 1. In Wave 3, we probed more deeply into the nature of self-study activities, asking respondents about the purposes, timing, and intensity of their self-study activities, the particular skills they had worked to improve, and the materials they used in self-study. We also were careful to distinguish, for respondents who reported both self-study and participation in formal literacy programs, teacher-assigned and self-initiated study activities.

Combining the information respondents provided in Wave 1 about their self-study prior to that time with the information they provided in Wave 3 about self-study over the 2 years between Waves 1 and 3, a chronology of self-study was pieced together for each respondent. Figure 14–3 displays the cumulative percentage over time of the LSAL population that had self-studied. The leftmost bar shows the percentage that had self-studied as of 1 year before the Wave 1 interview (i.e., had reported self-study activities occurring at least a year before their Wave 1 interview). The middle bar shows the percentage of the population that had self-studied prior to Wave 1. The rightmost bar shows the comparable percentage as of Wave 3. The estimated percentage rises from 29% a year prior to the onset of the study to 55% 3 years later at Wave 3. This is a steep rise but is consistent with high rates observed for other indicators of basic skill development activities in the population over the same time period, including program participation and GED test-taking.

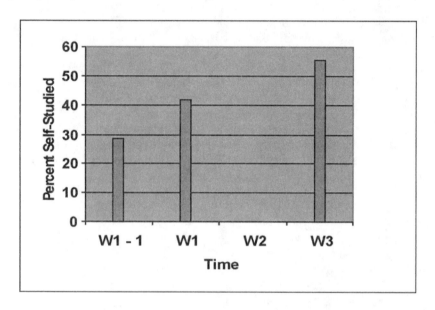

Figure 14.3. Percentage of Longitudinal Study of Adult Learning population that had ever self-studied at three time points: 1 year prior to Wave 1 ("W1-1"), Wave 1 ("W1"), and Wave 3 ("W3").

Individuals often engage in multiple periods (i.e., during disjointed time stretches) of self-study. Nearly half (46%) of those who had reported at least some self-study through Wave 3 had engaged in two or more discrete periods of self-study.

Figure 14–4 shows the percentages, cumulative through Wave 3, of the population in four exhaustive, mutually exclusive categories of participation: individuals who had neither self-studied nor attended a program (25%), individuals who had attended a program but who had never self-studied (10%), individuals who had self-studied but never attended a program (27%), and individuals who had both self-studied and attended a program (38%). Again we see that for this target population, self-study and program participation appear to be partially complementary approaches used to improve basic skills or prepare for the GED. There are individuals who use only one of the two approaches (and quite a few more use only self-study than use only program participation), many who use both, and of course, some individuals who use neither. The largest group within the target population has tried both approaches. When we look closely at the temporal patterns among those who use both approaches, we see examples of individuals who begin with a period of self-study and later attend a program, as well as individuals who attend a program and later engage in a period of self-study. These patterns are consistent with a notion of an active learner who considers both approaches as strategies or resources to support learning, perhaps using each as their life circumstances permit or needs for assistance require.

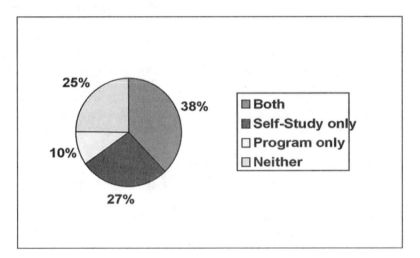

Figure 14.4. Percentage of Longitudinal Study of Adult Learning population that, through Wave 3, had participated in various combinations of self-study and formal programs to improve their basic skills or prepare for the General Educational Development (GED) tests.

Goals, Skills, Content, and Materials in Self-Study

Individuals who had self-studied were asked whether their self-study was intended to (a) prepare for the GED tests; (b) improve their reading, writing, or math skills; or (c) both prepare for the GED and improve their skills. About one in four (24%) of those who had self-studied indicated they had done so only to prepare for the GED, nearly half (45%) indicated they had self-studied to improve their skills (but not to prepare for the GED), and nearly one in three (30%) indicated that they had self-studied both to improve their skills and prepare for the GED. Thus over half (54%) of those who self-study do so (at least in part) to prepare for the GED.

Respondents who indicated their self-study was directed in part toward skill improvement were asked about the particular skills they had tried to improve

through their self-study. Interviewers listened to and probed respondents' descriptions of the skill content and categorized responses into the set of skill content categories shown in Table 14–2. The most commonly reported skills were
reading comprehension, vocabulary and spelling, arithmetic, and punctuation
and grammar. If the two categories of business writing and creative writing were
merged into a single category of writing, then writing would have been the single most common skill targeted by the self-study activities. It is important to
note that most individuals mentioned self-studying several of the skill areas. Not
all of the skills mentioned were necessarily "basic;" many individuals mentioned
levels of math, for example, considerably higher than arithmetic, including algebra and geometry and even more advanced math. These data help us appreciate
the wide range of skills individuals try to address through self-study. This is
consistent with our previously mentioned finding that many individuals in the
target population engage in self-study to improve their basic skills for reasons
other than GED preparation. The sophisticated level of some of the targeted
skills is consistent with the high level of literacy skills demonstrated by some
individuals in the population (as indicated by their TALS scores).

TABLE 14–2

Skills targeted by individuals engaged in self-study

Skill Studied	Percent
Vocabulary, spelling	45.4
Punctuation, grammar	40.8
Business writing	23.4
Creative writing	30.3
Reading comprehen-sion	48.1
Reading speed	29.6
Arithmetic	44.5
Algebra, geometry	36.9
Advanced math	11.6
Other	3.8

Note. For each skill, the percentage shown is based on individuals who reported
self-study was directed in part towards skill improvement. Percentages add to
more than 100% because individuals could report multiple skills.

Individuals who indicated their self-study was, at least in part, to prepare for the GED were asked about the topics (or tests) for which they were preparing. Table 14–3 shows the GED topics in which they had focused in self-study. Because obtaining a GED requires passing each of the individual tests, it is not surprising that the majority of those self-studying to prepare for the GED would focus on each of the test topics. Math is the topic that almost everyone focuses on, although more than three quarters also focus on writing and on language arts. We will be able to better interpret these content differences when we also examine the particular GED tests that individuals have taken.

TABLE 14–3

General Educational Development (GED) Topics of Self-Study

GED Topic Studied	Percent
Language Arts	76.9
Writing	78.9
Math	92.8
Science	70.5
Social Studies	68.5

Note. For each topic, the percentage shown is based on individuals who reported their self-study was directed in part on preparing for the GED (high school equivalency test). Percentages add to more than 100% because individuals could report multiple topics.

Table 14–4 exhibits the frequency that various types of materials were used in self-study activities. The most common types of materials used in self-study were workbooks–workbooks designed specifically for GED preparation and workbooks designed to help individuals improve their math skills or their vocabulary, spelling, or writing. It is notable that more than a third (35%) reported using computer-based materials for self-study. Apparently the computer is already more commonly used as an educational resource in this population than educational television.

TABLE 14–4.

Materials Used by Individuals Engaged in Self-Study

Type of Material	Percent
GED workbooks	48.6
Vocabulary/spelling/writing workbooks	57.0
Math workbooks	50.8
Educational TV/video	22.0
Audio cassettes	7.6
Computer	35.2
Other	13.1

Note. Percentages add to More Than 100% Because Individuals Could Report Multiple Materials.

Program Participation, Self-Study, and GED Attainment

By the time the Wave 3 interviews were conducted, 2 years after the Wave 1 interviews, 16% of the population had received a GED. Considering the broad age range of the target population, this seems to be a fairly high rate of obtaining the GED over just a 2-year period (we recall that, by definition, no one had a GED at Wave 1). Because many individuals in the target population are not interested in obtaining a GED, the effective "success" rate for obtaining a GED is considerably higher.

Figure 14–5 displays the percentage of various subpopulations that had received a GED by Wave 3. The four subgroups of the target population displayed in Figure 14–5 are the same as those shown in Figure 14–4: individuals who had never self-studied or participated in a program, individuals who had participated in a program but had never self-studied, individuals who had self-studied but never participated in a program, and individuals who had both self-studied and participated in a program.

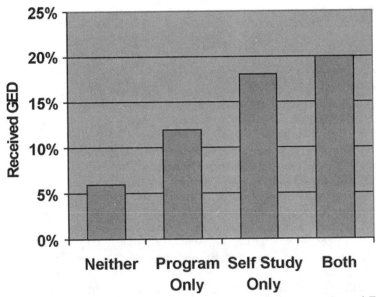

Figure 14.5. Percentage of individuals in target population receiving a General Educational Development (GED) Certificate as a function of whether they participated in a basic skills program or self-study.

Only 6% of individuals who neither participated in a program nor self-studied received a GED. Many in this "Neither" group have no intention of obtaining a GED, but those in this group who received a GED are among the sizable number of GED test takers who report not preparing at all for the tests (Baldwin et al., 1995). About 12% of those who participated in a basic skills program but did not self-study received their GED compared to 18% of those who self-studied but did not participate in a program. The highest percentage of GED attainment (20%) was observed among those who did both.

These data seem to indicate that both program participation and self-study, whether occurring alone or in combination, are associated with GED attainment. This is, of course, what we expect to see from program participation, because GED attainment has been the historical mission of adult education programs. Perhaps less expected is the apparent association between self-study and GED attainment, a relationship that appears at least as strong and perhaps stronger than that between program participation and GED attainment. Once LSAL data are complete, other variables such as age, gender, and whether individuals had the goal of obtaining a GED can be considered in more systematic interpretations of these outcome data.

Self-Study Summary

Self-study--defined in LSAL as working on one's own to prepare for the GED or improve reading, writing, or math skills–is a widespread mode of basic skills development among adults who did not complete high school. It occurs widely among participants in basic skills programs as well as among adults who do not participate in such programs. The utilization of self-study does not appear to be closely related to assessed literacy proficiency; individuals with relatively weak basic skills are just as likely to engage in self-study as those with higher levels of proficiency. For some learners, periods of self-study are followed by periods of participation in programs; for other learners, periods of self-study follow periods of program participation; and for yet other learners, both types of activities occur during the same time period. In general, self-study appears to be a bridge between periods of program participation and to facilitate persistence of learning. When we examine the percentages of individuals engaged in various combinations of self-study and program participation, self-study appears to be at least as strongly related to GED attainment as program participation. For the LSAL population through Wave 3, more individuals engage in self-study than in programs, and the GED attainment rate is higher for self-study than for program participation.

It is likely that many of these early findings from LSAL will endure as the longitudinal study continues over time. The longer-term impact of self-study on skill development, continuing education, and social and economic outcomes remains to be seen in future LSAL data. The extent to which these findings, based on a representative local, rather than national, target population, may generalize to other locales must of course be established by other research. It is reasonable to expect that the quantitative profiles of self-study may vary considerably from one area to another, depending on differences in local target populations, school systems, employment opportunities, and provision of adult education. With these caveats in mind, we can reasonably expect self-study to be an important component of adult literacy development in diverse locales and populations in the United States. There is much anecdotal evidence supporting such a generalization. The generality of self-study is also supported by other research. NCSALL's Persistence Study, for example, which looked closely at program participants from a range of programs in a different region of the United States, found qualitative evidence of the importance of self-study among the adult education students it followed (Comings et al., 1999).

IMPLICATIONS FOR ADULT LITERACY EDUCATION

The prevalence of self-study activities among adults seeking to improve their basic skills or prepare for the GED has major implications for policy and program design in adult literacy education. By broadening the conception and design of an adult literacy program to support self-study as well as provide classes, adult literacy programs could serve more learners (because many adults self-study who never come to formal classes), attract new learners to classes (because some adults who self-study might later attend classes), and increase the overall persistence of adult literacy learning (because many adult literacy learners engage in self-study and attend classes at different points in time). Comings and Cuban (this volume) explore some of the ways in which self-study and program participation might be combined to enhance the persistence of learners already in programs and thereby improve program quality. In addition to enhancing programs' capacity to increase the persistence of students who are already participating in programs, LSAL's findings on self-study also suggest increasing program quality through outreach efforts and delivery modalities that may engage new learners not participating in presently available programs.

Along with this broader model of the adult literacy program comes a broader conception of the adult literacy learner. This is an adult literacy learner who chooses among a range of literacy development strategies and resources, including self-study, attending classes, working with a tutor or mentor, and so forth (Wikelund, Reder, & Hart-Landsberg, 1992). Differences among learners' preferred modes of learning, their life circumstances, and the accessibility of learning resources such as classes shape their choices about how to pursue literacy development. Over time, as learners' needs and goals, life situations, and understandings of learning resources change, the literacy learning strategies and resources used may change as well (cf. Beder, 1991; Belzer, 1998).

To support this expanded notion of the adult literacy learner, programs need to expand their services to support learning among adults engaged in self-study activities as well as learning in the classroom. Such expansion may require changes in policy and program design. Policy changes at the federal, state, or local levels may be needed for programs to utilize adult education funds to support self-study. Issues may need to be resolved about the eligibility of self-study learners for official enrollment counts, about assessing their skills and progress, and about other aspects of accountability required by various categories of federal and state funds. In many respects, these policy and administrative issues may be similar to those already being addressed by some programs for students engaged in various forms of distance rather than on-site learning activities.

New program designs are needed to facilitate and support the learning of adults engaged in self-study and link self-study activities with program services. Learners engaged in self-study may benefit from various types of goal identification, skill assessment, selection of learning materials (whether print-based, online, or multimedia), mentoring or tutoring, progress assessment, and so forth. Not all such support materials and services may need to be newly developed; many usable materials and services may exist and others could be repurposed for use in facilitating self-study. LSAL has identified a range of materials in terms of content and media already being used by adults engaged in self-study. Examples already mentioned include study guides for the individual GED tests, workbooks for specific clusters of skills, and GED practice tests.

An important step in developing programmatic capacity to facilitate and support self-study will be mapping types of learners (specified perhaps in terms of their learning goals and life circumstances), skill development needs, and individually appropriate resources for supporting learning (which might be a classroom-based course, a distance-delivered course, a volunteer tutor, online or print-based materials for self-study, etc.). Such a system might assist learners with goal identification, needs assessment, direct instructional support, progress monitoring and feedback, advising and referral to other needed services. Not at all learners would choose or receive the same package of materials or services; the successful support and facilitation of self-study will likely entail customizing materials and services to learners in ways that fit their individual learning goals, meet their self-identified needs for skill development, and are compatible with their individual life circumstances and preferences for modes of learning.

Within this broad system of adult literacy education, self-study should be seen as being on a continuum with, rather than a polarized alternative to, classroom-based programs. The LSAL research points this out very clearly. Most adults who have tried in one way or another to improve their basic skills or prepare for the GED have tried both self-study and participating in a course. Furthermore, the majority of the LSAL population who had participated in programs, when asked to describe them, indicated that the programs included a substantial amount of individual work in nonclassroom settings as well as direct instruction in larger groups or classroom settings. Many of the local adult basic education and GED programs in Portland–and across the nation–include "learning centers" or "computer labs" or classroom-based "individualized group instruction" (Robinson-Geller, in press) where learners work individually, supplemented by on-demand instructional assistance. Thus, in some respects, existing program practices already include activities similar to forms of facilitated self-study. Other types of adult literacy services could also be included as learning support resources in the type of system being described here. On-demand tutoring or mentoring, for example, could effectively be provided to some learners engaged in self-study at home, similar to the way that program participants working in a learning center access direct instructional support from time to time. Models of "homework hotlines" developed by school districts, in which students working at home call in for assistance to teacher-staffed or volunteer-staffed tutoring call centers, may provide some useful experience from which adult programs can draw. Many community-based organizations–both those that provide adult literacy programs and those that do not--offer a range of services, social networks and contexts essential for engaging, motivating, and supporting adult learning. Library-based adult literacy programs have developed services, materials, and expertise that could be drawn on, linked into, and coordinated with a community-wide model of adult literacy education (Porter, Comings, & Cuban, 2005). Developing the appropriate tools and structures for coordinating such services with learner needs and goals would be the central challenge in such a system.

An important design element for such a system is active collaboration among adult literacy education providers, tutoring programs, libraries, and community-based organizations. The collaboration needs to be *learner-centered.* Although this term has been used with many other meanings, learner-centered in this context means mapping learning resources (whether classroom programs, online curricula, etc.) to the individual learner's characteristics, goals, skill needs, and desired mode of learning. It is essential that such a mapping of programs, services, and materials does not retrofit them to a narrowly prescribed framework. Instead, existing resources are to be evaluated and crosswalked with respect to a key set of learner characteristics. This would enable learners to be referred to appropriate resources, perhaps self-study materials at one point, perhaps a local program or tutor at another moment, and so forth. This learner-centered indexing of and referral to resources would promote continuity and persistence of learning from the learner's perspective and increase program retention from the perspective of the broadened adult literacy education system. The focus of the system would be on individual learners, not on self-study per se, although many learners would likely self-study at various points in their literacy development. Efforts to facilitate self-study, when appropriately implemented, will be leveraging important ethnopedagogical practices in adult literacy and thereby giving literacy away and increasing the capacity and quality of the adult literacy education system.

A project called the *Learner Web* is attempting to construct a prototype system in this manner. This project, with initial funding from the Oregon State Library through federal LSTA monies, involves a partnership among Portland State University; Oregon Literacy, a statewide nonprofit umbrella organization that supports local community partnerships and tutoring programs in adult literacy; and local adult education programs, libraries, and community-based organizations in three pilot communities.

Although this prototype system is being designed initially for three local communities, its design is scalable so that other communities' local resources and learners can be added to the system as it evolves and grows. Using an emergent, research-driven, and learner-centered design for the *Learner Web,* it is hoped that this system for facilitating self-study and connecting it with other elements of the adult literacy education system will help give literacy away.

REFERENCES

Baldwin, J., Kirsch, I. S., Rock, D., & Yamamoto, K. (1995). *The literacy profi-
    ciencies of GED examinees: Results from the GED-NALS Comparison
    Study.* Washington, DC/Princeton, NJ: American Council on Educa-
    tion/Educational Testing Service.

Barton, D., Hamilton, M., & Ivanic, R. (Eds.). (2000). *Situated literacies.* Lon-
    don: Routledge.

Beder, H. (1991). *Adult literacy: Issues for policy and practice.* Malabar, FL:
    Krieger Publishing Company.

Belzer, A. (1998). Stopping out, not dropping out. *Focus on Basics, 2A,*15-17.

Brandt, D. (2001). *Literacy in American lives.* Cambridge, England: Cambridge
    University Press.

Brookfield, S. (1985). Analyzing a critical paradigm of self-directed learning: A
    response. *Adult Education Quarterly, 36,* 60-64.

Candy, P. C. (1991). *Self-direction for lifelong learning.* San Francisco: Jossey-
    Bass.

Comings, J., Parrella, A., & Soricone, L. (1999). *Persistence among adult basic
    education students in pre-GED classes* (NCSALL Report No. 12).
    Cambridge, MA: National Center for the Study of Adult Learning and
    Literacy.

D'Amico, D., & Capehart, M. A. (2001). Letting learners lead: Theories of adult
    learning and TV411. *Focus on Basics, 5,* 35-41.

Garrison, D. R. (1992). Critical thinking and self-directed learning in adult edu-
    cation: An analysis of responsibility and control issues. *Adult Educa-
    tion Quarterly, 42,* 136-148.

Goody, J. (Ed.). (1968). *Literacy in traditional societies.* Cambridge, England:
    Cambridge University Press.

Goody, J., & Watt, I. (1963). The consequences of literacy. *Comparative Studies
    in Society and History, 5,* 304-345.

Hammond, M., & Collins, R. (1991). *Self-directed learning: Critical practice.*
    London: Kogan Page.

Johnstone, J. W. C., & Rivera, R. J. (1965). *Volunteers for learning: A study of
    the educational pursuits of American adults.* Chicago: Aldine.

Kirsch, I. S., Jungeblut, A., Jenkins, L., & Kolstad, A. (1993). *Adult literacy in
    America: A first look at the results of the National Adult Literacy Sur-
    vey.* Washington, DC: U.S. Department of Education, National Center
    for Education Statistics.

Knowles, M. (1975). *Self-directed learning.* New York: Association Press.

Long, H. B. (Ed.). (1993). *Emerging perspectives of self-directed learning.*
    Norman, OK: Research Center for Continuing Professional and Higher
    Education, University of Oklahoma.

Oddi, L. F. (1987). Perspectives on self-directed learning. *Adult Education Quarterly, 37,* 21-31.

Olson, D. R. (1977). The languages of instruction: The literate bias of schooling. In R. C. Anderson, R. Spiro, & W. E. Montague (Eds.), *Schooling and the acquisition of knowledge* (pp. 65-89). Hillsdale, NJ: Lawrence Erlbaum Associates, Inc.

Penland, P. (1977). *Self-planned learning in America.* Pittsburgh, PA: Book Center, University of Pittsburgh.

Penland, P. (1979). Self-initiated learning. *Adult Education, 29,* 170-179.

Porter, K., Comings, J., & Cuban, S. (2005). *One day I will make it: A study of adult student persistence in library literacy programs.* New York: Manpower Development Research Corporation.

Purcell-Gates, V., Degener, S., Jacobson, E., & Soler, M. (2000). *Affecting change in literacy practices of adult learners: Impact of two dimensions of instruction.* Cambridge, MA: National Center for the Study of Adult Learning and Literacy.

Reder, S. (1992). Getting the message across: Cultural factors in the intergenerational transfer of cognitive skills. In T. Sticht, B. McDonald, & M. Beeler (Eds.), *The intergenerational transfer of cognitive skills* (pp. 202-228). Newark, DE: Ablex.

Reder, S., & Green, K. R. (1983). Contrasting patterns of literacy in an Alaska fishing village. *International Journal of Sociology of Language, 42,* 9-39.

Reder, S., & Green, K. R. (1985). *Giving literacy away: An alternative strategy for increasing adult literacy development.* San Francisco: Far West Educational Laboratory.

Reder, S., & Strawn, C. (2001a). The K-12 school experiences of high school dropouts. *Focus on Basics, 4,* 12-13.

Reder, S., & Strawn, C. (2001b). Program participation and self-directed learning to improve basic skills. *Focus on Basics, 4,* 14-17.

Robinson-Geller, P. (in press). Individualized group instruction: A reality of adult basic education. In J. Comings, B. Garner, & C. Smith (Eds.), *The annual review of adult learning and literacy, volume 7.* Mahwah, NJ: Lawrence Erlbaum Associates, Inc.

Scribner, S., & Cole, M. (1981). *The psychology of literacy.* Cambridge, MA: Harvard University Press.

Street, B. V. (1995). *Social literacies: Critical approaches to literacy development, ethnography, and education.* Boston: Addison-Wesley.

Tough, A. (1971). *The adult's learning projects: A fresh approach to theory and practice in adult learning.* Toronto: The Ontario Institute for Studies in Education.

Wenger, E. (1998). *Communities of practice: Learning, meaning and identity.* Cambridge, England: Cambridge University Press.

Wikelund, K., Reder, S., & Hart-Landsberg, S. (1992). *Expanding theories of adult literacy participation: A literature* review (NCAL Tech. Rep. No. TR 92-1). Philadelphia: National Center on Adult Literacy, University of Pennsylvania.

Chapter 15

The Adult Learner in Adult and Family Literacy: Gender and Its Intersections with Role and Context

Vivian L. Gadsden
University of Pennsylvania

Images of adult learners in adult and family literacy discussions demonstrate the range of literacies that adults use and the complex relationships associated with their experiences and identities in and out of the classroom. Gender is a salient feature of these experiences and identities, including adults' (re)presentations of self, their social roles, and the contexts in which their gendered roles (as women, men, mothers, fathers, children, and workers) are assumed and enacted (Gadsden, 2002; Purcell-Gates & Waterman, 2000; Reder, this volume). Literacy programs—adult and family alike—are critical contexts for the enactment of these identities, roles, and expectations; they are as likely to be repositories for individuals' struggles and tensions . Similar to a focus on the social markers of race, culture, and class, a focus on gender is important to understanding how learners approach, resist, or embrace literacy support and how programs, as a special context and sphere of influence, can create balance between and among adults' sometimes competing gendered roles and learner identities. Gender, then, constitutes a provocative and useful lens into the lives of adult students and the ways in which adult learners shape and revise their purposes for literacy, their ability to sustain engagement in classroom practices, and their perceptions of what is possible for themselves and others in their social networks.

A primary premise of the discussion in this chapter is that gender is important to both adult and family literacy, which are discussed here in tandem. Gender issues have become a natural topic in adult literacy research, practice, and policy discussions—with some of the same possibilities and barriers as discussions of race, culture, and class. Adults are the target of attention as are the extensions and contexts of adults' learning (e.g., the workplace, home, and community). On the other hand, most family literacy discussions typically focus on literacy as a unidirectional activity, from parent (or designated caregiver) to child, with the child's literacy development being the target of attention. Thus, adult and family literacy are, at one and the same time, remarkably similar and remarkably different in how the adult is positioned; how gender definitions and roles are highlighted, discussed, and acted on; how learners in each are studied; and how policies attend to the diversity of adult learner needs. What is common to both areas is the fact that literacy is not neutral and that gendered practices in each may complicate or facilitate access and engagement. What is needed in both is a more concerted effort to understand adult learners within the context of their gendered role definitions, expectations, and experiences and the ways in which these dimensions of learners' identities are addressed by literacy practitioners and by the structure of programs themselves.

A second premise of the conceptual framework in this chapter is the multidimensionality of both identity and literacy (see Hull, Jury, & Zacher, this volume). It draws on the social practice theory of literacy (Barton & Hamilton,1998; Barton, Hamilton, & Ivanic, 2000) in which literacy is constructed as a set of social practices that are associated with different domains of life and are purposeful and embedded in broader social goals and practices. The personal behaviors and literacy practices of adults are seen as linked to socially constructed identities. In this way, the theory reinforces not only prior social practices but also current and future goals and behaviors. When generalized to a discussion of gender and literacy, it encompasses the idea that when adult learners enter programs, they do not leave the meanings, expectations, and struggles of past and current gender roles and responsibilities behind. How they come to define or refine definitions of self and how they choose to take up literacy in their personal, work, and family lives are grounded in and renegotiated against the backdrop of these roles and responsibilities; within the places in which they learn and use literacy; and in their own sense of self, ability, and possibility for learning.

In this chapter, I am interested in adults' identities and the gender definitions and expectations attached to their identities as literacy learners. With an eye toward the ways that programs facilitate access and engagement, I am similarly interested in the ways in which these definitions and expectations are situated in families and other social and cultural contexts and how they are situated, in turn, by the adult in framing and negotiating his or her own learning. This chapter is divided into four parts. The first presents a context for the discussion of gender definitions and conceptualizations. The second focuses on gender discussions in adult and family literacy. The third draws on two case studies of adults from my previous writing and current research. It examines the ways in which the adults' constructions of their gendered and family roles and responsibilities initially made their literacy and their participation in programs problematic, but eventually enabled them to embrace and engage learning in formal literacy programs, or mediated low literacy in home and work settings. The fourth part offers closing considerations.

GENDER DEFINITIONS AND THEIR VARIABILITY

Gender has been described as a highly political and politicized issue, although some argue that gender has yet to assume its rightful place in policy discussions (Di Pierro, 2000; Stromquist, 1998). Over the past 30 years, these political and politicized issues have ranged from educational and professional inequalities facing girls and women (Gilligan, 1982; Kantor, 1977; Pyke, 1996), to the implications of gender for learning and teaching (Datnow, Hubbard, & Conchas, 2001; Orellana, 1995), to the dichotomization of gender (Blackburn, 2005; Dutro, 2003). Global discussions have focused heavily on the limited opportunities for girls' schooling and the ways that traditions in Third World countries, in particular, fail to promote formal education for women. Because of financial constraints, geographic distance between homes and educational centers, and long-held social and cultural practices around family and women's roles in child care, Third World countries have often addressed the issues of gender and schooling in the barest and most fundamental terms—that is, creating modest schools for girls and women with limited resources that often lack sustained, systematic support (Filgueira, 1983; Rockhill, 1987a, 1987b). Gender, feminist, and women rights' scholars denote the inextricability of gender and poverty.

Compared to the problems in Third World countries, our challenges in the United States appear less severe on the surface, at least in relationship to literacy access. However, they are equally pressing in terms of quality, access, and financial support that constrain opportunities for women, minorities, and the poor—sometimes representing one and the same population. Moreover, in addition to connections between gender and poverty, the diversity of U. S. populations requires that we add a third intersecting factor—race—which, even at this point in our history, provokes a level of discomfort among educators at all levels of schooling (Gadsden, 2004; Sleeter, 2001).

Gender is similar to other fields of study that have a longer history of scholarly discourse in that it is linked to a range of conceptual frameworks and definitions that have changed over time. The discussion in this chapter is framed around the idea that the formation of identities and of a gendered identity may be considered an act of invention which individuals refine, reformulate, and recast as life changes, across time, and in different contexts or spaces—in other words, across the life course. Although more recent discussions of gender have been inclusive of gender identity and sexual orientation, gender typically is described as a binary construct which equates womanhood and manhood with femininities and masculinities, locking them into the hierarchies of power which these terms have come to denote in Western societies. This binary, as Michael Kimmel (2000) argued, suggests that "whether through biology or socialization, women act like women, no matter where they are, and that men act like men, no matter where they are" (p. 11). Gender identities based on this binary have been referred to as "essential identities," a concept which has been replaced in many discussions by references to *multiplicity of femininities and masculinities* which exist across peoples and contexts (Litosseliti & Sunderland, 2002). It is worth noting that although outside the scope of the discussion in this chapter, trans-gender identities further complicate this binary and also provide an interesting lens through which to examine traditional notions of gender itself.

Gender differences constitute a persistent theme in discussions of gender, particularly in reference to women's rights and efforts to single out unique char-acteristics of girls and women and boys and men (Maccoby, 1999; Maccoby & Jacklin, 1974; Pleck, 1984). For example, in the United States, the issue is raised every 4 years in reference to whether a woman can be President. Carol Tavris (1993) suggested that gender differences, in fact, represent differences in the individual's access to power. As a result, individuals are thrust into different positions in social hierarchies, with men having more access, historically, than women to higher status positions. In an interesting play on words that speaks to the importance of understanding how issues of gender are constructed, she ar-gued that a person's access and position determine some of what is thought to be gender differences rather than gender differences influencing access and posi-tion. In other words, if men are already in positions of power, they can assert further the superiority of their gendered identities and privilege themselves in different venues of life and society.

We might surmise that the focus on men and women or men versus women is misplaced at the very least, and flawed at the very most. It is difficult to con-sider women and men outside of other factors that contribute to their public presence or private experiences. Women and men do not simply assume a gen-dered identity outside of other identities which affect or determine access and position or outside societal expectations. Hence, as Kimmel (2000) pointed out, we should be examining differences among men and among women, particularly within-group diversity resulting from differences in age, race, ethnicity, culture, and class. He wrote the following:

> If gender varies across culture, over historical time, among men and women within any one culture, and over the life course, can we really speak of masculinity or femininity as though they were constant, uni-versal essences, common to all women and to all men? If not, gender must be seen as an ever-changing fluid assemblage of meanings and behaviors. In that sense, we must speak of masculinities and feminin-ities, and thus recognize the different definitions of masculinity and femininity that we construct. By pluralizing the terms, we acknowledge that masculinity and femininity mean different things to different groups of people at different times. (p. 10)

Another complementary theme in gender studies assumes gender to be what one does, not something possessed by an individual. In other words, it "is a relationship, not a thing" (Kimmel, 2000, p. 113) constructed by the individual and by society (Kimmel, 2000, drawing from Eduard P. Thompson's 1963 work on class). This argument suggests that individuals have the ability to renegotiate expectations associated with gender. However, forces external to the individual are as likely to dictate roles and create barriers to changing role expectations as forces internal to the individual and the immediate contexts of family and community. Kimmel (2000) wrote that we do not simply inherit a male or female sex role, but we actively—interactively—define and redefine what it means to be men or women in our daily encounters with one another. At the same time, "gender is a situated accomplishment, as much an aspect of interaction or identity, in which we produce forms of behavior seen by others in the same immediate situation as masculine or feminine" (Kimmel, 2000, p. 113). As a result, society and social institutions are contexts which reproduce gender differences and (re)inscribe gender inequality. Such inequality functions in concrete terms—in how children form ideas about the options available to them, the tolerance of society, and the roles and expectations attached to their evolving identities. These early perceptions of society and role denotations often travel with them to adulthood.

GENDER IN ADULT AND FAMILY LITERACY

In adult and family literacy, the focus on gender has been primarily on women: for example, as learners in adult literacy and as mothers or caregivers of learners in family literacy. However, the focus on women has a relatively recent history. Reports about adult literacy program participants almost 30 years ago to present (see Kim, Collins, Stowe, & Chandler, 1995) highlight the predominance of women in programs but examine little about the issues facing these women, despite the diversity of their backgrounds and roles.

The emergence of women's issues in literacy over the past two to three decades has provoked questions about gender more broadly. These questions are informed by other socially significant features of identity, including the large numbers of poor women in programs and the persistence of racial discrimination experienced by adult learners (men and women) who are ethnic minorities. This point is taken up in almost all discussions of women's literacy, whether the focus is global or local (Cortina & Stromquist, 2000; Gowen & Barlett, 1997; Stromquist, 1997). These studies describe the varied literacy experiences and practices with which women enter programs as being mapped onto and leveraged against a range of individual needs. These needs, on the surface, appear more appropriate for social service agencies to address than for literacy programs. Hence, both adult and family literacy grapple with the question of whether literacy programs should be concerned with reading and writing in isolation of other social, cultural, and human experiences and needs of learners.

The significance of learners' personal experiences is shared by both adult and family literacy. Accounts of women's participation in programs have chronicled their literacy practices, the familial and community responsibilities that they assume, their purposes for literacy, the economic and personal hardships they experience, and the ways that participation changes them, their families, and their relationships with others (Fingeret, 1983; Purcell-Gates & Waterman, 2000). Researchers such as Hanna Fingeret and others argue that it is virtually impossible to decouple these personal identities outside the classroom from learner identities within the classroom, suggesting that the two are deeply intertwined.

However, the two domains of literacy differ in the ways that the issues of women are identified and attended. Adult literacy practitioners have become increasingly aware of the complicated issues and problems (e.g., conflicts in the home) that are raised for women as well as the revisions of women's self-perceptions (e.g., employability or intolerance for spousal/partner abuse) that result from participating in programs (Cortina & Stromquist, 2000; Horsman, 1990). Much of the impetus for increased attention to these issues, as stated in the introduction of this chapter, is the direct result of international work with women in Third World countries, coupled with our observations of the unsettling similarities between these women's experiences and those of women in the United States. Just as analyses of local issues point to the inextricability of women's poverty and women's oppression, global efforts address the poignancy of women's attempts to participate in literacy learning and schooling, sometimes against apparently insurmountable odds (Evans, 2004; Horsman, 1990, 2000). They attempt to uncover not only the specific barriers to women's literacy and their roles in promoting family well-being but also a more challenging dialogue about the nature of women's experiences in home, program, and community contexts; the persistent demands of child care and family responsibility; tensions in the shifting relationships of women working in and outside the home; and change itself for women which often results from greater access to schooling and literacy instruction (Cortina & Stromquist, 2000). Locally and abroad, childbearing, child care, and household maintenance combine in the lives of poor women to create severe obstacles to their participation in programs, access to opportunity, and educational and social equity.

In family literacy, the attention to women has been less focused on women's gendered roles except as mothers or caregivers to children learning literacy. This prescribed attention to women eliminates women who are not parents or caregivers but who are family or community members and reinscribes the constraints assigned to women by society. In much the same way, issues related to men, until recently, have been ignored. Little research or written discussions about male involvement exists in the literature on practice and programs, and most analyses or reports are still written in venues outside family literacy, for example, early childhood journals (see *Vol. 57 of Young Children*).

Family literacy efforts that address the issues of men typically focus on the role of fathers, an attribution itself to programs' gendered expectations and learners' gendered identities. This interest in men as fathers has been spurred by national initiatives around father involvement. Programs often indicate that engaging fathers is difficult because, as the family's primary breadwinners, they are unavailable when classes are offered (Gadsden, 2002). Fathers who do not co-reside with children or have antagonistic relationships with the mothers of their children also present challenges. Practitioners are often hesitant to involve fathers because the practitioners are uncertain of what the boundaries should be of fathers' relationships with families in conflict. Involving fathers in programs raises questions about how gender is discussed and approached within the interventions themselves (Gadsden & Ray, 2002).

Posing questions and issues related to women and families is appropriate, warranted, and critical. The expectations of women, changing realities of women, and persistence of inequality continue to make women's issues a national and international priority. However, a discussion of gender involves more than a focus on women. A focus on gender needs to address issues and problems common to women and men as well as those unique to each. The importance of examining these issues has been heightened in the past few years as increasing numbers of men have entered adult and family literacy programs, often as a result of workplace downsizing or requirements for men's reentry to home from prison. These changes represent a particularly compelling set of programmatic and conceptual concerns. They are important in the context of education and welfare reform policies that affect gender roles and responsibilities of learners and adult literacy programs as contexts for learning; for example, the number of referrals of men from prisons, to the reduction in women participants resulting from welfare reform requirements, to concerns over the preparation of adult literacy practitioners (primarily women) to respond to new populations of learners.

A critical question for adult and family literacy programs is whether, and the degree to which, they are prepared to address the issues of gender in instructional support and program structure, in light of the changing expectations and social conditions that are related to gender. In other words, in what ways can programs respond appropriately to the gendered needs of both men and women who may share similar backgrounds of poverty, hardship, and low literacy but who are different in their experiences and the expectations assigned to them? Although men's participation in both adult and family literacy programs is still significantly smaller than that of women, an increasing presence of men in classes that have often been populated exclusively by women appears to affect the substance of classroom instruction, discussions, and interactions. In a series of interviews which I conducted with adult and family literacy practitioners, they commented on the shifts in classroom interaction, participation, and engagement when men are present; women participants reportedly share this view (Gadsden, 2003b). Even when the number of men is few, practitioners find themselves changing the topics for class discussion as well as the approaches and materials used and to build on real-life experiences. Most importantly perhaps is that classroom talk itself may change, with women revealing less about issues that affect them as women and mothers and men feeling uncomfortable in female-dominated settings. In other words, not unlike the dynamics in other adult academic contexts, such as postsecondary classrooms, the interactions between and among students and between the adult student and the instructor are affected; for example, in turn-taking, in who gets to talk, and in whose voices are heard, valued, and validated.

Improve My Literacy? Why? Negotiating Gendered Roles, Identity, and Uncertainty

It is not uncommon or unusual for us to weigh what is lost against what is gained when entering new situations because each new situation brings change and uncertainty. The uncertainty of change becomes more pronounced when we are entering a situation in which our backgrounds and vulnerabilities may be disclosed and compromises and negotiations may need to be made. Adult learners weigh gains and losses in determining whether and when they should enter a program. Practitioners and programs may not be prepared for the multiple roles and dimensions of the gendered experiences that learners bring and the ways in which these experiences and adults' prior learning shape their presentation of self and investment in the program. For example, it is possible for programs and practitioners to be sensitive to the issues of women but not attend to the diversity of women and women's experiences. They may welcome men but not create environments where men are engaged or, alternatively, create environments where men can assume center stage, relegating women to the background. Whatever the structure of learning opportunities in programs, learners may appear to struggle prior to and throughout their participation with different dimensions of their identity in relation to literacy learning, and how these dimensions are understood: low literate, provider, man, woman, mother, father, worker, heterosexual, homosexual. Both prior to and continuously through their participation in a program, this struggle can surface the following question: "Why do I need to improve my literacy?" "After all," one young father pointed out to me, "I'm makin' it okay."

In this section, I provide two short case studies of adult learners participating in adult literacy programs. These case studies are intended to inform the discussion of programs' work with adults by (a) highlighting adults' experiences in out-of-program contexts and prior to entering programs, and (b) demonstrating how these experiences are shaped by the gender expectations of society, of family and community, of programs, and of self; and the implications for program engagement and participation. Both of these purposes are cast against the importance of positioning adults' experiences within public policies that affect adults' personal dreams and their ability to sustain themselves.

Fred: Gender As a Struggle of Father Absence, Stereotypes, and Low Literacy

Fred Jones is an African American father who, along with his wife, Cindy, and son, Malik, participated in a family literacy portrait study in a New York City public school. Malik was a second grader at the time that the study and accompanying parent workshops were initiated. Fred and Cindy are parents to four children (two girls and two boys) and live in a low-income, low-middle-income community. Fred moved from the South to New York City with his parents when he and his siblings were young children. Both Fred and Cindy have managed generally to remain employed, despite having been laid off from several jobs because of downsizing. Fred takes pride in being the primary provider— "the man" in his household. He says proudly that his family has never been on public assistance: "We have always been able to make do. If we are ever in crunch, you know, I know we can depend on family members to chip in—as long as it looks like we're trying." Fred and Cindy have raised their children in a close-knit family whose members have supported each other in crisis. The family makes periodic pilgrimages to their southern home of origin, and the children are familiar with, if not close to, their maternal extended family members. Fred and Cindy have a good relationship with their children and regularly share stories from their own childhood and extended family experiences. They see and articulate the importance of education and of the responsibility of "men" and "women" as parents, wage-earners, and citizens.

As part of the parent workshops, parents and children were asked to paint or draw their own family portraits and to locate themselves in the family portrait. Malik and his classmates created these portraits with the help of their parents or other family members whereas other children brought in pictures. The parents themselves organized into small working groups in which they talked about the relationships between their cultural expectations and their family expectations, their hopes around literacy and schooling, and the contributions that they were willing to make to ensure their children's well-being. They were welcomed in the classroom as a site of learning for their children and for themselves—as a place in which reciprocity of learning between adult and child could take place. As a result, there was a deepened understanding by most about the processes of reading and writing, the ways that parents can assist their children and the teacher, and the role of classroom interactions. During these meetings, Fred was one of the few fathers in attendance and the most engaged. He consistently and publicly expressed the need for fathers to be active in these family literacy activities and children's school experiences, noting that "children need to see men involved" and "sometimes you have to give up somethin' to get somethin' for your kids."

Because Fred was the most active father in the program, his vocal resistance to the idea of the family portraits as well as the family and social history tasks about midway in the school year came as a surprise. His behavior was extremely perplexing to me because from the outset, he was generally cooperative and engaged in ways that led me to believe that we had developed a mutually trusting relationship. I was unsure as to why he was resistant to the activities and distrustful of the project's goals. Initially, I thought that he had been laid off or that there was some unrevealed dissonance between the activities in class and his experiences. I decided to observe, wait, and listen, and to be prepared to ask appropriate questions at the appropriate time. Fred grudgingly continued to participate in the project, being vocal in the focus groups about general issues but becoming distracted quickly and easily during actual literacy tasks. For example, at the same time that he seemed to like the idea of family portraits, he resisted the idea of including past generations. I assumed that his discomfort and distrust were a function of the added responsibility of the work along with a desire to forget the past, despite his focus on family history with Malik. In the workshops, Fred was exposed to texts about the conditions of the pre-Civil Rights South and discussions about the abject poverty among minorities throughout the urban North. I thought that it was possible that these images were overwhelming, making it more appealing (and useful as a coping mechanism) for Fred to disassociate himself from the past and live in a present in which race and racism are minimized and class differences are not seen as notable divides.

After visiting Fred and Cindy in their home a couple of times and talking more comfortably with Fred, Fred revealed the traumas of his life as a young boy in a low-income home with a father who, after vacillating between his family responsibilities and his inability to support his family, left the family. Fred stated, "I felt like I was the only kid whose dad left 'em, [although I knew other children with dads who had left them and their mothers]. I looked, you know, for the fathers … . Now, I still look for the Black fathers." We discussed the fact that throughout history such father evacuations have occurred across ethnic groups when men felt overwhelmed by the financial responsibilities of a wife, children, and other family members (see Mintz, 2001).

Fred continued to resist the idea of the family portraits. His inner struggles were being projected against a backdrop of low literacy, secrecy about his (in)ability to read, and apparently unresolved feelings of abandonment. After considerable conversations with Fred in person and by telephone, he revealed that he could barely read—reading only well enough to figure out his name, the names of his children, and landmarks and signs. Although we had given a short, informal assessment measure to the parents, only Cindy had completed it. Fred described himself to me as a "respectable con artist," noting that people often thought he was well-educated. Not unlike other low-literate adults, he was an astute observer of highly literate individuals in different settings. He worked in a hospital and spent considerable time talking to physicians, nurses, and other well-educated professionals.

By my sixth home visit, Fred had begun to embrace the project. He used the moment to remove the private nature of his low literacy and his personal conflict as a man. How, after all, could he maintain their respect if his children knew about his low literacy, a question that many low-literate learners ask. Because of Malik's interest in the project, Cindy's work with Malik, and Fred's spoken longing to unravel his family history, Fred made several important decisions that would affect him, his children, and the perceptions of those close to him. The first was to enroll in a formal adult literacy program. The second was to work on the assignments from the project during his class so that he was better prepared to work with Malik in the portrait study. He used the resources of the project as well to identify new and emerging interests and revise some of his expectations of manhood—cultural expectations he had adopted that both protected and made him vulnerable. The third was to chronicle the process of learning that he was experiencing in the research project and in the program. He did so by journaling, an activity which men often report that they do not enjoy. He acknowledged that to improve literacy, he had to grapple with negative stereotypes of Black men as disengaged with their children, his responsibility to "be there" for his children and assume the role of breadwinner, views on manhood and the public vestiges of "being a man" at all costs, and the fear that in revealing his low literacy he would disappoint his children.

Fred's early hardships were somewhat eased by a supportive mother and a school experience that was more social than academic. Later, he struggled with a sense of shame over "being a man and not knowing enough to help [his] kids." His mother had been his support as a child, but he believed that Cindy should not have to do the same for him in adulthood. "I am my wife's support," he proudly asserted ... "that's the way it should be." Thus, his carefully crafted role as man and provider made enrolling in an adult program one of the most difficult things he had ever done, according to Fred. It was critical that the program provide an inviting space and that the context and the instructional activities allow him to keep secret or disclose, as he felt it was appropriate, different dimensions of his experiences and struggles around masculinity, personal dissonance about his role as a Black father, societal stereotypes around Black men, and the images of strength and persistence which he hoped to transmit to his children and make public in his community. Although the adult literacy program and Fred's teacher were seeking to provide a place to support him, he noted that he was being challenged by the discussions about Black men with women—teacher and students—in the program he attended. Fred had hopes and continues to hope that he can claim a voice in his own familial history, specifically to grapple with his identity as man and father and the unfinished experiences of literacy learning.

Trudy: Transitioning Identities From Home to School[7]

Trudy is a White, middle-aged woman who grew up in an historically poor White neighborhood in a large Eastern city, where she resides today. She lives in a row house on a narrow one-way block. Unlike many houses near or in similar areas of the city, Trudy's house is not surrounded by vacant houses. There is no visible graffiti or any burned out or abandoned houses on her street. There is a small porch area in the front of Trudy's house. A large air conditioner is in the first floor front window. The house is in a community of Whites, where Blacks and other minorities do not generally travel. In fact, on the day the teacher-researcher, an African American woman who had been Trudy's instructor, visited to interview Trudy, the interviewer was met with long stares from community people and family as she emerged from her car. The apparent dissonance that the teacher's presence created was evident, in part, in the greeting the teacher received as she entered the porch. Trudy's son, without making eye contact or acknowledging the teacher, simply called out "Ma." Perhaps, Trudy had mentioned to her children that the teacher was visiting, or the son may have associated the teacher's visit with his own memories of why teachers would visit a student. However, the discomfort of having the teacher visit was evident, even in Trudy's interaction. On hearing the son's announcement of the teacher's arrival, Trudy came outside to meet the teacher, closed the door behind her, and talked to the teacher on the porch.

Trudy has had a difficult life; her mother died when she was 12. Her father was a sheet metal worker. None of her five brothers and sisters completed high school. In search of a decent life, Trudy dropped out of school at 17 to marry a young man who went on to become a firefighter. After 17 years of marriage, however, her husband left her. In the more than 10 years since, she has received welfare to support herself and four children. Prior to her divorce, Trudy felt certain about her culture's gender expectations of women: As a mother and wife, she was to provide a clean house for her husband and children, provide good meals, and take care of the children. That is what all the women did in her neighborhood and in her family. Even when couples separated, the woman assumed the role of protected—in Trudy's case, protected by the state. Although the source of her support changed, the fact that she would be supported did not.

The shifts in welfare policy that require women to work outside the home displaced Trudy's sense of herself as a mother and provider for her children and was inconsistent with the long-held familial, societal, and governmental identi-

---

7 This case summary is drawn from work conducted with Jacqueline Jackson, a doctoral candidate in the University of Pennsylvania Graduate School of Education.

ties that were assigned to women. Not only was Trudy negotiating old and new expectations and working to be strategic in caring for a family, despite meager personal resources, she was also faced with making her uncertainty about these expectations, her low literacy, and fears around literacy, public. It became urgent for her to improve her literacy and receive the General Educational Development (GED) certificate. When Trudy left school 20 years earlier, she stated that she saw the move "not as an end but a beginning." Employment at local mills, factories, and plants was plentiful with many opportunities for overtime, and the role of the husband was clear in making good on these opportunities.

Trudy had entered the adult literacy program while in the throes of uncertainty. The combination of urban blight, low literacy, and the termination of welfare made life difficult for her in the late 1990s. She had been enrolled in GED classes for 3 years prior to entering the adult literacy program. She had not been able to earn the score of 225 required to pass the test. In her initial conversation with her teacher, she admitted that she had always been painfully shy and that she got so nervous when she went to take the test that she could not remember anything. "It was," she stated, "as if [her] mind went blank." In subsequent sessions, she talked about her schooling experiences, stating that they left her anxious and exacerbated her shyness. After several meetings, she admitted to the teacher that she had been in "special classes," stating: "I never told no one about being, in special classes ... I was just too embarrassed." However, she could not recall ever being told why she had been placed in the classes, painfully sharing, "I guess I was just slow. I have to read and read it again. Everything takes me such a long time."

When Trudy contemplates the options available to her, her role as a mother is at the center—she considers the plight of her children. Trudy's sons left high school before graduating. Her hopes for the future are pinned on her youngest child, a daughter, now a high school student. Trudy stated, "She's part of the reason I stuck it out. I wanted my kids to respect me. I wanted them to think highly of me." Because her sons no longer attend school, they are not on Trudy's welfare budget, although they reside in the home, and she continues to provide some support for them.

Trudy's struggles as a literacy learner were complicated by the fact that she was experiencing a form of displacement at the time of the interview. With her welfare checks about to end and services at the program reduced, the likelihood that she could participate in the program and maintain her hopes as a learner and a role model to her daughter were slim. Context as the larger learning environment, and home as a specific domain unite with social class in ways that mitigate against the possibilities that Trudy will achieve her goals or that her hopes for her daughter will be realized. She relies on the literacy program in which she participates to help her construct new identities as a worker, a woman in contemporary times, and a learner. The script that she wrote for herself as a young 17-year-old bride is being rewritten by forces beyond her control with little reference to the travails that she endures as a low-income woman, mother, and learner.

CLOSING CONSIDERATIONS: GENDER, ROLE, AND CONTEXT IN LITERACY PROGRAMS

When the lives of Fred and Trudy are seen as the primary units of analysis, we observe them as connected in the shared goal to enhance their literacies. Their stories are intertwined with issues of gender—in relationship to their gendered histories (as a son or a daughter who did not learn to read and write well), in relationship to the present (as they reflect on the spaces in which they use literacy and seek to strengthen the bonds with their children as a man or father and a woman or mother), and in relationship to the future (as they contemplate the possibilities for their children). Intergenerational learning is a dominant image throughout the case studies, with parents viewing their literacy skills through the lens of their (gendered) children and relating their own literacy to their experiences as gendered children interacting with gendered parents.

The constructions of gender and role are complex and tightly interwoven in both case studies, and are also affected by issues of race and class. However, the degree to which the adults view themselves outside of a role-specific identity (mother, father, son, or daughter) is difficult to tease apart, raising questions about how they acknowledge their ideas of femininities and masculinities or the compartmentalization of roles ascribed to women and men. What are the implications of these structured genders, gendered differences, and role identities for how they construct literacy events, untangle the different dimensions of their lives, and make sense of the familiar and unfamiliar texts of literacy learning?

For Fred, gender is a deeply cultural experience. Here, I refer to culture in much the same way others have written about identity and gender—as fluid, changing, and dynamic. For Trudy, gender fits a small, externally defined set of behaviors and practices. For both Fred and Trudy, roles formerly assigned to men are taken up by women, and many roles assigned to women are taken up by men. The blurring of the divide for these adults is primarily a shifting line between role and context, with role being influenced by context and context shaping role. There is commonality across the kinds of responsibilities that they confront in relationship to spouses and extended family members—in how they talk about and unpack the issues of childhood. For example, context for Trudy has become increasingly problematic as home has changed—with the absence of her husband—and the community in which home is center has shifted dramatically. Concepts of self and a gendered self are deeply affected by these shifts, which ask Trudy, her sons, and her daughter to struggle with a new gendered identity in the midst of community and personal change. The case studies point to some of the ways in which the lives of adults are similar and how adults' personal interpretations of their cultural and social histories permeate their sense of present and future possibility and potentially their participation in programs.

Fred and Trudy struggle with multiple responsibilities and emerging identities as literacy learners. In each case, learning was initiated for family-related purposes. Both were restricted by the limits of social class—limits that prescribe their access to information about their options and the actual choices they can make. Their pathways to and participation in the programs are determined, in part, by the role they assumed or the role that was imposed—as parent, spouse or partner, caregiver to extended family, worker, and learner. If we were to add case studies of second-language learners such as those to which Strucker and Davidson (2003) and Wrigley (this volume) refer—from widely varying cultures and with diverse experiences of childbearing, employment, and class—the issues of role and gendered identities likely become considerably more complex.

Between home and program, the adults in the case studies rethought, revised, and reshaped their roles —influenced significantly over time by the emergence of new knowledge and a new sense of self. These roles can be considered as the multiplicity of responsibilities that contribute to a real or perceived identity as learner. They rarely exist in isolation from and are reciprocal with gendered identities and social statuses (as literacy learner, parent, provider, and family member). Context can be constructed as place or physical setting (e.g., home) as well as social space (e.g., gathering places) and familial relationships. In the case studies, gender dictated how the adults entered into their roles as learners, parents, women, men, and spouses; interpreted these roles, and attached meaning to them. This is perhaps no more vivid than in the case of Fred who, as an African American man, is one of a small group of men who typically participates in literacy programs. However, fathers are increasingly joining family literacy programs, bringing different ways of interacting with the staff, expectations, goals, perspectives, and sensitivities regarding the vulnerability associated with low literacy—vulnerability considered in terms of the problems of limited skill and ideas about masculinity, breadwinning roles, and power. The specific issues raised by fathers—particularly low-income, sporadically employed fathers—may represent unfamiliar territories of exclusion, racism, and discrimination that programs have not examined in the past (Gadsden, 2003a).

The issues facing Fred and Trudy could be presented in the contexts of either adult or family literacy programs. Although the specific course of activity may differ, both need to center the adult in its work. Adult and family literacy programs involve adults who both are learning for themselves and whose learning has the potential to affect others. Although this relationship of individual learner to others in home contexts is more explicit in family literacy, it has been chronicled in work on adults in adult literacy programs (Rodriguuez-Brown & Meehan, 1998; Street, 1995). Thus, a point of convergence for both domains of literacy is the adult learner and the ways that he or she approaches, accesses, and is engaged in learning. A focus on these issues helps in understanding why adults stay in programs, not only why they drop out. It calls for a more critical conceptual framework and set of actions, structures, and practices (Belzer, 2004; Purcell-Gates & Waterman, 2000).

In both domains of literacy, the issue of gender must be addressed in structural terms: for example, how programs are developed, how they see their missions, how they articulate these missions, and how the environments in which they are located speak to the diversity of gender experiences and lives of learners. This is no simple task, however. For example, simply putting pictures of men and women in full view may defeat the purpose unless reading selections are made that do not further stereotype. Recruiting men and fathers as participants and teachers may tip the balance of participation with unintended consequences. Providing for the perceived needs of diverse women may not cohere with the needs of the women. In other words, the structural issues that help to define gender directly intrude into the classroom, although little empirical data exist that describe this. Despite considerable writing and discussion by practitioners about the specific needs and problems faced by women, few critical analyses of how practitioners in general respond to student differences, particularly in the harshest scenarios, have been conducted (see Belzer, 2004). In addition to thinking about difference, what additional questions might adult and family literacy raise about other structural factors that originate in the different expectations of gendered roles for women and men and values we assign to these roles and responsibilities?

Child care and responsibility for children is a vital factor, with men increasing their role, but women continuing to carry the lion's share of care for children and carework for other family members (Stromquist, 1998). Income is another factor, which, in the larger population, differentiates men and women (although not necessarily minorities) but may be less divisive in adult and family literacy programs where participants typically share similar economic circumstances. It is the convergence of issues around class and poverty that may mediate other gendered and role differences between men and women in and out of the classroom contexts.

A third issue might revolve around prevailing assumptions about the value of literacy to men versus women. The relatively small number of men in literacy programs is both a function of their employment status and societal expectations of men as breadwinners and of the perception that there is no need to improve literacy if the man has a job. Another reason concerns the large presence of women in programs and programs being deemed spaces for women only. Hence, poor men who need literacy support are unlikely to take up with literacy programs, if acknowledgement of their limitations is a prerequisite.

Another area for consideration in thinking through gender is teaching and problematizing the work of teaching beyond the academic content to engage students and sustain their engagement over time. Although work on gender in kindergarten through grade 12 (K-12) settings has highlighted many critical issues regarding interactions between teachers and male versus female learners, the most comprehensive discussion of how teachers think about and approach issues of teaching difficult topics or socially and politically sensitive topics has come from discussions of multicultural education and diversity in K-12 teaching, and questions of who can teach whom most effectively. For example, in considering whether White, middle-class teachers are prepared to teach ethnically diverse students, Sleeter (2001) argued for a complicating of the idea to include the ways in which difference is understood. Perhaps the question, as Ladson-Billings (1997), Delpit (1999), Cochran-Smith (2004), and others might argue, is whether teachers—whatever their gender, ethnic, racial, or class background—have the will to seek the best approaches to teaching all learners. Ladson-Billings examined the possibilities of any teacher being able to teach any student, if the commitment to understanding the diverse needs as well as diverse cultural and social contexts in which learners access and use the literacies of school is present. The reality, it seems, is that we do not always know which students we will teach and that, in fact, over a teacher's professional life course, he or she should expect shifts in the populations that will be served.

Adult and family literacy programs are faced increasingly as well with responding to policy changes outside of education—for example, welfare reform in health and human service and reentry from the justice system. However, the effects of legislation outside of education receive relatively modest attention, although learners such as Trudy are affected, as are practitioners. With legislation focused on welfare reform and corrections or reentry, programs have experienced increases of men. Those programs are finding themselves needing to reimagine their roles and raise questions about what it means to participate in an adult or family literacy program and how the changing gender composition of literacy learning environments will influence learning for men and women. For example, practitioners and programs will need to examine a range of questions as a part of their preparation and planning for instruction and student support such as: will men feel comfortable reading essays about sexual behavior, abuse, or violence, particularly if they have been exposed to such behavior and have been the perpetrators of it; will women be hesitant to reveal themselves in these settings; and is candor and authenticity a casualty of classrooms in which gendered role identities are positioned in relation to each other and at the center of the work? Some would argue that an expansive and critical framework that addresses the broad dimensions of diversity and learners is needed to address such questions.

Last, what are the issues with which the field will need to struggle and address to begin a discourse and to develop a conceptual framework? How will this framework interrogate the literacy classroom as an open context, not bound by walls which shape and form thinking, but as spaces in which meaning is constructed and explored. Three issues emerge. One is linked to the pedagogical stance that the instructor assumes (Ellsworth, Healey, & Baratta, 1994). It becomes important to ask whether it is possible to interrupt typical ways of doing to examine the complexities of considering new issues (e.g., the issues of men), to examine existing understandings and perspectives in new ways (e.g., the diversity of women's experiences and the relational issues of women to men in an historically male-dominated society), and to open up discussions that have real-world impact? A second concern is an organizational and pedagogical one. Here the questions that need to be asked include the following: What is the content that will be used, and what are the forms in which it should be presented? As Purcell-Gates, Jacobson, and Degener, (2004) noted, the difficult problem of using real-life materials and examples is that real life changes. As a result, teaching must, by necessity, be a dynamic process in which the teacher acknowledges the diffuse nature of the work of teaching. However, there is a larger issue of how certain content that highlights gendered identity issues should be interrogated in classes—in relationship to adult learners or the possibilities for their children as people who are ascribed gendered identities?

In this chapter, I have been interested primarily in raising issues about gender as these issues are experienced in both adult and family literacy programs. Rather than separating the two, I have been more interested in highlighting the real and potential complementarity between both and the need for discussions between the two to address important issues of learning and teaching. It is possible that adult and family literacy efforts should work more aggressively to find and build the common ground between individual and family-focused literacy. In this way, both can identify critical propositions to be considered in refining their purposes, goals, and approaches to examining questions of gender rigorously.

Adults in family literacy programs are, similar to Fred and Trudy, motivated to attend programs primarily to participate in their children's schooling and to ensure their children's literacy development. Even if no additional assignments are given to address the specific needs of adults, the demands of parent-child activities in programs often result in parents recognizing the need to improve their own literacy if, in fact, they are to assist their children. As is often the case, however, parents, particularly young parents, want to reshape their own lives—to bring into the same lens—their adult persona and the multiple domains of their lives. They often seek change through employment and through increased understanding of how to navigate the "not-so-still" waters of schools and the educators in them, family configurations and practices, nutrition and health, the ways they spend their time, and a possible future self (Gadsden, 2004). These changes cut across multiple spheres and often require that the notions of role and responsibility, context and location, as well as gender, be examined carefully as they relate to changed practices.

It is important to note in these closing considerations that gender is a more complex concept than this chapter could cover. My discussion of gender in relationship to men and women primarily is itself a narrowing of current perspectives and a reifying of the binary. I, like others, am limited by the English language (see Blackburn, 2005) in expressing the continuum of gender identities and by the relative newness of these broader concepts in adult and family literacy. The growing efforts around women's rights have helped to construct a broader framework in which deeper analyses are possible, and the experiences of both women and men are considered outside of male-female dichotomies. A criticism across discussions of gender, and relevant to adult and family literacy, is the tendency to group women's experiences into one single reference and men's into another, except in the case of poor minority men whose experiences tend to be grouped together by researchers, practitioners, policymakers, and the public (Stromquist, 1998). Adult and family literacy programs will need to address the intersections of gender with race, class, and culture and the diversity within and across different individuals and the gendered identities they assume. These social markers do not exist in isolation. Rather they are part of a complex web of experiences and relationships that both derive from and contribute to gendered identities, roles, and contexts.

REFERENCES

Barton, D., & Hamilton, M. (1998). *Local literacies; reading and writing in one community.* New York: Routledge.

Barton, D., Hamilton, M., & Ivanic, R. (Eds.). (2000). *Situated literacies: Reading and writing in context.* New York: Routledge.

Belzer, A. (2004). Blundering toward critical pedagogy: True tales from the adult literacy classroom. In R. St. Clair & J. Sandlin (Eds.), *From critical theory to critical practice* (pp. 5-13). San Francisco: Jossey-Bass.

Blackburn, M. V. (2005). Disrupting dichotomies for social change: A review of, critique of, and complement to current educational literacy scholarship on gender. *Research in the Teaching of English, 39,* 398-416.

Cochran-Smith, M. (2004). *Walking the road: Race, diversity, and social justice in teacher education.* New York: Teachers College Press.

Cortina, R., & Stromquist, N. (Eds.). (2000). *Gender and education in Latin America: Distant alliances.* New York: Garland.

Datnow, A., Hubbard, L., & Conchas, G. Q. (2001). How context mediates policy: The implementation of single gender public schooling in California. *Teachers College Record, 103,* 184-206.

Delpit, L.. (1999). *Other people's children: Cultural conflict in the classroom.* New York: New Press.

Di Pierro, M. C. (2000). Public policy and adult education for women in Brazil. In R. Cortina & N. Stromquist. (Eds.), *Gender and education in Latin America: Distant alliances* (pp. 47–71). New York: Garland.

Dutro, E. (2003). "Us boys like to read football and boy stuff": Reading masculinities, performing boyhood. *Journal of Literacy Research, 34,* 465-500.

Ellsworth, N. J., Healey, C. N., & Baratta, A. N. (1994). *Literacy: A redefinition.* Hillsdale, NJ: Lawrence Erlbaum Associates, Inc.

Evans, K. (2004). Spaces of possibility: The place of writing in urban drug treatment. *Women's Studies Quarterly, 32,* 115-129.

Filgueira, C. (December). To educate or not to educate: Is that the question? *CEPAL Review, 21,* 56-86.

Fingeret, A. (1983). Social networks: A new perspective on independence and illiterate adults. *Adult Education Quarterly, 3,* 133-145.

Gadsden, V., & Ray, A. (2002). Engaging fathers: Issues and considerations for early childhood educators. *Young Children, 57*(6), 32-42.

Gadsden, V. L. (2002). *Family literacy: Issues in research and research-informed practice.* In J. Coming, B. Garner, & C. Smith (Eds.), *Annual review of adult learning and literacy* (Vol. 3, (pp. 248-287). San Francisco: Jossey-Bass.

Gadsden, V. L. (2003a). Expanding the concept of "family" in family literacy: Integrating a focus on fathers. In A. DeBruin-Parecki & B. Krol-

Sinclair (Eds.), *Family literacy: From theory to practice* (pp. 86-125). Newark, DE: International Reading Association.

Gadsden, V. L. (2003b). *Interviews with adult and family literacy practitioners.* Unpublished manuscript, University of Pennsylvania, Philadelphia.

Gadsden, V. L. (2004). Family literacy and culture. In B. H. Wasik (Ed.), *Handbook of family literacy.* Mahwah, NJ: Lawrence Erlbaum Associates, Inc.

Gilligan, C. (1982). *In a different voice.* Cambridge, MA: Harvard University Press.

Gowen, S.G., & Bartlett, C. (1997). Friends in the kitchen: Lessons from survivors. In G. Hull (Ed.), *Changing work, changing workers, critical perspectives on language, literacy, and skills* (pp. 131-158). New York: State University Press, Albany Press.

Horsman, J. (1990). *Something in mind besides the everyday.* Toronto, Ontario, Canada: Women's Press.

Horsman, J. (2000). *Too scared to learn: Women, violence, and education.* Mahwah, NJ: Lawrence Erlbaum Associates, Inc.

Kantor, E. M. (1977). *Men and women in the corporation.* New York: Harper & Row.

Kim, K., Collins, M., Stowe, P., & Chandler, K. (1995). *Forty percent of adults participate in adult education activities: 1994-95.* Washington, DC: National Center for Education Statistics.

Kimmel, M. (2004). *The gendered society.* New York: Oxford University Press.

Ladson-Billings, G. (1997). The dreamkeepers: Successful teachers of African-American children. Thousand Oaks, CA: Jossey-Bass.

Litosseliti, L., & Sunderland, J. (2002). *Gender identity and discourse analysis.* Philadelphia: Benjamins.

Maccoby, E. E. (1999). *The two sexes: Growing up apart, coming together.* Cambridge, MA; Harvard University Press.

Maccoby, E. E., & Jacklin, C. N. (1974). *What does this mean? The psychology of sex differences.* Stanford, CA: Stanford University Press.

Mintz, S. (2001). From patriarchy to androgyny and other myths: Placing men's family roles in historical perspective. In A. J. Cherlin (Ed.), *Public and private families: A reader* (pp. 42–51). New York: McGraw-Hill.

Orellana, M. F. (1995). Literacy as a gendered social practice: Tasks, texts, talk, and take-up. *Reading Research Quarterly, 30,* 678-708.

Pleck, J. (1984). The theory of male sex role identity: Its rise and fall, 1936 to the present. In M. Lewin (Ed.), *In the shadow of the past: Psychology portrays the sexes* (pp. 205-255). New York: Columbia University Press.

Purcell-Gates, V., Jacobson, E., & Degener, S. (2004). *Print literacy development: Uniting cognitive and social practice theories.* Cambridge, MA: Harvard University Press.

Purcell-Gates, V., & Waterman, R. A. (2000). *Now we read, we see, we speak: Portrait of literacy development in an adult Freirean-based class.* Mahwah, NJ: Lawrence Erlbaum Associates, Inc.

Pyke, K. D. (1996). Class-based masculinities: The interdependence of gender, class, and interpersonal power. *Gender & Society, 10,* 527-549.

Rockhill, K. (1987a). Gender, language and the politics of literacy. *British Journal of Sociology, 8,* 153-167.

Rockhill, K. (1987b). Literacy as threat/desire. Longing to be SOMEBODY. In J. Gaskell & A. McLaren (Eds.), *Women and education: A Canadian perspective* (pp. 315-331). Calgary: Detselig Enterprises/Temeron Books.

Rodriguez-Brown, F. V., & Meehan, M. A. (1998). Family literacy and adult education: Project FLAME. In M. C. Smith (Ed.), *Literacy for the twenty-first century: Research, policy, practices, and the National Adult Literacy Survey* (pp. 175-194). Westport, CT: Greenwood Publishing Group.

Sleeter, C. (2001). *Culture, difference, and power.* New York: Teachers College Press.

Street, B. V. (1995). *Literacy in theory and practice.* New York: Cambridge University Press.

Strucker, J., & Davidson, R. (2003). *Adult Reading Components Study* (ARCS). (NCSALL Research Brief No. X). Cambridge, MA: National Center for the Study of Adult Learning and Literacy.

Stromquist, N. (1998). The institutionalization of gender and its impact on educational policy. *Comparative Education, 34,* 85-100.

Stromquist, N.P. (1997). *Literacy for citizenship: Gender and grassroots dynamics in Brazil.* New York: State University of New York, Albany Press.

Tavris, C. (1993). The mismeasure of woman: Paradoxes and perspectives in the study of gender. In J. D. Goodchilds (Ed.), *Psychological perspectives on human diversity in America* (pp. 91-136). Washington, DC: American Psychological Association.

Thompson, E.P. (1963). *The making of the English working class.* London, UK: Victor Gollancz Ltd.

Chapter 16

Possible Selves:
Literacy, Identity, and Development in Work, School, and Community

Glynda A. Hull
University of California, Berkeley

Mark Jury
University at Albany, State University of New York

Jessica Zacher
California State University, Long Beach

In this chapter, we juxtapose ethnographic and qualitative data from three projects carried out over a period of approximately 10 years: studies of the literacy requirements of new and traditionally organized workplaces in the Silicon Valley, a vocational program designed to provide intensive training on information technologies and life skills, and a community technology center offering adults and youth accesses and introductions to new literacies and attendant technologies (cf. New London Group, 1996). Some of the participants in these studies were recent immigrants and still struggled with English, whereas others had been born in the United States but had struggled in school. Most would be categorized as "low income," and virtually all were looking—in school, in work, or through affiliations with community organizations—for opportunities to redesign their life chances, to start afresh, to get a new job, or simply to improve, grow, or accomplish (cf. Greene, 1990). Intertwined with these processes was an interest in and concern with literacy—a concern on our part, as literacy researchers, to be sure—but often a concern as well on the part of employers, workers, teachers, and students.

Over the course of our work in these contexts, we came to think a great deal about identity and development in adulthood. Admittedly, these are abstract and contested terms, and with them come decades of complex theorizing and research. Yet, they are terms that adult educators must of necessity appropriate and populate with their own intentions, to borrow Bakhtin's (1981) phrasing. We eventually came to frame identity and development as the narrative or storied construction and reconstruction over time of a sense of self as agent, as an actor able to influence present circumstances and future possibilities. Of special interest to us were adults' prospective visions, hence the "possible selves" of our title (cf. Emirbayer & Mische, 1998; Markus & Nurius, 1986). As is apparent, this framing reflects our philosophies as adult educators, as well as our theoretical orientation as students of sociocultural theory and our understandings of literacy and language as mediational tools (cf. Cole, 1996; Vygotsky, 1978). We have been interested, that is, in programs, curricula, and participant structures that enable "the initiation of relatively autonomous acts governed by our intentional states—our wishes, desires, beliefs, and expectancies" (Bruner, 1994, p. 41). We are aware that notions of agency and identity are culturally variable and follow Emirbayer and Mische (1998), who acknowledged that different conceptions of the relationships among past, present, and future enable distinctive forms of agentive activity.

A concern with the nature of personal identity was a leitmotiv of the 20th century and has assumed a special importance during the past quarter century. In the words of social psychologist Kenneth Gergen, "Under postmodern conditions persons exist in a state of continuous construction and reconstruction ... . Each reality of self gives way to reflexive questionings, irony, and ultimately the playful probing of yet another reality" (1991, pp. 5-6). Similarly, social theorist Anthony Giddens wrote of late modernity's "reflexive project of the self" and its "continuously revised, biographical narratives" (1991, p. 5). Proposing the related concept of ever evolving "possible selves" as an aspect of self-knowledge, psychologists Markus and Nurius (1986) added a developmental perspective, viewing human growth and change "as a process of acquiring and then achieving or resisting certain possible selves" (p. 955). Our interest in identity and development in the context of work, vocational school, and community, and about literacy as refracted through such an identity perspective, grew from a desire to understand the challenge, complexity, and richness of the self-constructive projects of our adult students, many of whom were alert to the need to, in some sense, reinvent themselves. With Maxine Greene (1990), we recognized the importance for these students of being able to "perceive alternate possibilities" (p. 37), and, hand in glove, to perceive themselves as capable in a range of ways, capable of new and different things. This is a crucial ability, she insists, "if people are to maintain their sense of agency and become capable of new beginnings" (p. 46).

One goal of this chapter, as has been the case for the research on which it is based, is to present the worlds of work, vocational training, and adult education from the points of view of adult students and workers. A second goal is to ask what such research can tell us that is useful for policy and practice. What guidance might this research offer educators and literacy specialists whose programs and classes provide the context, opportunity, and sometimes the impetus for the shaping of new selves?

AN IDENTITY FRAMEWORK

There is a massive literature on identity ranging from psychologist Erikson's (1963) stage model of development formulated in the United States a half century ago, to perspectives from anthropology, sociology, and most recently, from interdisciplinary fields such as cultural studies (cf. Holland, Lachicotte, Skinner, & Cain, 1998). Although early views of self privileged coherence, unity, consistency, and permanence, it has become customary to characterize identity as shifting, multiple, contradictory (Weedon, 1996), and reflexive (Giddens, 1991). In fact, through the work of Bruner (1994) and others (e.g., Ochs & Capps, 2001), we've learned to think of the construction of self as the making of a narrative, a story that one tells oneself about who one was and is and wants to become (cf. Markus & Nurius, 1986). With such a narrative perspective, there has been a shift from mining biographies for actual events in individual's lives toward understanding how people interpret their actions and represent themselves. With this project the importance of language and other forms of representation comes to the fore. There are several recent examples of taking such a narrative approach to development in the adult education literature (e.g., Clark, 2001; Rossiter, 1999).

Notions of identity have increasingly been brought to bear on studies of literacy and learning. Especially influential in the field of New Literacy Studies has been Gee's (1996) discourse framework, notably the idea of "identity kits," ways of writing and reading, along with ways of thinking, dressing, talking, acting, and valuing (cf. Foucault, 1979). Through this lens, researchers have moved from considering literacy primarily as an isolable skill or even a cultural practice, to considering literacy acquisition and learning as governed by participation in or incorporation by larger social projects. In other words, we can see acquisition and learning as central to the process of being or becoming particular kinds of people who participate with others in socially recognized and sanctioned ways (cf. Lave & Wenger, 1991; Wenger, 1998). Contemporary studies of literacy now regularly reference identity, with one prominent strand focused on how non-school-based literacy learning can position youth and adults to develop senses of self as competent and expert, as opposed to the less competent senses of self that sometimes derive from school-based literacy learning (cf. Hull & Schultz, 2001).

In adult education, there have been various efforts to theorize adult development and identity formation (see Clark & Caffarella, 1999; Merriam & Caffarella, 1999). However, relatively few studies in the domain of adult literacy have included such a focus. A notable exception is recent work that takes Kegan's (1982) model of adult development and applies it to adult literacy learners. This model posits a staged process whereby one's thinking and world view change in nature and complexity (see Drago-Severson et al., 2001). According to these researchers, adult development involves "a qualitative shift in how people know and understand themselves, their worlds, and the relationship between the two" (p. 6), and this qualitative shift is referred to as "transformational learning" (Drago-Severson et al., 2001). Because adult students in any program will represent each of the stages of development—termed instrumental, socializing, and self-authoring—one recommendation that derives from the work is for educators to be responsive to their learners' diversity, creating a "new pluralism" within the adult classroom.

As is detailed later, the work reported here derives from different traditions in terms of thinking about human development as a process of continual identity construction and the exploration of possible selves. For one thing, this conception is not centered on ordered stages of growth; also, as mentioned briefly earlier, the traditions we draw on place considerable emphasis on language as a key developmental tool, and especially the role of narrative in constructing a self and the notion of self as a story. Taking up this stance on identity development, in our view, may also allow an adult literacy educator a greater role in facilitating growth and change than might seem available through an ordered stage orientation. Yet, there are complementarities between these theoretical perspectives as well, especially in relation to the importance of the way of knowing that Drago-Severson et al. (2001) called "self-authoring." Interestingly, "authoring a self" is a phrase that also appears in the sociocultural literature, especially the writings of Bakhtin (see Holland et al., 1998). Although Kegan and colleagues emphasized self-authoring as a particular relationship to knowledge construction, socioculturalists frame self-authoring as an attempt to exercise agency in the face of cultural and social production.

Drawing from ethnographies of personhood, social theory, and sociohistorical research on literacy, learning, and human development, we think of identity as

- Enacted through and mediated by language and other cultural artifacts (cf. Cole, 1996; Vygotsky, 1978).

- Amalgamated from past experiences, available cultural resources, and possible subject positions in the present and future (cf. Eisenhart, 1995; Hall, 1996).

- Indexing social positions or one's privilege or lack thereof in relation to that of others (cf. Goffman, 1959; Holland et al., 1998).

- Inseparable from learning and especially mastery or the acquisition of expertise (cf. Lave & Wenger, 1991; Wenger, 1998).

- Allowing the possibility of agency or the capacity to direct or influence one's own behavior and life path (cf. de Certeau, 1984; Holland et al., 1998).

- Continuously revised (Giddens, 1991).

- Enacted most intensely during performative moments (Urciuoli, 1995).

- Articulated through story or narrative (cf. Bruner, 1994; Ochs & Capps, 2001).

- Influenced by and enacted in, across, and against particular places, spaces, and landscapes (cf. Mitchell, 2002; Soja, 1996).

We have written elsewhere in more detail about this conception of identity (Hull & Katz, in press) and also refer to and illustrate some of the features (listed earlier) in the sections that follow.

SCENES FROM A WORKPLACE

To embody the aforementioned theoretical language of identity and development, and to introduce what we believe is an important tension between the personal goals that adults bring to learning and literacy, and institutional goals that usually structure adults' participation in schooling and work, we turn next to studies of literacy and work from the Silicon Valley of northern California. In this section, we make three related points: (a) The project of creating new capitalist workplaces is at heart the project of shaping workers' identities, (b) language and literacy practices are intimately connected both with the work of these factories and the work of shaping workers' identities, and (c) adult workers exhibit a range of responses to attempts to shape their identities and attendant literacies, responses which are important to consider as we think about the design of adult literacy and literacy-related classes, particularly in workforce development and workplace programs.

The data reported in this section come from a larger ethnographic study (Hull, Jury, Ziv, & Katz, 1996) of two circuit board assembly factories over a 4-year period. In this study, we hoped to develop a view of how workplaces were changing under the pressures of global competition by examining the textual practices that play such a prominent role in the new work. At issue here was a new conceptualization of literacy, one that went beyond a notion of basic skills to incorporate something of the "higher order" thinking processes that many people believed then and still assert are at the heart of transformed workplaces and successful competition in a globalized world (Barton, 2000). "Is there a new literacy in new workplaces," we wanted to ask, "and if there is, how can we describe it, and how can workers best acquire it?"

At Teamco, a pseudonym for a company that had embarked on a quality enhancement program centered on autonomous work teams, our research team made over 200 visits between September 1994 and November 1995. We found that literacy saturated the world of electronics assembly, that there was a vastly increased demand that workers at all levels be able to deal with alphabetic texts and other forms of representation during their shifts, and that not only supervisors but all workers were required to monitor productivity and quality through detailed record-keeping and data analysis. Workers on the manufacturing floor were expected to physically manipulate circuit boards and sometimes manually affix components to the boards, but they were also increasingly asked to operate and monitor robots that did this work more efficiently and accurately than humanly possible. At the same time, as this work began to be mediated by literacy in quite fundamental ways, workers increasingly came to be judged in light of their performance around literacy and language-saturated activities. Our research eventually identified over 80 categories of literate activity among frontline workers, which we divided into 7 overall groupings: Performing Basic Literate Functions, Using Literacy to Explain, Taking Part in Discourse Around and About Texts and Literate Activities, Participating in the Flow of Information, Problem-Solving, Exercising Critical Judgment; and Using Literacy to Exercise or Resist Authority. These categories greatly extend the usual notions of basic skills as decoding or encoding simple texts (see Hull, 1999).

Another remarkable finding, given the tenor of the times (the mid-1990s), was that despite the fact that the workforce was comprised mostly of recent immigrants, many of whom were still learning English or settling into this country, these adults were able to manage successfully the massive and complex, multimodal and multirepresentational literate demands of their work. They were able to do so in large part because they worked in teams, due both to the new organizational structure of the company, and the informal ethnic networks that existed throughout the shop floor. We have written elsewhere about some of the literacy problems that did occur in workplaces (e.g., Hull, 1999), but these were largely due to workplace organizations that required workers to be self-monitoring, rather than self-directed, or that positioned workers as not responsible for literate activity. In 4 years of documenting work at two large companies, we simply did not find literacy problems of the sort that once were popularized by the press as accounting for U.S. failure to compete economically.

In fact, the most important variant in terms of workers' engagement with the new culture of teams, teamwork, problem solving, and paperwork had to do not with literacy per se, but with accepting or rejecting the working identities being promoted by the company. It has become almost commonplace to say that producing and regulating identities is a major aim for today's global companies (cf. Carnoy & Castells, 2001), and that, more than ever before, workplaces influence the social identities that workers develop. We found this to be the case, but also found much variation in workers' responses to their company's notion of an ideal worker as a self-directed team-player, a problem solver, and a symbol analyst. Some rejected or ignored the model, others embraced it, and still others turned it to their own purposes—all according to their backgrounds, present realities, and hopes for the future—and these responses of course also influenced workers' engagement with literacy practices (cf. Hull, 2002).

In the course of this research, we identified several categories of engagement and identification in relation to the company's model of an ideal worker. These ranged from "unengaged and unidentified," to "engaged and resistant," to "engaged and transformative," to "engaged and identified." Here we briefly illustrate one end of the spectrum, "unengaged and unidentified," by introducing Loi, who rejected the notion of teamwork. A Vietnamese woman in her 50s, she had been in the United States 5 years at the time of our interviews with her. In one particular interview (conducted in Vietnamese by Craig Wilson, a member of our research team who was fluent in the language), Loi initially adopted the party line regarding self-directed work teams (SDWTs), claiming teams are good not only for the product, but also for the company and "for everyone." Asked whether she saw any drawbacks in the program, she offered an interesting hedge: "No ... but there *could* be." Then, after again stating that she had no opinions on SDWTs or the classes that workers were required to take to learn what the company described as the principles of teamwork (e.g., accepting change), she offered an account of other people's opinions:

> The majority, most of the workers here don't like "SDWT." "They, they look like Communist. Yeah, they look like"-- All, most the people say like that. A majority, the great majority, everywhere, in every building I hear the same thing. Study, making them study is an act of extreme pressure, forcing them to study. They study because they are forced to. They don't like it. So they don't think it is something they should put any effort into.

She added that this forced "studying" was nothing new, that her coworkers had already experienced this in Vietnam, and "because of fear of communists they ran over here," only to meet up in the workplace with what seemed to her to be the VietCong's teacher.

Loi's history as an immigrant from Vietnam who had negative experiences with communism and attendant ideas of collective study and work clearly shaped her present notion of being a worker at Teamco. Certainly, some of her coworkers were enthusiastic about the self-directed work teams: Some participated willingly in the classes on teams and teamwork, seeing these classes as opportunities to practice their English; others welcomed the ways they believed the new team structure positioned them in the flow of work, in discussions about work processes, and in workplace hierarchies. As one of her coworkers put it, with the advent of teams and the expectation that line workers are observant data gatherers, problem-posers, and problem solvers, work and working relationships changed beyond the teams: "Now they (management) will come to me directly. So I explain why I get (a) problem like that. I can change my ability to work." During the weekly meetings of her self-directed work team, these particular co-workers would busy themselves with the latest quality and productivity reports and engineering changes, raising objections, seeking clarification, drawing fishbone diagrams on a whiteboard to troubleshoot a problem, debating possible solutions, and coaxing others to participate. Loi, however, remained silent throughout these meetings, despite her team leader's efforts to involve her. She engaged minimally in the requisite literate record-keeping and problem-solving activities. Unfortunately, Loi's silence and marginal participation in team meet-ings was often taken by supervisors and team coordinators as a sign that she and other reticent and disengaged teammates had not "grasped" the concept of teams due to their lack of formal education.

Loi, then, represented a segment of workers at Teamco who, for a variety of reasons, distanced themselves from the identity of self-directed worker and therefore took part in team-related and literacy-intensive activities only periph-erally. She steeled herself against participating in anything that would in any way compromise her view of herself as a person free from imposed ideologies. This very resistant stance was paralleled by other workers' almost total rejection of the team concept, although the situations surrounding their choices were not always so clear.

SCENES FROM A VOCATIONAL TRAINING PROGRAM

Having observed the sometimes brutal working conditions of high-pressure en-try work in the electronics industry, we searched for exemplary vocational pro-grams and turned up several that promised to train low-income residents of Oak-land, just 30 miles away from the Silicon Valley, for high tech, high-paying jobs. The program we chose to study—"City JOBS" (a pseudonym)—had a so-cial justice focus and represented itself as helping to "close the digital divide." Through intensive technical training and also regular instruction in what were called "life skills," City JOBS hoped to prepare economically disenfranchised area residents to become IT (information technology) technicians with high-paying jobs, computer professionals who would then be able to give back to the community. The data referred to in this section came from 18 months of field-work at City JOBS, consisting primarily of participant observation and inter-views (see Hull & Zacher, in press).

In this section, we illustrate the following points: (a) Vocational programs, like new capitalist workplaces, also focus on shaping workers' identities as much as they focus on imparting skills and knowledge; students in these pro-grams, like their counterparts in the workplaces we studied, had a range of responses to these attempts to shape particular selves; (b) language and literacy practices were integral parts of the vocational curriculum, even when not acknowledged; and (c) adult students attended vocational programs for a range of reasons, only some of which converged with the program's goals.

The West Oakland, CA, community that the program served had an extraordinarily high unemployment rate of over 60% and was beset by the crime and poverty patterns that have become such a part of the fabric of U.S. inner cities. People who came to City JOBS—mostly African Americans and a much smaller mixture of Latinos, Filipinos, and Asian Americans—were hoping to get their share of the economic boom that the Silicon Valley was still experiencing at the end of the 1990s. Like many people who attend vocational programs and literacy programs, they were hoping for second chances. This research project focused on understanding what kinds of identities participants were positioned to construct in a second-chance, social, justice-oriented vocational program and what kinds of language and literacy activities accompanied that process. The goals of City JOBS resulted in a number of worthy and rewarding experiences, but the enterprise was also fraught with unexpected tensions, complexities, and obstacles, many of them connected to issues of identity and representation for the program as well as its students.

The first finding we discuss here is that contradictory conceptions of students resulted in mixed messages about identity and development. For example, on the one hand, students were told by Ken, the charismatic founder of City JOBS, that they were "all geniuses" in at least one thing, and possibly two, and the challenge was to figure out what these things were. Yet, in the course of our data analysis, we found 7 times as many negative labels for students, and comments about them, as positive labels. Promotional flyers characterized the students whom City JOBS wanted to serve as "under-skilled," "poverty-level," "disadvantaged," "at-risk," "welfare-based," "unemployed," and "low-income." In speeches, promotional materials, and in conversations with visitors to the program, Ken often described his students by singling out characteristics and circumstances that focused on their needs. He mentioned, for example, that most had never left the neighborhood even to go across the Bay to San Francisco, whereas others were orphans or had criminal records, and most had few "options." He positioned himself and his program as offering strategies, knowledge, and skills that would make change possible for students. A central text in this enterprise was Stephen R. Covey's popular book, *Seven Habits of Highly Effective People* (1989), which offered "insights about adapting to personal and professional change" as well as ways to change "self-defeating behaviors." A second contradictory discourse arose from the tension between the stated social justice goals of the program (to help low-income residents gain the training needed to get good jobs, lead economically independent lives, and return to the community to give others a leg up) and the capitalist-centered texts and autobiographies they were asked to read and study (as models of corporate personas to develop). Several students braced against the push to develop such identities, and eventually began to voice their skepticism about Ken's belief in them and also about the impact of City JOBS on their futures.

Our second finding was the mismatch between the literate demands of IT training and participants' notions of what the work would be like. City JOBS focused on technical training, knowledge, and applied skills, but most of what had to be learned was mediated by print. This is true, of course, for information technologies in general, and is a perceived stumbling block for many technology-oriented organizations hoping to empower participants through the provision of access. Ken and the directors and teachers of other technical job training centers were worried about the literacy demands from the start; they saw reading as a real hurdle in a technical curriculum offered to students who, according to Ken, read on average at a seventh-grade level. One frustrated instructor, in a parking-lot conversation with us after her class, remarked that in the IT world, "there's just no way around it. You just have GOT to read." She went on explain that the technical manuals were dry and dense, and that the certification testing targeted "college educated and self-motivated people."

Ken's first solution was to modify the reading. Instead of giving students the actual texts used in IT, he tried to provide what he called simplified versions provided as weekly handouts. He recruited volunteers from the industry to help produce these simplified texts which the students referred to as "dumbing down" the curriculum. Students were still able to complete only a few such simplified units, and this struck the instructors as inadequate. At the end of the year, students complained bitterly about the lack of real textbooks in the beginning of the program, although when they did use industry books later on, they found them quite difficult to read. The instructor from a sister IT program approached local literacy programs for help in teaching students to read, but their weekly classes on non-IT materials didn't make a dent in the challenges students faced. Except for the small bit of help we provided or marshaled on how to read the real texts (our recommendation, in lieu of the simplification strategy), students were left to swim on their own. Most seemed to accept the reading and the technical tomes as part of the IT world, but for many students, the text-saturated nature of the program was a big disappointment. Following is one student's memorable words in an exit interview:

> It ain't what I thought it was gonna be. It's just a whole bunch of protocols and definitions to me … I thought we was gonna be fixing viruses and stuff like that. It's still the same paper and pencil stuff.

It is not surprising, then, that at the end of the program, although almost all of the students felt more confident around computer hardware and software, 90% were not able to pass the literacy-laden certification tests that are the coin of the realm in the IT world.

A third finding speaks to the ways in which participants accepted, rejected, modified, and ultimately made their own the notions of being a good worker that were promoted in the program. To illustrate this identity construction process, we'll introduce one of the students, Amy, an African American woman who began the program enthusiastically, hoping to get in on the "dot.com" phenomenon. Initially, she eagerly adopted the philosophies of work and workers promoted in the program, including *Seven Habits* (Covey, 1989). However, by midprogram, the heavy workload, dissatisfactions with the curriculum, and a growing suspicion that there would not be high-paying jobs at the end of the line, all began to take their toll. Amy had trouble picking up the discourse of the program. She inferred that learning the "lingo," as she put it, was more difficult for her because she was a woman, because she saw some men in the program talk the talk more easily.

Amy's deep desire to enter the field was not enough, and as the months progressed and the technical curriculum grew increasingly more complex, we observed a decline in her self-confidence and in her hopes for passing the technical certification tests. "At first I *expected* to pass the tests," she told us. "Now I'm just hoping I *might* be able to pass them." Although she continued to want a job in the industry, she was timid about applying, fearing she did not have the skills. In her exit interview with us, she expressed her disappointment that jobs weren't waiting for graduates of the program, as she had been led to believe. By the time graduation came, she had backed away from her original embrace of the identities, habits of mind, and promises of the program, as demonstrated in the spoof she composed and enacted at the graduate ceremony about the *Seven Habits* (Covey, 1989) curriculum. Amy produced her own version of the seven habits: "Habit #5 was 'teach yourself to read,'" she intoned. And then she paused for this punch line: "Teach yourself to read so you can understand why you're not employed!"

SCENES FROM A COMMUNITY TECHNOLOGY CENTER

The data that form the centerpiece of this section were collected across 4 years of participant observation at a community technology center, founded in 2001 by Hull and Michael James and located in the same section of Oakland, CA, as City JOBS. The overall goal of this project has been to understand the kinds of literate and social activities that can characterize the alternative learning space of a community technology center. Called "DUSTY," or "Digital Underground Storytelling for You(th)," the center provided afterschool programs for children and youth, and classes and workshops for adults on a form of multimedia, multimodal composing called "digital storytelling" (cf. Lambert, 2002). That is, participants typically wrote or told a narrative, often a personal account of a pivotal moment or person or event, recorded their voices reading the story, chose photographs and video to illustrate it, and selected or created background music to accompany it. The resulting compositions, 3- to 5-min movies, were shown to friends and family and to the larger community at public venues or via the Internet.

The "underground" in DUSTY's name referred to the fact that the program's first home was a basement, but also signified that the stories produced there represented discourses, identities, and practices that often departed from those more common and dominant narratives of school and work. For example, the opportunity to create digital multimodal compositions, with their marriage of sound, image, word, and music, is far from standard fare in adult education classes, as is the chance to participate in narrative practices that privilege the aesthetic, personal, or spiritual (cf. Belzer & St. Clair, 2003).

In this section, we illustrate the following points: (a) Although the great majority of literacy programs currently privilege instrumental forms of literacy, especially work-related competencies, many adults at DUSTY evinced considerable interest in literacy projects that foregrounded personal purposes and multiple modes; (b) given social and intellectual scaffolding, participants were successful at multimodal composing—this despite the complex array of technologies, skills, and practices involved, and regardless of the participants' initial levels of comfort and experience with Internet and Computer Technologies (ICT); and (c) in the act of making digital stories, participants created representations of self and sometimes tried on "possible selves." Of great interest to us were participants' efforts to exercise noticeably agentive selves, as they articulated pivotal moments or "turning points" (Bruner, 1994) in their own and their families' lives, and as they reflected on life trajectories and hopes and plans for the future.

By watching the approximately 200 digital stories created by children, youth, and adults at DUSTY, we inductively devised the following broad category schemes for genre and purpose. Genres included the following: Autobiographical Narratives; Poems and Raps; Social Critique and Public Service Announcements; Reenactments or Extensions of Stories, Cartoons, and Movies; Animations; Reports; Biographies and Interviews. The purposes of the stories ranged as follows: Offer a Tribute to Family Member(s), Friend(s); Recount or Interpret a Pivotal Moment or Key Event; Represent Place, Space, Community; Preserve History; Create Art or Artifact; Play or Fantasize; Heal, Grieve, or Reflect; Reach, Inform, or Influence Wider Audience. These simple lists belie the fact that many authors had multiple purposes and that digital storytelling is an internally diverse and necessarily dynamic and evolving genre.

Those caveats aside, we offer here a list of actual story topics devised by adult participants at DUSTY, meant to suggest the range: a recounting of the events of September 11, 2001, that ended with a tribute to family at Christmas time; the biography of a beloved brother, recently deceased; a description of a low-income neighborhood and social critique in prose and rap; an autobiography of recovery from drug abuse; a tribute to Tupac Shakur, as a role model for overcoming adversity and following your dreams; a portfolio of graffiti art and a history of the artist; a thank you to a daughter for standing by her mom in tough times; a memory as a girl of a family trip in China to attend a wedding; a survival story of discovering that a friend had been raped, followed by the revelation of the author's rape as child; an enactment of a poem, written previously, about growing up as an African American in the rural South. These topics suggest the challenging life worlds that many adult students navigate, and they testify as well to narrative desire, to a human need to reflect on and rerepresent one's experiences (cf. Bruner, 1994).

Of special interest to us have been those digital stories by adults that foreground the construction or reconstruction of self. Although most digital stories, as personal narratives broadly conceived, can generally be viewed as "identity texts" (cf. Hull & James, in press), some stories are especially evocative in this regard, offering accounts that are "thickly agentive," to borrow Bruner's (1994, p. 50) phrasing. Bruner commented on the universality of "turning points," moments when people report sharp change in their lives and accompanying dramatic changes in representations of self. So ubiquitous are such moments in autobiographical accounts that "it may well be that the culture's canonical forms for characterizing the seasons of a life encourage such subjective turning points" (1994, p. 42). Key features of these accounts are vivid detail and great affect, a connection between external events and internal awakenings, and agentive activity. These turning-point narratives thus serve as emblems, or tropes, for how a person conceives of his or her life as a whole.

A second strand of our research at DUSTY, then, has focused on understanding such "turning point narratives," those digital stories in which adults represent and interpret pivotal personal events partly to reframe themselves and their futures in relation to those events. To give two brief but striking examples, one participant centered his digital story on being diagnosed with a learning disability as an adult, and his determination to reconceptualize himself and his abilities thereafter (Hull & Paull, 2001). A different participant, distraught over the death of her brother and particularly the fact that she had not known of his illness, recreated and reinvented through a digital story her relationships with her departed brother and her other siblings. In these cases and others, adult authors developed and expressed agentive representations of their relationships to past events and to future selves. As Sennet (1998) noted, "Narratives are more than simple chronicles of events; they give shape to the forward movement of time, suggesting reasons why things happen, showing their consequences" (p. 30). We have begun to consider how multimodal narrative composition can potentially foreground and facilitate the reflective project of self. As the participant who wrote about his learning disability explained, "I had clarity because I lived it. I had even more clarity because I actually wrote it. I have even more clarity because I did the digital story. It just keeps coming clearer and clearer" (Hull & Paull, 2001).

Of course, the skills and technologies associated with digital storytelling are not sufficient in and of themselves. The teaching and learning that underpin this genre took place in a particular out-of-school context: a community center where it was possible to work outside the constraints of testing and school-based expectations and to promote multiple literacies, especially digital multimodal ones. In addition, threaded through the social cloth of DUSTY were particular values about ability, access, and learning. In fact, a belief in adults' and children's literate capacities to construct and represent an agentive and socially responsible self was a foundational principle. Also important were certain participant structures, such as the sharing of story ideas in small groups, one-on-one assistance throughout the process, and modeling and "fading," or the gradual decrease of technical support as participants become more confident and proficient. Most adults, even those who had had little or no experience with technology but plenty of cause to doubt their literacy skills, were able to successfully complete digital projects.

All of this is to emphasize that adults participated satisfactorily in self-reflective digital story projects not simply because the technology was available, but because a learning space had been constructed that fostered this particular use of the tools. We have conceptualized this space in two ways, as privileging literal, figurative, and virtual movement across communities (cf. Hull & James, in press), and as affording certain kinds of textual practices, especially what Bauman and Briggs (1990) described as the authority to appropriate others' texts and to "recenter" them, or recontextualize and repurpose them. We have seen especially vivid examples of the recentering of images, whereby DUSTY authors take well-known photographs, remove them from their particular historical contexts, and then recenter them in their own creative universes—literate acts full of agency and authorial authority (Hull & Katz, in press).

The strength of programs such as DUSTY, of course, is also their rub. They introduce digital literacies and the means to communicate multimodally, forms of signification that have an appeal for many adults and young people, and represent the new literacies. They privilege narrative forms and can encourage the envisioning of possible selves, social practices at the heart of identity formation. But typically they are not connected in any institutional or formal way to powerful instrumental and even academic uses of literacies that are themselves linked to certifications, employment, and advancement in the workplace and at school. To wit, one of the most prolific and talented digital storytellers at DUSTY was nonetheless marginalized in the world of work (Hull & Katz, in press). This same young man had also participated in City JOBS, a program designed for low-income residents, but was unable to get a job in the IT field, and moreover, his working identity had very little to do with IT per se.

CONCLUSION: IDENTITY AND LITERACY
DEVELOPMENT ACROSS CONTEXTS

In this chapter, we have called attention to the centrality of identity as a construct for thinking about adult learners. We have also illustrated how certain identities recruit certain literacy practices. And conversely, we have shown how certain literacy practices in tandem with new technologies can recruit especially powerful representations of self, which may in turn guide actions and behaviors. In the words of Markus and Nurius (1986), "ideas about what is possible for us to be, to think, to feel, or to experience provide a direction and impetus for action, change, and development" (p. 960). In addition, examining empirically how individuals construct senses of themselves in response to the cultural models that are offered, or imposed on them, drives home the ways in which personal goals, backgrounds, and habits of mind can conflict with institutional goals embedded in pedagogy, curricula, and day-to-day interactions with our students and workers.

At Teamco, for instance, particular literacies were required and resisted in various conditions. Opportunities to acquire, exercise, and further develop literate competencies were not separate from opportunities to enact particular kinds of identities, but were part and parcel of them. Although workers like Loi carried out the tasks required of them, they did not necessarily embrace the conceptions of self promoted by Teamco, or the literacy practices that went with them. On the other hand, some workers did identify with the company's notions of team-player and symbol-analyst, did trust that the new organization of the workplace would provide desirable opportunities, positions, and roles, ones that beckoned better futures and imagined selves. For them, the development of competencies was motivated by, strongly led by, their desire to construct particular working identities. Our findings from the Teamco site are also a reminder of the ways in which much work, even at the entry level, now has a literate overlay. This can mean more intensified and closely monitored work days, with only the possibility of more satisfying and self-directed work. Finally, the Silicon Valley study, like other research that has examined entry-level positions firsthand (cf. Gowen, 1993), brings home the extreme economic struggles of people who have to start out at this level.

Particular notions of self as workers, people, and citizens were promoted at City JOBS as well as at Teamco, and at both sites, students did not adopt the promoted versions of who they might become, but seemed to try them on for size and then reject or rework as they saw fit. At City JOBS, proficiency in certain kinds of literacy practices, although assumed by the program and necessary for IT certification, did not enter into most students' notions of themselves as workers at all, and were not a regular part of the curriculum. This program deserved praise for its attempts to provide an intensive course of study aimed as a pathway out of poverty and toward a more secure economic future for low-income adults. Yet it positioned students discursively, and in terms of material and symbolic resources, in ways that did not always help to achieve these aims. Ultimately, most of the students resented, as one man put it, being reduced to being low income—"sure, we're poor, but we're a lot more than that," he said. And he and the others also felt vastly cheated, having given up 9 months to participate in an intensive program, only to graduate from it with neither their IT certification nor a job.

Our notion of identity and development, which we have explored in these three contexts, centers on the narrative or storied construction and reconstruction of self over time. We have been especially interested in representations of self as agentive, as able to influence present circumstances and future possibilities, and able to situate oneself in relation to others in socially responsible ways. In our most recent work of helping to found a community technology center (DUSTY), and in teaching the social practices and technical skills that comprise digital storytelling, our aim has been to position adult students as narrators of their own stories (while acknowledging and examining the ways in which everyone's stories are parts of existing discourses, and therefore can never purely be our own). And in telling their stories, they are also positioned to craft a representation of self, family, and community. Thus, digital multimodal storytelling can sometimes be a radically self-altering act. Adult educators and adult literacy practitioners have of course long known the power of story, digital or print-based, although it is infrequent that we hear discussions of the power of narrative, or even the role of narrative in adult literacy classrooms, as a means for examining past, present, and future selves.

At this historical moment, the ways of thinking about adult development, identity, literacy, and technology that we have outlined here go against the grain (cf. Belzer & St. Clair, 2003). In adult literacy circles, we rarely conceptualize literacy as more than an alphabetic text, except for workplace innovators who know the importance of including graphs, charts, and other nonlinguistic forms of representation in functional context curricula. We rarely introduce our adult students to uses of new information technologies that go beyond the mundane and the pedestrian. In the United States, there has been a huge investment in instrumental skills that can be measured and that lead toward recognizable valued outcomes, like General Equivalence Degrees (GEDs), Tests of Adult Basic Education (TABE) scores, or some indicator of workplace readiness (Belzer & St. Clair, 2003). To attempt to bring identity development as the fostering of possible selves into this arena is a large task: How might we measure and report, not to mention explain the importance of, changes in understandings of self? Yet to ignore adults' identity projects, their attempts to fashion a self that they view as possible and desirable, is to risk losing their engagement in both school and work, a truth that many adult literacy educators have known all along. There is no better time, as the field moves toward more narrow understandings of literacy, teaching, and learning, to find individual and collective ways to go against the grain. After all, that is what our adult students do as they find their ways to our classes again and again despite great odds.

REFERENCES

Bakhtin, M. M. (1981). Discourse in the novel (C. Emerson & M. Holquist, Trans.). In M. Holquist (Ed.), *The dialogic imagination: Four essays by M. M. Bakhtin* (pp. 259-422). Austin: University of Texas Press.

Barton, P. (2000). *What jobs require: Literacy, education, and training, 1940-2006* (Policy Information Report). Princeton, NJ: Educational Testing Service.

Bauman, R., & Briggs, C. L. (1990). Poetics and performances as critical perspectives on language and social life. *Annual Review of Anthropology, 19,* 59-88.

Belzer, A., & St. Clair, R. (2003). *Opportunities and limits: An update on adult literacy education.* Columbus, OH: Center on Education and Training for Employment.

Bruner, J. (1994). The remembered self. In U. Neisser & R. Fivush (Eds.), *The remembering self: Construction and agency in self narrative* (pp. 41-54). Cambridge, England: Cambridge University Press.

Carnoy, M., & Castells, M. (2001). Globalization, the knowledge society, and the network state: Poulantzas at the millennium. *Global Networks, 1,* 1-18.

Clark, M. C. (2001). Incarcerated women and the construction of the self. In R. M. Cervero, B. C. Courtenay, & D. H. Monaghan (Eds.), *The Cyril O. Houle scholars in adult and continuing education program global research perspectives* (Vol. 1, pp. 14-27). Athens: University of Georgia Press.

Clark, M. C., & Caffarella, R. S. (Eds.). (1999). *An update on adult development theory: New ways of thinking about the life course. New directions for adult and continuing education* (No. 84). San Francisco: Jossey-Bass.

Cole, M. (1996). *Cultural psychology: A once and future discipline.* Cambridge, MA: Harvard University Press.

Covey, S. R. (1989). *Seven habits of highly effective people.* New York: Simon & Schuster.

de Certeau, M. (1984). *The practice of everyday life.* Berkeley: University of California Press.

Drago-Severson, E., Helsing, D., Kegan, R., Popp, N., Broderick, M., & Portnow, K. (2001). The power of a cohort and of collaborative groups [Electronic version]. *Focus on Basics, 5,* 15-22.

Eisenhart, M. (1995). The fax, the jazz player, and the self-story teller: How do people organize culture? *Anthropology & Education Quarterly, 26*(1), 3-26.

Emirbayer, M., & Mische, A. (1998). What is agency? *American Journal of Sociology, 103,* 962-1023.

Erikson, E. (1963). *Childhood and society* (2nd ed). New York: Norton.

Foucault, M. (1979). *The birth of the prison.* New York: Vintage.

Gee, J. P. (1996). *Social linguistics and literacies: Ideology in discourses.* Bristol, PA: Taylor & Francis.

Gergen, K. (1991). *The saturated self: Dilemmas of identity in contemporary life.* New York: Basic Books.

Giddens, A. (1991). *Modernity and self-identity: Self and society in the late modern age.* Cambridge, England: Polity Press.

Goffman, I. (1959). *The presentation of self in everyday life.* New York: Doubleday.

Gowen, S. (1993). *The politics of workplace literacy.* New York: Teachers College Press.

Greene, M. (1990). Revision and interpretation: Opening spaces for the second chance. In D. Inbar (Ed.), *Second chance in education* (pp. 37-48). London: Falmer.

Hall, S. (1996). Introduction: Who needs identity? In S. Hall & P. du Gay (Eds.), *Questions of cultural identity* (pp. 1-17). London: Sage.

Holland, D., Lachicotte Jr., W., Skinner, D., & Cain, C. (1998). *Identity and agency in cultural worlds.* Cambridge, MA: Harvard University Press.

Hull, G. (1999). What's in a label? Complicating notions of the skills-poor worker. *Written Communication, 16,* 379-411.

Hull, G. (2002). Enacting a self. In J. Searle & D. Roebuck (Eds.), *Envisioning practice—implementing change. Proceedings of the 10th Annual International Conference on Post-Compulsory Education and Training* (pp. 13-30). Brisbane: Australian Academic Press.

Hull, G., & James, M. (in press). Geographies of hope: A study of urban landscapes, digital media, and children's representations of place. In P. O'Neill (Ed.), *Blurring boundaries: Research and teaching beyond a discipline.* Cresskill, NJ: Hampton.

Hull, G., Jury, M., Ziv, O., & Katz, M. (1996). *Changing work, changing literacy? A study of skill requirements and development in a traditional and restructured workplace.* Berkeley: University of California, National Center for Research in Vocational Education and National Center for Study of Writing and Literacy.

Hull, G., & Katz, M. (in press). Crafting an agentive self: Case studies on digital storytelling. *Research in the Teaching of English.*

Hull, G., & Paull, C. (2001, February). *Fashioning selves through multiple media: An exploration of digital literacies and digital divides.* Invited address at the National Council of Teachers of English Research Assembly, Berkeley, CA.

Hull, G., & Schultz, K. (2001). Literacy and learning out of school: A review of theory and research. *Review of Educational Research, 71,* 575-561.

Hull, G., & Zacher, J. (in press). Enacting identities: An ethnography of a job training program. *Identity: An International Journal of Theory and Research.*

Kegan, R. (1982). *The evolving self: Problems and process in human development.* Cambridge, MA: Harvard University Press.

Lambert, J. (2002). *Digital storytelling: Capturing lives, creating community.* Berkeley, CA: Digital Diner Press.

Lave, J. & Wenger, E. (1991). *Situated learning: Legitimate peripheral participation.* Cambridge: Cambridge University Press.

Markus, H., & Nurius, P. (1986). Possible selves. *American Psychologist, 41,* 954-969.

Merriam, S.B., & Caffarella, R. S. (1999). *Learning in adulthood: A comprehensive guide* (2nd ed.). San Francisco: Jossey-Bass.

Mitchell, W. J. T. (Ed.). (2002). *Space, place, and landscape* (2nd ed.). Chicago: University of Chicago Press.

New London Group. (1996). A pedagogy of multiliteracies: Designing social futures. *Harvard Educational Review, 66,* 60-92.

Ochs, E., & Capps, L. (2001). *Living narrative: Creating lives in everyday storytelling.* Cambridge, MA: Harvard University Press.

Rossiter, M. (1999). A narrative approach to development: Implications for adult education. *Adult Education Quarterly, 50,* 56-71.

Sennet, R. (1998). *The corrosion of character: The personal consequences of work in the new capitalism.* New York: Norton.

Soja, E. W. (1996). *Thirdspace: Journeys to Los Angeles and other real-and imagined-places.* Malden, MA: Blackwell.

Urciuoli, B. (1995). The indexical structure of visibility. In B. Farnell (Ed.), *Human action signs in cultural context* (pp. 189-215). Lanham, MD: Scarecrow Press.

Vygotsky, L. (1978). *Mind in society: The development of higher psychological processes.* Cambridge, MA: Harvard University Press.

Weedon, C. (1996). *Feminist practice and poststructuralist theory.* Malden, MA: Blackwell.

Wenger, E. (1998). *Communities of practice: Learning, meaning, and identity.* Cambridge, England: Cambridge University Press.

Author Index

AUTHOR INDEX 321

Subject Index

A

A Nation at Risk, 50
Accountability, 11–14, 19, 21–22, 25–26, 30, 77, 172, 176
  Systems, 12, 19
Adult development, 39, 299, 301, 314, 316
Adult Education Act, 16, 96, 105
Adult learner, 2, 22–23, 33, 46, 71, 82, 96, 98, 104, 110, 113, 117, 125, 129, 131, 135, 140, 165, 170–171, 181, 187, 190–191, 193–194, 277, 308
  English language learners, 221–222, 234
Adult Performance Level Project, 96–97, 98, 100, 101, 105
Assessment, 2, 4, 19, 21– 25, 29, 35–36, 41–42, 46, 50, 66, 87, 98–99, 101, 122, 128, 131, 133, 156, 161, 171–173, 176–177, 183, 233, 253, 271–272, 286
  BEST Test, 243–244
  CASAS, 96, 98–102, 104
  Self-assessment, 171, 242
  Standardized tests, 56–57, 66–67, 91, 99, 104, 145, 161, 172, 232, 243, 262, 314
  Test of Adult Basic Education, 56, 91, 101, 243–244, 314

B

Basic skills, 88

C

Citizenship, 221, 232–233
Civics education, 231
Cognitive science, 39–40
Collaboration, 170, 225, 237, 248, 250–251, 273

Competency-based education, 98–99, 105
Critical literacy, 212
Critical pedagogy, 94
Cultural processes, 143

E

Economic Opportunity Act, 3
Emancipatory literacy, 94–95
English as a second language, 22–23, 83, 98, 111–113, 119, 169, 178, 217, 221–239, 241, 243–244
  English language literacy, 223, 231
  Generation 1.5, 228
Equipped for the Future, 4, 5, 7, 33–34, 37, 39–40, 42–51, 96, 99–102, 110–111, 113, 169, 174, 176, 250
Ethnopedagogy, 257
Evidence-based practice, 69–71, 73–74, 76–79

F

Family literacy, 241, 253, 283, 296–298
  Even Start, 241, 245–246, 250, 254
  FACE program, 242, 249–253
Funding, 174

G

Gender, 277, 279–280, 285, 296–298
General Educational Development (GED), 12, 23, 27, 57–58, 78, 88, 90, 92, 98, 129–130, 132, 140, 162, 165, 172, 180, 182, 184–186, 191, 196, 198, 200, 217, 228, 249, 253, 255, 259–260, 262–270, 272, 274, 289
Goals, 34, 50–51, 131, 151–152, 215, 265